Concepts in Applied Communication

A PRACTICAL ANALYSIS OF RESEARCH AND THEORY

First Edition

Edited by Bruce C. McKinney
University of North Carolina, Wilmington

cognella
San Diego, CA

Bassim Hamadeh, Publisher
Michael Simpson, Vice President of Acquisitions
Christopher Foster, Vice President of Marketing
Jessica Knott, Managing Editor
Stephen Milano, Creative Director
Kevin Fahey, Cognella Marketing Program Manager
Becky Smith, Acquisitions Editor
Erin Escobar, Licensing Associate
Sarah Wheeler, Project Editor

15 14 13 12 11   1 2 3 4 5

Printed in the United States of America

ISBN: 978-1-62131-298-7

www.cognella.com 800.200.3908

Contents

Dedicated to the Memory of the Pennsylvania State University

Speech Communication Professor

Gerald M. Phillips

Thank you for teaching how to believe in myself

Chapter 1

Human Communication

What and Why

Ronald B. Adler and George Rodman

In this introductory chapter, you are presented with some basic concepts about human communication, including the definition of communication, and the different types and functions of communication. Finally, you will come to terms with a concept that has been debated over the past thirty years: what exactly is communication competence?

Learning Objectives For This Chapter

- Define the term communication
- Know why communication is considered a symbolic process
- Identify the five different types of communication
- Describe what needs communication is used to satisfy
- Explain the difference between the linear and transactional models of communication
- Define the term communication competence
- Identify characteristics of competent communicators
- Describe the common misconceptions about communication

Communication Defined

Because this is a book about *communication*, it makes sense to begin by defining that term. This isn't as simple as it might seem because people use the term in a variety of ways that are only vaguely related:

- A dog scratches at the back door, signaling its desire to be let out of the house.
- Data flow from one computer database to another in a cascade of electronic impulses.
- Strangers who live thousands of miles apart spot each other's postings on a social networking website, and they become friends through conversations via e-mail, text messaging, and instant messaging.
- Locals approach a group of confused-looking people who seem to be from out of town and ask if they can help.
- In her sermon, a religious leader encourages the congregation to get more involved in the community.

There is clearly some relationship among uses of the term such as these, but we need to narrow our focus before going on. A look at the table of contents of this book shows that it obviously doesn't deal with animals. Neither is it about Holy Communion, the bestowing of a material thing, or many of the other subjects mentioned in the *Oxford English Dictionary's* 1,200-word definition of *communication*.

What, then, *are* we talking about when we use the term *communication?* As the reading on page 3 shows, there is no single, universally accepted usage. This isn't the place to explore the differences between these conceptions or to defend one against the others. What we need is a working definition that will help us in our study.

As its title suggests, this is a book about understanding *human* communication—so we'll start by explaining what it means to study communication that is unique to members of our species. For our purposes we'll define human **communication** as *the process of creating meaning through symbolic interaction.* Examining this definition reveals some important characteristics of human communication.

Communication is a Process

We often talk about communication as if it occurred in discrete, individual acts such as one person's utterance or a conversation. In fact, communication is a continuous, ongoing process. Consider, for example, a friend's compliment about your appearance. Your interpretation of those words will depend on a long series of experiences stretching far back in time: How have others judged your appearance? How do you feel about your looks? How honest has your friend been in the past? How have you been feeling about one another recently? All this history will help shape your response to the friend's remark. In turn, the words you speak and the way you say them will shape the way your friend behaves toward you and others—both in this situation and in the future. –

This simple example shows that it's inaccurate to talk about "acts" of communication as if they occurred in isolation. To put it differently, communication isn't a series of incidents pasted together like photographs in a scrapbook; instead, it is more like a motion picture in which the meaning comes from the unfolding of an interrelated series of images. The fact that communication is a process is reflected in the transactional model introduced later in this chapter.

Communication is Symbolic

Symbols are used to represent things, processes, ideas, or events in ways that make communication possible. The most significant feature of symbols is their *arbitrary* nature. For example, there's no logical reason why the letters in the word *book* should stand for the object you're reading now Speakers of Spanish call it a *libro,* and Germans call it a *Buch.* Even in English, another term would work just as well as long as everyone agreed to use it in the same way. We overcome the arbitrary nature of symbols by linguistic rules and customs. Effective communication depends on agreement among people about these rules. This is easiest to see when we observe people who don't follow linguistic conventions. For example, recall how unusual the speech of children and nonnative speakers of a language often sounds.

Animals don't use symbols in the varied and complex ways that humans do. There's nothing symbolic about a dog scratching at the door to be let out; there is a natural connection between the door and the dog's goal. By contrast, the words in the human utterance "Open the door!" are only arbitrarily related to the request they represent.

Symbolic communication allows people to think or talk about the past (while cats have no concept of their ancestors from a century ago), explain the present (a trout can't warn its companions about its close call with a fishing hook), and speculate about the future (a crow has no awareness of the year 2025, let alone tomorrow).

Like words, some nonverbal behavior can have symbolic meaning. For example, to most North Americans, nodding your head up and down means "yes" (although this meaning isn't universal). But even more than words, many nonverbal behaviors are ambiguous. Does a frown signify anger or unhappiness? Does a hug stand for a friendly greeting or a symbol of the hugger's romantic interest in you?

Types of Communication

Within the domain of human interaction, there are several types of communication. Each occurs in a different context. Despite the features they all share, each has its own characteristics.

Intrapersonal Communication

By definition, **intrapersonal communication** means "communicating with oneself."[1] You can tune in to one way that each of us communicates internally by listening to the little voice that lives in your mind. Take a moment and listen to what it is saying. Try it now, before reading on. Did you hear it? It may have been saying something like "What little voice? I don't have any little voice!" This voice is the "sound" of your thinking.

We don't always think in verbal terms, but whether the process is apparent or not, the way we mentally process information influences our interaction with others. Even though intrapersonal communication doesn't include other people directly, it does affect almost every type of interaction. You can understand the role of intrapersonal communication by imagining your thoughts in each of the following situations.

- You are planning to approach a stranger whom you would like to get to know better.
- You pause a minute and look at the audience before beginning a ten-minute speech.
- The boss yawns while you are asking for a raise.
- A friend seems irritated lately, and you're not sure whether you are responsible.

The way you handle all of these situations would depend on the intrapersonal communication that precedes or accompanies your overt behavior.

Dyadic/Interpersonal Communication

Social scientists call two persons interacting a **dyad,** and they often use the term **dyadic communication** to describe this type of communication. Dyads are the most common communication setting. One study revealed that college students spend almost half of their total communication time interacting with one other person.[2] Observation in a variety of settings ranging from playgrounds, train depots, and shopping malls to other settings shows that most communication is dyadic in nature.[3] Even communication within larger groups (think of classrooms, parties, and families as examples) consists of multiple, often shifting dyadic encounters.

Dyadic interaction is sometimes considered identical to **interpersonal communication,** but not all two-person interaction can be considered interpersonal in the fullest sense of the word. In fact, you will learn that the qualities that characterize interpersonal communication aren't limited to twosomes. They can be present in threesomes or even in small groups.

Small Group Communication

In **small group communication** every person can participate actively with the other members. Small groups are a common fixture of everyday life. Your family is a group. So are an athletic team, a group of coworkers in several time zones connected in cyberspace, and several students working on a class project.

Whatever their makeup, small groups possess characteristics that are not present in a dyad. For instance, in a group, the majority of members can put pressure on those in the minority to conform, either consciously or unconsciously, but in a dyad no such pressures exist. Conformity pressures can also be comforting, leading group members to take risks that they would not dare if they were alone or in a dyad. With their greater size, groups also have the ability to be more creative than dyads. Finally, communication in groups is affected strongly by the type of leader who is in a position of authority.

Public Communication

Public communication occurs when a group becomes too large for all members to contribute. One characteristic of public communication is an unequal amount of speaking. One or more people are likely to deliver their remarks to the remaining members, who act as an audience. This leads to a second characteristic of public settings: limited verbal feedback. The audience isn't able to talk back in a two-way conversation the way they might in a dyadic or small group setting. This doesn't mean that speakers operate in a vacuum when delivering their remarks. Audiences often have a chance to ask questions and offer brief comments, and their nonverbal reactions offer a wide range of clues about their reception of the speaker's remarks.

Public speakers usually have a greater chance to plan and structure their remarks than do communicators in smaller settings. For this reason, several chapters of this book describe the steps you can take to prepare and deliver an effective speech.

Mass Communication

Mass communication consists of messages that are transmitted to large, widespread audiences via electronic and print media: newspapers, magazines, television, radio, blogs, websites, and so on. As you can see in the Mass Communication section of the *Understanding Human Communication* website, mass communication differs from the interpersonal, small group, and public varieties in several ways. First, most mass messages are aimed at a large audience without any personal contact between sender and receivers. Second, many of the messages sent via mass communication channels are developed, or at least financed, by large organizations. In this sense, mass communication is far less personal and more of a product than the other types we have examined so far. Finally, mass communication is often controlled by many gatekeepers who determine what messages will be delivered to consumers, how they will be constructed, and when they will be delivered. Sponsors (whether corporate or governmental), editors, producers, reporters, and executives all have the power to influence mass messages in ways that don't affect most other types. While blogs have given ordinary people the chance to reach enormous audiences, the bulk of mass messages are still controlled by corporate and governmental sources. Because of these and other unique characteristics, the study of mass communication raises special issues and deserves special treatment.

Now that we have a working understanding of the term *communication,* it is important to discuss why we will spend so much time exploring this subject. Perhaps the strongest argument for studying communication is its central role in our lives. The amount of time we spend communicating is staggering. In one study, researchers measured the amount of time a sample group of college students spent on various activities.[4] They found that the subjects spent an average of over 61 percent of their waking hours engaged in some form of communication. Whatever one's occupation, the results of such a study would not be too different. Most of us are surrounded by others, trying to understand them and hoping that they understand us: family, friends, coworkers, teachers, and strangers.

There's a good reason why we speak, listen, read, and write so much: Communication satisfies many of our needs.

Physical Needs

Communication is so important that it is necessary for physical health. In fact, evidence suggests that an absence of satisfying communication can even jeopardize life itself. Medical researchers have identified a wide range of hazards that result from a lack of close relationships.[5] For instance:

- People who lack strong relationships have two to three times the risk of early death, regardless of whether they smoke, drink alcoholic beverages, or exercise regularly.
- Terminal cancer strikes socially isolated people more often than those who have close personal relationships.
- Divorced, separated, and widowed people are five to ten times more likely to need hospitalization for mental problems than their married counterparts.
- Pregnant women under stress and without supportive relationships have three times more complications than pregnant women who suffer from the same stress but have strong social support.
- Socially isolated people are four times more susceptible to the common cold than those who have active social networks.[6]

Studies indicate that social isolation is a major risk factor contributing to coronary disease, comparable to physiological factors such as diet, cigarette smoking, obesity, and lack of physical activity.[7]

Research like this demonstrates the importance of having satisfying personal relationships. Remember: Not everyone needs the same amount of contact, and the quality of communication is almost certainly as important as the quantity. The important point here is that personal communication is essential for our well-being. To paraphrase an old song, "people who need people" aren't "the luckiest people in the world," they're the *only* people!

Identity Needs

Communication does more than enable us to survive. It is the way—indeed, the *only* way—we learn who we are. Are we smart or stupid, attractive or ugly, skillful or inept? The answers to these questions don't come from looking in the mirror. We decide who we are based on how others react to us.

Deprived of communication with others, we would have no sense of identity. This fact is illustrated by the case of the famous "Wild Boy of Aveyron," who spent his early childhood without any apparent human contact. The boy was discovered in January 1800 while digging for vegetables in a French village garden.[8] He showed no behaviors one would expect in a social human. The boy could not speak but uttered only weird cries. More significant than this absence of social skills was his lack of any identity as a human being. As author Roger Shattuck put it, "The boy had no human sense of being in the world. He had no sense of himself as a person related to other persons."[9] Only after the influence of a loving "mother" did the boy begin to behave—and, we can imagine, think of himself as a human. Contemporary stories support the essential role that communication plays in shaping identity. In 1970, authorities discovered a twelve-year-old girl (whom they called "Genie") who had spent virtually all her life in an otherwise empty, darkened bedroom with almost no human contact. The child could not speak and had no sense of herself as a person until she was removed from her family and "nourished" by a team of caregivers.[10]

Like Genie and the boy of Aveyron, each of us enters the world with little or no sense of identity. We gain an idea of who we are from the ways others define us.

Social Needs

Besides helping to define who we are, communication provides a vital link with others. Researchers and theorists have identified a range of social needs we satisfy by communicating: *pleasure* (e.g., "because it's fun," "to have a good time"); *affection* (e.g., "to help others," "to let others know I care"); *inclusion* (e.g., "because I need someone to talk to or be with," "because it makes me less lonely"); *escape* (e.g., "to put off doing something I should be doing"); *relaxation* (e.g., "because it allows me to unwind"); and *control* (e.g., "because I want someone to do something for me," "to get something I don't have").[11]

As you look at this list of social needs for communicating, imagine how empty your life would be if these needs weren't satisfied. Then notice that it would be impossible to fulfill them without communicating with others. Because relationships with others are so vital, some theorists have gone as far as to argue that communication is the primary goal of human existence. Anthropologist Walter Goldschmidt terms the drive for meeting social needs as the "human career."[12]

Practical Needs

We shouldn't overlook the everyday, important functions that communication serves. Communication is the tool that lets us tell the hair stylist to take just a little off the sides, direct the doctor to where it hurts, and inform the plumber that the broken pipe needs attention *now!*

Beyond these obvious needs, a wealth of research demonstrates that communication is an important key to effectiveness in a variety of everyday settings. For example, a survey of over four hundred employers identified "communication skills" as the top characteristic that employers seek in job candidates.[13] It was rated as more important than technical competence, work experience, or academic background. In another survey, over 90 percent of the personnel officials at five hundred U.S. businesses stated that increased communication skills are needed for success in the twenty-first century.[14]

Communication is just as important outside of work. College roommates who are both willing and able to communicate effectively report higher satisfaction with one another than do those who lack these characteristics.[15] Married couples who were identified as effective communicators reported happier relationships than did less skillful husbands and wives.[16] In school, the grade point averages of college students were related positively to their communication competence.[17] In "getting acquainted" situations, communication competence played a major role in whether a person was judged physically attractive, socially desirable, and good at the task of getting acquainted.[18]

Modeling Communication

So far we have introduced a basic definition of *communication* and seen the functions it performs. This information is useful, but it only begins to describe the process we will be examining throughout this book. One way to understand more about what it means to communicate is to look at some models that describe what happens when two or more people interact. As you will see, over the last half-century scholars have developed an increasingly accurate and sophisticated view of this process.

A Linear Model

Until about fifty years ago, researchers viewed communication as something that one person "does" to another.[19] In this **linear communication model,** communication is like giving an injection: a **sender encodes** ideas and feelings into some sort of **message** and then conveys them to a **receiver** who **decodes** them. (Figure 1–1.)

One important element of the linear model is the communication **channel**—the method by which a message is conveyed between people. For most people, face-to-face contact is the most familiar and obvious channel. Writing is another channel. In addition to these long-used forms, **mediated communication** channels include telephone, e-mail, instant messaging, faxes, voice mail, and even videoconferencing. (The word *mediated*

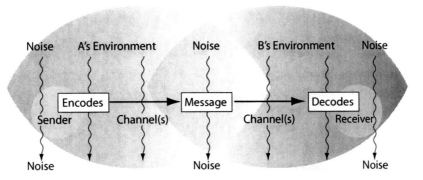

Figure 1–1: Linear Communication Model

reflects the fact that these messages are conveyed through some sort of communication medium.)

The channel you choose can make a big difference in the effect of a message. For example, a typewritten love letter probably wouldn't have the same effect as a handwritten note or card. Likewise, ending a relationship by sending a text message to your lover's cell phone would make a very different statement than delivering the bad news in person.

The linear model also introduces the concept of **noise**—a term used by social scientists to describe any forces that interfere with effective communication. Noise can occur at every stage of the communication process. Three types of noise can disrupt communication—external, physiological, and psychological. *External noise* (also called *physical*) includes those factors outside the receiver that make it difficult to hear, as well as many other kinds of distractions. For instance, too much cigarette smoke in a crowded room might make it hard for you to pay attention to another person, and sitting in the rear of an auditorium might make a speaker's remarks unclear. External noise can disrupt communication almost anywhere in our model—in the sender, channel, message, or receiver. *Physiological noise* involves biological factors in the receiver or sender that interfere with accurate reception: illness, fatigue, and so on. *Psychological noise* refers to forces within a communicator that interfere with the ability to express or understand a message accurately. For instance, an outdoors person might exaggerate the size and number of the fish he caught in order to convince himself and others of his talents. In the same way, a student might become so upset upon learning that she failed a test that she would be unable (perhaps *unwilling* is a better word) to understand clearly where she went wrong.

A linear model shows that communicators often occupy different **environments**—fields of experience that help them understand others' behavior. In communication terminology, *environment* refers not only to a physical location but also to the personal experiences and cultural backgrounds that participants bring to a conversation.

Consider just some of the factors that might contribute to different environments:

- A might belong to one ethnic group and B to another;
- A might be rich and B poor;

- A might be in a rush and B have nowhere to go;
- A might have lived a long, eventful life, and B might be young and inexperienced;
- A might be passionately concerned with the subject and B indifferent to it.

Notice how the model in Figure 1–1 shows that the environments of A and B overlap. This area represents the background that the communicators must have in common. As the shared environment becomes smaller, communication becomes more difficult. Consider a few examples in which different perspectives can make understanding difficult:

- Bosses who have trouble understanding the perspective of their employees will be less effective managers, and workers who do not appreciate the challenges of being a boss are more likely to be uncooperative (and probably less suitable for advancement).
- Parents who have trouble recalling their youth are likely to clash with their children, who have never known and may not appreciate the responsibility that comes with parenting.
- Members of a dominant culture who have never experienced how it feels to be "different" may not appreciate the concerns of people from nondominant co-cultures, whose own perspectives make it hard to understand the cultural blindness of the majority.

Differing environments make understanding others challenging but certainly not impossible. Hard work and many of the skills described in this book provide ways to bridge the gap that separates all of us to a greater or lesser degree. For now, recognizing the challenge that comes from dissimilar environments is a good start. You can't solve a problem until you recognize that it exists.

A Transactional Model

Despite its simplicity, the linear model doesn't do a very good job of representing the way most communication operates. The **transactional communication model** in Figure 1–2 presents a more accurate picture in several respects.

Simultaneous Sending and Receiving. Although some types of mass communication do flow in a one-way, linear manner, most types of personal communication are two-way exchanges.[20] The transactional model reflects the fact that we usually send and receive messages simultaneously. The roles of sender and receiver that seemed separate in the linear model are now superimposed and redefined as those of "communicators." This new term reflects the fact that at a given moment we are capable of receiving, decoding, and responding to another person's behavior, while at the same time that other person is receiving and responding to ours.

Consider, for instance, the significance of a friend's yawn as you describe your romantic problems. Or imagine the blush you may see as you tell one of your raunchier jokes to a

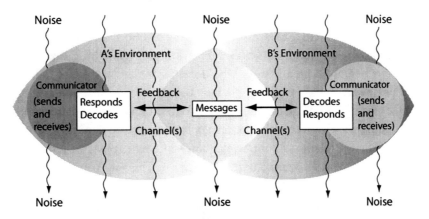

Figure 1–2 :Transactional Communication Model

new acquaintance. Nonverbal behaviors like these show that most face-to-face communication is a two-way affair. The discernible response of a receiver to a sender's message is called **feedback.** Not all feedback is nonverbal, of course. Sometimes it is oral, as when you ask an instructor questions about an upcoming test or volunteer your opinion of a friend's new haircut. In other cases it is written, as when you answer the questions on a midterm exam or respond to a letter from a friend. Figure 1–2 makes the importance of feedback clear. It shows that most communication is, indeed, a two-way affair.

Some forms of mediated communication like e-mail and text messaging don't appear to be simultaneous. Even here, though, the process is more complicated than the linear model suggests. For example, if you've ever waited impatiently for the response to a text message or instant message, you understand that even a nonresponse can have symbolic meaning. Is the unresponsive recipient busy? Thoughtful? Offended? Indifferent? Whether or not your interpretation is accurate, the silence is a form of communication.

Another weakness of the traditional linear model is the questionable assumption that all communication involves encoding. We certainly do choose symbols to convey most verbal messages. But what about the many nonverbal cues that occur whether or not people speak: facial expressions, gestures, postures, vocal tones, and so on? Cues like these clearly do offer information about others, although they are often unconscious and thus don't involve encoding. For this reason, the transactional model replaces the term *encodes* with the broader term *responds,* because it describes both intentional and unintentional actions that can be observed and interpreted.[21]

Communication Is Fluid, Not Static. It's difficult to isolate a discrete "act" of communication from the events that precede and follow it. The way a friend or family member reacts to a sarcastic remark you make will probably depend on the way you have related to one another in the past. Likewise, the way you'll act toward each other in the future depends on the outcome of this conversation.

Communication Is Relational, Not Individual. The transactional model shows that communication isn't something we do *to* others; rather, it is something we do *with* them.

In this sense, communication is rather like dancing—at least the kind of dancing we do with partners. Like dancing, communication depends on the involvement of a partner. And like good dancing, successful communication isn't something that depends just on the skill of one person. A great dancer who doesn't consider and adapt to the skill level of his or her partner can make both people look bad. In communication and dancing, even two talented partners don't guarantee success. When two talented dancers perform without coordinating their movements, the results feel bad to the dancers and look foolish to an audience. Finally, relational communication—like dancing—is a unique creation that arises out of the way in which the partners interact. The way you dance probably varies from one partner to another because of its cooperative, transactional nature. Likewise, the way you communicate almost certainly varies with different partners.

Psychologist Kenneth Gergen captures the relational nature of communication well when he points out how our success depends on interaction with others. As he says,"… one cannot be 'attractive' without others who are attracted, a 'leader' without others willing to follow, or a 'loving person' without others to affirm with appreciation."[22] Because communication is transactional, it's often a mistake to suggest that just one person is responsible for a relationship. Consider the accompanying cartoon. Both Cathy and Irving had good intentions, and both probably could have handled the situation better. As the humorous outcome shows, trying to pin the blame for a disappointing outcome on one person or the other is fruitless and counterproductive. It would have been far better to ask, "How did *we* handle this situation poorly, and what can *we* do to make it better?"

The transactional nature of communication shows up in school, where teachers and students influence one another's behavior. For example, teachers who regard some students negatively may treat them with subtle or overt disfavor. As a result, these students are likely to react to their teachers' behavior negatively, which reinforces the teachers' original attitudes and expectations.[23] It isn't necessary to resolve the "who started it" issue here to recognize that the behaviors of teachers and students are part of a transactional relationship.

The transactional character of communication also figures dramatically in relationships between parents and their children. We normally think of "good parenting" in terms of how well children turn out. But research suggests that the quality of interaction between parents and children is a two-way affair, that children influence parents just as much as the other way around.[24] For example, children who engage in what social scientists call "problematic behavior" evoke more high-control responses from their parents than do cooperative children. By contrast, youngsters with mild temperaments are less likely to provoke coercive reactions by their parents than are more aggressive children. Parents with low self-esteem tend to send more messages that weaken the self-esteem of their children, who in turn are likely to act in ways that make the parents feel even worse about them-selves. Thus, a mutually reinforcing cycle arises in which parents and children shape one another's feelings and behavior. In cases like this it's at least difficult and probably impossible to identify who is the "sender" and who is the "receiver" of messages. It's more accurate to acknowledge that parents and children—just like husbands and wives, bosses and employees, teachers and students, or any other people who communicate with one another—act in ways that mutually influence one another.

By now you can see that a transactional model of communication should be more like a motion picture film than a gallery of still photographs. Although Figure 1–2 does a fair job of picturing the phenomenon we call communication, an animated version in which the environments, communicators, and messages constantly change would be an even better way of capturing the process.

Communication Competence: What Makes An Effective Communicator?

It's easy to recognize good communicators, and even easier to spot poor ones. But what are the characteristics that distinguish effective communicators from their less successful counterparts? Answering this question has been one of the leading challenges for communication scholars.[25] Although all the answers aren't yet in, research has identified a great deal of important and useful information about communication competence.

Communication Competence Defined

Although scholars are still working to clarify the nature of **communication competence,** most would agree that effective communication involves achieving one's goals in a manner that, ideally, maintains or enhances the relationship in which it occurs.[26] This definition suggests several important characteristics of communication competence.

There Is No "Ideal" Way to Communicate. Your own experience shows that a variety of communication styles can be effective. Some very successful people are serious, whereas others use humor; some are gregarious, whereas others are quiet; and some are straightforward, whereas others hint diplomatically. Just as there are many kinds of beautiful music and art, there are many kinds of competent communication.

The type of communication that succeeds in one situation might be a colossal blunder in another. The joking insults you routinely trade with a friend might be insensitive and discouraging if he or she had just suffered a personal setback. The language you use with your peers might offend a family member, and last Saturday night's romantic approach would probably be out of place at work on Monday morning. For this reason, being a competent communicator requires flexibility in understanding what approach is likely to work best in a given situation.[27]

Competence Is Situational. Because competent behavior varies so much from one situation and person to another, it's a mistake to think that communication competence is a trait that a person either possesses or lacks. It's more accurate to talk about *degrees* or *areas* of competence.[28] You and the people you know are probably quite competent in some areas and less so in others. You might deal quite skillfully with peers, for example, but feel clumsy interacting with people much older or younger, wealthier or poorer, or more or less attractive than yourself. In fact, your competence with one person may vary from one situation to another. This means that it's an overgeneralization to say, in a moment of distress, "I'm a terrible communicator!" It would be more accurate to say, "I didn't handle this situation very well, even though I'm better in others."

Competence Is Relational. Because communication is transactional, something we do with others rather than to them, behavior that is competent in one relationship isn't necessarily competent in others.

A fascinating study on relational satisfaction illustrates that what constitutes satisfying communication varies from one relationship to another.[29] Researchers Brent Burleson and Wendy Sampter hypothesized that people with sophisticated communication skills (such as managing conflict well, giving ego-support to others, and providing comfort to relational partners) would be better at maintaining friendships than would be less skilled communicators. To their surprise, the results did not support this hypothesis. In fact, friendships were most satisfying when partners possessed matching skill levels. Apparendy, relational satisfaction arises in part when our style matches those of the people with whom we interact.

The same principle holds true in the case of jealousy. Researchers have uncovered a variety of ways by which people deal with jealousy in their relationships.[30] The ways included keeping closer tabs on the partner, acting indifferent, decreasing affection, talking the matter over, and acting angry. The researchers found that no type of behavior was effective or ineffective in every relationship. They concluded that approaches that work with some people would be harmful to others. Findings like these demonstrate that competence arises out of developing ways of interacting that work for you and for the other people involved.[31]

Competence Can Be Learned. To some degree, biology is destiny when it comes to communication style.[32] Studies of identical and fraternal twins suggest that traits including sociability, anger, and relaxation seem to be partially a function of our genetic makeup. Fortunately, biology isn't the only factor that shapes how we communicate: Communication is a set of skills that anyone can learn. As children grow, their ability to communicate effectively develops. For example, older children can produce more sophisticated persuasive attempts than can younger ones.[33] Along with maturity, systematic education (such as the class in which you are now enrolled) can boost communicative competence. Even a modest amount of training can produce dramatic results. After only thirty minutes of instruction, one group of observers became significantly more effective in detecting deception in interviews.[34] One study revealed that college students' communication competence increases over their undergraduate studies.[35] Even without systematic training, it's possible to develop communication skills through the processes of trial-and-error and observation. We learn from our own successes and failures, as well as from observing other models—both positive and negative.

Characteristics of Competent Communicators

Although competent communication varies from one situation to another, scholars have identified several common denominators that characterize effective communication in most contexts.

A Wide Range of Behaviors. Effective communicators are able to choose their actions from a wide range of behaviors. To understand the importance of having a large communication repertoire, imagine that someone you know repeatedly tells jokes—perhaps discriminatory ones—that you find offensive. You could respond to these jokes in a number of ways. You could:

- Say nothing, figuring that the risks of bringing the subject up would be greater than the benefits.
- Ask a third party to say something to the joke teller about the offensiveness of the jokes.
- Hint at your discomfort, hoping that your friend would get the point.
- Joke about your friend's insensitivity, counting on humor to soften the blow of your criticism.
- Express your discomfort in a straightforward way, asking your friend to stop telling the offensive jokes, at least around you.
- Simply demand that your friend stop.

With this choice of responses at your disposal (and you can probably think of others as well), you could pick the one that had the best chance of success. But if you were able to use only one or two of these responses when raising a delicate issue—always keeping quiet or always hinting, for example—your chances of success would be much smaller. Indeed, many poor communicators are easy to spot by their limited range of responses. Some are chronic jokers. Others are always belligerent. Still others are quiet in almost every situation. Like a piano player who knows only one tune or a chef who can prepare only a few dishes, these people are forced to rely on a small range of responses again and again, whether or not they are successful.

Ability to Choose the Most Appropriate Behavior. Simply possessing a large array of communication skills isn't a guarantee of effectiveness. It's also necessary to know which of these skills will work best in a particular situation. Choosing the best way to send a message is rather like choosing a gift: What is appropriate for one person won't be appropriate for another one at all. This ability to choose the best approach is essential because a response that works well in one setting would flop miserably in another one.

Although it's impossible to say precisely how to act in every situation, there are at least three factors to consider when you are deciding which response to choose: the context, your goal, and the other person.

Skill at Performing Behaviors. After you have chosen the most appropriate way to communicate, it's still necessary to perform the required skills effectively. There is a big difference between knowing *about* a skill and being able to put it into practice. Simply being aware of alternatives isn't much help, unless you can skillfully put these alternatives to work.

Just reading about communication skills in the following chapters won't guarantee that you can start using them flawlessly. As with any other skills—playing a musical instrument or learning a sport, for example—the road to competence in communication is not a short one. You can expect that your first efforts at communicating differently will be awkward. After some practice you will become more skillful, although you will still have to think about the new way of speaking or listening. Finally, after repeating the new skill again and again, you will find you can perform it without conscious thought.

Empathy/Perspective Taking. People have the best chance of developing an effective message when they understand the other person's point of view. And because others aren't always good at expressing their thoughts and feelings clearly, the ability to imagine how an issue might look from the other's point of view is an important skill. The value of taking the other's perspective suggests one reason why listening is so important. Not only does it help us understand others, but also it gives us information to develop strategies about how to best influence them.

Cognitive Complexity. Cognitive complexity is the ability to construct a variety of frameworks for viewing an issue. Cognitive complexity is an ingredient of communication competence because it allows us to make sense of people using a variety of perspectives. For instance, imagine that a longtime friend seems to be angry with you. One possible explanation is that your friend is offended by something you've done. Another possibility is that something upsetting has happened in another part of your friend's life. Or perhaps nothing at all is wrong, and you're just being overly sensitive. Researchers have found that the ability to analyze the behavior of others in a variety of ways leads to greater "conversational sensitivity," increasing the chances of acting in ways that will produce satisfying results.[36]

Self Monitoring. Psychologists use the term *self-monitoring* to describe the process of paying close attention to ones behavior and using these observations to shape the way one behaves. Self-monitors are able to separate a part of their consciousness and observe their behavior from a detached viewpoint, making observations such as:

"I'm making a fool out of myself."

"I'd better speak up now."

"This approach is working well. I'll keep it up."

Still, people who are aware of their behavior and the impression it makes are more skillful communicators than people who are low self-monitors.[37] For example, they are more accurate in judging others' emotional states, better at remembering information about others, less shy, and more assertive. By contrast, low self-monitors aren't even able to recognize their incompetence. (Calvin, in the nearby cartoon, does a nice job of illustrating this problem.) One study revealed that poor communicators were blissfully ignorant of their shortcomings and more likely to overestimate their skill than were better communicators.[38] For example, experimental subjects who scored in the lowest quartile on joke-telling skill were more likely than their funnier counterparts to grossly overestimate their sense of humor.

Commitment to the Relationship. One feature that distinguishes effective communication in almost any context is commitment. People who seem to care about the relationship communicate better than those who don't.[39] This concern shows up in commitment to the other person and to the message you are expressing.

Intercultural Communication Competence

What qualifies as competent behavior in one culture might be completely inept or even offensive in another.[40] On an obvious level, customs like belching after a meal or appearing nude in public, which might be appropriate in some parts of the world, would be considered outrageous in others. But as the "Understanding Diversity" box on page 19 shows, there are more subtle differences in competent communication. For example, qualities like being self-disclosing and speaking directly that are valued in the United States are likely to be considered overly aggressive and insensitive in many Asian cultures, where subtlety and indirectness are considered important.[41]

Cultures and Co-Cultures. National differences aren't the only dimensions of culture. Within a society, co-cultures have different communication practices. Consider just a few examples of co-cultures:

age (e.g., teen, Gen X, baby boomer)
socioeconomic status (e.g., high or low income; little or much education)
race/ethnicity (e.g., Native American, Latino)
sexual orientation (e.g., lesbian, gay male)
national heritage (e.g., Puerto Rican, Vietnamese)
different physical abilities (e.g., wheelchair users, deaf)
religion (e.g., Latter Day Saints, Muslim)
lifestyle (e.g., biker, gamer)

Some scholars have even characterized men and women as belonging to different co-cultures, claiming that each gender's style of communication is distinct. We'll have more to say about that topic throughout this book.

Members of various co-cultures may have different notions of appropriate behavior. One study revealed that ideas of how good friends should communicate varied from one ethnic group to another.[42] As a group, Latinos valued relational support most highly, whereas African Americans valued respect and acceptance. Asian Americans emphasized a caring, positive exchange of ideas, and Anglo Americans prized friends who recognized their needs as individuals. Findings like these mean that there can be no surefire list of rules or tips that will guarantee your success as a communicator. They also suggest that competent communicators are able to adapt their style to suit the individual and cultural preferences of others.[43]

Characteristics of Intercultural Competence. Communicating successfully with people from different cultural backgrounds calls for the same elements of competence outlined in the pages you have just read. But beyond these basic qualities, communication researchers have identified several other especially important ingredients of successful intercultural communication.[44]

Most obviously, it helps to know the rules of a specific culture. For example, the kind of self-deprecating humor that Americans are likely to find amusing may fall flat among Arabs from the Middle East.[45] But beyond knowing the specific rules of an individual culture, there are also attitudes and skills called "culture general" that help communicators build relationships with people from other backgrounds.[46]

Motivation. The desire to communicate successfully with strangers is an important start. For example, people high in willingness to communicate with people from other cultures report a greater number of friends from different backgrounds than those who are less willing to reach out.[47] Having the proper motivation is important in all communication, but particularly so in intercultural interactions because they can be quite challenging.

Tolerance for Ambiguity. Communicating with people from different backgrounds can be confusing. A tolerance for ambiguity makes it possible to accept, and even embrace, the often equivocal and sometimes downright incomprehensible messages that characterize intercultural communication.

For instance, if you happen to work with colleagues raised in traditional Native American co-cultures, you may find them much quieter and less outgoing than you are used to. Your first reaction might be to chalk this reticence up to a lack of friendliness. However, it may be a reflection of a co-culture in which reticence is valued more than extroversion and silence more than loquacity. In cross-cultural situations like this, ambiguity is a fact of life, and a challenge.

Open-Mindedness. It's one thing to tolerate ambiguity; it's another thing to become open-minded about cultural differences. There is a natural tendency to view others' communication choices as "wrong" when they don't match our cultural upbringing. In some parts of the world, you may find that women are not regarded with the same attitude of equality that is common in the West. Likewise, in other cultures, you may be aghast at the casual tolerance of poverty beyond anything at home, or with a practices of bribery that don't jibe with homegrown notions of what is ethical. In situations like these, principled communicators aren't likely to compromise deeply held beliefs about what is right. At the same time, competence requires an attitude that recognizes that people who behave differently are most likely following rules that have governed their whole lives.

Knowledge and Skill. The rules and customs that work with one group might be quite different from those that succeed with another. For example, when traveling in Latin America, you are likely to find that meetings there usually don't begin or end at their scheduled time, and that it takes the participants quite a while to "get down to business." Rather than viewing your hosts as irresponsible and unproductive, you'll want to recognize that the meaning of time is not the same in all cultures. Likewise, the gestures others make, the distance they stand from you, and the eye contact they maintain have ambiguous meanings that you'll need to learn and follow.

One way to boost your understanding of cultural differences is via mindfulness—awareness of your own behavior and that of others.[48] Communicators who lack this quality blunder through intercultural encounters mindlessly, oblivious of how their own behavior may confuse or offend others, and how behavior that they consider weird may be simply different. Communication theorist Charles Berger outlines three strategies for moving toward a more mindful, competent style of intercultural communication.[49]

- *Passive observation* involves noticing what behaviors members of a different culture use and applying these insights to communicate in ways that are most effective.
- • *Active strategies* include reading, watching films, and asking experts and members of the other culture how to behave, as well as taking academic courses related to intercultural communication and diversity.[50]
- *Self-disclosure* involves volunteering personal information to people from the other culture with whom you want to communicate. One type of self-disclosure is to confess your cultural ignorance: "This is very new to me. What's the right thing to do in this situation?" This approach is the riskiest of the three described here, since some cultures may not value candor and self-disclosure as much as others. Nevertheless, most people are pleased when strangers attempt to learn the practices of their culture, and they are usually more than willing to offer information and assistance.

Competence in Mediated Communication

Since the early 1990s, a growing number of researchers and theorists have studied the phenomenon of *mediated communication*: technologies that connect people who communicate without being face to face. Some forms of mediated communication are Internet-based: E-mail, instant messaging, and social networking websites are examples. These typically are labeled *computer-mediated communication* (CMC). Other mediated channels are phone-based: Cell phone conversations and text messaging are among the most common forms. As the "Understanding Communication Technology" box on page 21 shows, mediated communication calls for some skills that are different from those necessary in face-to-face interaction.[51]

Challenges of Mediated Communication. Nobody would downplay the challenges of communicating in face-to-face situations. But communicating via the Internet or phone presents its own set of issues.

Leaner Messages. Social scientists use the term richness to describe the abundance of nonverbal cues that add clarity to a verbal message. Face-to-face communication is rich because it abounds with nonverbal cues that give communicators cues about the meanings of one another's words and offer hints about their feelings.[52] By comparison, most mediated communication is a much leaner channel for conveying information.

To appreciate how message richness varies by medium, imagine you haven't heard from a friend in several weeks and you decide to ask "Is anything wrong?" Your friend replies, "No, I'm fine." Would that response be more or less descriptive depending on whether you received it via text message, over the phone, or in person?

You almost certainly would be able to tell a great deal more from a face-to-face response because it would contain a richer array of cues: facial expressions, vocal tone, and so on. By contrast, a text message contains only words. The phone message—containing vocal, but no visual cues—would probably fall somewhere in between.

Because most mediated messages are leaner than the face-to-face variety, they can be harder to interpret with confidence. Irony and attempts at humor can easily be misunderstood, so as a receiver it's important to clarify your interpretations before jumping to conclusions. As a sender, think about how to send unambiguous messages so you aren't misunderstood. (We'll discuss the value of "emoticons" and other text-based cues in Chapters 3 and 5.)

Disinhibition Sooner or later most of us speak before we think, blurting out remarks that embarrass ourselves and offend others. The tendency to transmit uncensored messages can be especially great in online communication, where we don't see, hear, or sometimes even know the target of our remarks. This **disinhi**bition can take two forms.

Sometimes online communicators volunteer personal information that they would prefer to keep confidential from at least some receivers. Consider the example of social networking sites like Facebook, MySpace, and Friendster. A quick scan of home pages there shows that many users post text and images about themselves that could prove embarrassing in some contexts: "Here I am just before my DUI arrest." "This is me in Cancun on spring break." This is not the sort of information most people would be eager to show a prospective employer or certain family members.

A second form of disinhibition is increased expressiveness. A growing body of research shows that communicators are more direct—often in a critical way—when using mediated channels than in face-to-face contact.[53]

Sometimes communicators take disinhibition to the extreme, blasting off angry—even vicious—e-mails, text messages, and website postings. The common term for these outbursts is *flaming*. Here is the account of one writer who was the target of an obscenity-filled e-mail:

> No one had ever said something like this to me before, and no one could have said this to me before: In any other medium, these **words** would be, literally, unspeakable. The **guy** couldn't have said this to me on the phone, because I would have hung up and not answered if the phone rang again, and he couldn't have said it to my face, because I wouldn't have let him finish....I suppose the guy could have written me a nasty letter: He **probably** wouldn't have used the word "rectum," though, and he probably wouldn't have mailed the letter; he would have thought twice while he **was** addressing the envelope. But the nature **of** E-mail is that you don't think twice. You write and send.[54]

Table 1-1: Factors to Consider When Choosing a Communication Channel

	Time Required for Feedback	Amount of Informatiion Conveyed	Sender's Control Over How Message is Composed	Control Over Receiver's Attention	Effectiveness for Detailed Messages
Face-to-face	Immediate (after contact established)	Highest	Moderate	Highest	Weak
Telephone	Immediate (after contact established)	Vocal, but not visual	Moderate	Less than in face-to-face setting	Weakest
Voice mail	Delayed	Vocal, but not visual	Higher (since receiver can't interrupt)	Low	Weak
E-mail	Delayed	Lowest (text only, no formatting)	High	Low	Better
Instant messaging	Immediate	Lowest (text only, no Formatting)	High	Modest	Weak
Hard copy (e.g., handwritten or typed message)	Delayed	Words, numbers, and images, but no nonverbal cues	Highest	Low	Good

Permanence. Common decency aside, the risk of hostile e-messages—or any inappropriate mediated messages—is their permanence. It can be bad enough to blurt out a private thought or lash out in person, but at least there is no permanent record of your indiscretion. By contrast, a regrettable text message, e-mail, or web posting can be archived virtually forever. Even worse, it can be retrieved and forwarded in ways that can only be imagined in your worst dreams. The best advice, then, is to take the same approach with mediated messages that you do in person: Think twice before saying something you may later regret.

Choosing the Best Medium. A generation ago, choosing which communication medium to use wasn't very complicated: If a face-to-face conversation wasn't desirable or possible, you either wrote a letter or used the telephone. Today's communicators have many more options. If you want to put your thoughts in writing, you can use e-mail, text messaging, instant messaging…or the traditional pen-and-paper approach. If you want to speak, you can either use a "landline" telephone, a cell phone, or an Internet-based system.

Sometimes the choice of a medium is a no-brainer. If a friend says "phone me while I'm on the road," you know what to do. If your boss or professor only responds to e-mails, then it would be foolish to use any other approach. But in many other situations, you have several options available. Table 1–1 outlines the advantages and drawbacks of the most common ones. Choosing the best channel can make a real difference in your success. In one survey managers who were identified as most "media sensitive" were almost twice as likely as their less savvy peers to receive top ratings in performance reviews.[55]

Having spent time talking about what communication is, we ought to also identify some things it is not.[56] Recognizing some misconceptions is important, not only because they ought to be avoided by anyone knowledgeable about the subject, but also because following them can get you into trouble.

Communication Does Not Always Require Complete Understanding

Most people operate on the implicit but flawed assumption that the goal of all communication is to maximize understanding between communicators. Although some understanding is necessary for us to comprehend one another's thoughts, there are some types of communication in which understanding as we usually conceive it isn't the primary goal.[57] Consider, for example:

- **Social rituals.** "How's it going?" you ask. "Great," the other person replies. The primary goal in exchanges like these is mutual acknowledgment: There's obviously no serious attempt to exchange information.
- **Many attempts to influence others.** A quick analysis of most television commercials shows that they are aimed at persuading viewers to buy products, not to understand the content of the commercial. In the same way, many of our attempts at persuading another to act as we want don't involve a desire to get the other person to understand what we want—just to comply with our wishes.
- **Deliberate ambiguity and deception.** When you decline an unwanted invitation by saying "I can't make it," you probably want to create the impression that the decision is really beyond your control. (If your goal was to be perfectly clear, you might say, "I don't want to get together. In fact, I'd rather do almost anything than accept your invitation.")
- **Coordinated action.** Examples are conversations where satisfaction doesn't depend on full understanding. The term **coordination** has been used to describe situations in which participants interact smoothly, with a high degree of satisfaction but without necessarily understanding one another well.[58] Coordination without understanding can be satisfying in far more important situations. Consider the words "I love you." This is a phrase that can have many meanings: Among other things, it can mean "I admire you," "I feel great affection for you," "I desire you," "I am grateful to you," "I feel guilty," "I want you to be faithful to me," or even "I hope *you* love *me*"[59] It's not hard to picture a situation in which partners gain great satisfaction—even over a lifetime—without completely understanding that the mutual love they profess actually is quite different for each of them. The cartoon on page 25 reflects the fact that better understanding can sometimes lead to *less* satisfaction. "You mean you mostly love me because I've been there for you? Hey, a *dog* is there for you!"

Communication Will Not Solve All Problems

"If I could just communicate better…" is the sad refrain of many unhappy people who believe that if they could just express themselves better, their relationships would improve. Though this is sometimes true, it's an exaggeration to say that communicating—even communicating clearly—is a guaranteed panacea.

Communication Isn't Always a Good Thing

For most people, belief in the value of communication rates somewhere close to parenthood in their hierarchy of important values. In truth, communication is neither good nor bad in itself. Rather, its value comes from the way it is used. In this sense, communication is similar to fire: Flames in the fireplace on a cold night keep you warm and create a cozy atmosphere, but the same flames can kill if they spread into the room. Communication can be a tool for expressing warm feelings and useful facts, but under different circumstances the same words and actions can cause both physical and emotional pain.

Meanings Rest in People, Not Words.

It's a mistake to think that, just because you use a word in one way, others will do so, too.[60] Sometimes differing interpretations of symbols are easily caught, as when we might first take the statement "He's loaded" to mean the subject has had too much to drink, only to find out that he is quite wealthy. In other cases, however, the ambiguity of words and nonverbal behaviors isn't so apparent, and thus has more far-reaching consequences. Remember, for instance, a time when someone said to you, "I'll be honest," and only later did you learn that those words hid precisely the opposite fact.

Communication is Not Simple

Most people assume that communication is an aptitude that people develop without the need for training—rather like breathing. After all, we've been swapping ideas with one another since early childhood, and there are lots of people who communicate pretty well without ever having had a class on the subject. Though this picture of communication as a natural ability seems accurate, it's actually a gross oversimplification.[61] Many people do learn to communicate skillfully because they have been exposed to models of such behavior by those around them. This principle of modeling explains why children who grow up in homes with stable relationships between family members have a greater chance of developing such relationships themselves. But even the best communicators aren't perfect: They often suffer the frustration of being unable to get a message across effectively, and they frequently misunderstand others. Furthermore, even the most successful people you know probably can identify ways in which their relationships could profit from better communication. These facts show that communication skills are rather like athletic ability: Even the most inept of us can learn to be more effective with training and practice, and those who are talented can always become better.

More Communication Isn't Always Better

Although it's certainly true that not communicating enough is a mistake, there are also situations when *too much* communication is a mistake. Sometimes excessive communication simply is unproductive, as when we "talk a problem to death," going over the same ground again and again without making any headway And there are times when communicating too much can actually aggravate a problem. We've all had the experience of "talking ourselves into a hole"—making a bad situation worse by pursuing it too far. As McCroskey and Wheeless put it, "More and more negative communication merely leads to more and more negative results."[62]

There are even times when *no* communication is the best course. Any good salesperson will tell you that it's often best to stop talking and let the customer think about the product. And when two people are angry and hurt, they may say things they don't mean and will later regret. At times like these it's probably best to spend a little time cooling off, thinking about what to say and how to say it.

One key to successful communication, then, is to share an *adequate* amount of information in a *skillful* manner. Teaching you *how* to decide what information is adequate and what constitutes skillful behavior is one major goal **of** this book.

Summary

In this chapter you have been introduced to some of the basic concepts of human communication which have been developed over the past fifty years. By understanding some of these concepts, you will have a greater ability to understand and interpret the chapters that follow. Understanding the symbolic nature of communication is essential to this goal. The following chapters will examine many of the concepts introduced in this chapter in greater detail: interpersonal communication, small group communication, public communication, and mediated communication. Additionally, you now have a good overview of the basic functions that communication may serve, be they physical, identity, social, or practical needs.

Another important aspect of this chapter is the introduction of the basic communication model which will be discussed in greater detail in Chapter Two. With knowledge of the linear, interactional, and transactional models of communication, you can see how the basic theories of human communication were developed. Finally, the concept of communication competence was introduced and discussed with respect to competence in a variety of communicative encounter.

It has often been said that a man or woman can only understand where they are going if they know where they have been. The purpose of the next chapter is to accomplish this very task—you will be introduced to the early theorizing about the concept of human communication, and how the basic model of communication was developed from Shannon and Weaver's mathematical model of communication.

Questions For Discussion

1. In what way can the symbolic nature of communication cause problems?
2. What are the key identity needs of college students today?
3. Why is the Linear Model of communication no longer accepted as a way to describe and analyze communication?
4. What is the essence of the term communication competence?
5. What are some of the basic misconceptions about human communication?

References

1. For an in-depth look at this topic, see S. B. Cunningham, "Intrapersonal Communication: A Review and Critique," in S. Deetz, ed., *Communication Yearbook* 15 (Newbury Park, CA Sage, 1992).
2. L. Wheeler and J. Nelek, "Sex Differences in Social Participation." *Journal of Personality and Social Psychology* 35 (1977): 742–754.
3. J. John, "The Distribution of Free-Forming Small Group Size." *American Sociological Review* 18 (1953): 569–570.
4. R. Verderber, A Elder, and E. Weiler, "A Study of Communication Time Usage among College Students" (unpublished study. University of Cincinnati, 1976).
5. For a summary of the link between social support and health, see S. Duck, "Staying Healthy… with a Little Help from Our Friends?" in *Human Relationships*, 2nd ed. (Newbury Park, CA: Sage, 1992).
6. S. Cohen, W.J. Doyle, D. P. Skoner, B. S. Rabin, and J. M. Gwaltney, "Social Ties and Susceptibility to the Common *Cold" Journal of the American Medical Association* 277 (1997): 1940–1944.
7. Three articles *m. Journal of the American Medical Association* 267 (January 22/29,1992) focus on the link between psychosocial influences and coronary heart disease: R. B. Case, A J. Moss, N. Case, M. McDermott, and S. Eberly, "Living Alone after Myocardial Infarction" (pp. 515–519); R. B. Williams, J. C. Barefoot, R. M. Calif, T. L. Haney, W. B. Saunders, D. B. Pryon, M. A Hlatky, I. C. Siegler, and D. B. Mark, "Prognostic Importance of Social and Economic Resources among Medically Treated Patients with Angiographically Documented Coronary Ar-

tery Disease" (pp. 520–524); and R. Ruberman, "Psychosocial Influences on Mortality of Patients with Coronary Heart Disease" (pp. 559–560).

8. J. Stewart, Bridges, *Not Walk: A Book about Interpersonal Communication*, 9th ed. (New York: McGraw-Hill, 2004), p. 11.

9. R. Shattuck, *The Forbidden Experiment: The Story of the Wild Boy of Aveyron* (New York: Farrar, Straus & Giroux, 1980), p. 37.

10. For a fascinating account of Genie's story, see R. Rymer, *Genie: An Abused Child's Flight from Silence* (New York: HarperCollins, 1993). Linguist Susan Curtiss provides a more specialized account of the case in her book *Genie: A Psycholinguistic Study of a Modern-Day "Wild Child"* (San Diego: Academic Press, 1977).

11. R. B. Rubin, E. M. Perse, and C. A Barbate, "Conceptualization and Measurement of Interpersonal Communication Motives." *Human Communication Research* 14 (1988): 602–628.

12. W. Goldschmidt, *The Human Career: The Self in the Symbolic World* (Cambridge, MA Basil Blackmun, 1990).

13. Job Outlook 2004, National Association of Colleges and Employers. *Report at* http://www.jobweb.com/joboutlook/2004outlook/

14. M. S. Peterson, "Personnel Interviewers' Perceptions of the Importance and Adequacy of Applicants' Communication Skills." *Communication Education* 46 (1997): 287–291.

15. M. W. Martin and C. M. Anderson, "Roommate Similarity: Are Roommates Who Are Similar in Their Communication Traits More Satisfied?" Communication Research Reports 12 (1995): 46–52.

16. E. Kirchler, "Marital Happiness and Interaction in Everyday Surroundings: A Time-Sample Diary Approach for Couples." Journal of Social and Personal Relationships 5 (1988): 375–382.

17. R. B. Rubin and E. E. Graham, "Communication Correlates of College Success: An Exploratory Investigation." Communication Education 37 (1988): 14–27.

18. R. L. Duran and L. Kelly, "The Influence of Communicative Competence on Perceived Task, Social and Physical Attraction." Communication Quarterly 36 (1988): 41–9.

19. C. E. Shannon and W. Weaver, *The Mathematical Theory of Communication* (Urbana: University of Illinois Press, 1949).

20. See, for example, M. Dunne and S. H. Ng, "Simultaneous Speech in Small Group Conversation: All-Together-Now and One-at-a-Time?" *Journal of Language and Social Psychology* 13 (1994): 45–71.

21. The issue of intentionality has been a matter of debate by communication theorists. For a sample of the arguments on both sides, see J. O. Greene, ed., *Message Production: Advances in Communication Theory* (New York: Erlbaum, 1997); M. T. Motley, "On Whether One Can(not) Communicate: An Examination via Traditional Communication Postulates." *Western Journal of Speech Communication* 54 (1990): 1–20; J. B. Bavelas, "Behaving and Communicating: A Reply to Modey." *Western Journal of Speech Communication* 54 (1990): 593–602; and J. Stewart, "A Postmodern Look at Traditional Communication Postulates." *Western Journal of Speech Communication* 55 (1991): 354–379.

22. K. J. Gergen, The Saturated Self: Dilemmas of Identity in Contemporary Life (New York: Basic Books, 1991), p. 158.

23. T. P. Mottet and V P. Richmond, "Student Nonverbal Communication and Its Influence on Teachers and Teaching: A Review of Literature," in J. L. Chesebro andj. C. McCroskey, eds., *Communication for Teachers* (Needham Heights, MA: Allyn & Bacon, 2001).

24. M. Dainton and L. Stafford, "The Dark Side of 'Normal' Family Interaction," in B. H. Spitzberg and W. R. Cupach, eds., *The Dark Side of Interpersonal Communication* (Hillsdale, NJ: Erlbaum, 1993).

25. For a thorough review of this topic, see B. H. Spitzberg and W. R. Cupach, *Handbook of Interpersonal Competence Research* (New York: Springer-Verlag, 1989).

26. See J. M. Wiemannj. Takai, H. Ota, and M. Wiemann, "A Relational Model of Communication Competence," in B. Kovacic, ed., *Emerging Theories of Human Communication* (Albany: SUNY Press, 1997).

27. For a review of the research citing the importance of flexibility, see M. M. Martin and C. M. Anderson, "The Cognitive Flexibility Scale: Three Validity Studies." *Communication Reports* 11 (1998): 1–9.

28. For a discussion of the trait versus state assessments of communication, see D. A. Infante, A. S. Rancer, and D. F. Womack, *Building Communication Theory*, 3rd ed. (Prospect Heights, IL: Waveland Press, 1996), pp. 159–160. For a specific discussion of trait versus state definitions of communication competence, see W. R. Cupach and B. H. Spitzberg, "Trait versus State: A Comparison of Dispositional and Situational Measures of Interpersonal Communication Competence." *Western Journal of Speech Communication* 47 (1983): 364–379.

29. B. R. Burleson and W. Samter, "A Social Skills Approach to Relationship Maintenance," in D. Canary and L. Stafford, eds., *Communication and Relationship Maintenance* (San Diego: Academic Press, 1994), p. 12.

30. L. K Guerrero, P. A Andersen, P. E Jorgensen, B. H. Spitzberg, and S. V Eloy. "Coping with the Green-Eyed Monster: Conceptualizing and Measuring Communicative Responses to Romantic Jealousy." *Western Journal of Communication* 59 (1995): 270–304.

31. See B.J. O'Keefe, "The Logic of Message Design: Individual Differences in Reasoning about Communication." *Communication Monographs* 55 (1996): 80–103.

32. See, for example, A D. Heisel, J. C. McCroskey, and V P. Richmond, "Testing Theoretical Relationships and Nonrelationships of Genetically-Based Predictors: Getting Started with Communi-biology," Communication Research Reports 16 (1999): 1–9; and J. C. McCroskey and K.J. Beatty, "The Communibiological Perspective: Implications for Communication in Instruction." *Communication Education* 49 (2000): 1–6.

33. S. L. Kline and B. L. Clinton, "Developments in Children's Persuasive Message Practices." *Communication Education* 47 (1998): 120–136.

34. M. A de Turck and G. R. Miller, "Training Observers to Detect Deception: Effects of Self-Monitoring and Rehearsal." *Human Communication Research* 16 (1990): 603–620.

35. R. B. Rubin, E. E. Graham, and J. T. Mignerey, "A Longitudinal Study of College Students' Communication Competence." *Communication Education* 39 (1990): 1–14.

36. See, for example, R. Martin, "Relational Cognition Complexity and Relational Communication in Personal Relationships." *Communication Monographs* 59 (1992): 150–163; D. W Stacks and M. A Murphy. "Conversational Sensitivity: Further Validation and Extension." *Communication Reports* 6 (1993): 18–24; and A L. Vangelisti and S. M. Draughton, "The Nature and Correlates of Conversational Sensitivity." *Human Communication Research* 14(1987): 167–202.

37. Research summarized in D. E. Hamachek, Encounters with the Self 2nd ed. (Fort Worth, TX: Holt, Rinehart and Winston, 1987), p. 8. See also J. A Daly, A L. Vangelisti, and S. M. Daughton, "The Nature and Correlates of Conversational Sensitivity," in M. V Redmond, ed., *Interpersonal Communication: Readings in Theory and Research* (Fort Worth, TX: Harcourt Brace, 1995).

38. D. A Dunning and J. Kruger, *Journal of Personality and Social Psychology* (December 1999).

39. Adapted from the work of R. P. Hart as reported by M. L. Knapp in Interpersonal Communication and Human Relationships (Boston: Allyn & Bacon, 1984), pp. 342–344. See also R. P.Hart and D. M. Burks, "Rhetorical Sensitivity and Social Interaction." Speech Monographs 39 (1972): 75–91; and R. P. Hart, R. E. Carlson, and W. F. Eadie, "Attitudes toward Communication and the Assessment of Rhetorical Sensitivity." *Communication Monographs* 47 (1980); 1–22.

40. See G. M. Chen and W. J. Sarosta, "Intercultural Communication Competence: A Synthesis," in B. R. Burleson and A W. Kunkel, eds., *Communication Yearbook* 19 (Thousand Oaks, CA: Sage, 1996).

41. See, for example, M. S. Kim, H. C. Shin, and D. Cai, "Cultural Influences on the Preferred Forms of Requesting and Re-Requesting." *Communication Monographs* 65 (1998): 47–66.

42. M.J. Collier, "Communication Competence Problematics in Ethnic Relationships." *Communication Monographs* 63 (1996): 314–336.

43. For an example of the advantages of cultural flexibility, see L. Chen, "Verbal Adaptive Strategies in U.S. American Dyadic Interactions with U.S. American or East-Asian Partners." *Communication Monographs* 64 (1997): 302–323.

44. See, for example, C. Hajek and H. Giles, "New Directions in Intercultural Communication Competence: The Process Model," in B. R. Burleson and J. O. Greene, eds., Handbook of Communication and Social Interactim Skills (Mahwah, NJ: Erlbaum, 2003); and S. Ting-Toomey andL. C. Chung, *Understanding Intercultural Communication* (Los Angeles: Roxbury, 2005).

45. M. Kalliny, K Cruthirds, and M. Minor, "Differences between American, Egyptian and Lebanese Humor Styles: Implications for International Management." *International Journal of Cross Cultural Management* 6 (2006): 121–134.

46. L. A Samovar and R. E. Porter, *Communication between Cultures* 5th ed. (Belmont, CA: Wadsworth, 2004).

47. J. W. Kassing, "Development of the Intercultural Willingness to Communicate Scale." *Communication Research Reports* 14 (1997): 399–407.

48. J. K Burgoon, C. R. Berger, and V R. Waldron, "Mindfulness and Interpersonal Communication." *Journal of Social Issues* 56 (2000): 105–128.

49. C. R. Berger, "Beyond Initial Interactions: Uncertainty, Understanding, and the Development of Interpersonal Relationships," in H. Giles and R. St. Clair, eds., *Language and Social Psychology* (Oxford: Blackwell, 1979), pp. 122–144.

50. L.J. Carrell, "Diversity in the Communication Curriculum: Impact on Student Empathy." *Communication Education* 46 (1997): 234–244.

51. For an overview of competence in mediated communication, see B. H. Spitzberg, "Preliminary Development of a Model and Measure of Computer-Mediated Communication (CMC) Competence." *Journal of Computer-Mediated Communication* 11 (2006): 629–666.

52. IC S. Surinder and R. B. Cooper, "Exploring the Core Concepts of Media Richness Theory: The Impact of Cue Multiplicity and Feedback Immediacy on Decision Quality." *Journal of Management Information Systems* 20 (2003): 263–299.

53. S. A Watts, "Evaluative feedback: Perspectives on media effects." *Journal of Computer-Mediated Communication* 12 (2007). Retrieved April 13,2007 from http://jcmc.indiana.edu/vol12/issue2/watts.html.

54. John Seabrook, "My First Flame." *New Yorker* (June 6,1994): 70–79.

55. J. Montague, "When E-Mail Just Won't Do." *Hospitals and Health Networks* 70 (October 20,1996): 10–11.

56. Adapted from J. C. McCroskey and L. R. Wheeless, *Introduction to Human Communication* (Boston: Allyn & Bacon, 1976), pp. 3–10.

57. R. K. Aune, "A Theory of Attribution of Responsibility for Creating Understanding." Paper delivered to the Interpersonal Communication Division of the 1998 International Communication Association Conference, Jerusalem, Israel.

58. W. B. Pearce and K. A. Pearce, "Extending the Theory of the Coordinated Management of Meaning (CMM) through a Community Dialogue Process. *Communication Theory* 10 (2000): 405–423. See also E. M. Griffin, *A First Look at Communication Theory*. 5th ed. (New York: McGraw-Hill, 2003), pp. 66–81.

59. J. A. M. Meerloo, *Conversation and Communication* (Madison, CT: International Universities Press, 1952), p. 91.

60. For a detailed rationale of the position argued in this section, see G. H. Stamp and M. L. Knapp, "The Construct of Intent in Interpersonal Communication." *Quarterly Journal of Speech* 76 (1990): 282–299. See also J. Stewart, "A Postmodern Look at Traditional Communication Postulates." *Western Journal of Speech Communication* 55 (1991): 354–379.

61. For a thorough discussion of communication difficulties, see N. Coupland, H. Giles, and J. M. Wiemann, eds., *"Miscommunication" and Problematic Talk* (Newbury Park, CA: Sage, 1991).

62. J. C. McCroskey and L. R. Wheeless, *Introduction to Human Communication* (Boston: Allyn & Bacon, 1976), p. 5.

Chapter 2

Communication Theory

John Fiske

In the last chapter you were given an overview of the concepts of human communication. You will now read the origin of this information, Shannon and Weaver's basic model of communication. This model was the start of many theories of communication, and understanding it will help you in your quest to master the concepts of human communication.

Learning Objectives For This Chapter

- Identify the basic elements of the Shannon and Weaver Model
- Explain the relationship between noise and information in communication
- Differentiate between redundancy and entropy
- Explain the importance of phatic communication
- Describe how channel, medium, meaning, and code interact in the communication process
- Explain the role that feedback plays in communication

Origins

Shannon and Weaver's *Mathematical Theory of Communication* (1949; Weaver, 1949b) is widely accepted as one of the main seeds out of which Communication Studies has grown.

Level A (technical problems)	How accurately can the symbols of communication be transmitted?
Level B (semantic problems)	How precisely do the transmitted symbols convey the desired meaning?
Level C (effectiveness problems)	How effectively does the received meaning affect conduct in the desired way?

It is a clear example of the process school, seeing communication as the transmission of messages.

Their work developed during the Second World War in the Bell Telephone Laboratories in the US, and their main concern was to work out a way in which the *channels* of communication could be used most efficiently. For them, the main channels were the telephone cable and the radio wave. They produced a theory that enabled them to approach the problem of how to send a maximum amount of information along a given channel, and how to measure the capacity of any one channel to carry information. This concentration on the channel and its capacity is appropriate to their engineering and mathematical background, but they claim that their theory is widely applicable over the whole question of human communication.

Their basic model of communication presents it as a simple linear process. Its simplicity has attracted many derivatives, and its linear, process-centred nature has attracted many critics. But we must look at the model (figure 2) before we consider its implications and before we attempt to evaluate it. The model is broadly understandable at first glance. Its obvious characteristics of simplicity and linearity stand out clearly. We will return to the named elements in the process later.

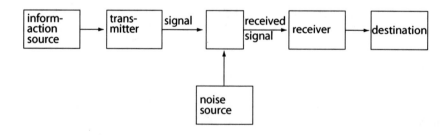

Figure 2: Shannon and Weaver's Model of Communication

Shannon and Weaver identify three levels of problems in the study of communication. These are:

The technical problems of level A are the simplest to understand and these are the ones that the model was originally developed to explain.

The semantic problems are again easy to identify, but much harder to solve, and range from the meaning of words to the meaning that a US newsreel picture might have for a Russian. Shannon and Weaver consider that the meaning is contained in the message: thus improving the encoding will increase the semantic accuracy. But there are also cultural factors at work here which the model does not specify: the meaning is at least as much in the culture as in the message.

The effectiveness problems may at first sight seem to imply that Shannon and Weaver see communication as manipulation or propaganda: that A has communicated effectively with B when B responds in the way A desires. They do lay themselves open to this criticism, and hardly deflect it by claiming that the aesthetic or emotional response to a work of art is an *effect* of communication.

They claim that the three levels are not watertight, but are interrelated, and interdependent, and that their model, despite its origin in level A, works equally well on all three levels. The point of studying communication at each and all of these levels is to understand how we may improve the *accuracy* and *efficiency* of the process.

But let us return to our model. The *source* is seen as the decision maker; that is, the source decides which message to send, or rather selects one out of a set of possible messages. This selected message is then changed by the *transmitter* into a *signal* which is sent through the *channel* to the *receiver*. For a telephone the channel is a wire, the signal an electrical current in it, and the transmitter and receiver are the telephone handsets. In conversation, my mouth is the transmitter, the signal is the sound waves which pass through the channel of the air (I could not talk to you in a vacuum), and your ear is the receiver.

Obviously, some parts of the model can operate more than once. In the telephone message for instance, my mouth transmits a signal to the handset which is at this moment a receiver, and which instantly becomes a transmitter to send the signal to your handset, which receives it and then transmits it via the air to your ear. Gerbner's model, as we will see later, deals more satisfactorily with this doubling up of certain stages of the process.

Noise

The one term in the model whose meaning is not readily apparent is noise. Noise is anything that is added to the signal between its transmission and reception that is not intended by the source. This can be distortion of sound or crackling in a telephone wire, static in a radio signal, or 'snow' on a television screen. These are all examples of noise occurring within the channel and this sort of noise, on level A, is Shannon and Weaver's main concern. But the concept of noise has been extended to mean any signal received that was not transmitted by the source, or anything that makes the intended signal harder to decode accurately. Thus an uncomfortable chair during a lecture can be a source of noise—we do not receive messages through our eyes and ears only. Thoughts that are more interesting than the lecturer's words are also noise.

Shannon and Weaver admit that the level-A concept of noise needs extending to cope with level-B problems. They distinguish between semantic noise (level B) and engineering noise (level A) and suggest that a box labelled 'semantic receiver' may need inserting between the engineering receiver and the destination. Semantic noise is defined as any distortion of meaning occurring in the communication process which is not intended by the source but which affects the reception of the message at its destination.

Noise, whether it originates in the channel, the audience, the sender, or the message itself, always confuses the intention of the sender and thus limits the amount of desired information that can be sent in a given situation in a given time. Overcoming the problems caused by noise led Shannon and Weaver into some further fundamental concepts.

Information: Basic Concept

Despite their claims to operate on levels A, B, and C, Shannon and Weaver do, in fact, concentrate their work on level A. On this level, their term information is used in a specialist, technical sense, and to understand it we must erase from our minds its usual everyday meaning.

Information on level A is a measure of the predictability of the signal, that is the number of choices open to its sender. It has nothing to do with its content. A signal, we remember, is the physical form of a message—sound waves in the air, light waves, electrical impulses, touchings, or whatever. So, I may have a code that consists of two signals—a single flash of a light bulb, or a double flash. The *information* contained by either of these signals is identical—50 per cent predictability. This is regardless of what they actually mean—one flash could mean 'Yes', two flashes 'No', or one flash could mean the whole of the Old Testament, and two flashes the New. In this case 'Yes' contains the same amount of information as the 'Old Testament'. The information contained by the letter 'u' when it follows the letter 'q' in English is nil because it is totally predictable.

Information: Further Implications

We can use the unit 'bit' to measure information. The word 'bit' is a compression of 'binary digit' and means, in practice, a Yes/No choice. These binary choices, or binary oppositions, are the basis of computer language, and many psychologists claim that they are the way in which our brain operates too. For instance, if we wish to assess someone's age we go through a rapid series of binary choices: are they old or are they young; if young, are they adult or pre-adult; if pre-adult, are they teenager or pre-teenager; if pre-teenager, are they school-age or pre-school; if preschool, are they toddler or baby? The answer is baby. Here, in this system of binary choices the word 'baby' contains five bits of information because we have made five choices along the way. Here, of course, we have slipped easily on to level B, because these are semantic categories, or categories of meaning, not simply of signal. 'Information' at this level is much closer to our normal use of the term. So if we say someone is young we give one bit of information only, that he is not old. If we say he is a baby we give five bits of information *if,* and it is a big *if,* we use the classifying system detailed above.

This is the trouble with the concept of 'information' on level B. The semantic systems are not so precisely defined as are the signal systems of level A, and thus the numerical measuring of information is harder, and some would say irrelevant. There is no doubt that a letter (i.e. part of the signal system of level A) contains five bits of information. (Ask if it is in the first or second half of the alphabet, then in the first or second half of the half you have chosen, and so on. Five questions, or binary choices, will enable you to identify any letter in the alphabet.) But there is considerable doubt about the possibility of measuring meaning in the same sort of way.

Obviously, Shannon and Weaver's engineering and mathematical background shows in their emphasis. In the design of a telephone system, the critical factor is the number of signals it can carry. *What* people actually say is irrelevant. The question for us, however, is how useful a theory with this sort of mechanistic base can be in the broader study of communication. Despite the doubts about the value of measuring meaning and information numerically, relating the amount of information to the number of choices available is insightful, and is broadly similar to insights into the nature of language provided by linguistics and semiotics, as we will see later in this book. Notions of predictability and choice are vital in understanding communication.

Redundancy and Entropy

Redundancy: Basic Concepts

Closely related to 'information' is the concept of *redundancy*. Redundancy is that which is predictable or conventional in a message. The opposite of redundancy is *entropy*. Redundancy is the result of high predictability, entropy of low predictability. So a message with low predictability can be said to be entropic and of high information. Conversely, a message of high predictability is redundant and of low information. If I meet a friend in the street and say 'Hello', I have a highly predictable, highly redundant message.

But I have not wasted my time and effort. The layman's use of the term to imply uselessness is misleading. Redundancy is not merely useful in communication, it is absolutely vital. In theory, communication *can* take place without redundancy, but in practice the situations in which this is possible are so rare as to be nonexistent. A degree of redundancy is essential to practical communication. The English language is about 50 per cent redundant. This means we can delete about 50 per cent of the words and still have a usable language capable of transmitting understandable messages.

Redundancy: Further Implications

So what use is redundancy? It performs two main types of functions: the first is technical, and is well defined by Shannon and Weaver; the second involves extending their concept into the social dimension.

Redundancy as a Technical Aid

Shannon and Weaver show how redundancy helps the accuracy of decoding and provides a check that enables us to identify errors. I can only identify a spelling mistake because of the redundancy in the language. In a non-redundant language, changing a letter would mean changing the word. Thus 'comming' would be a different word from 'coming' and you would not be able to tell that the first word was a misspelling. Of course, the context might help. In so far as it did, the context would be a source of redundancy. In a natural language, words are not equiprobable. If I say 'Spring is then I am creating a context in which 'coming' is more probable and thus more redundant than, say, 'a pane of glass'. It is, of course, possible that a poet, or even an advertiser for new windows, might write 'Spring is a pane of glass', but that would be a highly entropic use of language.

We are always checking the accuracy of any message we receive against the probable; and what is probable is determined by our experience of the code, context, and type of message—in other words, by our experience of convention and usage. *Convention* is a major source of redundancy, and thus of easy decoding. A writer who breaks with convention does not want to be easily understood: writers who desire easy communication with their readers use appropriate conventions. We will return to this question of convention and redundancy later.

Redundancy also helps overcome the deficiencies of a noisy channel. We repeat ourselves on a bad telephone line; when spelling words on radio or telephone we say A for apple, S for sugar, and so on. An advertiser whose message has to compete with many others for our attention (that is, who has to use a noisy channel) will plan a simple, repetitious, predictable message. One who can expect to have our undivided attention, as, for example, with a technical advertisement in a specialist journal, can design a more entropic message which contains more information.

Increasing redundancy also helps overcome the problems of transmitting an en-tropic message. A message that is completely unexpected, or that is the opposite of what would be expected, will need saying more than once, often in different ways. Or it may need some special preparation: 'Now, I've got a surprise for you, something you didn't expect at all...''

Redundancy also helps solve problems associated with the audience. If we wish to reach a larger, heterogeneous audience we will need to design a message with a high degree of redundancy. A small, specialist, homogeneous audience, on the other hand, can be reached with a more entropic message. Thus popular art is more redundant than highbrow art. An advertisement for soap powder is more redundant than one for a business computer.

The choice of channel can affect the need for redundancy in the message. Speech needs to be more redundant than writing because the hearer cannot introduce his or her own redundancy as a reader can by reading something twice.

This first function of redundancy, then, is concerned with the way it helps to overcome practical communication problems. These problems may be associated with accuracy and error detection, with the channel and noise, with the nature of the message, or with the audience.

Entropy

Entropy as a concept is of less value for the general student of communication in that it constitutes a communication problem, whereas redundancy is a means of improving communication. But entropy can best be understood as maximum unpredictability. On level A, entropy is simply a measure of the number of choices of signal that can be made and of the randomness of those choices. If I wish to communicate the identities of a pack of playing cards visually by showing all the cards singly, each signal will have maximum entropy if the pack is completely shuffled. If, however, I arrange the cards in order in their suits, each signal will have maximum redundancy, provided that the receiver knows, or can identify, the pattern or structure of a pack of cards.

Redundancy and Convention

Structuring a message according to shared patterns, or conventions, is one way of decreasing entropy and increasing redundancy. Imposing an aesthetic pattern or structure on material does precisely the same thing. Rhythmic poetry, by imposing repeatable and therefore predictable patterns of metre and rhyme, decreases entropy and therefore increases redundancy.

> Shall I compare thee to a summer's day? Thou art more lovely and more temperate: Rough winds do shake the darling buds of…

The convention or form of the sonnet has determined that the next word must, on level A, have a single syllable and must rhyme with 'day'. The choice of signal is restricted. Another convention which increases redundancy here is syntax. This reduces the possible choice further—to a noun. On level B, where we expect the word not only to fit the form but also to make sense, we restrict the choice even further. It could not really be 'hay', or 'way'. The word Shakespeare chose, 'May', must in fact be nearly totally redundant. But it feels absolutely right and is aesthetically satisfying. Redundancy is a critical part of the satisfaction provided by the form or structure of a work of art.

The more popular and widely accessible a work of art is, the more it will contain redundancies in form and content. Traditional folk-song or a television series provide obvious examples. Does it therefore follow that highbrow art is necessarily more entropic, in either or both level A (form) and level B (content)? It certainly may do, though communication theory would lead us to conclude that the crucial factor is not the 'level of brow', but the accessibility of the work of art to a wide audience. In other words, there can be popular, highbrow words of art, but these are nearly always conventional—think of Jane Austen or Beethoven as popular highbrows.

When we are dealing with entropy and redundancy in relation to works of art we must remember that we are not dealing with something static and unchanging. An art form or style may break existing conventions, and thus be entropic to its immediate audience, but may then establish its own conventions and thus increase its redundancy as these conventions become learnt and accepted more widely. The way that the Impressionist style of painting was at first rejected by its audience but has now become chocolate-box and calendar cliché is a good example.

Broadly, we may say that encoders, whether artists, preachers, or politicians, who build redundancy into their messages are audience-centred. They care about communicating. Those who do not are more concerned about subject matter, or (if they are artists) form. So redundancy is concerned primarily with the efficiency of communication and the overcoming of communication problems.

Redundancy and Social Relationships

But I said that there was an extension of this concept that could well perform a different, though related, function. Saying 'Hello' in the street is sending a highly redundant message. But there are no communication problems to solve. There is no noise; I do not wish to put over an entropic content; the audience is receptive. I am engaging in what Jakobson (see below) calls *phatic communication*. By this, he refers to acts of communication that contain nothing new, no information, but that use existing channels simply to keep them open and usable. In fact, of course, there is more to it than that. What I am doing in saying 'Hello' is maintaining and strengthening an existing relationship. Relationships can only exist through constant communication. My 'Hello' may not alter or develop the relationship, but not saying 'Hello' would certainly weaken it.

Social psychologists talk of the ego-drive, a need to have our presence noticed, recognized, and accepted. Not saying 'Hello', that is, cutting someone dead or looking right through them, is frustrating this need. It is socially necessary that I say 'Hello'. Phatic communication, by maintaining and reaffirming relationships, is crucial in holding a community or a society together. And phatic communication is highly redundant; it must be, because it is concerned with existing relationships, not with new information. Conventional behaviour and words in interpersonal situations, such as greetings, are phatic, redundant communication that reaffirms and strengthens social relationships. We call it politeness.

This points to similarities between the two functions of redundancy. The polite person, who indulges in phatic communication, is audience-or receiver-centred in the same way as the communicator who builds redundancy into his or her work. It is no coincidence that the word convention refers to both the behaviour of the polite person and the style of a popular artist.

We can extend this similarity further. A highly conventional art form such as folk-song performs a phatic function. Nothing can be more redundant than the refrain of a folk-song, but in singing it we reaffirm our membership of that particular group or subculture. Indeed, subcultures are often defined partly, if not mainly, by their shared taste in art. Teenage subcultures in our society are identified by the type of music they enjoy or the dance steps they perform. The music or dance is conventional: the shared conventions bind the fans into a subculture. Other forms of music or dance are excluded in so far as they deviate from the accepted conventions. The point is that it is the use of the conventional, redundant aspects of the music or dance that determines and affirms membership of the group. Individual variations are permissible only within the limits of the conventions—or entropic original elements are acceptable only within the redundancy of the form.

Another example of the way that the concept of redundancy enables us to link social behaviour and the form of messages may be seen in the common reception of avant-garde, unconventional, entropic art. The audience is frequently offended or outraged by the way an artist has broken artistic conventions, in just the same way as they would be if the artist had been socially impolite to them. The original reception of the Impressionists or of the early performances of *Waiting for Godot* are obvious instances of this.

If I have dwelt rather longer on redundancy than on other aspects of Shannon and Weaver's model, it is because I find it one of their most fruitful concepts. It does, I believe, offer unique insights into human communication in that it enables us to relate apparently very different elements of the process.

Analysis

Let us test this assertion. Look at plate 1a. Do you find it entropic or redundant? In *form* it is redundant, for it looks like a conventional news photograph, a moment of hot action caught by the camera. But a closer look at its *content* may give us second thoughts. We do not often see a ring of policemen apparently attacking a respectably dressed young lady (even if she is black). Conventionally, we think of our police as *defenders* of law and order, not as aggressors. Photographs are never as easy to decode as they may appear, and are usually open to a number of readings: one clearly possible reading of this one is that the police are aggressors and the blacks are victims. If this is the message it would be entropic for the typical *Daily Mirror* reader—though probably highly redundant for some urban blacks.

So, when the *Daily Mirror* decided that the dramatic impact of the photo was strong enough to front-page it, they had to do something to decrease the entropy and increase redundancy. In other words, they had to make this image of the police fit more closely with the way we conventionally think of them. Remember that the *Daily Mirror* is a mass-circulation popular newspaper whose stories will therefore be relatively predictable, relatively redundant. So what the editor did was to balance this picture with another one and to surround it with words (plate 1b).

The headlines push our understanding of who were the aggressors and who were the victims back towards the conventional. "CONFRONTATION" suggests that the balance of aggression was at least equal. 'Demo blacks clash with London police' pushes the balance firmly over to the blacks, as does the picture of the injured policeman. The editor has given the original picture a context that makes it fit better into conventional attitudes and beliefs. He has given it a higher degree of redundancy. We can see both types of redundancy at work here. On the technical level, the context simply makes the picture easier to decode, especially at a quick, first glance. On the level of social relationships we can see it reinforcing social bonds. It shows that we (the readers) are a community who share the same attitudes, the same social meanings. We see things in the same way. This reinforces both our social links with others and our sense of the rightness of our view of the world.

Redundancy is generally a force for the status quo and against change. Entropy is less comfortable, more stimulating, more shocking perhaps, but harder to communicate effectively.

Channel, Medium, Code

Basic Concepts

There are two other important concepts in the model that we have not yet commented on: these are *channel* and *code*. We can really only define them properly in relation to a word that Shannon and Weaver do not use, but that later authorities have found useful. This word is *medium*.

Channel

The channel is the easiest of the three concepts to define. It is simply the physical means by which the signal is transmitted. The main channels are light waves, sound waves, radio waves, telephone cables, the nervous system, and the like.

Medium

The medium is basically the technical or physical means of converting the message into a signal capable of being transmitted along the channel. My voice is a medium; the technology of broadcasting is what constitutes the media of radio and television. The technological or physical properties of a medium are determined by the nature of the channel or channels available for its use. These properties of the medium then determine the range of codes which it can transmit. We can divide media into three main categories.

Figure 3: *Media Relationships*

1. The presentational media: the voice, the face, the body. They use the 'natural' languages of spoken words, expressions, gestures, and so on. They require the presence of the communicator, for he or she is the medium; they are restricted to the here and now, and produce *acts* of communication.

2. The representational media: books, paintings, photographs, writing, architecture, interior decorating, gardening, etc. There are numerous media that use cultural and aesthetic conventions to create a 'text' of some sort. They are representational, creative. They make a text that can record the media of category 1 and that can exist independently of the communicator. They produce *works* of communication.

3. The mechanical media: telephones, radio, television, telexes. They are transmitters of categories 1 and 2. The main distinction between categories 2 and 3 is that the media in 3 use channels created by engineering and are thus subject to greater technological constraints and are more affected by level-A noise than those in category 2.

But the categories do leak into each other and you may find it convenient at times to merge them into one. Categorization involves identifying differences, but it is as important to think of the similarities between media as their differences.

Medium: Further Implications

A good example of an exploration of media similarities and differences is a study by Katz, Gurevitch, and Hass (1973). They explained the interrelationships of the five main mass media with a circular model (see figure 3). They used a large-scale audience survey to find out why people turned to a particular medium in preference to the others. They investigated the needs that people felt and their reasons for turning to a particular medium to satisfy them. People's responses enabled the researchers to arrange the media in the circular relationship shown in figure 3. The audience felt that each medium was most similar to its two neighbours, or, to put it another way, they felt that if one medium were not available, its functions would be best served by the ones on either side of it.

People tended to use newspapers, radio, and television to connect themselves to society, but used books and films to escape from reality for a while. The better-educated tended to use the print media; those with less education were inclined towards the electronic and visual media. Books were the medium most used for improving one's understanding of self.

Table 1: Audience needs

Needs	Media order of preference for satisfying needs				
	1st	2nd	3nd	4th	5th
A. Personal needs					
1. Understanding self	B	N	R	T	C
2. Enjoyment	C	T	B	R	N
3. Escapism	B	C	T	R	N
B. Social needs					
1. Knowledge about the world	N	R	T	B	C
2. *Self-confidence, stability, self-esteem	N	R	T	B	C
3. Strengthen connections with family	T	C	R	N	B
4. Strengthen connections with friends	C	T	N	R	B

* This need is articulated in theree main ways: the need to feel influential and the need to feel that others think in similar ways and hold similar aspirations.
Key: B=books, C=cinema, N=newspapers, R=radio, T=television

* This need is articulated in three main ways: the need to feel influential and the need to feel that others think in similar ways and hold similar aspirations. Key: B=books, C=cinema, N=newspapers, R=radio, T=television

If we look at the main needs that people use the media to satisfy, and then relate them to people's preferred choice of actual medium to provide that satisfaction, we can produce a table like table 1.

Code: Basic Concepts

A code is a system of meaning common to the members of a culture or subculture. It consists both of signs (i.e. physical signals that stand for something other than themselves) and of rules or conventions that determine how and in what contexts these signs are used and how they can be combined to form more complex messages. The way codes relate to and develop within their parent culture is complex.

Here I wish to do no more than to define the term, and to consider the basic relationships between codes, channels, and media.

The simplest is between code and *channel*. Clearly the physical characteristics of channels determine the nature of the codes that they can transmit. The telephone is limited to verbal language and paralanguage (the codes of intonation, stress, volume, etc.). We have evolved a number *of secondary codes* simply to make an already encoded message transmittable along a particular channel. A message in the primary code of verbal language may be re-encoded into a variety of secondary codes—morse, semaphore, deaf-and-dumb sign language, handwriting, Braille, printing. All of these secondary codes are determined by the physical properties of their channels, or mechanical media of communication.

The relationship between *medium* and code is not so clear cut. Television is a medium which uses the channels of vision and sound. Buscombe (1975) notes that a programme like *Match of the Day* uses both channel-specific codes and medium-specific codes. The channel-specific codes are:

visual channel—live action, studio shots, and graphics;

aural channel—recorded noises, speech, and music.

He then analyses the medium-specific codes used in the visual channel. These are the codes of lighting, colour, speed, definition, framing, camera movement and placing, and editing. He demonstrates that while the technical constraints of the medium define the range of possible uses open to each code, the actual use made of them is determined by the culture of the broadcasters.

But if we take a medium such as 'dress', for example, we find it difficult to distinguish between the codes and the medium. Is it useful to talk of different codes of dress, or simply of different messages being sent by the same code? The formally agreed meaning of a button or piece of braid on a military uniform differs certainly in degree but not necessarily in kind from the informally agreed less precise meaning of denim jeans. The medium and the code have the same boundaries, but the code is what we need to study, because the code is the significant use to which the medium is put. All cultures and societies have the medium of dress (including nudists, who are defined by its absence): communication occurs through the culturally based codes that the medium conveys.

Dress also has a non-communicative function—that of protection from the elements. Most cultural artefacts have this dual function—a physical, technological one and communication. Houses, cars, furniture are defined first by their technological function and second, through their design, by their communicative function. The constraints of the medium are technological: the codes operate within them.

Feedback

Basic Concepts

Like medium, *feedback* is a concept that Shannon and Weaver do not use, but is one that later workers have found useful. Briefly, feedback is the transmission of the receiver's reaction back to the sender. Models that emphasize feedback are ones with a cybernetic bias.

Cybernetics is the science of control. The word derives from the Greek word for helmsman and its origin can provide us with a good illustration. If a helmsman wishes to steer to port, he moves the tiller to starboard. He then watches to see how far the ship's bow will swing round to port and will adjust the extent to which he pushes the tiller to starboard accordingly. His eyes enable him to receive the feedback—that is, the response of the bow to his initial movement of the tiller. In the same way, the thermostat in a central-heating system sends messages to the boiler, and receives messages from the thermometer measuring the room temperature. This feedback enables it to adjust the performance of the boiler to the needs of the room. The same is true in human communication. Feedback enables the speaker to adjust his or her performance to the needs and responses of an audience. Good speakers are generally sensitive to feedback; pompous, domineering bores manage to filter out feedback almost entirely.

Some channels of communication make feedback very difficult. Two-way radios and telephones allow alternating transmission which can perform some of the functions of feedback, but the feedback is clearly of a different order from the simultaneous feedback that occurs during face-to-face communication. This is determined mainly by availability of channels. In face-to-face communication I can transmit with my voice and simultaneously receive with my eyes. Another factor is access to these channels. The mechanical media, particularly the mass media, limit access and therefore limit feedback. We cannot have constant access to the BBC, though its audience research unit tries to provide the Corporation with a formalized system of feedback. In the same way, when I am giving a lecture, my students' access to the channel of sound waves is limited—they give me less feedback than in a seminar, where they have a far greater share of the speaking time.

Feedback, then, has this one main function. It helps the communicator adjust his or her message to the needs and responses of the receiver. It also has a number of subsidiary functions. Perhaps the most important of these is that it helps the receiver to feel involved in the communication. Being aware that the communicator is taking account of our response makes us more likely to accept the message: being unable to express our response can lead to a build-up of frustration that can cause so much noise that the message may become totally lost. Though feedback inserts a return loop from destination to source, it does not destroy the linearity of the model. It is there to make the process of transmitting messages more efficient.

Summary

Though somewhat complex, the Shannon and Weaver model of communication is one of the important foundations of understanding communication. While it was originally designed to explain telephonic communication, its use has been used to explain many aspects of communication. Understanding the path of communication from sender to receiver along with all the problems that might arise to prohibit the meaning from the message sent being the same message received is essential to the study of communication.

In this chapter we have seen that information does not have the same meaning as it is used in everyday understanding. Information is seen as the basic predictability of the signal and not the content of the message. It is based on the choices the originator of a message makes, and how is related to the success of the message being understood. You were introduced to the concepts of redundancy and entropy and how they operate in the communication model. Additionally, you should now understand how the concepts of channel, medium, and code interact in the communication process, and how feedback may be used to improve the chances of success in communicating.

It could be argued that the most important function of communication is to form our identities as we interact with others. A crucial aspect of this process is perception, and how our perceptions interact with others in the process of creating our identities will be discussed in the next chapter.

Questions For Discussion

1. What is noise? How can it interfere with successful communication?
2. When we see an old friend you have not seen for a number of years, why might your problem be with entropy and redundancy?
3. What is phatic communication? Can you provide an example?
4. What is the medium of social media networks?
5. What helps a communicator adjust his or her message to the receiver?

Chapter 3

Identities and Perceptions

Steve Duck and David T. McMahan

Our abilities as communicators are largely influenced by our perceptual abilities. We never really describe reality when we communicate; we only describe our perception of reality. This chapter examines the perceptual process, and the key role this plays with respect to the ways we create and manage our identities.

Learning Objectives For This Chapter

- Identify the role that selection plays in perception
- Explain the way people organize and evaluate world around them
- Discuss the role that communication plays in the development of the self-concept
- Explain how narratives are used to create identities
- Understand the symbolic nature of identity
- Identify the two ways identity is transacted through interactions with others

We don't know you, and you don't know us. From reading this book you might have some impressions of us. You know who you are, though—not just name and address but the kind of person you are. You have an identity, and we don't just mean an ID that you show people to prove your age. You are an individual who is friends with other individuals, each perhaps quirky with a unique personality and identity. You might see these individuals and yourself as persons with a history deep inside, a childhood set of experiences that made them who they are and you who you are. You know things about yourself that no one else knows. You are you, you-nique!

This chapter will teach you that you have multiple identities and that these identities are transacted through communication. Some are created by the situation in which you find yourself or in the company of certain people but not others. (Do you really behave the same way with your mother as you do with your best friend?) Others are the result of cultural symbols attached to "being gay or lesbian" or "being a go-getter or a team player." Some are performed for an audience. In intimate relationships, you can perform and express most of your true self. In a police interview, you may want to conceal some of what you are. In a hospice at the end of your life, you may want to hang onto a little *dignity*. You lose control over the skills, performances, and parts of your body and self that used to compose your identity, and you become physically more dependent on others. Those old folks who look a lot older than you now could be how you will be someday. Think about it.

Identity is partly a *characteristic* (something that you possess), partly a *performance* (something that you do), and partly a *construction of society* For example, society tells you how to be "masculine" and "feminine" and indicates that "guys can't say that to guys" (Burleson, Holmstrom, & Gilstrap, 2005). This restricts the way in which men can give one another emotional support. Society also provides you with ways to describe a personality; the media focus you on some traits more than others. Categories like gluttonous, sexy, short, slim, paranoid, and kind are all available to you, but they are not all equally valued.

The ways you express yourself and the ways you respond to other people in your social context transact part of your identity. Your identity is partly constructed through your interactions with other people. Have you had the experience of being with someone who makes you nervous when you normally aren't nervous or who helps you relax when you feel tense? In these instances, your identity is molded by the person, situation, or communication. You'll get used to a rather odd phrase in communication studies: "doing an identity," used instead of "having an identity." Communication scholars now pay close attention to the ways in which people's behavior carries out, enacts, transacts, or does an identity in talk with other people.

The transaction of identities is guided in part through perceptions of yourself, others, and various components of an interaction. In other words, your internal views of yourself and others influence the external construction of identities. This notion may be somewhat difficult to comprehend, and we discuss this matter in more detail later in the chapter.

Up front, though, this is a very significant consideration and sets the discipline of communication and this textbook apart from others. Identities, relationships, cultural membership, and the like are not located within people or embedded within their minds waiting to be discovered. These things are instead created symbolically through interactions with others. At the same time, how a person views the world, organizes what is seen, and evaluates this information will influence the symbolic activity that does take place, and ultimately how that symbolic activity is viewed, organized, and evaluated. It is therefore important that these activities are also taken into account when exploring the transaction of identities.

Bob is a really nice guy. He is a good friend, loyal, trusting, open, honest, comforting, seriously devoted to his kids, caring, charitable, active in his religious community organizing charitable events (especially for mentally challenged kids), giving, respectful, a fabulous cook (he specializes in the cuisines of other cultures), and very caring to his aging parents (he never misses a visit and takes them on a short trip each weekend even though his father does not remember any longer who he is and his mother is seriously arthritic). Bob is the kind of guy who would give you one of his kidneys if he matched and you needed it. Everyone in the neighborhood knows and loves Bob; at some time or another everyone in Baxter Close has experienced his stellar generosity, whether the single-parent family that found groceries on their doorstep the week they ran out of food stamps or the feisty senior lesbian who just lost her lifetime partner and needed someone to talk to. He is active in the PTA, does long Saturdays coaching and refereeing the blossoming mixed-sex soccer group that he started, and does a spectacular comedic turn as George W. the Orangutan.

At work Bob is the most hated SOB in the Border Security branch of Homeland Security. There is no one who is such a completely ruthless, nasty, dogged, suspicious, awkward cuss. He is an officious, pettifogging a-hole, and there is no one better at interrogation. He nails people who make illegal applications for a green card and has the highest record in the whole border area for catching cheats. People lie to him, and he gets them every time; people fudge, and he owns them; people say things that do not match up with what they wrote on their forms, and he gets it right away without even looking. Nobody gets past Bob. He asks all the right probing questions, uncovers the half truth and the full-out lie, trusts no one, and never accepts at face value anything on an application form (he even caught the fact that one person could not spell his own name the same way in two different places on the same form). He regularly has grown men breaking down in tears in his office. If you get interviewed for immigration by Bob and are not 100% straight up, then he will get you. Believe it.

We all know a version of Bob. We all know a supervisor who is a pain in the buttermilk plant where he rules without mercy, gives no one any breaks, and cuts no slack, but in the rest of his life he is a beacon: a leading member of his church community, a giving and generous community member, and a social delight as long as there is no one there from the workplace.

Other examples surround us everywhere in everyday life. The same person may be unfriendly and distant on one occasion but funny and sociable on another. You may know someone whom you consider to be kind, yet one of your friends sees the person as nasty. In both cases you re talking about the same person, but people can have mood swings as a result of periodic hormonal imbalances, drinking too much, gluten intolerance, or just having had a series of really unfortunate events happen to them on a bad hair day.

That is perhaps not terribly surprising since many changes in mood are temporary, relatively unimportant, and reversible. Get the hormones back into balance, let them sleep off the hangover, and let the sun shine in, and then they will be back to their same old self.

What is much more complicated for communication scholars is the question of why different people disagree about whether someone is essentially good or bad. Why might two professors argue about whether a particular student is (a) intelligent or (b) someone who stands no chance of improving? Why might the bosses in an organization argue about whether someone should be promoted or passed over? If every person had just one identity at the core of his or her multi-layered onion of personality, then these kinds of questions would make no sense.

If people had a stable core inside a set of layers we could peel away to reach "the truth," then we would never be able to change our mind about someone. If someone were a good and loyal friend, he would never turn into an enemy unless he had a personality transplant. Yet you've most likely had the experience of seeing someone in a different light over time. This is a real problem for scholars of communication thinking about the nature of identity and self and why some people do not include "self" in their courses: far too mushy.

When a stranger does something unkind, your first thought may be to blame personality: This is an evil person, perhaps with psychopathic tendencies. Or you could put it down to the identity that had been constructed during childhood when there were some bad experiences. Lawyers often explain their clients' bad behavior in such terms. On the other hand, the "unkind stranger" probably saw identity in personality terms, too, but more favorable ones—as a good decent person who was being irritated by an annoying stranger (you!) and walked away thinking, "What a jerk [or some other nonspecific and dehumanizing term]!"

Of course, you (and your friends) have never done anything that dehumanizes, stereotypes, or depersonalizes others, have you? You have never called anyone "an illegal" or "a frat boy" or lumped someone together with all other "college kids" or chanted, "Oh, how I hate the team from State."

Framing Identity

Earlier chapters talked about frames for situations and thinking. Shotter (1984) sees identity as a frame for interpreting other people's actions: Your beliefs about other people set the stage for your understanding of how they act. Burke (1969) also saw motives and personality language as helpful frames for interpretation. In short, your identity will be revealed in a language that reflects the priorities of a particular culture or relationship and its frames for thinking about how humans should act and describe themselves.

Human beings talk about their identities in ways that are steered by social norms and conventions in their society. In return you expect other people to present such narratives and behaviors. Your culture frames identity as a stable inner self; it therefore feels quite normal for you to think in those terms, so you can easily understand the idea that someone would reveal a private self layer by layer. However, you would be thought crazy if you said, "My identity is blue with an elephant spirit inside." You'd soon be locked up.

You have to use terms and phrases that your audiences recognize as symbolically meaningful in the culture: "I'm a go-getter but quite private, ambitious yet introverted." In other words, you frame your talk about yourself and your identity in the language that your culture has taught you to use.

Perceiving Encounters and Transacting Identities

Your framing of an encounter is based, in part, on the perceptions you develop. **Perception** is a process of actively selecting, organizing, and evaluating information, activities, situations, people, and essentially all the things that make up your world. In what follows, we explore this process and its influence on identity construction.

Selecting

We have discussed how receiving stimuli does not necessarily mean you will recognize their presence or direct your attention to them. Imagine going up to a friend whose concentration is focused on a book (or a newspaper, a television program, a computer screen, a ball game, or any number of objects or activities). You greet her by saying hello or by saying her name, but she does not seem to recognize you are speaking. This person continues to focus solely on the book. You speak again, a little louder this time, and still receive no response. You may have to tap her on the shoulder, hit her over the head, or practically scream to get her attention away from that book. You are not being ignored; this person is simply not attending to, or selecting, the sound of your voice.

You select and focus more on some things going on around you and less on other things. Certain factors influence exactly to what extent you focus. If something stands out for whatever reason, you are more likely to focus your attention on that. For instance, if you scan a room of people wearing similar clothing, you will likely focus on a person whose clothing is dissimilar to that of the others. Another factor influencing focus is selective exposure, which means you are more likely to focus on and expose yourself to that which supports your beliefs, values, and attitudes. During your interactions with others, you will be more likely to pick up on activities that support your views of the world and pay less attention to those that do not. If you view yourself as a competent person, you will be more likely to pick up on the behaviors of others that uphold this view such as compliments and less likely to focus on behaviors that counter this view such as criticism. The opposite, of course, would happen if you viewed yourself as an incompetent person.

Organizing and Evaluating

Observations of the world are not floating randomly around in your head. Instead, they are organized in ways that allow you to retrieve them when necessary, and new information is connected to previous information that is already organized and stored. **Schemata** are mental structures that are used to organize information in part by clustering or linking associated material. For example, information about relationships can be stored and connected in "relationship" schemata and drawn from when needed. Since this information is stored in a relatively accessible manner, it can be used to make sense of what you are experiencing and to anticipate what might happen in a given situation.

This particular approach is based on the work of George Kelly (1955), who saw people as scientists making hypotheses about everyday life and then testing their effectiveness. When researchers conduct experiments, they make calculated guesses about what will happen and then decide if what they anticipated actually occurred once the experiment has been completed. Kelly maintained that people do the same thing in their everyday lives. For instance, upon meeting you may greet someone in a particular way because—based on past experience and observations—you believe doing so will lead to approval from the other person and a proper relational connection. If your expectations are proved correct, your existing way of viewing the world will be strengthened, and you will be more likely to perform the same action in the future. If your expectations are proved incorrect, you will likely revise your way of viewing the world, and you will be less likely to perform the same action in the future.

Your organizational system is constantly being updated and modified based on new experiences and as a result of evaluating its accuracy and usefulness. This system seems pretty efficient and beneficial. However, it is not without its disadvantages. Kelly (1955) maintained that a persons processes are "channelized" by the ways in which events are anticipated. As a result, certain ways of acting and viewing the world become more deeply ingrained in your thinking. Imagine running the end of a stick in a straight line over and over in the same spot on the ground. Eventually, an indentation begins to develop and becomes deeper and deeper as you continue to run the end of that stick in the same place. The same thing can be imagined with certain ways of behaving and viewing the world. The more you behave in a certain way and the more often you view the world in the same way, the deeper and more ingrained it becomes in your thinking. After a while, it becomes difficult to imagine behaving in another way or viewing the world in a different way.

Consequently, Kelly (1955) urged people to imagine a table as being soft. When touching a table, you probably anticipate that it will be hard, and most of the time you will be correct. However, you should always consider the possibility that the table will be soft. Always consider the opposite, and always consider other possibilities. When done consistently, a person's behaviors and views frequently become seen as correct and natural rather than things that should be constantly evaluated and reassessed. Alternatives may or may not be better, but they should always be considered.

Kelly's (1955) work has resulted in a better understanding of the ways in which people think and relate to others. It can also be used to better understand how our perceptions influence the transaction of identities through prototypes, personal constructs, and scripts.

Prototypes

A **prototype** is the best-case example of something (Fehr, 1993). You may have a prototype of an ideal romantic partner, for instance. This prototype could be a composite of different people or an actual person. Accordingly, your romantic partner prototype could be compiled from characteristics of past romantic partners, or it could be a single romantic partner. It could be made up of people you actually know, people you have observed, and media representations. All prototypes are influenced culturally.

When identities are transacted they are broadly measured using prototypes as standards. Someone attempting to construct the identity of a romantic partner would use his or her prototype as a model, and other people would use their respective prototypes of a romantic partner in order to evaluate and make sense of this person.

Personal Constructs

Personal constructs are bipolar dimensions used to measure and evaluate things. Whereas prototypes tend to be broad categories, personal constructs are narrow and more specific characteristics. These personal constructs can be used in the development of a prototype and to determine how close someone may come to meeting all the criteria. Using romantic partners again as an example, the following personal constructs could be used:

> Attractive-Unattractive
> Kind-Mean
> Passive-Aggressive
> Intelligent-Ignorant
> Humorous-Dull
> Employed-Unemployed

Like prototypes, personal constructs are used to make sense of the world and to evaluate what is taking place. Personal constructs, though, are more specific and detailed. They can be used to determine just how well a person measures up according to certain categories.

Scripts

Scripts are guides for behavior developed from our system of knowledge. A movie or television script informs actors what they should be doing and saying. Such scripts assist actors in performing a character. Likewise, you use scripts when performing social roles and enacting identities in everyday life. For example, you know what to say and how to act when performing the role or identity of a student. You are following the script of a student. Using the running example of romantic partners, you know what you should do and say as a romantic partner through scripts developed from personal experience and observations of others. You know when the other "actors" are following a script correctly and performing an identity accurately. You also know when they have forgotten their lines and are giving a horrible performance.

While following scripts is important, most actors are required to improvise their performance from time to time. They also explore the creation of a character by saying different things and behaving in different ways. You must do the same thing when you are performing particular identities. You develop your own spin on an identity. Furthermore, you must improvise and edit scripts when scenes or contexts change.

Scripts are subject to change and revision through experience and assessment. Sometimes a person discovers the table is soft! Beyond careful evaluation, however, scripts change with the passing of time. This change is especially noticeable with scripts involving identities associated with close personal relationships. For instance, the script of a friend in elementary school is different from the script of a friend in high school. Both scripts are different from the script of a middle-aged friend. Returning yet again to the example of romantic partners, the script of a romantic partner early in the relationship will likely be different from the script of a romantic partner after a number of years in the same relationship.

Ultimately, scripts focus our attention on the mutual influence of perception and the transaction of identities. Identities are performed though interactions with others, and perceptions guide our understanding of what should be done and the evaluation of symbolic performance. In what follows, we examine how people may view themselves as having an established inner core or identities to be revealed, but in actuality identities are performed though communication and personal relationships.

Identity as Inner Core: The Self-Concept

We start with the "commonsense" idea that you have a true inner self. By the end of the chapter, however, we will show that there is more to learn about personal identity built by relationships with other people. The chapter connects identity to language; to other people; to the norms, rules, and categories in society/culture; and to narratives of origin and belonging to other relationships. This identity may be represented by such statements as "I'm an African American" or, on a bumper sticker, "Proud parent of an Honor Roll student at City High." These examples make statements of identity that claim it through relationships with other people or membership in groups, not just as a person with an inner core.

Psychic/Reflective Self

When you think about persons as having some true personal, private, and essential core, covered with layers of secrecy, privacy, and convention, this is known as a **self-concept.** Because everyone is assumed to have this core, you are alarmed by people who have multiple personalities or are bipolar. Someone should have only one consistent personality; people who have more parts are disturbed or irrational. Your identity may be hard for other people to reach, but according to many self-help books and celebrity biographies, it is reachable. Communication serves to help people talk about or express what is inside, perhaps in greater depth as they get to know one another better. Communication scholars can teach you the skill of expressing yourself well or help you be open and honest and let "the real you" be heard.

The Weirdness of Consistent Expectations

A consistent inner self would be made up of the person's broad habits of thought (e.g., someone is kind, outward-looking, introverted, or self-centered). You might see that self revealed communicatively in styles of behavior (e.g., someone is aggressive, calm, ambitious, reliable, hardworking, or manipulative) or in characteristic styles of perception (e.g., someone is paranoid, trusting, insightful, or obstinate). Personality is the label that you would first use to describe someone's identity if you were asked about it casually in a conversation by someone who wanted to know what that person was like.

But it's a very odd idea indeed. People are too complex. A person can simultaneously be many identities. For example, a person can simultaneously be a loving parent, a vegetarian, a conservative, quick-tempered, a good dancer, a bad cook, business savvy, and a team player. You also have a choice in the identity you describe: a relational identity (friend/parent), an interactional identity (worker/customer/server), a sex or gender identity (male/female/masculine/feminine/GLBT), a racial/ethnic identity (the boxes to check on government forms), or a behavioral identity (extrovert/introvert). It's a choice, then, to describe your identity.

Unstable Behaviors

Another key point about identity comes from everyday experience. People are multi-layered and can have different moods, being good company on one day and bad on another. People can fluctuate during the course of the day, and events may happen to them that cause them to act "out of character." These fluctuations help demonstrate that it's a peculiar idea that somebody could have a fixed inner identity if it can also be so variable and complex over time.

The best you can hope for, then, is that the more you get to know someone through talk, the more you can understand the person's usual self. You can learn about what triggers a tailspin or a rant.

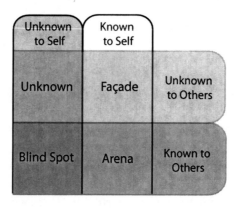

Figure 5.1: The Johari Window

Source: *Adapted from "The Johari Window: A Graphic Model of Interpersonal Awareness," by J. Luft and H. Ingham, 1955, in Proceedings of the Western Training Laboratory in Group Development (Los Angeles: University of California, Los Angeles).*

The upshot, though (and we are sorry to spoil it for you), is that all the magazine articles that offer to tell you about "the real [Lady Gaga/Beyoncé/Ashton Kutcher/Joseph Stalin/ Sarah Palin]" are always going to be nonsense. The notion that someone has a real single inner core is suspect for communication scholars from the get-go. Also, if identities could not be changed or reviewed, there would be no therapists or communication textbooks with advice on how to develop your communication and presentation skills (i.e., how to present your "true self" more effectively).

The Johari window, developed in 1955 by two guys called Joe (Luft) and Harry (Ingham)—and were not kidding—distinguishes between what a person knows about self and what others know about the person. As you can see in Figure 5.1, people have blind spots: Everyone but the person in question can see something obvious (for example, that Bob is "a pain"). In other cases we pretend (façade), concealing from people something that we know about ourselves (guilty secrets and so forth). The arena is basically where we openly act out a public identity that everyone else knows and recognizes.

Describing a Self

Ask people to tell you who they are. They will tell you their name and start revealing information about themselves, usually with a narrative that places their self in various contexts. Steve Duck indicates to someone in your culture that the person is male and has to put up with many very unoriginal jokes about his name. Although he has lived in the United States of America for more than 25 years, he is a Brit, or English as he prefers to think of it. His family comes from Whitby in North Yorkshire, England, where the first recorded Duck (John Duck) lived in 1288. John Duck and Steve Duck share the same skeptical attitude toward authority figures. John is in the historical record because he sued the Abbot of Whitby over ownership of a piece of land. John was descended from the Vikings who sacked and then colonized Whitby in about 800 a.d. Duck is a Viking nickname-based surname for a hunchback. (Have you ever ducked out of the way of anything? If so, you have crouched like a hunchback.)

Steve Duck is also relatively short for a man, is bald but bearded, likes watching people but is quite shy, and can read Latin, which is how he found out about John Duck while researching his family tree. Steve likes the music of Ralph Vaughan Williams, enjoys doing cryptic crosswords, knows about half the words that Shakespeare knew, and has occasionally lied. He resents his mother's controlling behavior, was an Oxford college rowing coxswain (cox'n), loves reading Roman history, and is gluten intolerant. He thinks he is a good driver and is proud of his dad, who was a Quaker pacifist (that antiauthority thing again) who won three medals for bravery in World War II for driving an unarmed ambulance into the front line of a war zone in order to rescue two seriously wounded (armed) comrades. Steve has lived in Iowa for 26 years. He has had two marriages and four children, carries a Swiss Army knife (and as many other gadgets as will fit onto one leather belt), and always wears two watches. He is wondering whether to get the new Swiss Army knife that has a data storage capacity, a laser pointer, and a fingerprint password. Sweet.

Self-Description and Stereotypes

Notice that some of this information about Steve's identity is self-description. That is, these words describe him in much the same way that anyone else could without knowing him personally (e.g., male, bearded, short, bald, two watches, magnetic sex appeal).

Self-description usually involves information about self that is obvious in public (or on your résumé). If you wear your college T-shirt, talk with a French accent, or are short, this evidence about you is available even to strangers who can see your physical appearance or hear how you sound. "Identity" in this sense is communicated publicly and physically. It parks the individual in categories (national, racial, or ethnic groups) or else lumps him or her into stereotypes. It isn't really an individual identity but is more about group membership.

Self-Disclosure

Some points in Steve's description of himself count as **self-disclosure:** the revelation of information that people could not know unless Steve made it known. In the above example, these are the points that describe particular feelings and emotions that other people would not know unless Steve specifically disclosed them. The resents, is proud of, enjoys, thinks, and is wondering parts give you a view of his identity that you could not directly obtain any other way, though you might work it out from what Steve says or does.

These parts, since they are spoken as insights, are self-disclosure, not self-description. The term self-disclosure is limited to revelation of private, sensitive, and confidential information relevant to identity. Values, fears, secrets, assessments, evaluations, and preferences all count as such confidences that you share with only a few people.

The Importance of Being Open

Jourard (1964, 1971) wrote about self-disclosure as making your identity "transparent" to others. People who make the most disclosures are acting in the most psychologically healthy manner. Early research also connected self-disclosure with growth in intimacy. Classic reports (e.g., Derlega, Metts, Petronio, & Margulis, 1993) found that the more people become intimate, the more they disclose to each other information that is both broad and deep. Also, the more you get to know someone's inner knowledge structures, the closer you feel to him or her.

Closeness generally develops only if the information is revealed in a way that indicates it is privileged information that other people do not know. For example, if a man lets you (and only you) know the secret that he has a serious invisible illness (such as diabetes, lupus, or prostate cancer), an unusually strong fear of spiders, or a significantly distressed marriage, you feel valued and trusted, because he let you into his inner life.

Openness and Closeness

There is an important relational process going on here: When someone tells you about inner identity, you feel honored and valued by someone's revelation of the inner self, or you may actually not care for what you are hearing. The important point is that disclosure itself does not make a difference to a relationship; the relationship makes a difference to the value of disclosure. If you feel the relationship is enhanced by self-disclosure, it is. If you don't, no matter how intimate the disclosure, the relationship does not grow in intimacy.

Later research has refined this idea (Dindia, 2000; Petronio, 2002). For example, too much disclosure of identity is not necessarily a good thing at all times. You've probably been bored by somebody telling you more than you wanted to know—TMI! By contrast, people who are closed and don't tell anything about themselves are regarded as psychologically unhealthy.

Communication scholar Kathryn Dindia (2000) points out that the revelation of identity is rarely a simple progression and is certainly not just the declaration of facts and then—bam!—intimacy. Self-disclosure is a dynamic process tied to other social processes that relate to your identity and how you disclose yourself over time. It continues through the life of relationships and is not a single onetime choice about whether to disclose or not. Part of your identity is the skill with which you reveal or conceal information about yourself and your feelings, as any good poker player knows.

Dynamics of Revelation

In fact, the revelation of your identity, like identity itself, is an open-ended process that continues indefinitely in relationships even after they have become deeply intimate. It is dynamic, continuous, and circular so that it is hard to say where self-disclosure or identity begins or ends. It is also influenced by the behavior and communication of the other person(s)—the audience. Both self-disclosure and identity occur in the context of a relationship that has ups and downs.

Dialectic Tensions

Everyone places a limit on the amount of information that he or she reveals to others, and some choose to remain private, even in intimate relationships. Baxter and Montgomery (1996) identify a push-pull **dialectic tension** of relationships. These tensions occur whenever you are in two minds about something or feel a simultaneous pull in two directions. Some communication scholars (e.g., Baxter, 2004, 2011; Baxter & Braithwaite, 2008) suggest that there simply is no singular core of identity but a dialogue between different "voices" in your head. For example, in relationships, you want to feel connected to someone else, but you do not want to give up all of your independence. You can see how you—and your identity—can grow by being in a relationship, but you can also see that this comes at a simultaneous cost or threat to your identity, independence, and autonomy.

The autonomy-connectedness dialectic is one dialectic tension, but another is openness-closedness, where people feel social pressure to be open yet also want to retain control over private information. This tension leads to people sometimes giving out and sometimes holding back information about themselves. Even in the same relationship, a person can feel willing to reveal information sometimes but crowded and guarded at other times. A personal relationship is not a consistent or a simple experience any more than identity is. Each affects the other over time. Also you may tell different versions of your identity to different audiences on different occasions.

Identity and Its Boundaries

In fact, people in relationships negotiate boundaries of privacy (Petronio, 2002). Part of the difference between friendship and mere acquaintance is that you have stronger boundaries around your identity for acquaintances than you do for friends.

As Jon Hess (2000) notes, you simply don't like some people. You don't want them to know "personal stuff" and may actively limit what they find out. Caughlin and Afifi (2004) have shown that even intimate partners sometimes prefer to completely avoid topics that may annoy or provoke the other person.

Petronio (2002) deals with the inconsistencies in the revelation of information by pointing to the importance of boundary management of the topics within different relational settings. People experience a tension between a desire for privacy and a demand for openness differently in different relationships. Couples make up their own rules for controlling the boundaries of privacy. So, for example, two people may define, between themselves, the nature of topics that they will mention in front of other people and what they will keep to themselves. A married couple may decide what topics it can discuss in front of the children, for instance, and these topics may change as the children grow older.

In other words, people show, employ, and work within different parts of their identity with different audiences at different times.

Self-Disclosure and Boundaries: Who Am I, for Whom?

One of Petronio's (2002) key points is that the suitability of something for disclosure is itself affected by relational context and by agreement between the partners. There are no absolutes.

She also draws attention to the ways in which a couple can decide how much to disclose. Amount, type, or subject of self-disclosure can be a topic for discussion (often called meta-communication or communication about communication). In contrast to Jourard's (1964, 1971) idea that there are absolute rules about self-disclosure of identity, Petronio (2002) demonstrates that it is a matter of personal preference, worked out explicitly between the partners in a relationship through communication.

The upshot of this discussion of self-disclosure questions identity as a straightforward, layered possession of your own inner being. Your self-disclosure and your identity are jointly owned by you and a partner. There is more to identity than just having or revealing one, then. The norms of appropriateness for reciprocity, the rules about amount of revealed information (especially negative information) show that there is a social context for communication about identity. Identity is revealed within that set of social rules, cultural norms, and contexts.

Identify and Other People

Saying that there is a social context for identity is basically making two points:

1. Society as a whole broadly influences the way you think about identity in the first place.
2. The other people who meet a person may influence the way that person's identity is expressed.

When you reveal your identity, you often use stories to tell the audience something about yourself and help its members shape their sense of who you are. As with self-disclosure, so too with stories: They are influenced by both society/culture and the specific persons or audience to which you do the telling.

Narrative Self and Altercasting

People tell stories about themselves and other people all the time and pay special care to what they will say, particularly for occasions like job interviews, sales pitches, and strategic communication of all sorts. You may have noticed that you adapt stories of your identity for consumption by other people in a social context.

Stories We Tell

A report about your identity characterizes you by means of a memory or history in its narrative or a typical or an amusing instance that involves character (your identity), plot, motives, scenes, and other actors Even when you reveal an internal model of self, this story organizes your identity in ways other people understand in terms of the rules that govern accounts, narratives, and other social reports. As Kellas (2008) has pointed out, narratives can be an ontology (how I came to be who I am), an epistemology (how I think about the world), an individual construction, or a relational process, such as when romantic partners tell the story about how they first met.

Origin Stories

Reports about an identity have a narrative structure that builds off both the sense of origin derived from early life and a sense of continuity. The self comes from somewhere and has roots—"I'm Hispanic," "I'm a true Southerner," "I'm a genuine Irish McMahan."

Identity comes in part from narratives of origin. These can be personal, cultural, or species ("What was my great-grandfather like?" "Where did I come from?" "Where did our culture come from?" "How did humans get started?"). A sense of origin leads, for most people, straight back to their family, the first little society that they ever experienced (Huisman, 2008). The specific context of family experience is the first influence on a person's sense of origin and identity. It gives the person a sense of connection to a larger network of others. Indeed, in African American cultures, "the family" can be seen as a whole community that goes beyond the direct blood ties that define "family" in other cultures. The earliest memories give you a sense of origin as represented by your experiences in a family-like environment.

Table 5.1: Early Experiences and Influences on Your Later Life

Early experiences affect your thought worlds/worlds of meaning.

They influence your sense of identity.

They create identity narratives about you and your history.
They influence feelings about self, the goals that you set for life, the levels of ability you feel yolu have, the ways you relate to other people, the dark fears that you hoard all your life, your beliefs about the way to behave properly (religious beliefs, rituals about birthdays, who cares for people emotionally, whether sports "matter"), and whether you see life as peacefully cozy or violently conflicted.

Origin, Memory, and the
Telling of Your Self

However, early memories are not neutral facts. They are loaded, like dice, by the experiences you think you had in your family. A childhood seen as terrible can make you absorb an identity that gives you low self-esteem, for example (Duck, 2011), and could lead you to treat later relational opportunities with great caution. People treated respectfully by parents end up confident and secure about themselves, whereas those treated by their parents as nuisances come to see themselves that way. They also become anxious in relationships or avoid them altogether.

A key point, then, is that by both direct and indirect means, your interactions and communication with other people shape your views of yourself. This happens even when you don't realize it or necessarily want it to happen—and this influence is not automatically something you just grow out of. Therapists get paid to put clients' childhood into better perspective! Early experiences in "the family" lay down many of the tracks upon which your later life will run.

Stories about you must fit with what your audience believes to be coherent and acceptable. It is not just that you have a self but that you shape the telling of your identity in a way that your audience (culture, friends) will accept.

This distinction is like the difference between the words in a joke and the way someone tells it: The telling adds something performative to the words, and a person can spoil a joke by telling it badly. Likewise with identity, it has to be performed or told in appropriate ways. When Bob, the nontraditional student, the Purdue fan, or the frat boy brags about his achievements to friends, he probably tells his identity differently than he would to former workmates, the police, Indiana University fans, or the dean of students.

Labeling

Identity is also made by **labeling** the characteristics that you want to stand out. One of our faculty colleagues refers to himself as "Dr. Dave," which creates a certain kind of image, a mixture of professionalism and accessibility that is also an amusing cross-reference to the cultural icon Dr. Phil. Such nicknames and labels can be used for reinforcement of a type of identity. In the case of other people, a technical term used in discussion of communication and identity is **altercasting.** Altercasting refers to how language can give people an identity and then force them to live up to the description, whether positive or negative (Marwell & Schmitt, 1967), For example, you are altercasting when you say, "As a good friend, you will want to help me here" or "Only a fool would…" These label the listener as a certain kind of person (or not), by positioning the person to respond appropriately (as a friend or not as a fool). Even such small elements of communication transact your identity and the identities of those people around you.

When you communicate about yourself, therefore, you assume that the audience will understand you, so you assume a shared basis for understanding other people. On top of that, you assume that special people—friends, for example—not only understand your "self" but also do reality checks for you. When people talk about identity, then, they assume their audience will be able to comprehend, interpret, and probably support it.

The earlier description of Steve, for example, mentions a Swiss Army knife because that particular item is well known in the culture. Any description of an identity is therefore steered by beliefs about the criteria, categories, and descriptions that will matter to, or even impress, the audience. For example, people project a professional identity by wearing smart business clothes to a job interview. People also communicate their cultural identity through their accent and behavior. Thus "who you are" is a relational point.

Symbolic Identity

Your sense of self is influenced by language frames, culture, origin, membership, and other people's thoughts about you. But don't you actually do a lot of your identity for specific people, such as your priest, your neighbor, your best friend, and your coworkers and customers?

The Many Yous

Most people have a range of identities that they can turn on as necessary according to where they are and who is there with them. In that case, identity is not so much something that you have as it is something that you do in ways that people recognize as suitable.

Do you ever feel like a different person when you are with your friends compared to when you're talking to your mother? Are you the same person all the time, or do you have good and bad days? Do you ever do things you regret or regard as not typical? Ever say things you regret?

Most people have protested that someone has misrepresented them. Until now you would not have called that resistance to an altercasting by refusing to accept it, but that is what it is. A hostile or negative person can make you feel very bad about yourself. Have you ever met anyone who didn't really "get" what you are about?

On the other hand, you may have had a close relationship with a partner that felt good because you were able to be your true self around the other person or because the person helped bring out sides of you that other people could not. Did you struggle to assert an identity independent from your parents when you were a teenager?

You must already be wondering how any of that is possible if "you" are one identity. You may also have started to think about how advertising, religion, and social fashions influence the ways you dress and act. Other people can affect your values, the choices you make, and how these feed into your sense of identity. Your culture and your identity at the very least interact with one another. At most, culture and its icons (pop stars, fashion models, celebrities) account for quite a lot of your identity, by showing you how to dress and how to behave and what standards of belief are "OK."

Symbolic Self

The lesson is simple: Your identity is shaped by culture and the people you interact with. This is because you can reflect that your "self" is an object of other people's perceptions and that they can do critical thinking or listening about you as well. In short, your identity is a **symbolic self,** a self that exists for other people and goes beyond what it means to you; it arises from social interaction with other people. As a result, you fit identity descriptions into the form of narratives that your society and your particular acquaintances know about and accept. Hence, any identity that you offer to other people is based on the fact that you all share meanings about what is important in defining a person's identity.

Symbols and Identity: Reflection

Another way of thinking about identity, then, is in terms of how broad social forces affect or even transact an individual's view of who he or she is. This set of ideas is referred to as **symbolic interactionism.** In particular, George Herbert Mead (1934) suggested that people get their sense of self from other people and from being aware that others observe, judge, and evaluate one's behavior. How many times have you done or not done something because of how you would look to your friends if you did it? Has your family ever said, "What will the neighbors think?"

Mead (1934) called this phenomenon the human ability to adopt an **attitude of reflection.** You think about how you look in other people's eyes or reflect on the fact that other people can see you as a social object from their point of view. Guided by these reflections, you do not always do what you want to do but what you think people will accept. You may end up doing something you don't want to do because you cannot think how to say no to another person in a reasonable way. You cannot just stamp your foot and shout "SHAN'T!"

Your identity, then, is not yours alone. Indeed, Mead (1934) also saw self as a transacted result of communicating with other people: You learn how to be an individual by recognizing the way that people treat you. You come to see your identity through the eyes of other people, for whom you are a meaningful object. People recognize you and treat you differently from everyone else, as distinct in their eyes and so in your own.

Self as Others Treat You

Relationships connect through communication to the formation of your identity. If other people treat you with respect, you come to see yourself as respected, and self-respect becomes part of your identity. If your parents treated you like a child even after you had grown older, they drew out from you some sense that you were still a child, which may have caused you to feel resentment. If you are intelligent and people treat you as interesting, you may come to see yourself as having different value to other people than does someone who is not treated as intelligent. You get so used to the idea that it gets inside your "identity" and becomes part of who you are, but it originated from other people, not from you.

If you are tall, tough, and muscular (not short, bald, and carrying a Swiss Army knife), perhaps people habitually treat you with respect and caution. Over time, you get used to the idea, and identity is enacted and transacted in communication as a person who expects respect and a little caution from other people (Duck, 2011). Eventually, you will not have to act in a generally intimidating way in order to make people respectful. Your manner of communicating comes to reflect expected reactions to you. Although your identity began in the way you were treated by other people, it eventually becomes transacted in communication.

Society as Other Individuals:
Society's Secret Agents

Another way of thinking about this is to see how "society" gets your friends to do its work for it. You have never met a society or a culture, and you never will. You will only ever meet people who (re) present some of a society's key values to you. This contact with other folks puts them in the role of Society's Secret Agents. These people you meet and talk with are doing your society's work by enacting ways that culture represents the values that are desirable within it.

When you communicate with other people in your culture, you get information about what works and what doesn't, what is acceptable and what isn't, and how much you count in that society—what your identity is "worth." For example, the dominant culture in the United States typically values ambition, good looks, hard work, demonstration of material success, and a strong code of individuality. People stress those values in their talk ("The American Dream"/"Winners") or else feel inadequate because they don't stack up against these values ("Losers").

Of course, you are forced to interact with some people whether you like them or not (coworkers, professors, or relatives, for example). The principle is the same even though you most often think of the influence of your friends and relatives or key teachers on your identity. Nonfriends may challenge aspects of your sense of identity and make you reflect on the question, "Who am I?" Sometimes this reflection results in reinforced confidence in your opinions, but sometimes it undermines, modifies, or even challenges them. Either way, discussions of everyday communication transact some effect on your view of self, your identity. Your sense of self/identity comes from interactions with other people representing society as a whole.

Individuals acquire their individuality through the social practices in which they carry out their lives. Accordingly, they encounter powerful forces of society that are enacted by Society's Secret Agents in ordinary interactions. That "raised eyebrow" from your neighbor/instructor/team fan was actually society at work! Your "self" is structured and enacted in relation to those people who have power over you in formal ways, like the police, but most often you encounter the institutions within a society through its secret agents: public opinion. The people you know who express opinions about moral issues of the day and give you their judgments—they are Society's Secret Agents, guiding what

Table 5.2: Embarrassments and Predicaments

Embarrassment is when you perform a behavior that is inconsistent with the identity you want to present (Cupach & Metts, 1994; metts, 2000), Someone who wants to impress an interviewer but instead spills coffee on his or her lap undercuts "face" of professional competence by being clumsy. Someone who wants to present a "face" of calmness and confidence but who suddenly blushes or twitches allows nonverbal behavior to contradict the identity of being cool and composed. The *performance* of an identity (face) is undercut by a specific behavior that does not fit.

Predicaments present a longer challenge to the performative self (think of predicaments as extended embarrassment). If you go to a job interview and your very first answer makes you look stupid, you still have to carry on, with the interviewers all thinking you are a hopeless, worthless, and unemployable idiot. You cannot leave; you have to sit it out watching their polite smiles and feeling terrible.

other people do and thinking just as they do. And for that matter, your talk with other people makes you an agent also. Every time you comment on someone else's behavior, dress, relationships, or speech, you (yes, you) are helping to enforce social norms and practices.

Transacting a Self in Interactions With Others

In keeping with this book's theme, you can't have a self without also having relationships with other people—both the personal relationships you choose and the social relationships you reject. A person cannot have a concept of self without reflection on identity via the views of other people with whom he or she has relationships. Your identity is transacted or constituted in part from two things: First, you take into yourself the beliefs and prevailing norms of the society in which you live. Second, you are held to account for the identity that you project. As a football fan, you lose face if you don't know the score during a game or cannot name your own team's quarterback. As a student, you are expected to know answers about the book you are reading for your class.

Banality of Life as an Identity Maker

Again, your identity is a complex result not only of your own thinking, history, and experience but also of your interaction with other people and their influence on you, both as individuals and as Society's Secret Agents. Behind all those things that you think of as abstract social structures, like "the law," are real individuals acting in relation to one another (you and the police officer). These social relations get internalized into yourself. You slow down at speed-limit signs not because you want to but because you saw the police car and don't need another ticket.

The routine ordinary banality of everyday life talk with friends who share the same values and talk about them day by day (a) actually does something for society and (b) helps make you who you are. Daily routines like meeting at 11 a.m. for coffee in the coffee room put events in a predictable framework of meaning through trivial and pedestrian communication (Wood & Duck, 2006). But—here's the point of this section, so remember it well—you do your identity in front of the audiences, and they might evaluate and comment on whether you're doing it right.

The same kinds of processes occur in interaction when you profess your undying allegiance to one football team and your supposed hatred of the opposing team, or say that murder is wrong or that bankers are gouging customers. The people around you do not resent it but actually encourage you and reinforce your expression of ideas that make up your identity. They share it and support it. Just as Bob and his colleagues dehumanize "illegals" as targets for his most diligent attention and scrutiny—and his colleagues admire him for it—so do you when you categorize the opposing team as some kind of enemy. The underlying idea—that a group of people can be treated as nothing more than depersonalized, dehumanized others with no appreciable individuality—runs through team loyalty and rivalry, town versus college kids, treating older students as aliens, and any other kind of stereotyping.

Performative Self

Other people influence who you are and how you are treated. Other people use labels and judge your behavior. You are not just an inner core but part of a heritage. You are not just you; you are a symbol in a cultural and social structure.

On top of that, add the curious idea that you don't just have an identity; you actually do one. Identity is not just having a symbolic sense of self but doing it in the presence of other people and doing it well in their eyes. This is an extremely interesting and provocative fact about communication: Everyone does his or her identity for an audience, like an actor in a play. **Performative self** means that selves are creative performances based on the social demands and norms of a given situation. As we will now discuss, you try to present the right face to people you are with and do your identity differently in front and back regions.

Facework Revisited

Facework is part of what happens in everyday life communication, and people have a sense of their own dignity. This gets transacted in everyday communication by polite protection of the person's "face."

This idea is about the performance of one's identity in public, the presentation of the self to people in a way that is intended to make the self look good.

Erving Goffman (1959) indicated the way in which momentary social forces affect identity portrayal. Goffman was interested in how identity is performed in everyday life so that people manage their image to make everyone "look good" (Cupach & Metts, 1994). The concept of "looking good" of course means "looking good to other people" It is therefore essentially a relational concept. (Table 5.2 provides challenges to a persons face.)

It takes you one step closer to looking at the interpersonal interaction that occurs on the ground every day. Rather than looking at society in an abstract way, Goffman (1959) focused on what you actually do in interactions. In part, your portrayal of yourself is shaped by the social needs at the time, the social situation, the social frame, and the circumstances surrounding your performance. Remember the server from Chapter 1? She does not introduce herself that way to her friends ("Hi, I'm Alice, and I'll be your server tonight") except as a joke, so her performance of the server identity is restricted to those times and places where it is appropriate.

Front and Back Regions

Goffman (1959) differentiated a **front region** and **back region** to social performance: The front region/front stage is not a place but an occasion where your professional, proper self is performed. For example, a server is all smiles and civility in the front stage of the restaurant when talking to customers. This behavior might be different from how he or she performs in the back region/backstage (say, the restaurant kitchen) when talking with the cooks or other servers and making jokes about the customers or about being disrespectful to them. But again, the back region is not just a place: If all servers are standing around in the restaurant before the customers come in and they are just chatting informally among themselves, the instant the first customer comes through the door, their demeanor will change to "professional" and they will switch to a front-region performance.

That means the performance of your identity is not sprung into action by your own free wishes but by social cues that this is the time to perform your "self" in that way. An identity is a performance. It shows how a person makes sense of the world not just alone but within a context provided by others.

Any identity connects to other identities. You can be friendly when you are with your friends, but you are expected to be professional when on the job and to do student identity when in class. So is this what allows Bob to be "two people," one at work and one in the social community? Is he just doing a front-region SOB performance at work?

Individuals inevitably draw on knowledge shared in any community, so any person draws on information that is both personal and communal. If you change from thinking of identity as about "self as character" and instead see it as "self as performer," you also must consider the importance of changes in performance to suit different audiences and transactive situations.

Self Constituted/Transacted in
Everyday Practices

We have seen that identity is not just a personal inner core but a communicative performance molded by surrounding cultural influences, the way that you do your identity and how you are recognized as having one. Your practical performance of "being yourself" is affected by the social norms that are in place to guide communication in a given society. People judge your identity performance in a practical world and expect you to explain or account for yourself.

Practical Self

Your identity is performed in a material world that affects who you are. For example, the fact that you can communicate with other people more or less instantaneously across huge distances by mobile telephone materially affects your sense of connection to other people. This practical self is born from the ability to do practical things and is illustrated by the importance to many young people of learning to drive a car. When you can drive, not only do you go through the transformation of self as "more of a grown-up," but when you have a car you also can do what you cannot do when you do not have one. The ability to drive and obtain access to a car expands your identity in a practical way.

Part of your performance of self is connected to the practical artifacts, accompaniments, and "stuff" that you use in your performance. If you have the right "stuff" (professional suit, bling, or a sports car), the self that you project is different from the self you perform without it.

Accountable Self

An important element of doing an identity in front of an audience is that you become an **accountable self,** which essentially allows your identity to be morally judged by other people. What you do can be assessed by other people as right or wrong according to existing habits of society. Any performance of identity turns identity into a moral action. That is, identity becomes a way of living, based on choices made about actions that a person sees as available or relevant. Others will judge and hold the performance to account. The social construction of identity is influenced by societal value systems. Society as a whole encourages you to take certain actions (do not park next to fire hydrants, protect the elderly and the weak, be a good neighbor, recycle!).

Moral accountability is a fancy way of saying that society as a whole makes judgments about your actions and choices. It holds you to account for the actions and choices that you make, but it also forcefully encourages you to act in particular ways and to see specific types of identity as "good" (patriot is good, traitor is bad; loyalty is good, thief is bad; open self-disclosure is good, passive aggression is bad, for example). As noted before, "society" does this through everyday performances and communications by Society's Secret Agents—including you.

Table 5.3: Some Ways to See Identity Communication and Relationships

Psychic/ reflective self	*Habits of thought/of behavior/of perception identify a person's "personality."* What you normally think of as identity a priori: Your communicative behavior just expresses the inner self.
Symbolic self	*Broad social forces affect self differentiation/characterization.* Self arises out of social interaction and not vice versa; hence, it does not "belong to me." You are who you are because of the people you hang out with, interact with, and communicate with; you can be a different identity in different circumstances.
Performative self	*Present social situation affects self-portrayal.* Selves are acted out in a network of social demands and norms; you do your identity differently in front and back regions and try to present the right "face" to the people you are with.
Practical self	*Material world affects self/how you think of self.* Practical aspects of materiality transform the concept of self. Your identity is represented by objects that symbolically make claims about the sort of person you are.
Accountable self	*Social contex influences broad forms of portrayal.* Personality is just an abstract concept. People act within a set of social ideas and habitual styles of thinking, allowing other people to comment and steer how they behave.
Improvisational performance	*There is a rhetorical spin to this and how "self" is presented.* Ideology affects the manner of presentation of terms, characteristics, and so on. We try to narrate ourselves in the way that our society expects us to represent identity.

Improvisational Performance

The identity that you thought of as your own personality, then, is not made up of your own desires and impulses but is formed, performed, and expressed within a set of social patterns and judgments. These are reinforced by the practices in a community through the relationships that people have with one another. The Indiana University fan is not asked why she is cheering for Indiana University by other Indiana University fans; Bob is not asked by his colleagues why he is so tough on "illegals."

A person's identity is a complex and compound concept that is partly based on history, memory, experiences, and interpretations by the individual, partly evoked by momentary aspects of talk (its context, the people you are with, your stage in life, your goals at the time), and partly a social creation directed by other people, society and its categories, and your relationship objectives in those contexts. Your performance of the self is guided by your relationships with other people, as well as your social goals. Even your embodiment of this knowledge or your sense of self is shaped by your social practices with other people. Your self-consciousness in their presence influences the presentation of yourself to other people. Although a sense of self/identity is experienced in your practical interactions with other people, you get trapped by language into reporting it abstractly as some sort of disembodied "identity," a symbolic representation of the routine practices and communication styles that you experience in your daily interactions with other people. Once again, then, another apparently simple idea (identity, personality, self) runs into the relational influences that make the basics of communication so valuable to study.

Summary

This chapter discussed the basic elements of identities and perceptions and how these are related to the development of the self-concept. Identity is seen as a performance that is conducted when we interact with other people, and they way others respond to our performance is seen as an important aspect in the development of the self-concept.

It is important to remember that there are influences on one's ability to perceive, and these influences can cause significant differences in perception from one person to another. Physiological factors are perhaps the biggest influence: we can't perceive what we can't sense. Once we do perceive something, we organize these perceptions in such a manner that we can retrieve this information as needed via prototypes, personal constructs, and scripts.

Our self-concept is the inner core of our identity, however the number of identities an individual can have varies from person to person. Our identity is influenced by many factors, but perhaps the most significant influence on our self-concept is our interaction with other people. Another important aspect in the development of our self-concept is self-disclosure; however the kind and amount of information revealed through self-disclosure is different with each individual. If there is anything to learned about our identities it is that they are dynamic; it is a process that continues to change as our lives evolve.

We each have narratives or stories about our lives that we share with other people, and this helps create a symbolic identity about ourselves. Finally, this chapter reinforces the point that you cannot have an identity without having relationships with other people, and the identities we have are transacted through interaction with these individuals.

The next chapter focuses on a communicative skill that is also influenced by perception, and is probably one of the more under-utilized skills in communication: listening. Understanding how to listen actively will enable one to distinguish the significant differences between simply hearing and making a conscious effort to listen.

Questions For Discussion

1. Can you identify some the most basic perceptual problems in human communication?
2. Why is the answer to the question, "Who are you?"so difficult to answer?

3. What is the difference between a script and a prototype?
4. What do you consider to be the key narrative about your life?
5. Why are people so surprised when they discover that there is a significant difference between a person's "front stage" and "back stage" behavior?

References

Baxter, L. A. (2004). Distinguished scholar article: Relationships as dialogues. Personal Relationships, 11(1), 1–22. Baxter, L. A. (2011). *Voicing relationships: A dialogic perspective.* Thousand Oaks, CA: Sage.

Baxter, L. A., & Braithwaite, D. O. (2008). Relational dialectics theory: Crafting meaning from competing discourses. In L. A. Baxter & D. O. Braithwaite (Eds.), *Engaging theories in interpersonal communication* (pp. 349–361). Thousand Oaks, CA: Sage.

Baxter, L. A., & Montgomery, B. M. (1996). *Relating: Dialogs and dialectics.* New York: Guilford Press.

Berscheid, E., & Reis, H. T. (1998). *Attraction and close relationships.* In D. T. Gilbert, S. F. Fiske, & G. Lindzey (Eds.), *The handbook of social psychology* (4th ed., pp. 139–281). Boston: McGraw-Hill.

Burke, K. (1969). *A grammar of motives.* Berkeley: University of California Press.

Burleson, B. R., Holmstrom, A.J., & Gilstrap, C. M. (2005). "Guys can't say that to guys": Four experiments assessing the normative motivation account for deficiencies in the emotional support provided by men. *Communication Monographs, 72*(4), 468–501.

Caughlin, J. P., & Afifi, T. D. (2004). When is topic avoidance unsatisfying? Examining the moderators of the association between avoidance and dissatisfaction. *Human Communication Research, 30*(4), 479–513.

Cupach, W. R., & Metts, S. (1994). *Facework.* Thousand Oaks, CA: Sage.

Derlega, V.J., Metts, S., Petronio, S., & Margulis, S. T. (1993). *Self-disclosure.* Newbury Park, CA: Sage.

Dindia, K. (2000). Self-disclosure, identity, and relationship development: A dialectical perspective. In K. Dindia & S. W. Duck (Eds.), *Communication and personal relationships* (pp. 147–162). Chichester, UK: Wiley.

Duck, S. W. (2011). *Rethinking relationships: A new approach to relationship research.* Thousand Oaks, CA: Sage.

Fehr, B. (1993). How do I love thee: Let me consult my prototype. In S. W. Duck (Ed.), *Understanding relationship processes* (Vol. 1, pp. 87–120). Newbury Park, CA: Sage.

Goffman, E. (1959). *Behaviour in public places.* Harmondsworth, UK: Penguin Books.

Hess, J. A. (2000). Maintaining a nonvoluntary relationship with disliked partners : An investigation into the use of distancing behaviors. *Human Communication Research,* 26, 458–488.

Huisman, D. (2008). *Intergenerational family storytelling.* Iowa City: University of Iowa Department of Communication Studies.

Jourard, S. M. (1964). *The transparent self.* New York: Van Nostrand Reinhold.

Jourard, S. M. (1971). *Self disclosure.* New York: Wiley.

Kellas, J. K. (2008). Narrative theories: Making sense of interpersonal communication. In L. A. Baxter 8c D. O. Braithwaite (Eds.), *Engaging theories in interpersonal communication* (pp. 241–254). Thousand Oaks, CA: Sage.

Kelly, G. A. (1955). *The psychology of personal constructs.* New York: Norton.

Luft, J., & Ingham, H. (1955). *The Johari window: A graphic model of interpersonal awareness.* Proceedings of the Western Training Laboratory in Group Development. Los Angeles: University of California.

Marwell, G, & Schmitt, D. R. (1967). Dimensions of compliance-gaining behavior: An empirical analysis. *Sociometry*, 30, 350–364.

Mead, G. H. (1934). *Mind, self, and society.* Chicago: University of Chicago Press.

Metts, S. (2000). Face and facework: Implications for the study of personal relationships. In K. Dindia & S. W. Duck (Eds.), *Communication and personal relationships* (pp. 74–92). Chichester, UK: Wiley.

Norwood, K. M. (2010, April 26). *Here and gone: Competing discourses in the communication of families with a transgender member.* Unpublished PhD thesis, Department of Communication Studies, University of Iowa.

Payne, A. (Director). (2004). *Sideways* [Motion picture]. United States: Fox Searchlight Pictures.

Petronio, S. (2002). *Boundaries of privacy.* Albany: State University of New York Press.

Shotter, J. (1984). *Social accountability and selfhood.* Oxford, UK: Basil Blackwell.

Wood, J. T., & Duck, S. W. (Eds.). (2006). *Composing relationships: Communication in everyday life.* Belmont, CA: Thomson Wadsworth.

Chapter 4

Active Listening

James G. Clawson

This chapter introduces you to the components of the active listening process. In the last chapter you were introduced to the process of perception and how it influences communication—listening is a key part of that process. If we hear but do not listen, perceptions will have a greater chance of being incorrect.

Learning Objectives For This Chapter

- Identify the four keys to active listening
- Describe the purpose of active listening
- Explain the benefits of active listening
- Describe the disadvantages of active listening

I think real listening is something you do with your whole self. You have to hear what people are really saying beneath all the words. You have to pick up the messages that have a certain urgency and then respond to these nuances with further questions. Over the years, I've learned that the really attentive listening requires conversational responsiveness. You have to try to listen in such a way that you can respond with your own ideas and feelings and aspirations—so that you show the speaker that you've truly been paying attention. I'm talking about a strong human connection here: How do we understand one another? How do we give ourselves to someone else, and possibly even become one?

—Robert Coles[1]

Introduction

What if you had a magic wand and could, with one stroke, become a more effective leader, closer to your significant others, more influential in your professional relationships, a better friend, and a wiser, more mature adult? Active listening is a social skill that promises all of these things and more. Most people fall prey to a variety of social pitfalls in their conversations that erodes their influence, undermines their attempts to lead, and deepens the chasms between them and others. Those pitfalls include the almost universal tendency to judge others from our own points of view, to try to lead the conversation even when talking about the other's interests, and the desire to convince others of the correctness of our points of view. Effective listening or active listening helps us to overcome those gaffes and become more influential and more effective in our relationships, professional and personal.

Effective listening is essential to good leadership. Unless you understand the position, views, beliefs, values, opinions, and conclusions of others, your attempts to manage others, to offer advice, directions, instructions, comments, or opinions will be blind ventures based on your experience and perhaps totally inappropriate to the other. The more you know about the views of the other person, the better you can frame not only what you say, but how you say it. The "magic wand" of active listening can be an enormous asset in your interpersonal tool kit—if you're willing to develop it.

Active or "reflective" listening was originally developed and refined by psychologist Carl Rogers for use in personal counseling. Rogers wrote extensively about his very successful approach and gave seminars teaching others how to use it to help their patients. The technique can be very useful in settings outside counseling, including everyday conversations, formal discussions, teaching, managing, and in marriage—in virtually every situation where people interact. Active listening is particularly useful when the speaker has a problem or is animated about some topic and the listener either wants to help the person with that problem or to learn more about the speaker's perspective.

Active listening consists of two major components; first, seeking genuinely to understand the other person at two levels, and second, communicating or reflecting that understanding back to the speaker. This latter characteristic has caused the approach to be referred to often as "reflective listening." The reflection is important, because it reassures the speaker and the listener that what is being communicated is being understood. Without that link, neither the speaker nor the listener is really sure whether clear communication is taking place.

Active listening is a learnable skill. But it is more than the lay language implies; it is more than simply "paying attention." The approach includes a cluster of skills—and perhaps more importantly—a mindset. This mindset is the desire to see and understand how another person sees and experiences the world. Most of us, having grown up as we have within our own experience set, tend to think that the rest of the world sees the world as we do. We are surprised when we see people behaving in ways that seem irrational to us. The first step in developing active listening skills is to have a genuine interest in seeing the

Figure 1: Four Key Active Listening Skills

1. Suspending judgment of the speaker
2. Focusing on emotion as well as content
3. Following, not leading the conversation
4. Reflecting accurately what you understand, so the speaker can "see" it more clearly

world as others do. Given that desire, one must develop some, perhaps unnatural skills to become effective at the technique (Figure 1).

Suspending Judgment

Perhaps the central skill in active listening is the ability to *momentarily* suspend our own judgments and beliefs about what may be right or wrong. That is difficult for most people to do. We all want to believe that we are "right." If we cannot let go of that for a moment or two, however, we will be unable to see the world as the other person sees it. When we listen to a person actively, we suspend for the moment our own views and values, beliefs and attitudes, judgments, and conclusions. Whenever we say, "I know exactly what you mean!" we are probably still locked in our own experience perspective. We've picked up on something the speaker said—immediately we've jumped to our own similar experience and concluded that they must have responded the same way. Often that is not true. And our presumption shifts leadership of the conversation from the speaker to us.

We approach active listening by clearing our own minds of our thoughts and priorities, *for the moment,* and understanding as deeply as we can how the other person thinks and feels and then reflecting or mirroring that understanding to the speaker. Any judgment—negative or positive—will cloud our ability to hear and connect with the speaker. When we suspend judgment, we give the speaker "breathing room"—space to be honest and to do so without defensiveness.

People find it difficult to stop judging others for a variety of reasons. First, they infer that suspending judgment means that they are agreeing with the speaker, which is not so. Our goal is not to confirm their viewpoint but to understand it. If we confuse these two, it makes it harder for us to let go of our own views. Second, some people are afraid that if they listen to another's views carefully it may affect their own views in negative ways. Suspension of judgment requires some confidence in our own abilities to put aside and then reassume our own values and priorities. Consider for a moment the kind of people that you have the most difficulty not judging. Is it a religious group, a political group, a race? Whatever it is, unless you are able to pause in your tendency to judge people immediately, you will likely find it difficult to become a good listener. And listening to someone who believes deeply and differently from you does not mean that your thinking will be "contaminated." Rather, you may learn something that will benefit you for the rest of your life, professionally and personally.

Focusing on Emotion as Well as Content

The second active listening skill is the ability to pay attention to both the content and the related emotions contained in what another is communicating. This is what Daniel Goleman has called "emotional intelligence" and I have referred to as "social quotient."[2] At first blush, this seems simple, but for those who practice active listening, figuring out quickly what a person is saying while simultaneously paying attention to the feelings surrounding that content is quite a challenge. Emotions are important because they reflect the intensity of the person's thoughts and experience. If you can see what another person is feeling and then articulate that accurately back to them, you can signal to the speaker the depth of your understanding of their world.

Identifying a speaker's emotions is not so simple. Sometimes their emotions may be obvious: anger, fear, depression. In those cases, it may be easy to identify what they're feeling. Other times, however, the feelings washing over a speaker may be ambivalence, confusion, or a vague uneasiness. These emotional states may be more difficult to see and even more difficult to articulate. Good listeners understand the wide range of emotions and are able to see and describe them in conversations.

Following, Not Leading the Conversation

The primary goal of active listening is to give the speaker complete freedom to pursue issues and topics of their choosing, and in so doing, to use the listener—yourself—as a sounding board for ideas and options about handling personal situations and concerns. Most would-be listeners are unable to allow this because they begin judging and asking questions, thereby focusing on what's important to the *listener* rather than on what's important to the speaker. Good active listeners are willing and able to allow the speaker to go where he or she wants to by virtue of their competency in letting the other lead the conversation. Paradoxically, one must let go of the desire to lead the discussion along lines of one's own interests in order to become more influential with the other.

Reflecting Accurately What You Understand

Another active listening skill is the ability to reframe the content and emotion of the other person's statement in a way that makes it easy for the speaker to understand that you, the listener, understand *accurately* what the other has been saying and feeling. If one simply repeats what the other has said (parroting), the speaker may come to feel that the listener is playing some pop psychological game with them or is mocking by mimicry. If the listener overstates what the speaker has said, the speaker may feel manipulated or invaded and retreat from the conversation.

Active listening is hard work, and it can be frightening. To lay one's own beliefs and values aside for the moment and to concentrate on how someone else thinks and believes and feels—to wrap one's self inside another's view of the world—can be unsettling. This willing suspension of one's own view of the world requires a certain self confidence in one's own views and beliefs and in one's ability to pick them up again in a moment at will. This suspension requires you to understand that others have and utilize a rationale different from your own. The goal of active listening is to understand their rationale— and emotional experience—from *their* vantage point. Learning to be an effective active listener by suspending judgement, paying attention to content and emotion, following not leading, and reflecting your understanding is hard, even exhausting work. When you first begin to practice active listening, you are likely to find that you feel worn out. But don't give up! Active listening serves a valuable purpose.

Purpose of Active Listening

The primary purpose of active listening is to allow another person an unfettered, unguided opportunity to articulate what they are concerned about so that both you—and, more important—*they* may understand that concern more clearly and then deal with it. A major side purpose here is to allow you, the listener, to expand your horizons and to learn more about how other people in the world think about and react to events around them. Unless we do this, we are doomed to offer advice from our own perspectives and experience—which may or may not be appropriate for another.

In other words, the goal of active listening is to allow the speaker to lead the conversation without fear or inhibition—for a time—so that they can take the conversation in the direction they want. If a person is afraid of the reactions of the listener in any way, he or she is likely to maintain a certain defensiveness. This defensiveness inhibits both the speaker and the listener from clearly "seeing" the speaker's true thoughts and feelings. Active listeners seek to see the world, for the moment, through the other person's biases and filters, to be clearly aware of what the speaker is both saying and feeling, to clearly see the way the speaker thinks and to reflect that understanding back to the speaker. However difficult this may seem at first, if one can achieve this purpose, one can accomplish several important benefits.

Benefits of Active Listening

Understanding Another Person's Point of View

We all see the world differently. The more clearly we understand how others see the world, the better able we are to understand their behavior. This will broaden and strengthen our understanding of human behavior and guide our efforts at motivating and leading others. We are often perplexed about why other people are behaving the way they are. Active listening can help us to understand their behavior better and thus be better equipped for working with them.

Stronger Interpersonal Relationships

Skilled reflective listening tends to strengthen interpersonal commitments. When a speaker senses that a listener has suspended judgment and is working hard to see the world through his or her eyes, he or she appreciates the effort. Good active listening allows the speaker to feel safe. The speaker senses the respect that the listener must have for the speaker in order to be able to do this, and he is likely to return the favor. The unspoken message from the listener is: "I respect what you have to say and what you are feeling, I will take the time (and the talent required) to listen to it." Sensing this message, the speaker feels safe, less defensive, and closer to the listener.

Helping the Speaker

When a person can speak without fear of being judged, he or she is more likely to speak openly and completely. At the same time, when one does this and both the content and emotion of the speech are mirrored in the listener, the speaker sees and hears more clearly what he or she is saying and feeling than he can do when simply listening internally. Sometimes the speaker may even say, "Did I say that?" or "Yes, I guess that's what I'm saying." When that happens, the speaker's positions and concerns are clarified, and the person is then often better able to decide what to do about the question at hand.

We can point out here that people do not always "know" what they think and feel. Carl Rogers spoke about two "translations" that must occur for a person to communicate clearly (see Figure 1). First, one must be aware of one's own experience, the things one is feeling and thinking. Current work on the nature of emotional intelligence[3] suggests that people vary widely in this "skill." Being aware of one's experience to the point that one can

Figure 1: Carl Rogers's two translations in communication.

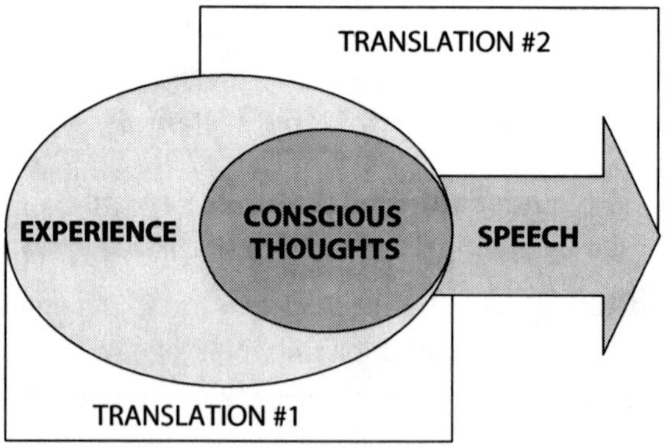

formulate a thought about it is the first translation. The second translation comes when one tries to put his or her thoughts into spoken words. If your experience is like mine, you find daily examples of others who struggle to say clearly "what they mean." You may even find yourself struggling from time to time throughout the day to communicate clearly to others what you're thinking and feeling. When we "see" or hear reflected back to us what we're saying, two things happen: first, we gain a sense of validation in the world, that someone else out there understands us, and second, we are able to understand ourselves better by virtue of that "mirroring" effect.[4] Instructors in the classroom will often write what students say on the chalkboard so that others and the speaker may "see" and explore the functionality of their comments. Yet, while active listening does much to strengthen relationships and to help people deal with each other, these benefits come at a certain cost.

Disadvantages of Active Listening

Active listening has some disadvantages. Perhaps the most obvious is that it takes time. Active listening is not the sort of thing one can do in one minute in a hurried exchange with a subordinate or colleague.[5] But the old advertisement adage, "You can pay me now, or you can pay me later," applies here. If one does not take the time to understand the other person in a relationship early on, the prices or costs of lack of trust, lack of respect, lack of communication, lack of motivation, and loss of ability to influence or lead make the accounting more difficult. The time commitment in active listening, both in learning to do it well—as well as to use it—is heavy on the front end, but rewarding in the end.

A second disadvantage is that many think they are good listeners when they are not. People who "parrot" what another says and believe themselves to be good reflective listeners are fooling themselves—but probably not those they are talking with. Skill in active listening requires above all else the ability to put one's own view of the world aside *for the moment* and then to focus exclusively on the other person's content and emotion. Unless the genuine intent and the skill to back it up are there, attempts to use active listening as a management "tool" may actually undermine a relationship.

Consider the 2-by-2 table shown in Figure 2. If a person does not have a genuine interest in understanding another's point of view, this "attitude" will probably come through sooner or later to the speaker. Having some skill at reflective listening then is not enough; genuine interest is a critical foundation. On the other hand, if one has a genuine interest but weak skills, the other person may forgive technical gaffs because they know you are really trying. If you can add a degree of skill to your genuine attempts to listen actively, you may hope for deeper, more aware, more productive relationships. If you have neither skill nor interest in active listening, you may spend your time in superficial relationships never really knowing why others do what they do—especially around you. That suggests a need to clarify the fundamental principles of using active listening.

There are some seemingly simple principles to active listening that you should keep in mind as you begin to try it—they seem easier to do than they really are.

Respond, Don't Lead

While you are in the reflective listening mode, your goal is to understand as completely as possible, not to direct. The goal is to let the speaker determine *what* will be talked about next and to what degree. The speaker should choose what is important, not the listener. If you begin to direct the discussion, it will focus on your interests, not the speaker's. If you begin to ask questions, you will begin to lead the discussion and you will have lost an opportunity to learn more about the other person and what *he or she* wants to talk about.

Respond to the Personal Rather Than the Impersonal

Whenever we respond to what another person has said, we are faced with multiple choices. A key choice is whether to respond to the personal or the impersonal components of what has been said. When one responds to the impersonal, one directs the discussion away from the speaker's beliefs and values, when often those are the very things he or she is trying to communicate or understand better. Some people find it difficult to talk with others about personal things. That is a choice we all have, speakers and listeners. The choice to remain impersonal has a consequence of keeping the relationship on a relatively superficial level. If you are willing to listen personally, you must still respect the speaker's choice about how much to open up—or not. The speaker may not want the listener to get that close. More often than not, however, the choice to focus on the impersonal, arm's-length content of the discussion is a result of the discomfort of the listener in dealing with (that is, listening to) personal matters. If you feel this way, remind yourself that your goal is not to offer advice about what to do about a particular personal problem, rather only to *understand*

Figure 2: Impact of sincerity and active listening skill on relationships.

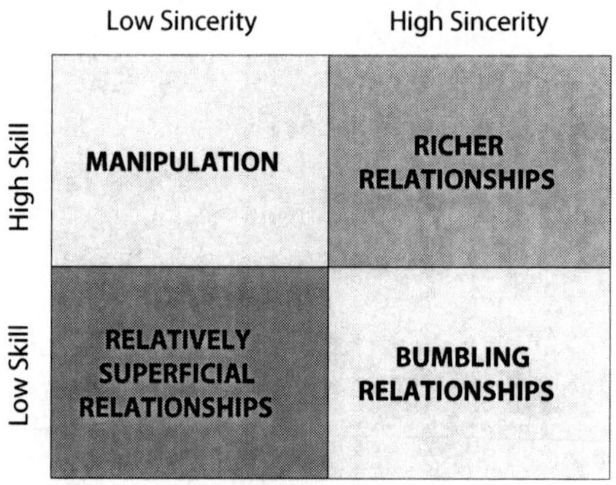

it. Ultimately, it is the speaker's responsibility to take action about the issue. Perhaps this will make it easier to participate in a more personal conversation.

Recognize Feelings as Well as Content

Emotions are an important determinant of behavior. The skill of recognizing feelings is an essential part of understanding another person. If we cannot recognize and reflect the emotions that speakers have, we may not be able to understand their values and the strength of those values. Learn to watch for and be able to identify the *feelings* associated with what a person is saying. Some managers find it almost impossible to recognize feelings—perhaps, because the demands of their jobs have taught them over the years to suppress the emotional side of their personalities.[6] Each of us has learned patterns that determine how much emotion we show in our relationships. Whether we show them or not, they are there, and if listeners can watch for and reflect them, we can learn more about what bothers us, what we like, what we dislike, and how to manage those emotions at work as well as in our nonwork activities.

Know When to Use Active Listening

Active listening is in some ways like a carpentry tool or a golf club in that it has specific purposes and predictable outcomes, and therefore, is not applicable to every situation. In the way that judgments about which tool or golf club to use when are important skills for the carpenter and golfer, knowing when to use active listening is a key skill for the effective manager. Ideally, one will sense these times and be able to slip in and out of active listening so smoothly that the speaker is hardly aware of the change in structure yet feels better understood and ready to proceed without concern.

Many managers claim that they have a "communication problem" in their organizations. When asked what this means, they often say, "I can't get them to understand what I want them to do!" This answer reflects a theory of communication that begins with the desire to *be* understood. We suggest that a more productive theory of communication would *begin with the desire to understand* and only secondly move to the desire to be understood.[7] The reason is that when other people feel understood, they are much more likely to be willing to listen to what you have to say (later) and, therefore, will allow you to be understood. Although (a topic for another discussion) the means one uses to be understood are critical, too.[8] Unless one can be clear, stimulating, respectful, and congruent, others will probably not respond well. Further, sharing the raw data from which you have drawn your own conclusions, rather than sharing only your conclusions, lets others draw their own conclusions and tends to lead to more productive working relationships.

Choose Appropriate Response Types

Whenever we respond to what someone else has said, we choose a type of response. We can array these responses on a continuum of directiveness, as shown in Exhibit 1. The goal of active listening is to be nondirective. As you review this array, you will be surprised at where some response types appear. You may be surprised, for example, that questions rank so highly on the scale toward "directive." If you think about it, when we ask a question, we are focusing the discussion on what *we* want to know—not necessarily on what the speaker wants to talk about. When we ask questions, immediately the speaker is asked to take a secondary role, one of responding to your inquiries. Questions send a message, however subtle or unrecognized, that you are leading the discussion and not really interested in what the speaker wants to talk about. Active listening seeks to use the responses on the nondirective end of the spectrum so that the speaker will feel free to say what is on his or her mind.

Then What?

You should not try to use active listening all the time. Eventually, people may want to know what you think and what your view is. This is one of the points in Coles's quote at the beginning of this note. Active listening could be another tool in your social toolkit. If you know how to use it, you must also know when to use it and when to put it aside and move on to another tool, perhaps questioning or giving advice. Active listening will help you understand another person better and help them to understand themselves better. Often, a person who has a good active listener will come naturally to the course of action they wish to pursue by hearing and seeing the reflections of their listener. In these cases, the listener need never switch to giving advice or direct instructions. This is good for both parties: the speaker feels more autonomous and powerful while the listener feels more influential and powerful.

Sometimes, though, the speaker runs out of steam. While Rogers, in a counseling session, would carefully avoid giving advice at these points, in a managerial setting you may feel it appropriate to switch over to giving suggestions. Just beware, though. Most of us are way too quick to do this, and in so doing we undermine the development of our relationships. This tendency is what William Glasser has called "control theory," the desire of most people to assume that they know what's right and that they have a right and obligation to get others to agree with them and to accede to their point of view.[9] We will be better leaders if we can resist this urge to control others.

Summary

In this brief chapter you learned the four keys of active listening: suspending judgment, focusing on emotion and content, following as opposed to leading conversations, and reflecting back to the speaker what you have understood from them, not simply repeating what they have said.

By understanding the benefits of active listening you can more easily understand another person's viewpoint, develop stronger interpersonal relationships, and listen without judging. With all the advantages of active listening, there are a few pitfalls: it takes more time to listen actively, people may mistake active listening for "parroting" back what the speaker says without taking a genuine interest in what the other person says. Finally, the principles of active listening were presented to give you the best chance of being successful when you attempt to listen actively.

In our next chapter we look at verbal communication, and all the complexities of language and communication. While active listening is important, if you do not understand the many aspects of verbal communication and how they are related, you will not be very successful in communicating.

Questions For Discussion

1. What do you think are some of the most common errors people make when they listen?
2. How does active listening differ from just repeating back what the speaker has said to you?
3. Why can better listening improve interpersonal relationships?
4. What is the difference between hearing and listening?
5. When is it not a good idea to employ active listening?

Notes

1. Robert Coles, "The Inner Life of Executive Kids: A Conversation with Child Psychiatrist Robert Coles," *Harvard Business Review* (November 2001): R0110A.
2. Daniel Goleman, *Emotional Intelligence* (New York: Bantam, 1995); and James G. Clawson, "Leadership and Intelligence," *Level Three Leadership 2e,* (Upper Saddle River, NJ: Prentice Hall, 2002).
3. See Daniel Goleman, *Emotional Intelligence* (New York: Bantam, 1995).
4. Alice Miller's classic book, *The Drama of the Gifted Child* (New York: BasicBooks, 1997), for example, points out how fundamental an impact mirroring has on the development of small children. Simply put, when we are allowed to see ourselves in our relationships with others, we gain an ego strength and self-confidence that cannot be gotten elsewhere.

5. Ken Blanchard, author of *The One Minute Manager* (New York: William Morrow, 1982) might disagree. Actually, a person skilled at moving in and out of active listening could probably use it to good effect from moment to moment throughout any given day.

6. Again, the work on emotional intelligence is revealing here. See footnote 3.

7. See Stephen Covey's best-selling book, *The Seven Habits of Highly Effective People* (New York: Simon and Schuster, 1989).

8. For more information here, see the discussion on the language of leadership in the chapter on "Leading Others" in James G. Clawson, *Level Three Leadership 2e* (Upper Saddle River, New Jersey: Prentice-Hall, 1999).

9. William Glasser, *Choice Theory* (New York: Harper Collins, 1999).

Chapter 5

Verbal Communication

Steve Duck and David T. McMahan

W hen you begin to understand the dynamics of verbal communication, you begin to understand that it is incredible that there are not more misunderstandings when people communicate. This chapter introduces you to the various aspects of verbal communication and how to understand better the way words influence or lives through such concepts as intentionality, facework, and narratives.

Learning Objectives For This Chapter

- Understand how langue and parole are used to understand the relationship between the speaker and listener
- Describe how polysemy can cause misunderstandings in communication
- Explain the role that frames and naming have in communication
- Differentiate between connotative and denotative meanings of words
- Describe how intentionality functions in communication
- Identify the three functions of talk in relationships
- Explain the role of facework in communication
- Understand the difference between low code and high code
- Explain the function or narratives
- Identify the five dimensions of Burke's Pentad

A man walked into a bar. A second man walked into a bar. A third one didn't, because he ducked. You know the word *bar,* and you know that in our culture jokes and stories often start with the phrase "A man walked into a ban" Such cultural knowledge frames your expectations about the story you are being told. *A frame,* you recall, is a context that influences the interpretation of communication. However, the word *bar has* different meanings. If you were faintly amused by the opening sentences here, it is partly because the word is used in the first sentence differently than you expected on the basis of the frame of the story. The punch line works only because you are misled—twice—into thinking of a different kind of "bar." Familiarity with the story's cultural form frames your expectations in a way that pulls the last sentence right out from under you.

Verbal communication involves the use of language. Whenever you speak, you *use* language in ways that take much for granted, and the study of *language use in talk* is the subject of this chapter. Language has a grammatical structure, but when used conversationally, it uses cultural and, relational assumptions. These are represented by symbols, frames, and meanings. In this chapter you will learn more about the workings of these aspects of the spoken language of everyday life and how they serve to build and sustain relationships.

In everyday talk, words weave together seamlessly within a context that includes nonverbal communication. Examples of nonverbal communication include facial expressions, hand gestures, movements, changes in posture, and pacing or timing of speech. In practice, nonverbal aspects of communication help frame your expectations and interpretation of what someone means. For convenience, though, we have to separate verbal and nonverbal communication into two parts: verbal, or language. Keep in mind, however, that this split is artificial when it comes to understanding everyday life.

How Do You Know What Talk Means?

When you use the word *cat,* everyone assumes you are referring to an animal. You know what animals are and, specifically, what a cat looks like. When you started to learn to read, "The cat sat on the mat" may have been one of the first sentences you ever came across. In everyday life talk, however, if you say to a person, "You really are catty" (Norwood, 2007), you are speaking not literally but relationally or metaphorically. A listener would understand what you mean, even though the words are literally not true: He or she is not a cat. This example emphasizes an important point: The formal grammar of a language is different from use of that language in everyday talk.

Linguists like Ferdinand de Saussure (Komatsu, 1993) therefore draw a distinction between *langue* (pronounced "longg") and *parole* (pronounced "pa-rull"). Langue is the formal grammatical structure of language that you will read about in books on grammar. **Parole** is how people actually use language, with informal and ungrammatical phrases that carry meaning to us all the same. "Git er done!" is an example of parole but would earn you bad grades in an English grammar course (langue). When people feel relaxed in a close relationship, they are much more likely to use parole. People in a formal setting are more likely to use langue. Communication is used loosely in close personal relationships because they are quite informal, but formal relationships are more uptight. Relationships frame both what gets said and how it gets understood.

Language and your use of talk are also based on other frames. One is familiarity with the other person: The friendlier you are with the other person, the more you use relaxed, informal language. Other influences on your speech affect the words you choose or the relational messages sent by the words you pick out ("Hey, you!" is different from "Excuse me, sir").

Other frames for talk depend on the times that you live in and the items that are familiar to you. Your great-grandparents may have called their father "sir" whereas you probably call yours "Dad" or something less formal.

A final frame requires that you know how the strict rules of grammar may be bent when you speak language out loud. We are sure that our readers normally speak in perfectly polished grammatical sentences; after all, you are educated people. However, quite probably you also know that in everyday talk you can speak in ungrammatical ways that everyone else understands. For example, "Ain't no way I'm gonna do that!" does not make a lot of sense from a strictly grammatical point of view. All the same it sends messages of defiant resistance to anyone who speaks a current modern form of English. "A pox on you, knave" means something when you are reading Shakespeare, but you would be unlikely to say it in everyday life today.

Multiple Meanings: Polysemy

Words, gestures, and symbols can have different meanings on different occasions/circumstances according to the particular frame for talk. Communication scholars and philosophers call this **polysemy,** multiple meanings for the same word (Ogden & Richards, 1946). Even though you already knew that the same word could carry multiple meanings, knowing the academic term for it becomes important for deepening your insights into the Way that everyday conversation actually works. You need to know how, in a particular sentence, you work out which meaning a person is using. If every communication—whether words, facial expressions, or gestures—can have several different meanings, then each time you speak or hear a word, you must determine which meaning applies.

Ambiguity

Polysemy exists as a feature of all communication, and you must always deal with the ambiguities that it creates. Ability to deal with this ambiguity is very important in everyday communication because that talk consists of many types of utterance (both formal and informal). Some examples of everyday talk are technical jargon, ordinary slang, put-downs, boasting, euphemisms, and even occasional cursing.

In the course of a single conversation, the partners can switch between styles and vocabularies. So they need to be sure that the context/frame clarifies what is going on when these switches occur. If a friend moves from informal to formal talk, suddenly curses, or switches from slang to technical talk, is he or she angry with you, or is there another explanation? Look at it the other way, too. If an acquaintance switches from formal to informal talk, this might mean that he or she wants to develop a friendly relationship in place of a previously more formal one. The most important point in this chapter, then, is that *relationships frame the meaning of talk.* So a strong and close connection exists among language, talk, and relationships.

Uncertainty

Uncertainty about meaning decreases as your understanding of frames that relationships and other contexts give you increases. The best and most helpful guide to a person's meaning is the personal knowledge you have from a close relationship with him or her. People tend to hang around with others who share their general system for understanding meanings (Duck, 2007). That familiarity helps narrow down the uncertainty in meaning.

You are better able to communicate with another person when both of you can assume you are in the same frame and know what you are talking about. You make assumptions about the best choice of meaning based on what you know about the frame you are in. You signal the frames you are using by means of various relational, cultural, and personal cues. For example, "Let's not be so formal" is a direct way of saying that you are in the "friendly frame," but "Take a seat and make yourself comfortable" has the same effect. More subtly, the fact that therapists have cozy offices with comfortable furniture, rather than hard benches, sends the same framing message in a different (nonverbal) way. Such cues place an interaction into a frame of informal relaxation rather than emphasizing toughness, distance, business, or threat.

Reading Conversational Frames

People can work out what you mean on a given occasion by reading these broad cues. The more familiar you are with the meanings available in a culture, the easier it is to read them. But the key to deeper understanding—the crucial guide to interpreting what someone means—is your relationship to others and how well you know them and their thinking styles. Talk is more than just language: It is the *use* of language, and the use of language can be personalized. In fact, the more closely two people get to know each other—what they know, how they think, how they talk—the more personal their talk becomes.

Conversational Yellow Pages: Categories That Frame Talk

Having culture or relationships is like having the Yellow Pages for conversation in a particular language. There are lots of phone number categories, so it helps if you know you are looking for a plumber and can find the page with the plumber numbers listed. So, too, with talk: It helps if you know that when your partner talks about love, you are on the "romance" page, not the "tennis" page. Probably the strongest clue in language is provided by naming.

Naming and Defining

anguage splits our world in many ways, dividing it into those items for which there are names. **Naming** is important because it seems both *arbitrary* ("It doesn't matter if you call it salad or dessert; it's still just Jell-O") and *natural* ("What do you mean, 'What's Jell-O?' It's Jell-O. Everybody knows Jell-O"). Naming involves another process, too: distinguishing items from other items for which we also have (different) words.

Several thinkers from both rhetorical studies (Burke, 1966) and psychology (Kelly, 1969) have observed that definition involves negation or contrasting. That is, whenever you say what something is, you also say either explicitly or implicitly what it is not. When a behavior is named as "sexual harassment," it is not "a joke" or "flirting." Some thinkers even suggest that you cannot know some concepts without knowing their opposites (for example, the concept of light makes no sense without the concept of darkness).

An even stronger version of this idea was proposed by Edward Sapir and Benjamin Whorf (Sapir, 1949; Whorf, 1956). The **Sapir/Whorf hypothesis** proposes that "you think what you can say." In other words, the names that make verbal distinctions also help you make conceptual distinctions rather than the other way around.

Naming and Understanding the World

The words that a person or culture uses will have a direct influence on how the person or culture understands the world: The words make the world rather than the opposite, as you might typically think. You have no doubt heard the urban myth that the Eskimos have some different words for snow because people in that part of the world want to be able to differentiate between sorts of snow that "mean" or carry different implications for their activities in life. For example, assume that *snow1* indicates a kind of snow that means the coming of a storm, and *snow2* indicates a kind of snow that means the coming of spring. Using different words *(snow1, snow2)* helps the Eskimos make this and other important distinctions that matter in their lives.

Naming something not only sticks a label on it but also differentiates it from the rest of the world; your name tag, for example, goes on only *your* stuff. So a major function of language is to separate the world into different categories of objects and concepts (chairs, dogs, ideas, papers, professors, students, taxes, death, justice, freedom).

Phrased in a more academic way, language—and, in particular, the names we use in talk—will classify our world by giving things separate identities and properties. These serve to structure our worlds into *thought units* or items that we consider quite different from each other. Naming is incredibly powerful, and it makes a huge difference, for example, whether you name someone "an insurgent" or "a freedom fighter." Because there are two subtypes of meaning, we can connect them to the distinction we made in Chapter 1 concerning representation and presentation.

Types of Meaning

Communication studies draw a distinction between *denotative* and *connotative* meaning as a way of splitting the world into finer thought units. **Denotative meaning** refers to the identification of something by pointing it out. If you point at a cat and say, "Cat," everyone will know that the sound denotes the object that is furry and whiskered and currently eating your homework. **Connotative meaning** refers to the overtones, implications, or additional meanings associated with a word or an object. For example, cats are seen as independent, cuddly, hunters, companions, irritations, allergens, stalkers, stealthy, and incredibly lucky both in landing on their feet all the time and in having nine lives. If you talk about someone as a "pussycat," you are most likely referring to the connotative meaning and implying that he is soft and cuddly and perhaps stealthy, companionable, and lucky. You are unlikely to be referring to the denotative meaning and warning people that he is actually, secretly a cat and has fur and eats homework.

A handy way of thinking about this distinction is that "denotative meaning" basically identifies something, and "connotative meaning" gives you its overtones. You can see that denotative meaning roughly corresponds with representation/facts and connotative meaning roughly corresponds with presentation/spin.

Denoting

Once you understand this distinction, you can see its importance in everyday talk. Conversation works only when both people can assume that they split the world by using the same words to denote and connote items. Denoting the same object or idea by the same words is an obviously fundamental requirement for communicating. If you point to something and use the applicable word *(bar, cat, food, witchety grub),* but the other person does not understand what you're pointing to, the communication is not effective. What occurs is action, not interaction; that is, the message is sent but not received.

When parents teach their children to communicate, they spend lots of time pointing out objects and repeating the correct words (communication as action) so the child learns to connect the object with the label ("Look at the cat." "Yes, that's a cat"). At the moment when the child gets what is going on, communication as interaction begins (message sent and received). Something even more magical begins to happen as the child starts to understand his or her world more effectively and to see connections and meaning and learns to *go beyond.* "That's a fire. It's hot. Don't touch it, or you will hurt yourself" turns the communication into transaction. Constitutive activity occurs as the child learns to associate fire as an object with the possibility of heat and therefore pain.

Connoting

On the other hand, connoting is about the implications and background behind the same words. For example, some words carry baggage that makes you feel good, and some do not. Consider the different emotions stirred up by the words *patriot and traitor*. The first connotes many good feelings of loyalty, duty, and faithfulness. The second connotes bad qualities like deceit, two-facedness, untrustworthiness, and disloyalty. These connotations are extra layers of meaning atop the denotation of a person as one kind of citizen or the other. You would feel proud to be called a patriot but ashamed to be called a traitor.

Words carry strong connotations in your particular culture, but connotations can be personal and complex the better you know someone. A consequence of this association is that your ability to understand people improves as you know more about their minds and helps you to understand their specific intentions on a particular occasion. If you know where someone's "buttons" are, you know whether he or she responds irritably to an exclamation ("Go, Hawks!") because he or she is feeling defensive, just tired, or not particularly playful.

Intentionally

Communication scholars have spent considerable time discussing the notion of **intentionality.** A basic assumption in communication studies is that messages indicate somebody's intentions or that they are produced intentionally or in a way that gives insight, at the very least, into the senders mental processes. For example, if someone says something apparently insulting ("You dork!"), it makes a great deal of difference whether you believe he or she did it intending to be funny and didn't mean it to be hurtful (for example, if he or she said it with a smile or a joking tone of voice).

People usually assume that communication cannot happen unless someone sends an intentional message. However, the issue of intentionality is not whether it was actually present but more accurately depends on whether you *assume* that it was (for example, whether you believe that someone was really joking or is just saying that he or she was). Intentionality matters, then, not as an objective issue about what is really on the other person's mind but as a subjective judgment. What does an observer attribute to and project onto the other person? To interpret messages more accurately, you must develop a good feel for the speaker's intentions.

Culture, context, past history, and your relationship to the other person in a conversation help you know what meanings are listed on the relevant "Yellow Page." Otherwise, you'd end up having constant arguments and conflicts about what was going on. One person might assume that the other person meant something other than intended. That would create confusion, ill will, and suspicion, which would threaten the relationship.

Suspicion and Mistrust of Intent

Interactions between enemies and rivals or conversations based on mistrust show exactly this characteristic. Rivals are always looking for, or suspecting, a hidden meaning or agenda. Communication scholar Dan Kirkpatrick and colleagues (Kirkpatrick, Duck, & Foley, 2006) noted that enemies do not trust each other to mean what they say, always suspecting a lie or a "setup." This suspicion makes the conversation unproductive and very difficult to handle.

On the other hand, the deeper and more trusting your relationship with someone, the more likely you are to understand his or her intentions. Once again, the close connection among relationships, communication, and meaning solves social dilemmas for you and helps you understand what is going on.

Relationships and Connotation

The more personal your relationship with them, the more you are able to understand people's intentions and meanings. Part of becoming closer to other people is learning how they tick—an informal way of saying that you understand their worlds of meaning. When you know people better, you also know better than strangers what they mean when they make certain comments.

Relationships and the Taken-for-Granted

In a relationship context, your assumptions, shared understandings, and forms of speech encode/transact the relationship by means of shared understanding. The understandings shared by you and your friends represent not only common understanding but also your relationship. No one else shares the exact understandings, common history, experiences, knowledge of the same people, or assumptions that you take for granted in that relationship.

Think for a minute about what happens when a friend from out of town comes to visit, and you go out with your in-town friends. You probably notice that the conversation is a bit more awkward even if it is still friendly: You do a bit more explaining, for example. Instead of saying, "So, De'Janee, how was the hot date?" and waiting for an answer, you throw in a conversational bracket that helps your friend from out of town understand the question. For example, you may say, "So, De'Janee, how was the hot date?" and follow it with an aside comment to the out-of-towner ("De'Janee has this hot new love interest she has a *real* crush on, and they finally went out last night").

When you talk to people, you use words that refer to your shared history and common understandings that represent your relationship or shared culture. As you talk, you monitor that knowledge and occasionally must explain to outsiders, but the very need for explanation—particularly important when you are giving a speech to an audience that does not know what you know—indicates a level of relationship, not just a level of knowledge. Relationships presume common, shared knowledge.

Words and Relationships

Words differentiate the world into objects and thought units and then name them. Talk does this relationally, too: With friends, we draw on words differently than we do in work relationships, family relationships, enemy relationships, and competitive relationships. It is very important to recognize that there is more to talk than just use of language (enshrouded in nonverbal communication) to denote something in the world.

You do not just do things with words when you talk. You do things with *relationships,* too, and the words you use in conversation transact your relationships. As well as the naming that *language* does, people adopt different styles of *speaking* according to their relationship. Restaurant servers, for example, identify items strictly relevant to their task, such as broccoli, witchety grub, and prices. Friends can refer to their previous experience together, their common history, their knowledge of particular places and times, and other experiences they likewise understand ("Remember when we went to Jimmie's?"). Because both friends know what is being referred to, neither of them needs to explain.

Words and Hidden Values

Let's take this a little further: Words make value judgments and these judgments are built into talk in relationships, and vice versa. A society or culture not only uses different words from those current in another language (obviously!) but also prefers some subjects to others. For example, how do you react to the words *spider, ice cream, class test, Porsche, sour, Republican, liberty, death, and justice?*

God Terms and Devil Terms

Communication philosopher Kenneth Burke (1966) made a distinction between **God terms** and Devil **terms** in a particular culture. God terms are powerful terms that are viewed positively in a society, and Devil terms are equally strong terms that are viewed negatively. The obvious difference is that both are powerful, but each in a different way; terms like *justice* and *liberty,* for example, are seen very positively in U.S. society (God terms), whereas *Osama bin Laden* may be a Devil term (see Table 2.1 for some other examples).

Depending on your political point of view, such words as *Bush* or *Clinton* or *Obama* may be one or the other, so you can see that God and Devil terms are not absolutes for everyone in the same society. The terms apply in relationships, too, because the partners in a relationship will have special references for people and events. Both of you will

Table 2.1: God and Devil Terms

God terms in the United States	Liberty, Freedom, Justice, American Dream
Devil terms in the United States	Communism, Torture, Ineuality, Prejudice, King George III

know what topics may not be mentioned or topics that you know your partner is sensitive about—his or her Devil terms—and that you steer away from. Sometimes your partner may act on behalf of society: "Oh! You shouldn't say such things! You're bad!"

Other Values in Words

We noted previously that symbols indicate not only what is true but also what you would like people to think, and we used the terms *presentation* and *representation* to describe this difference. At times, your speech is persuasive or preferential; it makes distinctions that you want your audience to accept as valid.

Kenneth Burke's (1966) point about the value judgments built into words is very similar—namely, that your words encode your values and you see some concepts as good (communication studies) and some as bad (pedophilia). Every time you talk, you are essentially using words to argue and present your personal preferences and judgments, as well as simply describing your world. Your culture has preferences, as do you and your friends. Your communications express values in both obvious and hidden ways. Start paying more attention to those expressions of the values embedded in the words that you use to talk in your everyday lives. If you tell your instructor about your grade and say, "I think I deserved a B-, but you gave me a C+," both you and the instructor recognize that a B- is "better than" a C+ in the framework of meaning taken for granted in school. Your words are going beyond what they seem to be saying and are taking for granted the context, the relationship, and the culture in which the conversation occurs.

Keep In mind that nonverbal communication is a constant context for all talk. Not only the words themselves but also how you choose Frames can also be created by the style in which something is said. If talk is friendly, chances are that an ambiguous comment is friendly and not hostile, so previous context helps you make the decision about its meaning.

Everyday Life Talk and the Relationships Context

Duck and Pond (1989), apart from being our favorite combination of authors' names, came up with some ideas about the way relationships connect with talk in everyday life. They pointed out that talk can serve three functions for relationships: It can make something happen in relationships (instrumental function), indicate something about the relationship (indexical function), or amount to the relationship and make it what it is, creating its essence (essential function). Although these functions might sound complicateci at first, you practice each of them every day without knowing it. Let's take a closer look.

Instrumental Functions

Whenever you ask someone out for a date, to a party, to meet you for a chat or a coffee, to be your friend, or to be just a little bit more sensitive and caring, you are performing an **instrumental function of talk** in relationships. What you say reveals a goal that you have in mind for the relationship, and talk is the means or instrument by which you reveal it. Anything you say that serves the purpose of bringing something new to or changing anything about the relationship is an instrumental function of talk in relationships.

Indexical Functions

An **indexical function of talk** demonstrates or indicates the nature of the relationship between speakers. You index your relationship in the *way* that you talk to somebody. If you say in a sharp tone, "Come into my office; I want to see you!" you are not only being discourteous, but you are indicating that you are superior to the other person and have the relational right to order him or her around. The content and relational elements of the talk occur together. In your talk with other people, you constantly weave in clues about your relationships.

Conversational Hypertext and Hyperlinks

We have already slipped in one form of indexical function in talk: *hyperlinks*. Duck (2002) noticed that lots of talk involves a kind of **conversational hypertext.**

You know what hypertext is from your use of computers and the Internet, and how you talk to people works the same way. In conversation, we often use a word that suggests more about a topic and would therefore show up on a computer screen in blue, pointing you to a hyperlink. For example, you might say, "I was reading Duck and McMahan, and I learned that there are many more extra messages that friends pick up in talk than I had realized before." This sentence makes perfect sense to somebody who knows what "Duck and McMahan" is, but others may not understand. On a computer, they would use their mouse to find out more about Duck and McMahan by going to <u>www.sagepub.com/bocstudy</u>, but in a conversation, they would "click" on the hypertext by asking a direct question: "What's Duck and McMahan?"

Conversational hypertext, therefore, is the idea that all of our conversation contains coded messages that an informed listener will effortlessly understand. In relationships, the shared worlds of meaning and the overlap of perception make communication special and closer. Uninformed listeners, however, can always request that the hypertext be unpacked, expanded, or addressed directly.

How Friends Understand One Another

You and your friends talk in coded, hypertextual language all the time. Only when you encounter someone who does not understand the code do you need to further explain. In the previous example, "De'Janee" is hypertext until you have been introduced to her, and the "hot date" is hypertext until you learn that De'Janee has a new love interest. After that initial explanation, the term *hot date* might become a shared reference. Even the friend from out of town now knows what it means. If, later in the conversation, someone starts to talk about "De'Janee's hottie," the out-of-town friend will be included in the shared knowledge. At that point, the group of friends will have created a new hypertext to the conversation and the relationship that even the out-of-town friend understands.

Research shows how you can tell, just from their talk, whether people know one another because of the way they treat conversational hypertext as needing no further explanation. Planalp and Garvin-Doxas (1994) reported studies where they played tapes of talk to an audience and asked the listeners to say whether the people on the tape were friends. Listeners were very skilled at making this identification. They could easily tell whether two conversational partners were acquainted or merely strangers. What made the difference was whether the talkers took information for granted or whether they explained the terms used. Said without explanation, "Jim was worried about his foot again" identified the two conversers as friends. On the other hand, the following showed them to be unacquainted: "Jim—that's my friend from high school—was worried about his foot again. He has gout and has to be careful about setting it off. It is a problem that keeps coming back. It worries him a lot, so he usually calls me when it flares up, and I help him deal with it."

Essential Functions

People very easily underestimate the extent to which talk and its nonverbal wrapping *are* a relationship. Of course, even when you are in a relationship, you and your partner do not spend every moment with each other. You experience absences, breaks, and separations: They may be relatively short (one person goes shopping), longer (a child goes to school for the day), or extended (two lovers get jobs in different parts of the country, go on vacation separately, or are involved in a commuter relationship).

Because these breaks occur, there are ways to indicate that, although the interaction may be over, the relationship itself continues. For example, you might say, "See you next week," "Talk to you later," or "Next week we will be discussing the chapter on informative and persuasive speeches." All of these phrases are examples of the **essential function** of talk. Talk makes the relationship real and talks it into being by simply assuming that it exists. The above examples, talking about the continuance of the relationship beyond an upcoming absence, demonstrate that the relationship will outlast the separation.

Most of the time, however, talk creates and embodies relationships in other ways, both implicitly ("I've got you, babe") and explicitly ("You're my friend"). There can be direct talk that embodies the relationship ("I love you") or indirect talk ("What shall we do this Friday night?") that recognizes the relationship's existence but does not mention it explicitly. The essential function of talk operates in hidden ways as simple as more frequent references to "we" and "us" or inclusion in talk where joint planning is carried out or nicknames are used. Linguistic inclusion *(let's, we, us),* also known as **immediacy,** is a seemingly small but powerful way to essentialize the relationship in talk. Nicknames, even as obvious as *honey* or *Jimbo* rather than *James,* clearly show familiarity. Inclusion in planning ("Let's do something really special tonight") signals the essentializing of the relationship as a taken-for-granted part of the speaker's life.

Politeness and Facework

Different kinds of talk essentialize relationships in different ways. For example, a polite conversation is different in style from an impolite one and essentializes a different type of relationship. Of course, other frames may indicate whether the impoliteness results from dislike or the informality that characterizes close friendship.

Politeness

Let's start with politeness, since in one way or another, most of our everyday talk is polite even with strangers. Communication scholars Bill Cupach and Sandra Metts (Cupach & Metts, 1994; Metts, 2000) speak of **facework,** a term that refers to the management of people's "face," meaning dignity or self-respect. When people are ashamed or humiliated, you might talk of them "losing face." Although that is a metaphor, it is worth noticing how often people who are embarrassed or who feel foolish cover their faces with their hands. An almost automatic reaction to shame or to the recognition that we have done something foolish, it makes our point that "face" is connected to moral appearance in the social world as a composed and centered social being. You might also see that the term *boldfaced lie,* used for a particularly daring falsehood, refers to the same idea. Doing facework or presenting a strongly favorable image of yourself, a particularly important aspect of giving talks, speeches, or interviews, is even more basic to daily conversation.

Saving Face

Sociologist Erving Goffman (1971) promoted the notion that "face" is something managed by people in social interactions, noting that you "save face" for yourself and other people. Many times, for example, you try to save someone else's face by trivializing an embarrassing mistake ("Oh, don't worry about it; I do that all the time"; "Think nothing of it"; "No big deal"). In effect, you are saying that you don't see the person's behavior truly as an indication of who he or she really is: You are trying to let him or her off the hook as a person and are distinguishing his or her momentary *actions* from his or her deep, true *self.*

Face Wants

People have positive face wants and negative face wants: **Positive face wants** refer to the need to be seen and accepted as a worthwhile and reasonable person; **negative face**

wants refer to the desire not to be imposed upon or treated as inferior. The management of this last type of face want is perhaps the most familiar: "I don't mean to trouble you, but would you..."; "I hope this is not too inconvenient, but would you mind..."; "Sorry to be a nuisance, but..."; and our personal favorite from students, "I have a *quick* question" (implying that it will not be a lot of trouble or a big imposition to answer it).

Although this management of people's negative face wants is quite common, positive face wants are also dealt with quite frequently, and you often hear people pay compliments like "You are doing a great job!"; "How very nice of you"; or "You're too kind."

Use of either type of behavior allows you to manage your relationships by paying attention to the ways people need to be seen in the social world. The behaviors are therefore a subtle kind of relational management done in talk. It may not have been obvious—or at least not obviously connecting talk to relationships—but it is a basic feature of communication.

Ways of Speaking

In everyday conversation with people you know, other aspects of talk are worth noticing as ways to transact relationships. The form of language through which you choose to express your thoughts carries important relational messages. You sometimes use that knowledge as part of what you choose to say on a particular occasion.

Codes of Speech

When people talk to very young children, they tend to adopt baby language; when students or employees talk with professors or supervisors, they try to sound "professional." When talking with friends, you use informal language, but in class or in conversation with your boss, your language may be a bit more complicated.

High Code/Low Code

Think about the difference between saying, when you're hungry, "I'm so hungry I could eat a horse" and "My state of famishment is of such a proportion that I would gladly consume the complete corporeality of a member of the species *Equus przewalski poliakov*" The first example is written in what communication scholars call **low code,** and the second is written in **high code** (Giles, Taylor, & Bourhis, 1973). Low code is an informal and often ungrammatical way of talking; high code is a formal, grammatical, and very correct—often "official"—way of talking. You might be able to look around your lecture hall and see a sign that says something like "Consumption of food and beverages on these premises is prohibited." That is a high-code way of saying the low-code message "Do not eat or drink here."

Polysemy and Speech Style

By now, then, you can see that not just individual words are polysemic. The whole structure of language and the *way in which* you speak can be polysemic. Let's spend some time elaborating on this so that you come to understand how it plays out in relationships with an audience, whether public or intimate.

The language you use contains more than one way of saying the same thing—a sort of stylistic polysemy. Although this may not have struck you as particularly important yet, the form of language you use to express essentially the same idea conveys its own messages about something other than the topic you're talking about.

In fact, it connotes and essentializes the relationship between you and your audience, as well as conveys something about you as a person. A high form is formal, pompous, and professional; a low form is casual, welcoming, friendly, and relaxed. By choosing one form over another at a particular point, you are not just sending a message but

1. delivering *content* about a particular topic,
2. *presenting yourself* as a particular sort of person (projecting identity), and
3. *indexing* a particular sort of relationship to the audience.

Part of your connotative meaning at a given time is always an essentializing commentary about "the state of the relationship" between the speaker and the audience, whether a large or small group or an individual. Just as public speakers adopt particular ways of talking depending on the group with which they strive to identify, so too a person can choose a friendly, informal style or a more distant, formal style with a stranger.

Accommodation: Convergence and Divergence

Just as you can set the frame, you can change it. You can choose a particular way to say something. You may change or adapt it either to suit an audience or to see changes in feelings or in the relationship that occurs during the course of the interaction.

Giles and his colleagues (1973) have shown that people will change their accent, their rate of speech, and even the words they use to indicate a relational connection with the person to whom they are talking. They called this process **accommodation** and identified two types: convergence and divergence. In **convergence,** a person moves toward the style of talk used by the other speaker. For example, an adult converges when he or she uses baby talk to communicate with a child, or a brownnosing employee converges when he or she uses the boss's company lingo style of talk. In **divergence,** exactly the opposite happens: One talker moves away from another's style of speech to make a relational point, such as establishing dislike or superiority. A good example is how computer geeks and car mechanics insist on using a lot of technical language with customers, instead of giving simple explanations that the nonexpert could understand. This form of divergence keeps the customer in a lower relational place.

The different ways of sending the same content in a message are another instance of how meaning and relationships are inextricably tied together. Talking conveys content and something about your identity. It conveys even more about your sense of the ongoing changes in your relationship with others and how it may be altered by the course of an interaction.

Narration; Telling Stories

The multilayered framing aspect of talk is quite noticeable when people tell stories. Communication scholars use the term *narrative* to cover what is involved when you say *what* people are doing and *why* they are doing it. This applies whether talk includes funny events, tragic events, significant emotional experiences, or relational stories (meeting new people, falling in love, breaking up). You may not always notice that talk has the features of a story. You have heard many examples—"How We Met," "How My Day Was," and even "I Couldn't Do the Assignment," which may not at first strike you as a story. A **narrative** is any organized story, report, or prepared talk that has a plot, an argument, or a theme, or can be interpreted as having one. In a narrative, speakers do not just relate facts but also arrange the story in a way that provides an account, an explanation, or a conclusion. Often stories make the speakers look good or are told from their own particular point of view (i.e., their talk appears representational when it is really presentational). Some remarks do not appear story-like but follow the same pattern all the same: for example, "I couldn't do the assignment; it was way too hard." This relates a fact and presents a conclusion. You said you couldn't do it because it was too hard. Your instructor may have thought you did not do enough work. Different stories!

Everyday Stories: Part of Human Nature

Much of everyday life is spent telling stories about yourself and other people, whether or not they walk into bars. For example, you may tell a story about when you went into a shop and something funny or unexpected happened. Or you may tell your friends how when you were, like, working in the pizza parlor, some guy came in and couldn't, like, make his mind up about whether he wanted, like, double cheese or pepperoni, and you, like, stood there for, like, 5 minutes while he made up his mind.

Communication scholar Walter Fisher (1985) pointed out that much more of human life than we suspect is spent telling stories. He even coined the term *homo narrans* (Latin for "the person as a storyteller or narrator") to describe this human tendency. Indeed, he suggested that storytelling is one of the most important human activities. Stories are also a large part of relating, so we need to spend some time exploring how people narrate and justify their action in stories.

Everyday talk can be "a story." Narratives often appear to be special kinds of talk, but they are hidden in straightforward talk. They are elaborate frames, too, that provide excuses for your actions. For example, in the cheese and pepperoni case, the end of your story might be "I was so mad." The details about the person failing to make up his mind are used to justify (frame) the fact that you felt irritated.

People often give excuses and tell stories that help explain their actions within a set of existing frames. This section looks at how stories use, and provide, frames for your talk to present you incidentally as a relationally responsible and attractive person (facework).

Burke's Pentad

All stories have particular common elements that were identified by Kenneth Burke (1969) as a **pentad**; *pentad* is a word derived from the Greek for "five" (see Table 2.2 for a listing of the elements).

The outcome usually offers a moral result (the moral of the story). The next time you hear people telling stories in everyday life communication, you can check how far their reports fit this framework for justifying and explaining their actions.

Elements of the Pentad

Stories start out with a *scene* in which something happened *(act)* ("I was working in a pizza parlor last night, and this guy came in…"; "My professor told me yesterday during office hours that…"; "My mom was driving home from work last night and realized…"; "I was talking with my boyfriend yesterday, and we decided to break up because…"). These elements of talk introduce the main characters *(agents),* often yourself and some-one you know ("I was working…this guy came in"). Stories involve the interaction and intersection of characters *(agency)—*"He couldn't make up his mind"; "I stood there for 5 minutes waiting"—and their plotlines are based on a sequence of events that result in an *outcome* ("I was so mad").

The simple pizza story now looks quite different. For one thing it is organized and structured in the way Burke (1969) proposed. Although you may not previously have been able to name the terms this story encompasses, you now know more about stories than you did before.

Table 2.2 Common Elements of Stories That Make up Burke's Pentad

1. Scene (setting)	*Where* it happened
2. Agent (character)	*Who* was involved
3. Act (single event or sequences of events)	*What* (facts) unfolded in time
4. Agency (plotine)	*How* (the way in which) acts happened
5. Purpose (outcome)	*Why* (What was the result or goal?)

Burke's Pentad as Frame

The important point is how the story is used to frame its outcome as reasonable and inevitable. Table 2.3 shows how the punch lines of stories—even news stories and scientific reports or tales of people walking into bars—are seen as reasonable and acceptable. It all depends on how they are set up in such ratios of justification and presentation.

Stories and People's Frames

The elements of the pentad that show up in a person's typical accounts of everyday life experience give insight into how the person thinks. The terms of the pentad used by a narrator present selected aspects of the world. When a person highlights an element of the pentad, that gives insight into the way he or she thinks about the world. From this point of view, stories are not simply narrations of events but personalized ways of telling: The narration indicates presentation of a perspective or personal frame.

One significant frame that sets the scene for all narratives comes from

1. the character of the agent telling the story, making the speech, giving a toast, reporting the gossip, or talking the talk, and
2. the relationship between the speaker and the audience (a latent agent-to-agent ratio).

In formal settings a toastmaster may wear a uniform, a priest who is speaking may wear the clothes of office, or speakers may wear business clothes to clarify their importance, professionalism, and seriousness. However, even in informal settings all speakers invite you to accept the important frame that they *matter* whether or not they are giving a formal presentation.

The bottom line of many stories really comes down to "I'm a decent person, and what I'm telling you is essentially a good idea/I did the right thing, didn't I?" Outside of therapy, you rarely meet anyone who does not, at root, like to think he or she is a good person, essentially decent and OK. Now you may recognize that these story "bottom lines" are offering justifications and accounts for acts. Also the features in this chapter relate the speaker and the audience. Speaking to any audience is always an act set in a relational scene.

Character as Frame

A speaker's character frames what he or she says and justifies his or her attempts to persuade an audience. It is the same whether the speaker addresses a formally seated audience at a political rally or gives a business speech or is just talking with a friend.

All speakers want to make relational partners, potential friends, and other audiences appreciate or even like them. In most everyday life conversations, the chances are that you are already speaking to friends, family, and people who like you quite a bit to begin with.

Table 2.3 How a Story Is Used to Frame Its Outcome as Reasonable or Inevitable

Agent:act ratio	• Uses a person's character to explain actions • For example, "He's the kind of guy who does that": "Friends don't let friends drive drunk."
Scene:act ratio	• Uses a situation or circumstances to justify action • For example, "Desperate times call for desperate measures"; "This is war and we need to use harsh methods to obtain the truth from prisoners."
Scene:agent ratio	• Uses a situation to explain the kinds of characters who are found there For example, "Politics makes strange bedfellows"; "Miami is a sunny place for shady people."
Scene:agent:act ratio	• Uses a situation or circumstances (e.g., a disintegrating parental marriage) to explain a person's actions • For example, "Children of divorced parents are more likely to be insecure in relationships and get divorced themselves later in life."

Your relationship then frames, or sets the scene for, what you are going to say, just as much as your argument and your words do.

Scenes as Frames

Other scenes also exist. Narratives, stories, and all daily talk are framed by assumptions about the culture and what works within it. They may be framed by assumptions about justice, responsibility, free will, personality, "speaker truth," and audience.

When you talk with your friends, you most likely do not find it necessary to keep convincing them that you are speaking the truth. You assume that *they* assume that you speak the truth. In other circumstances, it may be more important for you to tell stories in a way that reflects assumptions based on your own particular reasons. For example, if you are talking about the terrible character of a person who just broke off a relationship with you, the frame is that you are a decent person while the other person is a jerk.

At other times, you may want to describe yourself in a way that helps other people understand how you "tick." You may want to reveal personal information that helps them understand you better. Again, remember that you do this very much from your own point of view and personal motives. Don't ever believe that when someone tells you a story, it is a neutral and simply representational view of the world.

All stories and speech are presentational. When listening to politicians, you can expect them to present events in a way that suits their personal interests best. You have to learn to recognize that *everyone* is a politician for his or her own party: the "vote for me because I am a good person" party.

Giving Accounts

Although narratives appear on the surface just to report (represent) events, they frequently account for (present) the behaviors. **Accounts** are forms of communication that offer *justifications* ("I was so mad"), *excuses* ("I was really tired"), *exonerations* ("It wasn't my fault"), *explanations* ("And that's how we fell in love"), *accusations* ("But he started it!"), and *apologies* ("I'm an idiot"). Accounts "go beyond the facts."

Presentation, Representation, and Frames

Psychologists, communication scholars, and sociologists would talk about the above pizza parlor story as "giving an account" (Scott & Lyman, 1968): telling a story in a way that justifies, blames someone for, or calls for someone to account for what happened. Even the "facts" in reports can turn out to be presentational. Your description of something contains "spin" that explains the "facts" you are reporting. For example, you tell your friend, "I just failed a math test. It was way too hard." Both statements appear to be facts. One is actually an explanation for why you failed (the test was too hard). It is also a *presentational* account—a personal view about the reason for your failure (the test was too hard). Your teacher may think you failed because you did not do the homework.

Listen with fresh ears to everyday conversation, and you will start to hear framing justifications much more often. Think about their structure and what it tells you about communication and the implied relationship between the speaker and the audience. For example, you don't bother to justify yourself to people whose opinions you do not care about. You would not justify yourself to an enemy in the same way you would to a friend. You expect the friend to know more about your background and to cut you some slack. This familiarity influences the style of your report, once again connecting talk to relationships.

Remember what we wrote at the start of this chapter: that a whole system of nonverbal communication frames what we say, too. If I say "I love you" but wince when I say it, that frames the words in a different way than if I smile and look all gooey when I say it. The next chapter covers nonverbal communication on its own and then reconnects it as a frame for interpreting talk. Although we have separated talk from its real behavioral context so that you can understand features of talk itself, talk never happens in life in a way that is separated from nonverbal behavior. The next chapter shows you how nonverbal behavior works and how it is used not only to send messages on its own but also to affect how the messages in talk are modified or understood.

Summary

So, do you know what talk means? Hopefully you should after reading this chapter. To understand talk, you need to discriminate between langue and parole. Unfortunately, the multiple meanings of words (polysemy) can be further complicated by ambiguity, uncertainty that encompasses all language. It is important to understand that all words can have two meanings—connotative and denotative, and all the ambiguities that these meanings carry. The significance of talk in relationships is further complicated by the aspects of instrumental, indexical, and conversational hypertext and hyperlinks in communication.

In communication facework is an essential term to comprehend, for it influences how people manage politeness, and their efforts to balance positive face wants and negative face wants. Along with facework, low code and high code further differentiate the complexity of verbal communication. The concept of narration is essential to understand how and why human beings communicate to others about their lives—it represents an organized story that people tell about their life experiences, and these narratives are framed by the language we use. Finally, Kenneth Burke's Pentad was introduced to give further insight into verbal communication through an understanding of scene, agent, act, agency, and purpose.

Complementing all verbal communication is the equally intricate nonverbal communication. It is no less rich than verbal communication, and is just as complex and intricate as verbal communication. That will be the focus of the next chapter.

Questions For Discussion

1. Why are people successful at communicating in light of all the problems that can take place?
2. What is the difference between a denotative and a connotative meaning?
3. What are some good examples of God terms and Devil terms that are used in political campaigns in the U.S.?
4. How is conversational hypertext used by people in a relationship?
5. What is a common narrative that is used as support for U.S. military action?

References

Burke, K. (1966). *Language as symbolic action: Essays on life, literature and method.* Berkeley: University of California Press.

Burke, K. (1969). *A grammar of motives.* Berkeley: University of California Press.

Cupach, W. R., & Metts, S. (1994). *Facework.* Thousand Oaks, CA: Sage.

Duck, S. W. (2002). Hypertext in the key of G: Three types of "history" as influences on conversational structure and flow. *Communication Theory, 12*(1), 41–62.

Duck, S. W. (2007). *Human relationships* (4th ed.). London: Sage.

Duck, S. W., & Pond, K. (1989). Friends, Romans, Countrymen; lend me your retrospective data: Rhetoric and reality in personal relationships. In C. Hendrick (Ed.), *Review of social psychology and personality: Close relationships* (Vol. 10, pp. 17–38). Newbury Park, CA: Sage.

Fisher, W. R. (1985). The narrative paradigm: An elaboration. *Communication Monographs, 52,* 347–367.

Giles, H., Taylor, D. M., & Bourhis, R. Y. (1973). Towards a theory of interpersonal accommodation through language use. *Language in Society* 2, 177–192.

Goffman, E. (1971). *Relations in public: Microstudies of the public order.* New York: Harper & Row.

Kelly, G. A. (1969). Ontological acceleration. In B. Mather (Ed.), Clinical psychology and personality: *The collected papers of George Kelly* (pp. 7–45). New York: Wiley.

Kirkpatrick, C. D., Duck, S.W., & Foley, M. K. (Eds.). (2006). Relating difficulty: The processes of constructing and managing difficult interaction. LEA *Series on Personal Relationships.* Mahwah, NJ: Lawrence Erlbaum.

Komatsu, E. (Ed.). (1993). *Saussure's third course of lectures on general linguistics* (1910–1911) (R. Harris, Trans.). London: Pergamon.

Metts, S. (2000). Face and facework: Implications for the study of personal relationships. In K. Dindia & S. W. Duck (Eds.), *Communication and personal relationships* (pp. 72–94). Chichester, UK: Wiley.

Norwood, K. M. (2007). *Gendered conflict? The "cattiness" of women on "Flavor of Love."* Paper presented at the Organization for the Study of Communication, Language, and Gender, Omaha, NE.

Ogden, C. K., & Richards, I. A. (1946). *The meaning of meaning* (8th ed.). New York: Harcourt Brace Jovanovich.

Planalp, S., & Garvin-Doxas, K. (1994). Using mutual knowledge in conversation: Friends as experts in each other. In S. W. Duck (Ed.), *Dynamics of relationships* (Understanding relationship processes 4, pp. 1–26). Newbury Park, CA: Sage.

Sapir, E. (1949). *Selected writings in language, culture and personality* (D. Mandelbaum, Ed.). Berkeley: University of California Press.

Scott, M. B., & Lyman, S. M. (1968). Accounts. *American Sociological Review,* 33,46–62.

Whorf, B. (1956). *Language, thought, and reality: Selected writings of Benjamin Lee Whorf* (J. Carroll, Ed.). Boston: MIT Press.

Chapter 6

Nonverbal Communication

Walid A. Afifi

No less important than verbal communication, the nature of nonverbal communication is just as complex—to fully the understand process of human communication it is necessary to analyze all of the various aspect of nonverbal communication. In fact, many believe that that nonverbal messages are more important than verbal messages, and people are more apt to believe a nonverbal message even if it conflicts with a verbal message. The reasons behind this belief are discussed in this chapter.

Learning Objectives For This Chapter

- Explain why nonverbal communication is often deemed more important than verbal communication
- Identify nonverbal codes and their function in the communication process
- Describe the functions of nonverbal codes and their use
- Discuss why deceiving others is seen as an important aspect of nonverbal communication
- Understand the critical role that nonverbal communication plays in explaining interaction outcomes

Sayings that attest to the importance of nonverbal communication in our lives vary from "A picture is a worth 1,000 words" to "Appearances are deceiving." But what are we talking about when discussing nonverbal elements of communication? Many people think of "body language" when discussing nonverbal messages. However, thinking of nonverbal only as body language ignores several important elements. For our purposes, nonverbal communication will be defined as "those behaviors other than words themselves that form a socially shared coding system" (Burgoon, 1994, p. 231). Two primary aspects of this definition are worth noting: First, it includes a wide variety of behaviors besides "body language." Second, it assumes people recognize the meaning of these behaviors within their social or cultural setting. These two aspects of nonverbal will become very clear by the end of this selection.

Scholars often claim that nonverbal messages are more important than verbal ones (see Burgoon, Buller, & Woodall, 1996). Their claim is based on several arguments. First, studies suggest that nonverbal messages make up a majority of the meaning of a message (see Andersen, 1999). Think of the times you've watched people from a distance, not being able to hear what they're saying but being able to see them. Based only on their nonverbal messages, you are able to understand a lot about their relationship and their interaction. You may be able to determine whether they are friends or dating partners, whether they are having a pleasant or unpleasant interaction, and whether they are in a hurry or not; all these interpretations occur without hearing a word. Although the importance of nonverbal messages for the meaning of an interaction varies, they play at least some role in every interaction. Second, nonverbal communication is omnipresent. In other words, every communication act includes a nonverbal component; nonverbal behavior is part of every communicative message. From how we say something to what we do and how we look when saying it, nonverbal messages are constant influences on our interpretation of what others are communicating to us. Third, there are nonverbal signals that are understood cross-culturally. Unlike verbal messages, which carry meaning strictly within the relevant language culture, nonverbal messages can be used as a communication tool among individuals from vastly different language cultures. For example, individuals from a wide variety of cultures recognize smiles to indicate happiness or recognize hunger from the act of putting fingers to your mouth. Finally, nonverbal messages are trusted over verbal, messages when those two channels of information conflict. Because we (somewhat erroneously) believe that nonverbal actions are more subconscious than verbal messages, we tend to believe the nonverbal over the verbal. All these arguments for the importance of nonverbal messages will be defended by the end of this selection.

In part because nonverbal behaviors are an important aspect of every communication message, this selection will be organized somewhat differently than some others in this book. Rather than focus on one theory or one concept, the primary goal of this selection is to make you aware of the many aspects of our behavior that fall under the rubric of nonverbal communication. As part, of that goal, several theories will be briefly reviewed when they seem to apply particularly well to a type or function of nonverbal behavior. However, it is important to keep in mind that all theories described in this book are behaviorally represented through nonverbal messages; the theories noted in this selection are simply a small sampling of the many theories that could be used as illustrations of nonverbal messages "in action."

The selection is divided into roughly two sections. The first section overviews the various types of nonverbal messages (i.e., codes), starting with body movements (i.e., kinesics) and ending with physical aspects of the environment that affect behavior (i.e., artifacts). You should have a good sense for the breadth and importance of nonverbal communication by the end of that section. The next part of the selection overviews the ways we use nonverbal messages (i.e., functions). Nonverbal messages can be used to accomplish a wide variety of outcomes, from allowing the smooth flow of an interaction to deceiving others. Theories will be applied throughout the selection but will be concentrated in the discussion of functions.

Nonverbal Codes

As noted earlier, nonverbal behaviors include a lot more than "body language." Although scholars disagree on the exact number, there are seven codes (or categories) of nonverbal behavior that will be reviewed in this selection: kinesics, haptics, proxemics, physical appearance, vocalics, chronemics, and artifacts. I will define each code in turn and discuss some of the associated behaviors.

Kinesics

What do you think of when you ponder nonverbal behavior? If you're like many people who have not studied nonverbal communication, you think of gestures, body movements, eye contact and the like. In other words, you think of only one of the seven codes that exist to describe nonverbal behavior. The kinesic code includes almost all behaviors that most people believe make up nonverbal ways of expression, including gestures, eye contact, and body position. Burgoon et al. (1996) defined kinesics as referring to "all forms of body movement, excluding physical contact with another" (p. 41). As you can imagine, these movements number in the hundreds of thousands, but there are classifications of kinesic activity that help us better place the movements into discrete categories. Perhaps the most, widely used is Ekman and Friesen's (1969) distinction among emblems, illustrators, regulators, affect displays, and adaptors. This typology describes kinesic behaviors according to their intended purpose.

Emblems are body movements that carry meaning in and of themselves. Emblems stand alone, without verbal accompaniment, and still convey a clear message to the recipients. Common examples of emblems include a thumbs-up gesture, "flipping someone the bird," using the thumb and index finger to signal "OK," and moving two fingers across your throat to signal someone to stop. In fact, sports are often an arena where celebratory emblems are displayed or become a part of our cultural fabric. An example is the "raise the roof" signal, an emblem signaling celebration that quickly caught on among sports players and is now understood relatively widely in this culture. The historical development of emblem form and meaning is fascinating and varies dramatically from culture to culture. Certain cultures (e.g., Italy, France, Egypt) rely on emblems for the delivery of meaning much more so than other cultures, but all cultures include emblems as part of their communication channel.

Unlike emblems, **illustrators** do not carry meaning without verbal accompaniment. Instead, illustrators are body movements that help receivers interpret and better attend to what is being said verbally. The sort of "nonsense" hand gestures that often accompany a person's speech, especially when speaking publicly, are one form of illustrators. Yet these "nonsense" gestures actually serve important functions: They help focus the receiver's attention on what is being said, they help the sender emphasize a part of his or her speech, they help the sender clarify what is being said, and so on. A father who scolds his child may accentuate the seriousness of the message by waving a finger in the youngster's face, or a traveler may clarify a description of her lost luggage by drawing a "picture" of its shape in the air as she describes it; these are simply two examples of how we use illustrators to assist the verbal component.

Regulators are body movements that are employed to help guide conversations. They may be used to help signal a desire to speak, or a desire not to be called on, or to communicate to the speaker that you are or are not listening. Perhaps the most common example of a regulator is the head nod. We consistently use head nods during conversation to signal to speakers that we are listening, a sign that encourages them to continue. Other behaviors that function as regulators of our conversation include maintaining eye contact, turning our bodies toward or away from the speaker, and looking at our watch.

Adaptors are body movements that "satisfy physical or psychological needs" (Burgoon et al., 1996, p. 42). These movements are rarely intended to communicate anything, but they are good signals of the sender's physiological and psychological state. There are three categories of adaptors: self-adaptors, alter-directed adaptors, and object adaptors. **Self**-adaptors are movements that people direct toward themselves or their bodies; examples include biting fingernails, sucking on a thumb, repeatedly tapping a foot, adjusting a collar, and vigorously rubbing an arm to increase warmth. **Alter-directed** adaptors include the same sorts of behaviors found among self-adaptors except that they are movements people direct to the bodies of others; examples include scratching a friend's back itch, caressing a partner's hair, adjusting a partner's collar, or dusting off a friend's rarely worn jacket. Alter-directed adaptors often signal to the target person or to the audience the level of attachment between the individuals in the exchange. **Object** adaptors are movements that involve attention to an object; common examples include biting on a pen, holding a (sometimes unlit) cigar, or circling the edge of a cup with a finger.

Finally, **affect** displays are body movements that express emotion without the use of touch. Like emblems, affect displays often do not require verbal accompaniment for understanding. In fact, several studies have shown that people across cultures understand certain nonverbal facial expressions as reflective of particular emotions (see Ekman & Oster, 1979; Izard, 1977). By manipulating three facial regions (the eyes and eyelids, the eyebrows and forehead, and the mouth and cheeks), people can create affect displays that are recognizable world wide. For example, sadness is expressed by somewhat constricting the eyes and forehead region, while flattening the cheeks and displaying a slight down-ward curvature of the mouth.

Although Ekman and Friesen's category system captures most gestural movements, it doesn't describe all kinesic behaviors. Perhaps most importantly, it gives short shrift to the types and functions of eye contact. A popular saying exults that "the eyes are the window to the soul" Research on eye behavior supports these beliefs. Eye contact has been shown to vary dramatically in form and to differ significantly in function (for review, see Gramet, 1983). It clearly occupies a central place as a channel for message transmission and will emerge in studies reviewed throughout the selection.

One concept that captures several aspects of our kinesic activity and has received con-siderable research attention is **immediacy.** Included as part of the cluster of immediacy behaviors are the kinesic behaviors of eye contact, body orientation (i.e., the degree to which the interactant's body is oriented toward or away from the other), body lean (i.e., the degree to which the person's body is leaning forward or back), head nods, interper-sonal distance (part of the proxemic code), and touch (part of the haptic code). Together, this set of behaviors communicates the degree to which an individual is involved in the interaction. Studies have shown that changes in immediacy behavior strongly affect the outcome of interactions, from having important consequences for the success of job in-terviews to influencing the attentiveness of patients during interactions with physicians (Buller & Street, 1992; Forbes & Jackson, 1980).

Haptics

A second general category of nonverbal behavior is labeled haptics and refers to all aspects of touch. Perhaps no other code has stronger communicative potential than does touch. Research has shown that individuals place considerable weight on the meaning of touch and that touch has important developmental benefits (see Jones & Yarbrough, 1985). In fact, several studies have found that the absence of touch from parents has seri-ous consequences for children's growth (for review, see Montagu, 1978). Close, physical contact with the caregiver seems to give children the critical sense of protection and security that cannot be attained in other ways. As such, it is not surprising that holding babies is often the behavior that can best calm them and that physicians spend some time explaining baby-holding techniques to new parents.

Touch does not only play an important role during early childhood, it is a critical part of our life as we age as well (see Barnard & Brazelton, 1990). Indeed, the elderly may be most affected by the harmful consequences of touch deprivation (see Montagu, 1978). When lifelong partners pass away, the elderly often lose the one source of affectionate touch on which they have relied for much of their lives. Although certain associations (e.g., long-time neighbors, family members) may help alleviate some potential for loneli-ness, it is unlikely that their needs for touch will be fully satisfied by these connections.

As with kinesics, haptic behaviors may be classified in multiple ways, some focused on type and others focused on function. Among the type of haptics discussed, scholars have distinguished between the form of touch and its qualities. On the one hand, the form of the touch sends an important communicative message. For example, we could easily separate nuzzles from kisses, rubs from hugs, pokes from hits, pushes from punches, and so on. In fact, Morris (1971) observed 457 different types of touch that seemed to signal the presence of a relationship between the parties. He then categorized the touches into 14 categories of what he labeled tie signs. Among these tie signs are hand-holding, patting, arm-linking, several types of embraces, and kissing. Afifi and Johnson (1999) compared dating partners and male-female friends in their use of these tie signs in college bars. Interestingly, they found more similarities than differences in the frequency that the tie signs were used across the two relationship types. Specifically, all types of tie signs were used in both dating relationships and friendships. However, daters were more likely than friends to lean against one another, use shoulder and waist embraces, and to kiss. Given the relative similarity between daters and friends of the opposite sex in their use of tie signs in bars, it is no wonder that young adults often report confusion about the status of their cross-sex friendships (see Monsour, 2002). Although not assessed by Afifi and Johnson, qualities of the touch, such as the duration and intensity (e.g., amount of pressure) undoubtedly play an important role in their meaning. Both friends and daters may exchange kisses, but a "peck" is different from a longer and more intense kiss. Similarly, a hug can differ dramatically in duration and intensity, aspects that are much more meaningful than simply recognizing that a hug occurred. In other words, both the type of touch and its characteristics serve to define its meaning and affect its outcome.

A final way that touches have been categorized is by their intended purpose. Heslin (as cited in Andersen, 1999) differentiated between five purposes of touch, each increasing in intimacy. **Functional/professional** touches have a specific task-related purpose. They are considered the least intimate forms of touch. Although the type and quality of touch may be considered intimate in other contexts, the receiver of the touch recognizes the function of the touch as being necessary for the task at hand. For example, physicians sometimes touch us in highly intimate areas, but the touch is not considered an intimate one because its function is recognized as being part of the required task of health maintenance. The next function of touch is labeled **Social/polite** and is characterized by relatively formal touches that accompany greetings and departures. A common example of social/polite touches is the handshake. Although other cultures utilize more intimate sorts of greetings (e.g., kisses), the context again defines the otherwise intimate touch as functioning as a polite expression rather than an intimate one. **Friendship/warmth** touches are the sort typically exchanged between friends. The formality of social/polite touches is gone and replaced with qualities of touch that signal increased bondedness. Examples of friendship/warmth touches include partial embraces, full embraces, and pats. **Love/intimacy** touches function to signal elevated closeness and are less likely to be enacted publicly. Touches such as a kiss or a prolonged embrace may serve the love/intimacy function. Finally, touches that function to increase sexual arousal are the most intimate types of touch. The sort of touch that occurs during sexual activity is the most common example of this function. In sum, rather than consider touches as differing by type, this category scheme focuses on their function. The same type of touch (e.g., a backrub) may serve a functional/professional purpose when conducted by a masseuse or sports therapist but act to increase sexual arousal when conducted by a romantic partner. Unfortunately, the existing categorization schemes do not adequately capture the many types of more harmful touches or the more negative purposes of touch (e.g., to harm, to intimidate).

Proxemics

The proxemic category of nonverbal behavior captures the way we use space. From analyses of overpopulation in certain nations, to the impact of small dorm room space, to overcrowding in prisons, studies consistently show harmful, effects of limited space. Although cultures differ dramatically in the amount of space that is typically given, we are all born with at least minimum needs for space. Threatening those space needs, especially for prolonged periods, produces high stress that, in turn, affects our psyche and behavior dramatically (see Edwards, Fuller, Vorakitphokatorn, & Sermsri, 1994). It is not surprising then, that confinement in a very small and dark room is commonly used as a method of torture (www.amnesty.org) and that such torture has devastating psychological impact. Indeed, Lester (1990) found an increase in suicide rates associated with overcrowding in prisons. Donoghue (1992) reported overcrowding as a factor contributing to stress among teenagers in the Virgin Islands. Curiously, he noted that sexual activity (sometimes leading to pregnancy) was one of consequences. Also, Gress and Heft (1998) showed that, the number of roommates in college dorms negatively affected the residents both emotionally and behaviorally. One way in which this need for space is expressed is through our behavior around territories.

Territories are physically fixed areas that one or more individuals defend as their own (Altman, 1975). To maintain the spatial needs provided by these territories, we set up markers so that others know the territory's boundaries (Buslig, 1999). For example, students may put books on the seat next to them to ensure that the seat is not taken, or spread their belongings across a wide area of a table to indicate the area as their own. Fences around property, "Keep Away" and "Do Not Disturb" signs, and markers around beach blankets are other common examples of signaling territory. Interestingly, locations where space is limited are particularly prone to markers of territory. Roommates often send very clear signals about the boundaries of their territory by hanging unique posters or signs that mark the area as their own. The importance of these territories to our well being is evident in the way individuals react to their violation. Intrusions into territory have been shown to produce elevated stress, and behavioral responses varying from withdrawal to confrontation (for review, see Lyman & Scott, 1967).

Unlike territories, which are fixed physical entities, **personal space** is a proxemic-based need that moves along with the individual. It is an "invisible bubble" that expands and shrinks according to context, but follows each individual, protecting him or her from physical threats (Hall, 1966). Violation of that personal space bubble produces responses similar to those found for the violation of territory. In North America, typical personal space has a circumference of approximately 3 ft, but the size of that space varies dramatically and is influenced by a variety of factors, from the target of your conversation to its location (see Burgoon et al., 1996). For example, you would likely feel much more uncomfortable standing 2 ft away from someone in a relatively empty elevator than in a crowded elevator. We recognize that certain contexts necessitate the temporary violation of our personal space, but we also keenly anticipate extracting ourselves from that context and restoring the security that comes with maintaining those personal space needs. A behavior that is commonly used both to violate personal space and restore it is eye contact. Have you ever felt that your personal space has been violated by someone simply staring at you, even from a distance? Many people report such a sensation. Have you ever looked away from someone who got too close physically? That sort of behavior is a common response to the violation of personal space in elevators, for example (see Rivano-Fischer, 1988).

Physical Appearance

The physical appearance category of nonverbal behavior includes all aspects related to the way we look, from our body type, to body adornments (e.g., tattoos, rings), to what we wear. Perhaps no other category of nonverbal behavior has a stronger effect on initial impressions than our physical appearance. The two general types of physical appearance that will be addressed in this selection are body type and attire.

Researchers have identified three general body types: ectomorphs, mesomorphs, and endomorphs (see Burgoon et al., 1996). **Ectomorphic** bodies are characterized by thin bone structures and lean bodies, **mesomorphic** bodies have strong bone structures, are typically muscular and athletic, and **endomorphic** bodies have large bone structures, and are typically heavy-set and somewhat rounded. An individual's body type is partly based on genetic elements such as bone structures and partly based on other elements such as diet and levels of activity. Regardless of the source of one's body structure or the degree to which it has any actual effect on behavior, research has clearly shown that people have strong impressions of others based on their body type. Specifically, ectomorphs are perceived to be timid, clumsy, and anxious, but also intelligent; mesomorphs are seen as outgoing, social, and strong; and endomorphs are considered lazy, jolly, and relatively unintelligent (Burgoon et al., 1996). Some factors may affect these perceptions. For example, women ectomorphs and male mesomorphs may be perceived more favorably than their other-sex counterparts. Unfortunately, research has not sufficiently addressed these possibilities. However, one pattern that has been well documented is that, regardless of actual body size, women are more likely than men to perceive their bodies negatively (for review, see Cash & Pruzinsky, 1990). Such "body image disturbances" have devastating consequences, affecting self-esteem, leading to eating disorders, and even increasing suicide rates (e.g., Phillips, 1999; Stice, Hayward, Cameron, Killen, & Taylor, 2000). Why do many women have such dislike for their bodies? Although the answer to this question is not at all simple, it is undoubtedly based, at least in part, on a cultural obsession with images of overly thin women (see Botta, 1999).

However, body shape is not the only aspect of physical appearance that has been shown to affect people's perceptions of us. Another strong influence on perceptions is height. Taller men and women are more likely to be seen as competent, dominant, and intelligent (see Boyson, Pryor, & Butler, 1999). Interestingly, however, the advantage of height does not extend to perceptions of women's attractiveness. Instead, shorter women are perceived as more attractive and date more frequently than taller women (Sheppard & Strathman, 1989). Men and women who fall well above or below this preferred standard encounter lifelong difficulties, including a diminished likelihood of relational success and struggles with perceptions of credibility across a wide range of evaluative contexts (see Martel & Biller, 1987). To combat these perceptions, short people sometimes change their environment to hide their height. For example, Robert Reich, who served on three presidential administrations and is under 5 ft tall, would speak behind a podium and use a step stool, making media viewers unaware of his short stature.

One explanation for the strong perceptions associated with body type and height comes from Evolutionary Theory. Evolutionary theorists (otherwise called sociobiologists) argue that our attraction to others is based in large part on our perceptions of their genetic makeup (see Buss, 1994). They suggest that, much like other mammals, the strongest members of our species receive the greatest attention and are considered the most attractive. For us, signs of health, wealth, and intelligence are the primary determinants of "strength." As such, it is not surprising to these scholars that people's body type (which may be associated with health) and height (which often translates to physical superiority) affect their life success.

Finally, the clothes we wear are a part of our physical appearance that also affects people's perceptions of us. The clothes we wear strongly influence perceptions of credibility, status, attractiveness, competence, and likability (e.g., Kaiser, 1997). This should come as no surprise to anyone who has seen students proudly display their **Abercrombie & Fitch** shirts, observed the respect often afforded to those wearing their military uniforms, or shook their head in frustration at someone who leaves for an interview in completely disheveled clothes. Indeed, individuals wearing formal clothes are seen as more credible and more persuasive than those wearing informal clothes, affecting their success across a range of interaction contexts, from job interviews to dates. Other aspects of physical appearance that relate to people's judgments include tattoos, rings, and hair styles, in sum, studies unequivocally demonstrate that physical appearance, both things under individuals' control (e.g., attire) and those not (e.g., height), strongly influence perceptions.

Vocalics

Vocalics, a category that people sometimes have difficulty recognizing as a nonverbal component, reflect all aspects of the voice, including loudness, pitch, accent, rate of speech, length of pauses between speech, and tone, among many others. Vocalic elements carry much of the meaning of a message and communicate a lot about the sender. Its importance can be reflected by a simple exercise. Try saying the same words (e.g., "Come over here") with slightly different vocalic qualities. Depending on how we say these words, we could communicate anger, passion, sadness, love, or a variety of other emotions. Indeed, studies have shown that we make relatively accurate judgments about a person's sex, age, height, and cultural background based on vocal cues alone (see Argyle, 1988). Like many of the codes discussed so far, vocalic elements also affect perceptions of attractiveness and competence (Semic, 1999). Deeper voices among men, like that of Barry White for example, are considered sexual and romantic, whereas high-pitched voices among men are considered feminine and weak. Other vocal qualities such as accent and speech rate are also associated with intelligence. For example, certain accents (e.g., British accents) may be considered sophisticated whereas others may not (e.g., thick Boston accents). This difference in the attractiveness of accents is illustrated in the movie **My Fair Lady** which is based on the premise that individuals sometimes must change their accent to affect judgments of their credibility.

One theory that has been applied to understand vocalic shifts is Communication Accommodation Theory (CAA, see chap. 16, this volume). Central to CAA is the belief that we converge our speech toward the style of individuals with whom we want to be associated and diverge away from that of individuals with whom we do not want association (see Giles, Mulac. Bradac, & Johnson, 1987). Examples of this behavior can be found across a wide range of contexts, including interactions between individuals of different ages (e.g., adults and the elderly), individuals from different cultures, individuals with different levels of status, even individuals of different sexes (see Gallois, Giles, Jones, Cargile, & Ota, 1995). So, if you were from the eastern United States and were to spend considerable time in the South, you would likely develop somewhat of a Southern accent, at least when around your friends from the South. That accent accommodation is a way of signaling connectedness with the South. Not surprisingly, the degree to which you are willing to accommodate others in your language has also been shown to significantly affect their perceptions of you. Failure to accommodate your vocalic patterns to others implicitly signals to them that you are not interested in joining their cultural group. On the other hand, a willingness to accommodate communicates attraction.

Chronemics and Artifacts

Chronemics and artifacts are the last two categories of nonverbal behavior that we will discuss in this selection. Rarely considered when discussing nonverbal messages, these codes nevertheless play a strong role in our interactions. The chronemic code captures our use and perception of time, including (among other things) our perception of the "appropriate" duration of an event, the number of things we do at once, the importance of punctuality, our use of time in our language, and the desired sequencing of events (Andersen, 1999). The North American culture is preoccupied with the notion of time; life is fast-paced and individuals are seemingly always struggling against time constraints. Two hours seems to be the maximum time that one expects to allot for entertainment or food events; movies are typically 2 hr or less, plays may go 3 hr but will have a prolonged recess to affect the perception of time, and quests often start getting anxious when meals take longer than 2 hr. Other countries differ dramatically from this North American norm. Although we rarely think of these time norms, they become very evident when we visit other countries. For example, Mediterranean countries often take 3 to 4 hr for a meal, making it as much a social event as it is time for nourishment. This selection will focus on three chronemic elements: duration, punctuality, and the distinction between polychronism and monochronism.

The expectations surrounding event duration are captured in part by the example provided previously. For every event or interaction, we have culturally and socially based expectations about its duration (Gonzalez & Zimbardo, 1999). Whether it be the amount of time a professor spends in an office meeting with a student, the amount of time set aside for a lunch date, or the amount of time before contact is made following a successful first date, these expectations strongly affect our perceptions of others' competence or attractiveness. Imagine if you had strong expectations that someone not call you back until 2 or 3 days after a first date but the person calls you within minutes after dropping you off. That violation of your chronemic expectations would undoubtedly affect your perceptions of him or her. In a similar vein, perceptions associated with punctuality vary according to the context and have important consequences. Punctuality is held with relatively high esteem in the North American culture, especially for more formal engagements. Arriving late to an interview, even if 5 min, is considered inexcusable, but 5 min late for a lunch date may be acceptable. However, even informal occasions have relatively strict punctuality expectations; arriving 30 min late for a lunch date is not appropriate, for example. In other cultures, however, there is a recognition that the time set for an appointment is rarely adhered to, and expectations are that the appointment may begin 30 to 45 min following the originally set appointment time. Failing to meet these culturally and contextually driven expectations have important implications for assessments of individuals (see Burgoon & Hale, 1988).

A final concept related to chronemics that will be considered in this selection is the distinction between polychronism and monochronism (Hall & Hall 1999). Polychronism reflects the act of doing multiple activities at once, whereas monochronism characterizes a focus on one activity at a time. For example, interacting with someone while you are cleaning your apartment, or watching TV while talking to someone reflects polychronistic behavior. Although sometimes necessary, such behavior is often considered a reflection of (dis)interest in the conversation. Of course, certain careers (e.g., secretarial work, CEOs) require that individuals are adept at polychronistic activity, and some cultures consider polychronism a sign of importance, so monochronism is not universally preferred.

The final nonverbal code is **artifacts,** a category that includes "the physical objects and environmental attributes that communicate directly, define the communication context, or guide social behavior in some way" (Burgoon et al., 1996, p. 109). Hall (1966) classified artifacts into two main types: fixed-feature elements and semifixed-feature elements. Fixed features include aspects of our surroundings that are not easily movable and are unlikely to change. Among these features is the structure of our surroundings, including the architectural style, the number and size of windows, and the amount of space available. Studies have shown that such architectural features directly impact the sort of communication that occurs (see Sundstrom, Bell, Busby, & Asmus, 1996). For instance, people who work in small cubicles are much less productive and less satisfied than people who work in their own office space, especially when the office space includes windows. Semifixed features are defined as aspects of our surroundings that are somewhat easily movable. Examples include rugs, paintings, wall color, the amount of lighting, and the temperature, among others. Considerable evidence suggests that these features also strongly affect both psychological health and communication outcome (for review; see Sundstrom et al., 1996). For example, research has shown that the semifixed aspects of a hospital affect the speed of patient recovery (Gross, Sasson, Zarhy, & Zohar, 1998).

In sum, nonverbal messages affect our interactions in hundreds of ways, from movement in our face, to our body posture, our gestures, the space between us, the ways we touch, the intonations in our voice, the way we use time, and the surroundings in which we find ourselves. Together, these nonverbal features inescapably guide the way we act and the outcome of our interactions. However, noting the population of nonverbal message types is only part of the equation. Each of these nonverbal behaviors can serve a variety of functions or purposes.

Functions of Nonverbal Codes

There are three assumptions about nonverbal behavior that shape the research reviewed in the remainder of this selection (for review, see Cappella & Street, 1985). First, all behavior is motivated by particular goals. In other words, all behavior is functional in some way. You gesture to someone with a specific purpose in mind, you look at someone to get his attention, you touch someone to let her know you're here, you yell at someone to communicate your anger, and so on. Second, each function or purpose can be achieved in multiple ways. For instance, you are not limited to only one way that you can show affection to people. You may hug them, kiss them, hold their hand, or take them out to a fancy restaurant. The third assumption related to this perspective on nonverbal messages is that a single behavior can serve multiple functions. For example, a hug can show someone you care, while simultaneously signaling to others that you and the recipient of the hug are in a committed relationship. These three assumptions are an inherent part of almost all studies of nonverbal communication and guide our understanding of nonverbal messages and their use.

Although scholars disagree on the exact number of functions served by nonverbal behaviors, there are six functions that seem to emerge in most discussions on this issue and that will be highlighted in this selection. These six functions are (a) structuring and regulating interaction, (b) creating and managing identities, (c) communicating emotions, (d) defining and managing relationships, (e) influencing others, and (f) deceiving others.

Structuring and Regulating Interaction

Each of the nonverbal codes serves to shape the quality of the interactions in which we find ourselves. By so doing, they structure and regulate these encounters. For example, Robinson's (1998) analysis of physician-patient interaction reveals the way in which the kinesic behaviors of eye gaze and body orientation signal to patients the physician's willingness to begin the interaction. Patients learn to stay silent until the physician kinesically signals that he or she is ready to start the interaction. Indeed, as noted earlier, many studies of immediacy reach similar conclusions, with varying levels of nonverbal involvement strongly affecting the quality of the interaction. Research on our use of vocalics also demonstrates the many ways that we nonverbally structure interactions. Conversations are typically considered a series of turns at talk. Each turn is requested, given, and ended in subtle, but clearly understood, nonverbal ways. For example, turns at talk are requested by such behaviors as establishing eye contact with the speaker, abruptly and noticeably inhaling a short breath, and starting to gesture toward the speaker (Wiemann & Knapp, 1975). In contrast, we communicate that our turn is ending by subtly changing the rhythm, loudness, and pitch of our voice (Boomer, 1978). In another interesting study on the potential of nonverbal message to structure interactions, Eaves and Leathers (1991) compared the physical layouts of McDonald's and Burger King to determine whether they affected interactions. Their study demonstrated that customers at McDonalds showed considerably higher levels of nonverbal involvement than did Burger King customers. Given these differences within two relatively similar fast-food chains, you can imagine how more noticeable differences in the level of restaurant formality affect our interactions.

One of the clearest signs that nonverbal behavior serves to structure the flow of interactions comes from examining how people adapt behavior during interaction. Indeed, a long history of research has shown that we react and adapt to one another's nonverbal expressions during interaction (for review, see Burgoon, Stem, & Dillman, 1995). Interaction Adaptation Theory (Burgoon, Stern, & Dillman, 1995) argues that people carry certain nonverbal needs for affiliation, recognize societal expectations for levels of affiliation, and have preferences for particular levels of affiliation from each interaction partner. The levels of these components differ in each context. For example, you may be may upset 1 day and feel the **need** for some autonomy. You **expect** your roommate to greet you and welcome you home. But, your **preference** is that your roommate not interact with you at all for the next few hours. The combination of these three elements produces what is called the **Interaction Position,** a concept that reflects the amount of distance you anticipate from your roommate. The argument in this theory is that your needs and preferences act together with your general social expectations to affect what behavior you anticipate from your interaction partner (i.e., the interaction position, the IP). In the previous example, the IP may be that your roommate will greet you but recognize your mood and give you some space. This IP is then compared to the actual behavior you receive (A). The theory argues that the comparison between your IP and the A determines how you will nonverbally adapt. If the actual behavior (i.e., the A) is better than you anticipated (i.e., the IP) you will converge toward the person's behavior, but if the actual behavior is worse than you anticipated, you will diverge away from that behavior. This "dance" is perhaps the greatest example of concerning the effect of nonverbal behavior on the structure of interactions.

Creating and Managing Identities and Impressions

Another general function of nonverbal messages is to communicate to others the groups to which we belong and to convey particular impressions of ourselves to others. I will review two theoretical frameworks that apply this function. Social Identity Theory (Tajfel & Turner, 1979) focuses on our identity as group members, whereas theoretical work on self-presentation (e.g., Goffman, 1959) focuses on our identity as individuals. Together, these theories help explain the way in which we use nonverbal behavior to achieve the function of creating and managing identities and impressions.

Communicating Group Identities. The main premise of Social Identity Theory is that we develop and maintain our self-concept in large part from the social groups with which we affiliate or to which we belong (e.g., ethnicity, sports team, club membership, department, organizational unit). The importance of these group memberships vary according to context (e.g., the importance of your status as a member of a particular fraternity decreases when with your parents), but each group has specific ways through which membership is communicated to others. So, when group membership becomes relevant, we act in ways that convey to others that we are a part of that group, while also letting people who are not in that group become more aware of their out-group status. Not surprisingly, the primary method of communicating these group memberships is nonverbal.

Take membership in a high school clique, for example. Members of a particular clique are likely to dress in relatively similar ways (physical appearance), and often have specific gestures they use to greet one another or that they use during conversation (kinesics). Individuals can indicate group membership by standing close to one another or by sitting next to each other at the lunch table (proxemics). Group members may spend a significant portion of their day with others in their clique (chronemics), place indicators of affiliation (signs, letters, etc.) on their lockers (artifacts), and may whisper to one another in the presence of an outgroup member (vocalics). Given the importance of group membership (Worschel & Austin, 1986), it is not surprising that we go to such lengths to identify with groups that we consider enhancing to our self concept.

It is also the case that we distance ourselves nonverbally from groups with which we want to remain independent. A look around college campuses shows a lot of the ways that people accomplish this distancing. Individuals often make little effort to include members of ethnic groups other than their own in their conversations. Eder's (1985) study of behavior among midadolescent females showed that group members communicated distance from group outsiders by avoiding interaction, body contact, or eye contact with nonmembers. Although these are examples of interpersonal ways in which we send group-related identity messages, there are ways in which societies or cultures communicate outgroup status to entire groups. Certainly laws discriminating against where particular cultural groups can gather—let alone eat, sit, or stand—are examples of such societal messages that become translated through nonverbal means. Everything from kinesics gestures (e.g., lack of eye contact) to proxemic decisions (e.g., maintaining large distances) to artifacts (e.g., signs indicating that entrance is prohibited to certain groups) communicate exclusion. For example, laws prohibiting the homeless from loitering in certain parks or communities are violations of public territorial rights that reflect one of many ways through which the homeless are shown their status as a societal "outgroup."

Communicating Individual Identities. Besides communicating our identity as members of particular groups, we also send nonverbal messages that are intended to convey our individual identities. Several theories have been advanced to capture this aspect of our behavior. The labels of these frameworks include Politeness Theory (Brown & Levinson, 1987), the Theory of Self-Identification (Schlenker, Britt, & Pennington, 1996), and Facework (Tracy, 1990). Within each of these theories are such concepts as self presentation, impression management, and identity management. In general, they all refer to the idea that we are motivated by a desire to maintain a positive impression of ourselves in the eyes of others. In other words, we generally want others to see us in a positive light. DePaulo (1992) defined self-presentation as "a matter of regulating one's own behavior to create a particular impression on others, of communicating a particular image of oneself to others, or of showing oneself to be a particular kind of person" (p. 205). For many reasons, we often manage our impression in front of others nonverbally (see DePaulo, 1992). For example, Albas and Albas (1988) examined ways in which students reacted after receiving graded exams. They found that individuals who received good grades smiled (kinesics), displayed an open body posture (kinesics), and left their exams open with the grade showing, whereas those who received poor grades displayed a closed body posture (kinesics) and left immediately following the class (chronemics).

The use of nonverbal methods to manage impressions is obviously not limited to students' reactions to exam scores; evidence for other applications can be found across a whole host of contexts. Daly, Hogg, Sacks, Smith, and Zimring (1983) reported that people in early stages of relationships spend more time adjusting their clothes, fixing their hair, and attending to their physical appearance than those in later stages. In a similar vein, Montepare and Vega (1988) showed that women's vocalic cues communicated greater approachability and sincerity, among other characteristics, when talking over the phone with men with whom they had an intimate relationship, as compared to those with whom they had no relationship. Finally, Blanck, Rosenthal, and Cordell (1985) reported that judges were more likely to display nonverbal cues associated with warmth, professionalism, and fairness when facing older, more educated jurors than younger, less educated jurors. In sum, the function of creating and managing identities is a common purpose of our nonverbal activity and involves actions from all codes.

Communicating Emotions

Another common purpose of nonverbal behavior is to communicate emotion. In fact, as noted earlier, the majority of emotion messages are communicated through facial cues (i.e., kinesically). Particularly impressive is the evidence that some of these expressions are recognized cross-culturally. The argument underlying the Universality Hypothesis on emotion expression is that humans are innately equipped to decode certain expressions of emotion (for review, see Ekman, 1978), leading to cross-cultural recognition of these emotions. Initially, several studies supported that claim (e.g., Ekman, 1973; Izard, 1977). However, when researchers improved their studies, they found dramatic differences in individuals" nonverbal responses. To reconcile the differences in the research and to help account for both cultural-specific and universal patterns of expression, Ekman and colleagues developed the Neurocultural Theory of emotion expression (Ekman & Friesen, 1969). The theory argues that there is an element of biological innateness in our expression of emotion that accounts for the consistency across cultures in recognition of emotion expressions. For example, an experience of joy produces an upward curvature of the mouth and lips. However, differences in actual expression of emotion occur across cultures due to (a) cultural differences in the association between events and the experience of particular emotions and (b) culturally learned and context-based rules about the appropriateness of expressing particular emotions (labeled **display rules).** The first of these two factors makes sense once you consider the way that cultures shapes the emotions we experience (for review, see Nussbaum, 2000). For instance, some cultures emphasize individuality and are likely to encourage intense emotional responses to events that threaten individuality, whereas other cultures emphasize the collective and are likely to shape emotional responses accordingly. In other words, the same events are unlikely to produce the same emotions across cultures. However, researchers have devoted much more energy toward understanding the second of these factors: display rules. **Display rules** are defined as "socially learned habits regarding the control of facial appearance that act to intensify, deintensify, mask, or qualify a universal expression of emotion depending on the social circumstance" (Kupperbusch et al., 1999, p. 21).

Studies have shown that infants' emotional expressions abide by cultural, gender, and familial display rules before their first birthday (e.g., Malatesta & Haviland, 1982). These rules are communicated by parents from infancy but reinforced throughout life by the media, family members, peers, and even strangers. Common examples of these display rules are those generally discouraging overt public displays of affection, or those directing people on appropriate methods of emotional expression in movie theatres, funeral homes, classrooms, concerts, and so on. Display rules also direct people regarding the appropriateness of emotion expression in close relationships. Considerable evidence demonstrates that "negative" emotions (e.g., anger, jealousy) are considered inappropriate to express in early stages of relationships (for review, see Aune, 1997). Moreover, studies show the way that these display rules affect our expression of emotion even in our most intimate relationships. For example, Cloven and Roloff (1994) found that one fifth of relational irritations were not expressed in couples at the most advanced relational stages, and Aune,

Buller, and Aune (1996) found that positive emotions were considered more appropriate to express than negative emotions, regardless of relationship stage.

Defining and Managing Relationships

Another important function of nonverbal messages is to help people negotiate and express the quality or status of the relationship they have with others. These relational messages vary along five dimensions (see Burgoon & Hale, 1987). Labeled the topoi (themes) of relational communication, the five dimensions along which nonverbal messages can differentially communicate relational qualities are (a) the amount of dominance, (b) the level of intimacy, (c) the degree of composure or arousal, (d) the level of formality, and (e) the degree to which the interaction is focused on task or social elements. Evidence associated with how each of these dimensions is communicated nonverbally will be briefly summarized.

Dominance. Nonverbal messages help indicate the degree to which one member of the interaction is powerful dominant, and controlling. The way in which men and women communicate power nonverbally has been examined frequently, most notably by Henley (1977). Behavior from each nonverbal code can be applied to study how dominance is conveyed (see Burgoon et al., 1996). For example, people communicate dominance by refusing to engage in eye contact (kinesics), by initiating touch (haptics), by arriving late for a meeting (chronemics), by having access to large office space or by displaying awards (artifacts), by demanding large personal space needs or unilaterally changing the amount of space between themselves and their interactants (proxemics), by speaking loudly and in a lower pitch (vocalics), and by emphasizing their body size or dressing in formal attire (physical appearance).

Intimacy: Nonverbal messages help communicate the amount of affection, inclusion, involvement, depth, trust, and similarity there is between interactants. As noted earlier in this selection, several studies have shown the benefits of expressing nonverbal involvement in interactions. Displays such as gestural activity, direct body orientation, forward body lean, and close (but socially acceptable) conversational distance increase the success of job interviews, increase liking, and produce perceptions of personality warmth (Burgoon et al., 1996). Whereas expressing involvement is one method of communicating relational intimacy and interest, more intimate messages are communicated in other ways, such as the use of tie signs and an increase in the frequency and intimacy of touch. Interestingly, the eyes are often the best indicator of attraction (Grumet, 1983). Establishing eye contact is typically the first way individuals communicate attraction and people who are attracted to one another look into each other's eyes more than others do. Also, our pupils involuntarily increase in size when we are talking to someone to whom we are attracted, a fact that, in turn, subconsciously seems to make us more attractive to others (Hess, 1975). In sum, the nonverbal methods for communicating intimacy are numerous.

Composure and Arousal. The degree to which individuals are relaxed and calm in an interaction has also been shown to communicate qualities of their relationship. As a general rule, people in close relationships are more likely to be relaxed around one-another than acquaintances. In fact, people sometimes manipulate their levels of composure to send messages about their comfort in the interaction or the relationship. For example, job candidates or people on first dates usually do their best to hide the amount of anxiety being felt in part because they want to show a level of relational comfort. In other words, we make efforts to appear composed in certainty situations precisely because we know what anxiety communicates about relationships.

Formality. Another way in which individuals can communicate qualities of the relationship is through the degree of casualness conveyed in their nonverbal behavior. Although relatively few studies have examined it, the level of formality, like other dimensions of relationship quality, can be communicated in many different ways. Three common methods of indicating the formality of the relationship are through the formality of the attire, through kinesic rigidity, and through conversational distance (Burgoon, 1991; Burgoon et al., 1996). The more casual the clothing, the more relaxed the body posture, the more frequent the hand gesturing, and the greater the distance between interactants, the greater the perception that the interaction is an informal one. Not surprisingly, studies have shown that the likelihood of communicating formality differs across status and that these differences affect people's perceptions. For example, Lamude and Scudder (1991) reported that upper level managers are more likely to be formal than lower or middle-level managers. Interestingly, research has also shown that college teachers are perceived as more effective when they dress informally (Butler, & Roesel, 1991; Lukavski, Butler, & Harden, 1995), whereas physicians and interview candidates are perceived as less effective when behaving or dressing informally (Burgoon et al., 1987; Gifford Ng, & Wilkinson, 1985).

Task or Social Orientation. Nonverbal messages reflecting the degree to which the interaction is one focused on a task constitute the final dimension through which people communicate qualities of their relationships nonverbally. This dimension is typically communicated through the chronemic code and, again, the desirability of communicating a focus on task is strongly affected by context. On the one hand, managers who focus on task, to the exclusion of relational maintenance behaviors, receive the lowest ratings of satisfaction by subordinates (Lamude, Daniels, & Smilowitz, 1995). On the other hand, teachers whose in-class behavior focuses on task produce better student outcomes (Harris, Rosenthal, & Snodgrass, 1986). In general, the communication of a task orientation has been shown to convey lower levels of relational connectedness than socially oriented messages (Burgoon & Hale, 1987).

Influencing Others

A long history of research has examined the methods we use to attempt to change someone's attitudes or behavior or to strengthen already established attitudes or behaviors (see O'Keefe, 1990). In general studies find that we are most influenced by people who we find attractive (i.e., likeable), credible, or powerful (see O'Keefe, 1990).

Social Attractiveness or Liking. Scholars have shown many ways in which individuals can increase their attractiveness to others. For example, studies demonstrate that establishing eye contact increases the likelihood of influencing others in a wide variety of situations including persuading strangers to give a dime for a phone call, donate to a charity, take pamphlets, or pick up a hitchhiker (for review, see Segrin, 1999). Also, light touching is linked to bigger tips, an increase in petition signings, and a greater willingness to sign up for volunteer work (e.g., Goldman, Kiyohara, & Pfannensteil, 1985). Physical appearance cues also strongly affect perceived attractiveness and the potential to influence others. In one study, a confederate gave the same speech to two different audiences but varied her physical appearance through differences in the messiness of her hair and the fit of her clothes (Mills & Aronson, 1965). Results showed that she was more convincing when she was dressed more neatly. In a similar vein, physically attractive political candidates are more likely to get elected for office and physically attractive defendants are less likely to be found guilty (Mazzella & Feingold, 1994; Sigelman, Thomas, Sigelman, & Ribich, 1986). However, other studies suggest that the advantage of physical attractiveness depends at least somewhat on context. Juhnke, Barmann, Cunningham, and Smith (1987) found that strangers were more willing to give detailed directions to college students who were poorly dressed and asking about the location of a lower status location (i.e., a thrift shop) than students who were well dressed or asking for directions to a higher status location (e.g., the Gap). In sum, physical appearance has repeatedly been shown to be a nonverbal signal that functions to increase or decrease the success of social influence attempts.

Credibility. Besides physical attractiveness, research has shown that our perceptions of someone's credibility affect the degree to which they influence us. The notion of credibility refers to "the judgments made by a perceiver (e.g., a message recipient) concerning the believability of a communicator" (O'Keefe, 1990, pp. 130–131). Kinesic behaviors that are related to perceptions of credibility include eye contact, moderate amounts of gesturing, use of supportive head nods, facial expressiveness, and moderately forward leans, all indicators of conversational immediacy (see Burgoon, Birk, & Pfau, 1990). For example, Badzinski and Pettus (1994) showed that jurors determined a judge's credibility by attending to his or her kinesic behavior. Equipped with this knowledge, many lawyers approach the bench of jurors during opening and closing remarks, establish eye contact with each juror, and use other kinesic behaviors that are known to increase credibility **ratings.**

Besides kinesic elements, vocalic cues also affect perceptions of credibility. Among the most common findings is that nonfluencies in speech strongly decrease credibility ratings and the potential for successful persuasion. Nonfluencies include pauses in speech (e.g., "Auh," "Aummm"), repetition of "nonsense" words (e.g. "like"), and difficulty in articulation (O'Keefe. 1990). Besides the absence of nonfluencies, credible speakers use more varied intonation, speak more loudly and with more intensity, and talk faster (see Burgoon et al., 1996). But perhaps no other nonverbal code has received more attention for its effect on perceptions of credibility than physical appearance. For example, studies have shown that women who have specific eye shapes, short hair, appear older (although not elderly), wear a moderate amount of makeup, and are conservatively dressed were rated as more credible than their counterparts (Dellinger & Williams, 1997; Rosenberg, Kahn. & Tran, 1991). The final aspect known to increase persuadability is the perceived power of the speaker.

Power. Power will be defined in this selection as a perception that the speaker holds a position of authority. Like most assessments, this perception of authority is primarily established through nonverbal means. Again, perhaps the most common method of affecting perceptions of power is through physical appearance. Attire and physical size go a long way toward establishing a speaker's authority. For example, individuals wearing suits or uniforms, and those standing tall, as opposed to those with a slumped posture, are immediately afforded greater perceptions of power than their counterparts (see Andersen & Bowman, 1999). An extreme example of the effect of physical appearance on the success of influence came from Milgram's (1974) research program on obedience. In his studies, he showed that individuals dressed in lab coats were able to convince research participants to administer what participants believed to be fatal levels of electric shock to others. The result of Milgram's research program starkly demonstrated the degree to which people will obey others who they perceive to hold power positions, a perception primarily guided by nonverbal cues.

Deceiving Others

The last purpose of nonverbal messages that will be reviewed in this selection is to deceive others. Deception is defined as "a message knowingly transmitted by a sender to foster a false belief or conclusion by a receiver" (Buller & Burgoon, 1996, p. 205). Although people assume that most interactions involve truth-telling, some studies suggest that a majority actually involve some element of deception (e.g., O'Hair & Cody, 1994). So, how is it that we get away with so much deception and when is it that we're likely to be caught? The answer to both questions lies in our manipulation of nonverbal behavior.

Interpersonal Deception Theory (Buller & Burgoon, 1996) is a framework that, combines several perspectives to help explain the process of deception in interactions. Although the theory is quite complex, it relies primarily on the idea that deception is an interactive activity and that its detection is a process affected by the behavior of both sender and receiver, as well as contextual and relational factors. In other words, whether you are successful at lying is partly based on your nonverbal cues, but it is also affected by the receiver's behavior, the relationship you have with him or her, and the context surrounding the interaction, among other elements. Given the emphasis of this selection, I will focus on the nonverbal behaviors that have been shown to affect the success of the deceiver.

Research suggests that successful liars are those who maintain eye contact, display a forward body lean, smile, and orient their bodies toward the other person (for review, see Buller & Burgoon, 1994). That is, people who can display elevated levels of immediacy are more likely to get away with a lie (Burgoon, Buller, Dillman, & Walther. 1995). Burgoon and colleagues offer at least two explanations for this finding. First, the high immediacy by receivers may produce an adaptational response by the deceiver—increased immediacy. That response, in turn, makes the deceiver appear honest. So, the receiver's immediacy "pulls" the liar into that behavioral pattern and causes him or her look more honest. Another possibility is that the receiver's immediacy makes the deceiver feel better about the success of his or her deception and lessens the anxiety cues that often "leak" from deceivers. In addition to the previously noted cues, successful liars display vocalic fluency and kinesic composure, while also being generally expressive nonverbally and avoiding extended pause rates during conversation. In contrast, unsuccessful liars "leak" their anxiety nonverbally through heightened pitch, greater nonfluencies, negative expressions, nervous behaviors, and generally lowered immediacy levels (for review, see Burgoon, Buller, & Guerrero, 1995).

Although the research on deception is vast and includes much more detailed analysis of factors affecting deception success and failure, among other aspects of the deception episode, the previously noted cues seem to capture some of the essential elements of deceiver behavior.

Summary

The study of nonverbal codes—from kinesics to chronemics to artifacts, is an essential aspect of human communication. In fact, after reading this chapter you will now understand why some think that the nonverbal meaning of a message is more important than the verbal aspect of the same message. The functions of nonverbal codes operate for a variety of reasons, including structuring and regulating interactions, creating and managing identity and impressions, communicating our emotions, and defining and managing relationships.

The reader should be aware that the study of nonverbal communication is much more complex than many books in the personal help section of bookstores. The idea that one can completely "read" a person by analyzing their nonverbal communication is missing the other half of the message (verbal), and only focusing on the nonverbal aspect of the message could lead to many inaccurate impressions. When possible, individual's should use perception checking to determine if their analysis of the nonverbal aspects of a message is correct—interpreting nonverbal messages without verbally checking to see if perceptions are correct can lead to many misunderstandings. If the observer does not have the ability to check their perceptions based on nonverbal interpretations are correct, they should remember that any such perceptions are only inferences, and need to be checked verbally as soon as possible to determine the successfulness of the perception.

Questions For Discussion

1. Why do you think that when presented with contradicting verbal and nonverbal communication, people are more apt to believe the nonverbal message?
2. Do you think nonverbal communication is more important than verbal communication?
3. What are some non-written laws about proxemics in the U.S. with respect to standing in line?
4. In what way have you used nonverbal communication to create your personal identity?
5. What are some nonverbal gestures that you have seen when people have tried to deceive you?

References

Afifi, W. A. & Johnson, M. L. (1999). The use and interpretation of tie signs in a public setting: Relationship and sex differences. *Journal of Social and Personal Relationships, 16,* 9–38.

Albas. D., & Albas. C. (1988). Acers and bombers: Post-exam impression management strategies of students. *Symbolic Interaction, 2,* 289–302.

Altman, I. (1975). *The environment and social behavior.* Monterey, CA: Brooks/Cole.

Andersen, P. A. (1999). *Nonverbal communication: Forms and functions.* Mountain View, CA: Mayfield.

Andersen, P. A., & Bowman, L. L. (1999). Positions of power: Nonverbal influence in organizational communication. In L. K. Guerrero, J. A. DeVito, & M. L. Hecht (Eds.), *The nonverbal communication reader: Classic and contemporary readings* (2nd ed., pp. 317–334). Prospect Heights, IL: Waveland.

Argyle, M. (1988). *Bodily communication* (2nd ed.). London: Methuen.

Aune, K. S. (1997). Self and partner perceptions of the appropriateness of emotions. *Communication Reports, 10,* 133–142.

Aune. K. S., Buller, D. B., & Aune, R. K. (1996). Display rule development in romantic relationships: Emotion management and perceived appropriateness of emotions across relationship stages. *Human Communication Research, 23,* 115–145.

Badzinski, D. M., & Pettus, A. B. (1994). Nonverbal involvement and sex: Effects on jury decisions making. *Journal of Applied Communication Research, 22,* 309–321.

Barnard, K. E. & Brazelton, T. B. (Eds.). (1990). *Touch: The foundation of experience.* Madison, CT: International Universities Press.

Blanck, P.D., Rosenthal, R., & Cordell, L. H. (1985). The appearance of justice: Judges' verbal and nonverbal behavior in criminal jury trials. *Stanford Law Review, 38,* 89–164.

Botta. R. A. (1999). Televised images and adolescent girls' body image disturbance. *Journal of Communication, 49,* 22–41.

Boomer, D. S. (1978). The phonemic clause: Speech unit in human communication. In A. W. Siegman & S. Feldstein (Eds.), *Nonverbal behavior and communication* (pp. 245–262). Hillsdale, NJ: Lawrence Erlbaum Associates, Inc.

Boyson. A.R., Pryor, B., & Butler, J. (1999). Height as power in women. *North American Journal of Psychology, 1,* 109–114.

Brown, P., & Levinson, S. (1987). *Universals in language usage: Politeness phenomena.* Cambridge, England: Cambridge University Press.

Buller, D. B., & Burgoon, J. K. (1994). Deception: Strategic and nonstrategic communication. In J. A. Daly & J. M. Wiemann (Eds.), *Strategic interpersonal communication* (pp. 191–223). Hillsdale, NJ: Lawrence Erlbaum Associates, Inc.

Buller, D. B., & Burgoon. J. K. (1996). Interpersonal Deception Theory. *Communication Theory, 6,* 203–242.

Buller, D. B., & Street, R. L., Jr. (1992). Physician-patient relationships. In R. S. Feldman (Ed.), *Applications of nonverbal theories and research* (pp. 119–141). Hillsdale, NJ: Lawrence Erlbaum Associates, Inc.

Burgoon, J. K. (1991). Relational messages interpretations of touch, conversational distance, and posture. *Journal of Nonverbal Behavior, 15,* 233–259.

Burgoon, J. K. (1994). Nonverbal signals. In M. L. Knapp & G. R. Miller (Eds.), *Handbook of interpersonal communication* (2nd ed., pp. 229–285). Thousand Oaks, CA: Sage.

Burgoon, J. K., Birk, T., & Pfau, M. (1990). Nonverbal behaviors, persuasion, and credibility. *Human Communication Research, 17,* 140–169.

Burgoon, J. K., Buller, D. B., Dillman, L., & Walther, J. B. (1995). Interpersonal deception: IV. Effects of suspicion on perceived communication and nonverbal behavior dynamics. *Human Communication Research, 22,* 163–196.

Burgoon, J. K., Buller, D. B., & Guerrero, L. K. (1995). Interpersonal deception: IX. Effects of social skill and nonverbal communication on deception success and detection accuracy. *Journal of Language and Social Psychology, 14,* 289–311.

Burgoon, J. K., Buller, D. B., & Woodall, W. G. (1996). *Nonverbal communication: The unspoken dialogue* (2nd ed.). New York: McGraw-Hill.

Burgoon, J. K., & Hale, J. L. (1987). Validation and measurement of the fundamental themes of relational communication. *Communication Monographs, 54,* 19–41.

Burgoon, J. K. & Hale, J. L. (1988). Nonverbal expectancy violations: Model elaboration and application to immediacy behaviors. *Communication Monographs, 55,* 58–79.

Burgoon, J. K., Pfau, M., Parrott, R., Birk, T., Coker, R., & Burgoon, M. (1987). Relational communication, satisfaction, compliance-gaining strategies, and compliance in communication between physicians and patients. *Communication Monographs, 54,* 307–324.

Burgoon, J. K., Stern, L. A., & Dillman, L. (1995). *Interpersonal adaptation: Dyadic interaction patterns.* Cambridge, England: Cambridge University Press.

Buslig, A. L. S. (1999). 'Stop' signs: Regulating privacy with environmental features. In L. K. Guerrero, J. A. DeVito. & M. L. Hecht (Eds.), *The nonverbal communication reader: Classic and contemporary readings* (2nd ed., pp. 241–249). Prospect Heights, IL: Waveland.

Buss, D. M. (1994). *The evolution of desire.* New York: Basic Books.

Butler, S., & Roesel, K. (1991). Students perceptions of male teachers: Effects of teachers' dress and students' characteristics. *Perceptual and Motor Skills, 73,* 943–951.

Cappella, J. N., & Street, R. L. (1985). A functional approach to the structure of communicative behavior. In R. L. Street & J. N. Cappelia (Eds.), *Sequence and pattern in communicative behavior* (pp. 1–29). London: Edward Arnold.

Cash. T. E, & Pruzinsky, T. (Eds.). (1990). *Body images: Development, deviance, and change.* New York: Guilford.

Cloven, D. H., & Roloff, M. E. (1994). A developmental model of decisions to withhold relational irritations in romantic relationships. *Personal Relationships, 1,* 143–164.

Daly, J. A., Hogg, E., Sacks, D., Smith, M., & Zimring, L. (1983). Sex and relationship affect social self-grooming. *Journal of Nonverbal Behavior, 7,* 183–189.

Dellinger, K., & Williams, C. L. (1997). Makeup at work: Negotiating appearance rules in the workplace. *Gender and Society, 11,* 151–177.

DePaulo, B. M. (1992). Nonverbal behavior and self-presentation. *Psychological Bulletin, 111,* 203–243.

Donoghue, E. (1992). Sociopsychological correlates of teenage pregnancy in the United States Virgin Islands. *International Journal of Mental Health, 21,* 39–49.

Eaves, M. H., & Leathers, D. G. (1991). Context as communication: McDonald's vs. Burger King. *Journal of Applied Communication, 19,* 263–289.

Eder, D. (1985). The cycle of popularity: Interpersonal relations among female adolescents. *Sociology of Education, 58,* 154–165.

Edwards, J. N., Fuller, T. D., Vorakitphokatorn, S., & Sermsri, S. (1994). *Household crowing and its consequences.* Boulder, CO: Westview.

Ekman, P. (1973). *Darwin and facial expression: A century of research in review.* New York: Academic.

Ekman, P. (1978). Facial expression. In A. W. Siegman & S. Feldstein (Eds.). *Nonverbal behavior and communication* (pp. 96–116). Hillsdale, NJ: Lawrence Erlbaum Associates, Inc.

Ekman, P. & Friesen, W. V. (1969). The repertoire of nonverbal behavior: Categories, origins, usage, and coding. *Semiotica, 1,* 49–98.

Ekman, P., & Oster, H. (1979). Facial expression of emotion. *Annual Review of Psychology, 30,* 527–554.

Forbes, R. J., & Jackson, P. R. (1980). Nonverbal behavior and the outcome of selection interviews. *Journal of Occupational Psychology, 53,* 67–72.

Gallois, C, Giles, EL Jones, E., Cargile, A. C, & Ota, H. (1995). Accommodating intercultural encounters: Elaborations and extensions. *International and Intercultural Communication Annual, 19,* 115–147.

Gifford, R., Ng, C. R, Wilkinson, M. (1985). Nonverbal cues in the employment interview: Links between applicant qualities and interviewer judgments. *Journal of Applied Psychology, 70,* 729–736.

Giles, H., Mulac, A., Bradac, J. J., & Johnson. P. (1987). Speech Accommodation Theory: The first decade and beyond. In M. IVlcLaughlin (Ed.), *Communication Yearbook* (Vol. 10, pp. 13–48). New-bury Park, CA: Sage.

Goffman, E. (1959). *The presentation of self in everyday life.* Garden City. NY: Doubleday.

Goldman, M., Kiyohara, O., & Pfannensteil, D. A. (1985). Interpersonal touch, social labeling, and the foot-in-the-door effect. *Journal of Social Psychology, 125,* 143–147.

Gonzalez, A., & Zimbardo. P. G. (1999). Time in perspective. In L. K. Guerrero. J. A. DeVito, & M. L. Hecht (Eds.), *The nonverbal communication reader: Classic and contemporary readings* (2nd ed., pp. 227–236). Prospect Heights, IL: Waveland.

Gress, J. E., & Heft, H. (1998). Do territorial actions attenuate the effects of high density? A field study. In J. Sanford & B. R. Connell (Eds.), *People, places, and public policy* (pp. 47–52). Edmond, OK: Environmental Design Research Association.

Gross, R., Sasson, Y., Zarhy, M., & Zohar, J. (1998). Healing environment in psychiatric hospitals. *General Hospital Psychiatry, 20,* 108–114.

Grumet, G. W. (1983). Eye contact: The core of interpersonal relatedness. *Psychiatry, 48,* 172–180.

Guerrero, L. K., Devito, J. A., & Hecht, M. L. (Eds.). (1999). *The nonverbal communication reader: Classic and contemporary readings* (2nd ed.). Prospect Heights, IL: Waveland.

Hall, E. T. (1966). *The hidden dimension* (2nd ed.). Garden City, NY: Anchor/Doubleday.

Hall E. T., & Hall. M. R. (1999). Monochrome and polychrome time. In L. K. Guerrero, J. A. DeVito, & M. L. Hecht (Eds.), *The nonverbal communication reader: Classic and contemporary readings* (2nd ed., pp. 237–240). Prospect Heights. IL: Waveland.

Harris, M. J. Rosenthal, R., & Snodgrass, S. E. (1986). The effects of teacher expectations, gender, and behavior on pupil academic performance and self-concept. *Journal of Educational Research, 79,* 173–179.

Henley, N. M. (1977). *Body politics: Power, sex, and nonverbal communication.* Englewood Cliffs, NJ: Prentice-Hall.

Hess, E. H. (1975). The role of pupil size in communication. *Scientific American, 233,* 110–119.

Izard, C. E. (1977). *Human emotions.* New York: Plenum.

Jones, S. E., & Yarbrough, A. E. (1985). A naturallistic study of the meanings of touch. *Communication Monographs, 52,* 19–56.

Juhnke, R., Barmann, B., Cunningham, M., & Smith, E. (1987). Effects of attractiveness and nature of request on helping behavior. *Journal of Social Psychology, 127,* 317–322.

Kaiser, S. B. (1997). *The social psychology of clothing: Symbolic appearances in context* (2nd ed.). New York: Fairchild.

Kupperbusch, C, Matsumoto. D., Kooken, K., Loewinger, S., Uchida, H., Wilson-Cohn, C., et al. (1999). Cultural influences on nonverbal expressions of emotion. In P. Philippot, R. S. Feldman. & E. J. Coats (Eds.), *The social context of nonverbal behavior* (pp. 17–44). Cambridge, England: Cambridge University Press.

Lamude, K. G., Daniels, T. D., & Smilowitz, M. (1995). Subordinates(satisfaction with communication and managers' relational messages. *Perceptual and Motor Skills, 81,* 467–471.

Lamude, K. G. & Scudder, J. (1991). Hierarchical levels and type of relational messages. *Communication Research Reports, 8,* 149–157.

Lester, D. (1990). Overcrowding in prisons and rates of suicide and homocide. *Perceptual and Motor Skills, 71,* 274.

Lukavsky. J., Butler, S., & Harden, A. J. (1995). Perceptions of an instructor: Dress and students' characteristics. *Perceptual and Motor Skills, 81,* 231–240.

Lyman, S. 1VL, & Scott, M. B. (1967), Territoriality: A neglected sociological dimension. *Social Problems, 15,* 236–249.

Malatesta, C. Z., & Haviland, J. M. (1982). Learning display rules: The socialization of emotion expression in infancy. *Child Development, 53,* 991–1003.

Martel, L. F., & Biller, H. B. (1987). *Stature and stigma: The biopsychosocial development of short males.* Lexington, MA: Lexington.

Mazzella, R., & Feingold, A. (1994). The effects of physical attractiveness, race, socioeconomic status, and gender of defendants and victims on judgments of mock jurors: A meta-analysis. *Journal of Applied Social Psychology, 24,* 1315–1344.

Milgram, S. (1974). *Obedience to authority: An experimental view.* New York: Harper & Row. Mills. J., & Aronson, E. (1965). Opinion change as a function of the communicator's attractiveness and desire to influence. *Journal of Personality and Social Psychology, 1,* 74–77.

Monsour, M. (2002). *Women and men as friends: Relationships across the life span in the 21st century.* Mahwah, NJ: Lawrence Erlbaum Associates, Inc.

Montagu, A. (1978). *Touching: The human significance of the skin* (2nd ed.). New York: Harper & Row.

Montepare, J. M., & Vega, C. (1988). Women's vocal reactions to intimate and casual male friends. *Personality and Social Psychology, 14,* 103–113.

Morris, D. (1971). *Intimate behavior.* New York: Random House.

Nussbaum, M. C. (2000). Emotions and social norms. In L. P. Nucci & G. B. Saxe (Eds.), *Culture, thought, and development* (pp. 41–63). Mahwah, NJ: Lawrence Erlbaum. Associates, Inc.

O'Hair, H. D., & Cody, M. J. (1994). Deception. In W. R. Cupach & B. H. Spitzberg (Eds.), *The dark side of interpersonal communication* (pp. 181–214). Hillsdale, NJ: Lawrence Erlbaum Associates, Inc.

O'Keefe, D. J. (1990). *Persuasion: Theory and research.* Newbury Park, CA: Sage.

Phillips, K. A. (1999). Body dysmorphic disorder and depression: Theoretical considerations and treatment strategies. *Psychiatric Quarterly, 70,* 313–331.

Rivano-Fischer, M. (1988). Micro territorial behavior in public transport vehicles: A field study on a bus route. *Psychological Research Bulletin, 28,* 18.

Robinson, J. D. (1998). Getting down to business: Talk, gaze, and body orientation during openings of doctor-patient consultations. *Human Communication Research, 25,* 97–123.

Rosenberg, S. W., Kahn. S., & Tran, T. (1991). Creating a political image: Shaping appearance and manipulating the vote. *Political Behavior, 13,* 345–367.

Schlenker, B. R., Britt, T. W., & Pennington, J. (1996). Impression regulation and management: Highlights of a theory of self-identification. In R. M. Sorrentino & E. T. Higgins (Eds.), *Handbook of motivation and cognition: The interpersonal context* (Vol. 3, pp. 118–147). New York: Guilford.

Segrin, C. (1999). The influence of nonverbal behaviors in compliance-gaining processes. In L. K. Guerrero, J. A. DeVito, & M. L. Hecht (Eds.), *The nonverbal communication reader: Classic and contemporary readings* (2nd ed., pp. 335–346). Prospect Heights, IL: Waveland.

Semic, B. (1999). Vocal attractiveness: What sounds beautiful is good. In L. K. Guerrero, J. A. DeVito, & M. L. Hecht (Eds.), *The nonverbal communication reader: Classic and contemporary readings* (2nd ed., pp. 149–155). Prospect Heights, IL: Waveland.

Sheppard, J. A., & Strathman, A. J. (1989). Attractiveness and height: The role of stature in dating preference, frequency of dating, and perceptions of attractiveness. *Personality and Social Psychology Bulletin, 15,* 617–627.

Sigelman, C. K., Thomas, D. B., Sigelman, L., & Ribich, F. D. (1986). Gender, physical attractiveness, and electability: An experimental investigation of voter biases. *Journal of Applied Social Psychology, 16,* 229–248.

Stice, E., Hayward, C, Cameron, R. P., Killen. J. D., & Taylor, C. B. (2000). Body-image and eating disturbances predict onset of depression among female adolescents: A longitudinal study. *Journal of Abnormal Psychology, 109,* 438–444.

Sundstrom, E., Bell, P. A. Busby, P. L., & Asmus, C. (1996). Environmental psychology 1989–1994. *Annual Review of Psychology 47,* 482–512,

Tajfel, H., & Turner, J. C. (1979). An integrative theory of group conflict. In W. G. Austin & S. Worchel (Eds.), *The social psychology of intergroup relations* (pp. 33–47). Monterey, CA: Brooks-Cole.

Tracy. K. (1990). The many faces of facework. In H. Giles & W. P. Robinson (Eds.), *Handbook of language and social psychology* (pp. 209–226). Chichester, England: John "Wiley & Sons.

Wiemann. J. M., & Knapp, M. L. (1975). Turn-taking in conversation. *Journal of Communication, 25,* 75–92.

Worschel, S., & Austin, W. G. (Eds.). (1986). *The social psychology of intergroup relations.* Chicago: Nelson Hall.

Chapter 7

Tides in the Ocean

A Layered Approach to Communication and Culture

Sandra L. Faulkner and Michael L. Hecht

Each of us is born into a particular culture—we have no choice in this matter. However, the culture into which we are born will affect our life until the day we die. Culture is so much more than just speaking a different language, it consists of many layers that we may or may not be aware of as we go about our daily lives. Understanding how these layers operate is essential to understand the significance of communication and culture.

Learning Objectives For This Chapter

- Explain the role that codes play in intercultural communication
- Describe how conversation and culture interact in the communication of culture
- Discuss why cultures can be seen as communities
- Identify the four layers that exist in all cultures
- Explain the difference between individualistic and collectivist cultures
- Understand the components of a co-culture
- Explain how the dialectical approach helps understand how the various elements of culture are related to each other
- Identify how co-cultural groups communicate within dominant social structures
- Discuss how ethnography of communication can help understand problems that arise when people from different cultures interact

Culture is a lens for viewing the connections and relationships that define the human experience. Just as physics has become more and more focused on the connections and relationships among energy and matter, so too have the human sciences come to focus on these sources of connectivity. We believe that the construct of "culture" provides a means for understanding and explaining the connections among people as well as between people and their environment. At the same time, it helps explain how people's various identities come together to create the self. We consider culture to be like a "lens" because it focuses us on these connections, helping us see more clearly something that, while containing material objects, is actually symbolic.

In this chapter we will attempt to describe and explain the lens of culture, and show you how it can be used to understand everyday occurrences as well as the more complex and enduring patterns of human experience. We hope to demonstrate how something can be both abstract and concrete, complex and simple. We invite you to look into our chapter through your own lens of culture and hope that the following will help you interpret this lens while lending understanding to those used by others.

But lenses are not passive or benign pointers. Rather, they may change the observation itself by bringing it closer or moving it further away, and by clarifying or distorting an image. Think of a camera lens that zooms in and out. Think also of what we mean by getting a camera lens "in focus"—we see more clearly what is in the middle of the picture while the edges or borders are fuzzy. In this way, the lens of culture calls our attention to parts of our experience, putting those parts in the foreground and center of our world picture. And what do we see most clearly through the lens of culture? We believe that culture highlights most clearly three concepts: *code, conversation,* and *community.* Culture helps us understand the codes of conduct and thought, the ways in people converse and interact, and the communities in which they live.

Gerry Philipsen (1987) was among the first to point out these three unifying concepts of culture. We use his approach as a starting point and offer definitions of cultural codes, conversations, and communities as well as discuss what it means to define culture as a code, conversation, and community. We will use Michael's culture to illustrate these concepts. Michael is of Eastern European Jewish American descent and was raised in New York City.

Cultural Code

A *code* is a system of symbols, rules, meanings, beliefs, values, and images of the ideal. It is a world view or source of order. Geertz (1973) described culture as "webs of significance" (p. 5) and goes on to discuss the patterns of meanings and symbolic forms. Similarly, Carbaugh (1985) discussed culture as "a system of meaning or process of sense making" (p. 32), while Gudykunst and Kim (1992) referred to it as "a unified set of symbolic ideas" (p. 4). There are many ways to see these codes. One way is to examine the types of ceremonies that different cultures perform. These ceremonies reflect what is valued, and each has its own rules and customs. Think about the ceremonies you attend (e.g., weddings, funerals, graduation). What does a funeral mean to you? How do you behave at one? What clothing do you wear for it? In some cultures (e.g., Japan) white is preferred to show respect for death, and others (e.g., United States) prefer dark colors. Think about the rules for job interviewing. When starting a new job, what codes will you need to master to succeed as an employee? Cultures teach us about how to interpret events; how to behave; how to be. This is what we mean when we say, culture is a code.

Jewish American Code: Hebrew/Yiddish, Knowledge, Religion

Michael was encouraged to speak Hebrew, the language of the Jewish Bible when growing up. As eastern Europeans, his grand parents spoke Yiddish, a language combining Hebrew and German that had been used by previous generations of immigrants to assimilate to German culture. His parents, aunts, and uncles spoke this language, though all but the eldest of the next generation were discouraged from its use because of the belief it would interfere with learning Hebrew and would mark them as lower class and foreign.

But this marks only the "language code" of the culture. Remember, that in our definition we discussed code as meaning and values. One of the unifying values in this culture is knowledge—the quest for information and wisdom through study. Historically, Jewish culture has emphasized knowledge, reserving the Sabbath for study.

Finally, Judaism invokes a religious code. This more formal system is cataloged in the Jewish Testament, though it is not used as a rigid set of laws as much as a set of guidelines for life within Michael's cultural group.

Culture as Conversation

Conversation involves patterns of verbal and nonverbal interactions. Borman (1983) talked about culture as "the sum total of ways of living, organizing, and communing" (p. 100), while E. T. Hall and Hall (1989) described it as a program for behavior. Hymes (1974) thought of culture as a speech community, in a sense combining culture as conversation with culture as community. For example, Black English represents a distinctive language code (Hecht, Jackson, & Ribeau, 2003). Culture tells us how to interact with others. Think about traveling to another culture as a salesperson. Who would you contact at a company to make the sale? How should you start the conversation? Now think about meeting people in another culture. Can you ask about personal topics? How quickly is it appropriate to invite someone to your home? Our cultures give us the answers to these questions about how to carry on a conversation.

Jewish American Conversation: Expressive, Aggressive, Political

The conversational style that Michael's culture invokes is a highly expressive and aggressive one. Conversations are animated and issues are engaged in a direct and sometimes provocative manner. Often, these discussions turn to political issues. Michael remembers family dinners becoming debates about the issues of the day, often between him and his elder sister with his father moderating. Just as Jewish religion and biblical interpretations are debated in religious practice, so to is this style of interaction pervasive in the group's cultural conversation.

Culture as Community

A *community* represents a group, shared identities, a sense of membership, who "we" are and the way people organize themselves. Linton (1955) defined culture as an organized group, and Winkelman (1993) talked about it as the people who share the culture. Carbaugh (1989) wrote extensively about "personhood"—what we consider a person to be and how they constitute part of a group. For instance, what does it mean to be a student and how does a student become part of a university student body? Many writers refer to culture as a "way of life," clearly implicating the community or collectivity. Nations are perhaps the most common way of thinking about a culture. Nations have a sense of place but, more importantly, are a group of people. We talk about the French culture, the Russian culture and the Chinese culture.

Jewish American Community:
Temple, Other Jews

Being a Jewish American means feeling part of a group or community. This community is often defined locally around the Temple or Synagogue but more broadly includes all Jews. However, within Judaism there are sects or denominations (Orthodox, Conservative, Reform, and, recently, Reconstruction), and these may define the boundaries of group membership for some. Clearly, non-Jews are defined as outsiders and the pervasiveness of Yiddish words that mark this status is a clear sign of the importance of distinguishing Jews from non-Jews.

Your Cultural Code, Conversation,
and Community

Stop for a moment and think about your own cultural group membership(s). Do you feel aligned with a particular group? Or, perhaps, more than one? Choose a group and see if you can describe its code, conversation, and community. In our college classes, students sometimes describe their fraternity or sorority as a culture, or even the entire university (e.g., Here at Penn State there are people who consider themselves "Penn Staters"). Others choose their ethnic or racial group, religious group, or nationality. Still others define their group by sexual orientation.

Thus far, we have described culture as a lens for viewing the human experience and explained that the lens focuses us on code, conversation and community. We noted, however, that in addition to focusing on a particular picture (e.g, codes or conversations or communities) the lens also provides a perspective on the content—in a sense zooming us in on the details or zooming us out to see the overview.

We approach this issue from a layered perspective—that is, we assume that culture exists on different layers or levels. Some people define culture as only the group (e.g., African Americans) ignoring individuals. We believe that culture is present in individuals as well as shared by collectivities and communities. Philipsen (1987) commented that we need to understand how people manage the tension between the pull of communal life and the impulse of individuals to be free, and that we need a definition of culture that addresses this dynamic push and pull (or "dialectic" as Baxter and Braithwaite explained).

Examining culture from this perspective allows one to consider the polarities and contradictions in social life, rather than viewing culture as simply the group or the individual, or even as existing at some point along a continuum from one to the other (Hecht, 1993). Using a layer metaphor lets us see that polarities are present in all interaction, and it broadens the view of contradictions as polar opposites between two elements (e.g., individual and society). This seems especially relevant to the examination of culture given that culture exists and is expressed on multiple levels. Culture is not only a characteristic of the individual or society; it is a characteristic of both the individual and society as well as the interrelationships between the two. The notion of layering is a metaphor used to represent people's experiences and how they understand their experiences. We experience our social worlds in many ways including behaviorally, emotionally, spiritually, physiologically, experientially, and cognitively. These various realms are like "tides in the ocean, each integrated into the whole ocean (i.e., human experience) and yet each with identifiable characteristics (i.e., a separable realm of the experience)" (Hecht, 1993, p. 77). Thus, the final characteristic of the cultural lens is to identify layers or levels at which culture can be viewed.

The Layers of Culture

The Layered Approach (Baldwin & Hecht, 1995, 2000; Hecht, 1993; Hecht & Baldwin, 1998; Hecht, Jackson, Lindsley, Strauss, & Johnson, 2001) identifies four layers of culture: the personal, enacted, relational, and communal.

The *personal layer* examines one's self-concept or spiritual sense of well-being. Culture can be conceptualized as a characteristic of a person—who they think they are and how they see themselves (self-concept). Above, we illustrated code, conversation, and community by showing how Michael saw himself, his personal take on his culture.

But culture is also expressed in the way people communicate. This is called the *enacted layer* and focuses on how messages express culture. There are both direct and indirect ways of expressing culture. For example, you telling someone directly you are Morman or you can mention specific Morman people who you know to express it indirectly. In addition, culture is enacted through specific practices such as putting up a Christmas tree, singing the National Anthem, fasting during Ramadan, or wearing a dashiki. Not all communication is about expressing identity, but much in what we say and do expresses who we are.

The *relational layer* refers to how one's culture is *formed* through one's relationships, is *invested* in one's relationship to other people, and *exists* in relation to one's other identities. We learn about culture through our families and teachers—through our relationships. We practice our culture with other people (e.g., religious and cultural celebrations, national holidays). Sometimes we even define ourselves in terms of our relationships (e.g., as someone's relational partner, someone's father, someone's friend). Often our cultural groupings are defined in terms of others, a process labeled ingroup or outgroup distinction. These group distinctions are commonly evoked in intercultural communication. Dividing the world into ingroups and outgroups or us versus them is a natural phenomenon and thus, necessary to consider in intercultural research and practice. In fact, this is one of the key concepts in intercultural communication theory. The "intergroup perspective" has been developed by authors such as Tajfel, Giles, and others, and focuses on how people make distinctions between groups in which they feel memberships and those in which they do not, as well as how people communicate' across group lines. Our national cultures, for example, are often contrasted with other groups, particularly if they are traditional enemies and rivals (e.g., England and France). Other examples of ingroups include professions, families, religions, and social clubs. Among adolescents, they can include distinctions based on interests, like the skaters versus the jocks, or based on musical interests. Consider all of the world conflict that results from religious differences. These ingroup and outgroup distinctions play a major role in intergroup relations and underlie some of the most serious problems the world faces today (e.g., in the Middle East and the Balkans-Eastern Europe). At times, just the act of categorizing people into two groups fosters intergroup discrimination (Tajfel, 1981).

What determines the nature of intergroup conflict? Intergroup threats are present when individuals experience anxiety about interacting with outgroups (Tajfel, 1981). Individuals tend to experience high levels of anxiety if there has been little prior contact with or knowledge about outgroup members. Conversely, anxiety also results from a history of intergroup hostility and competition, especially if one group has been in a minority or low-status position. This is evident in recent international conflicts (e.g., Bosnia, Middle East) as well as interracial relations in the United States. Anxiety about interaction also is related to ethnocentricity. Being able to only see your own country or groups' point of view is ethnocentrism. When people want to show solidarity with an ingroup, communication tends to converge and when differences between ingroups and outgroups are being expressed, communication tends to diverge (Giles & Coupland, 1991). Research by Hecht et al. (2003) revealed that satisfaction in ingroup conversations depends on feeling you have some power or control over the conversation as well as the establishment of relational solidarity; satisfaction with outgroup conversations is contingent on establishing common ground through the communication of acceptance, shared world view, not stereotyping, and understanding.

Finally, the *communal layer* focuses on how a group of people or some particular community shares an identity, such as being Jewish or Gay. A community possesses its own identity and shared visions of personhood. This is perhaps the most common way to see culture—as a group of people. When we talk about "Japanese culture" we are not focusing on individual Japanese people but, instead, talking about the collective or group as a whole. This notion of collectivity or community is certainly important to how culture is defined and should not be neglected. In fact, the communal layer is probably the most common way of thinking about culture. Unfortunately, focusing on culture as communal can also be the source of problems because if you assume that members of the culture automatically share common characteristics, you will have stereotyped them. That's why it is important to remember that most of the time when we talk about culture we are talking about characteristics of the community or collectivity, not the individuals.

Connections Among Layers

These four levels, or layers, can work individually, in pairs, or in any combination. For example, you might ask about the values of a specific cultural group (communal level). Or, you might wonder how an individual's view of herself (personal level) effects how she interacts with members of the outgroup (relational level).

In addition, the layers may be in conflict with each other such as a person who feels pride in his or her own religious identity, yet does not wish to participate in religious practices. Another conflict may be a couple who come from two differing groups' (e.g., Muslim and Christian)—they see themselves as possessing a relationship or relational culture of their own (relational level), though the larger collectivity (communal level) may not approve.

Moreover, the layers are considered to be interpenetrating, that is they can be found within each other. For example, relationships help shape personal understandings while at the same time relationships are formed out of a person's culture. Thus, the relational layer is in the personal layer and the personal is in the relationship.

When these four layers are considered, culture can be seen as a *negotiation* among the individual, the enacted, the relational, and the communal layers, or any combination of the four. For example, think of how a gay Jew in a committed relationship with a non-Jew negotiates identity and culture at these various levels.

This ends our discussion about conceptualizing culture. Certainly, there are many other factors to consider. Culture is intergenerationally transmitted (e.g, handed down from generation to generation; Murphy, 1986); it is the human-made part of the environment (Triandis, 1990); it encompasses our practices and behaviors that signal our differences (Fiske, 1992). Some would argue that the most important aspect of culture are the power relations and hierarchies it creates (Hall 1986). However, for our purposes the concepts of code, conversation, and community considered at personal, enacted, relational and communal levels is adequate for understanding of culture.

In the remainder of this chapter we will consider a theory of culture at each of the four layers. We hope this review will provide you with some idea about how culture and communication have been conceptualized (although it is not meant to be exhaustive). It should be clear that culture and communication are inseparable. There can be no culture without communication that constitutes and creates the code, is the conversation, and binds and organizes the community. Similarly, communication requires a code to give it meaning and is a set of cultural practices engaged in within and between communities.

Personal Layer

A number of writers have talked about how culture shapes or creates the individual or self. For instance, Hofstede (1991) focused on cultural values. While he was interested in describing the values of entire cultures, other writers have shown how individuals in cultures use these values and are influenced by them (e.g., Triandis, 1994). Communal values influence individual's (e.g., being Japanese in a collectivistic country) selfconcepts and behavior. Space precludes a discussion of all such values, so here we focus on *Individualism/ Collectivism* and *Gender* as cultural characteristics of individuals.

Individualism/Collectivism. Individualism versus collectivism is one of the most basic cultural dimensions. According to Tomkins (1984), an individual's psychological makeup is the result of this cultural dimension. For example, he reported that human beings in Western Civilization have tended toward positive or negative self-celebration, and in Asian thought harmony between humans and nature is another alternative that is represented. Whether people live alone, in families, or tribes depends on the degree of individualism-collectivism in a culture (Anderson, 1985). An emphasis on community, shared interests, harmony, tradition, the public good, and maintaining face characterize collectivistic cultures. Collectivism "pertains to societies in which people from birth onwards are integrated into strong, cohesive ingroups, which throughout people's lifetime continue to protect them in exchange for unquestioning loyalty" (Hofstede, 1991, p.51). Societies in which people look after themselves and those in their immediate families and where ties are loose characterize individualistic cultures (Hofstede, 1991).

In individualistic Western cultures, people rely on personal judgments (Triandis, 1994), whereas an emphasis on harmony among people, between people and nature, and on collective judgement can be seen in people from Eastern cultures (Gudykunst et al., 1996). People living in the United States, for example, tend to place a very high value on individualism (Bellah, Madsen, Sullivan, Swidler, & Tipson, 1985; Kim, 1994). More traditional and collectivist cultures place value on the interdependence among individuals and conforming to social roles and norms whereas individualistic and less traditional cultures stress independence in the pursuit of personal goals and interests and self expression. The best and worst in U.S. culture can be attributed to individualism. If we think of some of the positive elements, we may consider individualism as the basis of freedom, creativity, and economic incentive. The majority of Americans believe "that a man [or woman] by following his [or her] own interest, rightly understood, will be led to do what is just and good" (Tocqueville, 1945, p. 409).

On the other hand, individual consciousness may disrupt the systemic nature of life on earth by pulling humans out of their ecological niche, that is separating humans from nature with the increasing isolation and industrialization (Bateson, 1972). The downside of individualism includes alienation, loneliness, materialism and difficulty interacting with those from less individualistic cultures (Condon & Yousef, 1983; Hofstede, 1991). Thus, our individualism leads us to value creative ways of expressing ourselves (e.g., the person who is the "life of the party") but may challenge our ability to work together as a team (e.g., sacrifice for the common good).

Even though the United States is the most individualistic country (Hofstede, 1984/1990), certain ethnic groups and geographic regions vary in their degrees of individualism. For instance, African Americans place a great deal of emphasis on individualism (Collier, Ribeau, & Hecht, 1986; Hecht et al., 2003; Hecht & Ribeau, 1984: Kochman, 1981), whereas Mexican Americans place greater emphasis on relational solidarity and their families (Hecht & Ribeau, 1984; Hecht, Ribeau, & Sedano, 1990). This translates into a general tendency for African Americans to "tell it like it is" in conversations in order to preserve authenticity and Mexican Americans to focus on the relational with others in conversations, sometimes avoiding negative information in the process. There is a tendency to relay on *simpatia,* a preference for harmony in interpersonal, relations such that negative comments may be ignored in a conversation.

Of course, the very notion of individualism suggests that a person's own values may transcend his or her cultural group membership. In fact, there is evidence that personal individualism may transcend cultural differences for certain variables. Singelis (1996) urged us to examine the connection between context and individual variables. Schmidt (1983), for example, compared the effects of crowding on people from the United States (an individualistic culture) and Singapore (a collectivist culture). Schmidt hypothesized that similar psychological variables would underlie people's stress and annoyance responses to crowding. He studied students at a U.S. university bookstore during the first 3 days of the quarter (a typically crowded time) and Singaporean high school students in their places of residence and found similar perceptions for both cultures on the relationships among personal control on annoyance and stress about environmental crowding. What we conclude is that no culture or individual is completely individualistic or collectivistic. All have some conception of the person as well as the group. What differs is the relative value placed on each and how people work out the competing pressures (e.g., the role of sacrifice).

Gender. Although gender is typically thought of (and investigated as) as an individual characteristic, it has been neglected as a cultural dimension. We conceptualize this dimension of culture as the rigidity and definition of gender roles. Cultures that are more rigid expect members to act within a narrow range of gender-related behaviors and stress traditional gender-role identification. Hofstede (1984/1990) described masculine traits within such a world view typically as attributes such as strength, assertiveness, competitiveness, achievement, and ambitiousness, whereas feminine traits are attributes such as affection, compassion, nurturance, and emotionality. More rigid societies prescribe masculine behavior for men and feminine behavior for women, although there is a tendency for women in masculine societies to be "tougher" than women in feminine societies (Hofstede, 1998). "The masculinity-femininity dimension relates to people's self-concept: Who I am and what is my task in life" (Hofstede, 1984/1990, p. 84). A cross-cultural study comparing advertisements from Japan, Russia, Sweden, and the United States suggests that countries can be characterized along these masculine feminine dimensions. Milner and Collins (2000) discovered that television advertisements from feminine countries (Sweden, Russia) compared with more masculine countries (Japan, United States) contained more depictions of relationships for male and female characters. They conclude that a feminine country's dominant orientation is reflected in media, specifically television advertising and the depiction of characters in relationships.

Cross-cultural research shows that while young girls are expected to be more nurturant than boys though there is considerable variation from country to country (E. T. Hall, 1984). An important area to explore are the kinds of goals individuals value in their lives. Hofstede's (1984/1990) work examined the degree to which people of both sexes in a culture endorse primarily masculine or feminine goals. Goals such as competitiveness, assertiveness, ambitiousness, and a focus on material success are considered masculine, whereas nurturance, compassion, modesty, and a focus on the quality of life are considered feminine goals (Hofstede, 1998). A cross-cultural study with male and female Israeli Arab students (more traditional collectivist culture) and male and female Israeli Jewish students (more individualistic less traditional culture) demonstrated the role that culture plays in discriminatory behavior (Lobel, Mashraki-Pedhatzur, Mantzur, & Libby, 2000). Lobel et al. (2000) presented students with candidates for class representative, one male with traditional feminine interests (ballet) and characteristics (slight build) and one male with masculine interests (football) and characteristics (broad-shouldered build). The study revealed that all participants discriminated against the feminine male, but the Arab students discriminate more explicitly. They were less likely to elect him, to believe that others would freely choose him, and to think that he should be elected. Additionally, they liked him less than the masculine candidate and compared with the masculine candidate were less likely to report engaging in activities with him. The authors conclude that any transgression against gender norms in Arab culture is looked upon more harshly because of the collectivist tradition while more individualistic Israeli Jews are judged less critically for deviating from gender norms.

Given all of the differences we have described, what goals should we adopt? Research suggests that androgyny (combinations of both feminine and masculine goals) results in more self-esteem, social competence, success, and intellectual development for both men and women. In other words, it is actually healthier for both male and females to adopt more androgynous patterns of behavior. For instance, males may harm their health by internalizing emotions rather than externalizing them as women are usually apt to do (Buck, 1984). It would be helpful for those used to a "masculine" style to express their emotions. Being concerned with both the task (traditionally "masculine" qualities) and emotional issues (traditionally "feminine" pursuits) is important in our intimate relationships. Inman's (1996) research on men's same sex friendships showed that self-disclosure and expressivity were as vital to men's friendships as "continuity, perceived support and dependability, shared understandings, and perceived compatibility" (p. 100). Self-disclosure and expressivity benefit friendships, both male and female (Jones & Dembo, 1989). Furthermore, over time romantic partners are more less satisfied if partners adhere to stereotyped gender role expectations (Ickes, 1993). Quakenbush (1990) discovered that in dating and sexual relationships, androgynous men compared with men with masculine and undifferentiated gender roles, reported the most comfort.

Jackson (1997) provided yet another argument for the advantageousness of androgyny when he speaks of the cultural crossroads Black masculinity occupies. Black men alternate between embracing and rejecting the more rigid gender roles of American mainstream culture and the more androgynous and interdependent gender roles with their own culture. He believes that androgyny is an approach that should be taken given the difficulty of separating masculine and feminine characteristics. Individuals need all characteristics to get a sense of a cultural self and to foster a strong community (Jackson & Dangerfield, 2003).

In short, we discussed the dimensions of individualism-collectivism and gender as part of how culture shapes or creates the individual or self. Individualism refers to cultures where individuals are more loosely connected and focus on personal achievement whereas collectivism references cultures were strong and cohesive groups are the norm. However, all cultures display characteristics of both. Similarly, we argue that displaying masculine and feminine qualities is advantageous, even though cultures can be characterized broadly as masculine and feminine and gender roles vary to a great extent.

Relational Layer

The relational level focuses on relationships between different elements of a culture (e.g., how it balances individualism and collectivism), how a culture defines relationships between people, and on the relationships between people that are culturally based (i.e., intergroup relations; relations between members of different cultural groups). For example, Hecht et al. (1993) talked about how African Americans attempt to balance the desire for sharing or commonality with the group and the value placed on individuality (i.e., the relationship between different elements of the culture). Gaines and his colleagues (1996; Gaines & Ickes, 1997) studied interethnic romantic relations, concluding that people in these types of relationships are often more romantic (i.e., relationships between people that are culturally based). Others have been concerned with prejudice and discrimination between groups (Hecht, 1998), that is how a culture defines relationships between people. Thus, the relational level can focus us on the relationships between individual members of groups or between and among the groups themselves.

Co-Cultural Communication Theory is one example of a relational layer approach that focuses on the relationships between groups and their members. *The Dialectical Approach* (see chap. 15, this volume) focuses on how elements of a particular culture relate to each other (e.g., how competing values are balanced) as well as how the balances struck among the elements within one culture (e.g., individualism and collectivism) relate to the balance in a second culture.

Co-Cultural Communication Theory. Co-Cultural Communication Theory examines an assortment of domestic co-cultures in the United States in terms of elements such as age, class, sex, education, ethnicity, religion, abilities, affection or sexual orientation. Orbe (1996, 1998a, 1998b) described this perspective as an examination of how those traditionally without societal power communicate "within oppressive dominant structures" (Orbe, 1998a, p. 1). The term co-culture is used in order to avoid negative connotations from terms that have been employed to describe the many cultures within the United States. The connotations of "subculture" and "minority communication" suggest that less importance is attached to a group member's communication among the variety of co-cultures that exist in our society (e.g., people of color, women, gays/lesbians/bisexuals). Orbe preferred co-culture "to signify that no one culture in our society is inherently superior over other co-existing cultures" (Orbe, 1998a, p. 2).

Co-Cultural Theory is predicated on the belief that some co-cultures have gained dominance in major social institutions over time. As a result, these co-cultural groups (e.g., European Americans and men) figure centrally in predominant social structures such as religion, corporations, and legal entities rendering other co-cultural groups marginal. Co-Cultural Communication Theory examines how dominant and under-represented group members interact with each other and across groups and is based on the assumption that some co-cultural groups (e.g., people of color) have developed communication orientations in the United States to survive because of their marginalized positions. Orbe (1998a) identified two premises of the theory:

1. Although representing a widely diverse array of lived experiences, co-cultural group members including women, people of color, gays/lesbians/bisexuals, people with disabilities, and those from a lower socioeconomic status will share similar societal positioning that renders them marginalized and underrepresented within dominant structures, and;
2. To confront oppressive dominant structures and achieve any measure of success, co-cultural group members adopt certain communication orientations when functioning within the confines of public communicative structures. These communication strategies will be addressed later in the chapter.

These premises recognize the similarities in co-cultural group members experiences of sexism, racism, heterosexism, ableism (i.e., discrimination against those who are not able-bodied), and classism, while acknowledging different experiences in the daily lives of co-cultural group members. For example, two women can both be African American, but one could also be lesbian and experience homophobia in addition to racism. Co-cultural group members may overhear racist and sexist comments in the workplace (e.g., "Since we hired more women, there has been more gossip around here." "You know how lazy Mexicans are…") and use an avoidance strategy with co-workers.

Dialectical Approach. A Dialectical Approach, while not a theory, highlights another aspect of the relational nature of intercultural communication. Whereas, Co-Cultural Communication Theory is concerned with how members of groups as well as the groups themselves relate to each other, the Dialectical Approach focuses us on how the elements of culture are related. How does one cultural value relate to another value? For example, a fraternity may value good grades but also see itself as a "party" group. How does a member balance the need to study for an important exam with the pressure to party that night? A school may be trying to develop a strong sense of community that includes responsibility to the group at the same time it wants its students to be creative. How does a student balance the individuality needed for creativity with the need to be part of the collective whole?

Drawing on previous theory, Baxter and colleagues suggested that the elements of communication are dialectically related to each other (for a summary of this approach to communication and relationships, see Baxter & Montgomery, 1996; Rawlins, 1992). This means that concepts like academics and partying, and creativity and community are not separate from each other. That is, we don't focus on one or the other, or even a fixed combination of each. Instead, they are competing or opposite pressures that work at the same time. If the culture values both we are unlikely to escape their influence. In fact, one would not want to, from a dialectical perspective, because we are interested in multiple points of view that affect each other. Rather than looking for a resolution in a middle ground or compromise, the Dialectical Approach highlights the continuing need to balance and rebalance competing forces. In fact, these forces are seen as part of the same whole or entity rather than as separate and inconsistent with each other. Thus, the dialectics or contradictions cause tension in relationships and cultures, but this tension is necessary and not necessarily antagonistic (Werner & Baxter, 1994). For example, individual autonomy and interdependence with another person defines any relationship. A person desires to be an individual while at the same time establishing a connection with another person. Both elements are necessary even though they are in opposition.

The Dialectical Approach has been applied to the study of culture by a number of authors (e.g., Carbaugh, 1989; Hecht et al, 2003; Martin, Nakayama, & Flores, 1998). We can identify at least two additional implications for the study of communication and culture that the Dialectical Approach gives us. First, it implies that both culture and the members of the culture change are in process. When we communicate with others, we can not assume that if a person belongs to a particular culture he or she will have certain characteristics. Individuals change during their lifetime, as does the cultural environment in which they live. For instance, the United States in the 1980s is not the same as the United States in the 21st century.

Second, dialectics places an emphasis on the relational rather than individual characteristics of people and culture. Looking at culture dialectically means that we look at the holistic relationships, that we focus attention between the aspects of intercultural communication, individuals and individuals in relationship to other groups. Martin et al. (1998) asked "Can we understand culture without understanding communication and vice versa (p. 6)?" They provide an example of the former Yugoslavia by asking "Can we understand the conflict in the former Yugoslavia by only looking at the Serbian experience" (p. 6)?

Cultural studies have described a number of specific dialectics. Some of these are characteristic of a particular culture (e.g., the dialectic between sharing and individuality with African American culture described above), while others tend to be present in most, perhaps all cultures. We will discuss more of the general dialectics in greater detail.

The first of these is the *cultural-individual* dialectic which refers to the idea that intercultural communication contains elements of both culture and individuals, that is individuals may have behaviors that are not shared by anyone else (e.g., a certain, idiosyncratic way of using language), and they may share communication patterns with others whom they share cultural practices (e.g., family members). For instance, your younger brother may call a lemon a neebee, but he may also call your Aunt, Tante, like everyone else in your family. A second dialectic, that of *present-future/history-past*, represents the need to balance our past with the present and future. What is the relationship between past, present and future? Does the culture value one more than the other? Or does the culture value the flow from one to another? For some, the past is viewed through the present. Think about the Israeli-Palestinian conflict. Both Israelis and Palestinians share an important tie to Jerusalem, their holy city. To understand the conflict, we need to know the history of each people, yet the current view of the conflict depends on the context of what occurs today.

The relational elements are also emphasized in the final two dialectics: personal-social and privilege-disadvantaged. The *personal-social* dialectic emphasizes the connection between an individual's social roles and his or her personal characteristics. When a police officer talks about certain topics he or she may be interpreted in certain ways depending on the context. Imagine how differently you would interpret what the officer was saying if it were uttered while writing a ticket versus while relaxing with you at a local pizza pub. The final dialectic, *privilege-disadvantage*, involves the role of power in intercultural communication. We have different types of privilege and power (e.g., social position and political preference) as individuals, which we carry with us into interactions. For instance, the intercultural interactions of a U.S. tourist in Africa will be influenced by economic power and this establishes a different relationship with the citizens of the country than if the visitor was a worker who came from a poor nation in Southeast Asia.

Enacted Layer

It is important to understand that culture is not merely an abstract way of understanding the world. Rather, an important element of culture are the ways it is enacted—that is, how it is expressed by behavior, particularly communication, and how these behaviors are themselves cultural practices. So, our messages can announce our culture to others. But at the same time, culture cannot exist without its being expressed. So when we communicate we create and recreate our culture. *Communication Accommodation Theory* provides an excellent example of culture as enactment. It examines the process of how identity may affect communication and references how individuals are motivated to move towards or away from others through language and nonverbal communication. In addition, *Co-Cultural Communication Theory,* introduced in the previous section, not only talks about the relationships between groups but also how these relationships get enacted in communication. We continue our discussion of this theory below and link it to research on ethnic similarities and differences in communication.

Orbe (1996, 1998a, 1998b) revealed six factors that influence how co-cultural group members communicate within dominant social structures by examining oral narratives of individuals possessing a wide variety of co-cultural experiences. These factors include preferred outcome, communication approach, abilities, perceived costs and reward, field of experiences, and situational context. The six interrelated factors affect the communication and communication orientation group members possess. Each of these factors is intimately connected to the others. *Preferred outcome* refers to the goal that a person has for an interaction and may affect the *communication approach* an individual adopts, that is the voice that a person uses which can be assertive, aggressive, or nonassertive. "Each person asks herself or himself the following question, 'What communication behavior will lead to the effect that I desire'" (Orbe, 1998a, p. 5)? Consciously or unconsciously, co-cultural group members answer this question about how their communication behavior affects the relationship between themselves and dominant group members. Nonassertive behavior describes actions where a co-cultural member puts others' needs before his or her own by being inhibited and nonconfrontational. Aggressive communication includes hurtfully expressive actions that are self-promoting and controlling (Orbe, 1998a). Somewhere in the middle of these two is assertive behavior that is characterized by expressive communication that enhances the self and takes others into consideration. Orbe (1996) described 12 strategies that co-cultural group members use when communicating with dominant group members. These include:

1. Avoidance is maintaining a distance with others, not getting involved, and only communicating with people that are different from yourself when necessary. A young gay man described this:

   "I don't get involved too much…They will have these conversations…but I don't get involved because I don't want to lead them on one way or the other (concerning his closeted identity). I just communicate what has to be done" (p. 163)

2. Idealized communication refers to no change in communication when conversing with others different from yourself. The idea that "people are people," means a person emphasizes individuals' similarities and ignores differences.

3. Mirroring is like assimilation. This strategy is used when a person wants "to make their co-cultural identities less visible while adopting those behaviors of the dominant culture" (p. 163). This is when a person "talks white" and avoids the use of slang and ethnic idioms.

4. Respectful communication is marked by graciousness, being less threatening and less assertive, and the use of formal titles. When talking to male supervisors, a 20 year-old woman stated "I am very aware of their expectations of me and try to follow them."

5. Self-censorship occurs when a person says nothing and "swallows it." A person could be afraid of another's reaction to an open and honest response, so they "blow it off" and say nothing.

6. Extensive preparation entails cognitive rehearsal and research. An African American man talked about how he prepared talking with European American men so that "I am much more through and pointed" (p. 165). Before an encounter with someone outside of your group, you extensively prepare.

7. Countering stereotypes refers to the negation of existing stereotypes. "I guess you can say that I make more of an effort to be a positive person so that people can see that those qualities [black, lesbian, woman] are not negative ones" (p. 165). A person tries to set a positive examples through their behavior without debating dominant group members about stereotypical beliefs.

8. Manipulating stereotypes is a reaction to dominant's cultures stereotypes by conforming to these stereotypes for personal gain. For instance, crying, flirting, or sweet-talking to "manipulate men."

9. Self-assured communication occurs when a person simply is themselves. This means exhibiting positive self-esteem. "I let my accomplishments and personality speak for me," said a Mexican American man (p. 166).

10. Increased visibility means increasing other people's awareness of the self. Things such as wearing signs of your background and occupying space where others can see you are ways to increase visibility.

11. Utilization of liaisons is using other individuals when interacting with those from the dominant culture. Liaisons include friends, advisors, colleagues, and empathetic supervisors.

12. Confrontational tactics are using direct and belligerent "in your face" methods when interacting with the dominant culture. A European American gay man discussed how he liked confronting heterosexuals with his homosexuality, "Flaming was not the word for me, I mean I wanted everyone to know and deal with it" (p. 167).

Assimilation, accommodation, and separation are three major outcomes of these interactions. If a person "adopts" mainstream culture and eliminates cultural differences to fit in with dominant society, this is assimilation. On the other hand, if a person, rejects

Table 20.1

Nine General Co-Cultural Communication Orientations

Strategy	Examples
Nonassertive assimilation	Emphasize similarities Develop positive face Self-censorship Avert controversy
Assertive assimilation	Bargaining Manipulating stereotypes Overcompensating Extensive preparation
Aggressive assimilation	Dissociating Mirroring Strategic distancing Self-ridicule
Nonassertive acco0mmodation	Increasing visibility Dispelling stereotypes
Assertive accommodation	Communicating self Intergroup networking Using liaisons Educaiting others
Aggressive accommodation	Confronting tactics Power moves
Nonassertive separation	Avoidance Maintaining interpersonal barriers
Assertive separation	Communicating self Intragroup networking Exemplify strengths Embrace stereotypes
Aggressive separation	Exert personal power Verbal attacking Sabotaging dominant group efforts

Note. Adapted from Orbe (1998a, 1998b).

the idea of forming a common bond with dominant groups or even other co-cultural groups and limits the amount of interaction with "outsiders," the outcome is separation. Accommodation falls in the middle and refers to an insistence that the dominant cultural rules change to incorporate the life experiences of co-cultural group members. Orbe (1998a, 1998b) crossed the three outcomes with the three communication approaches described earlier to arrive at nine general communication strategies co-cultural members use shown in Table 20.1.

Research by Hecht and colleagues (e.g., Hecht et al, 2003; Hecht et al, 1990) focuses attention on what some co-cultural members, specifically Mexican Americans and African

Americans, find to be satisfying communication with European Americans and with one another. Their work provides examples of what a co-cultural perspective would call preferred outcome. They (Hecht & Ribeau, 1984; Hecht et al., 1990) found that Mexican American's preferred a comfortable communication climate developed by both parties where individuals could honestly express themselves without fear of retaliation, judgment, or rejection. Work with African Americans revealed similar themes; acceptance, emotional expressiveness, understanding, authenticity, achieving desired outcomes, and not feeling controlled and manipulated were important (Hecht et al., 2003).

We do need to recognize that individuals will have different *abilities* to establish and enact strategies that work for their goals. A person may not have the skill to surmount a nonassertive orientation to communication in an organization, for example, when a more assertive approach may be warranted for success in promotions (Orbe, 1998b).

Individuals may consider the *costs and rewards* of different communicative practices before they engage in them. For instance, Orbe's (1998b) work in organizations shows that taking an assertive assimilation stance may bring benefits to co-cultural group members in the form of social approval and salary increases. These costs and rewards are often determined by *field of experiences* which are the sum of a person's lived experiences. Past experience helps individuals recognize the consequences and efficacy of certain strategies in different situations. Orbe (1998b) quoted a young Mexican American man who believes that "my father's influence and general background has a lot to do with the way I act in public" (p. 250). Finally, given that situations influence how an individual decides on communication choices, the notion of *situational context* plays a central role in co-cultural theory. The number of other co-cultural members present in a situation, for instance, may affect whether a person manipulates stereotypes in the work place.

Communal Layer

Finally, we come to the communal layer, the layer probably most commonly thought about as culture. Communities, or collectivities, are the groups that share a common culture. Culture can be defined as these groupings, although we prefer to see the community as one way of viewing culture in order to avoid defining culture exclusively as people rather than as codes, enactments, and relationships discussed above. The *Ethnography of Communication* approach provides an excellent example of the communal layer.

The ethnography of communication provides us with a useful way of describing the place of speaking for people from different cultures and misunderstandings that can arise when people from different social groups interact (Carbaugh, 1985, 1989, 1993; Fitch, 1998; Philipsen, 1975, 1987, 1998). This method focuses on collecting and analyzing information about how social meaning is conveyed. More specifically, it illuminates how distinct cultural groups instill styles of communication among themselves and interpret others' communication (Saville-Troike, 1989). "The ethnography of communication takes language first and foremost as a socially situated cultural form, while recognizing the necessity to analyze the code itself and the cognitive process of its speakers and hearers" (Saville-Troike, 1989, p. 3). The ethnography of communication would be useful for exploring the interactions of ethnic groups that use the same language such as English-speaking Cuban Americans and European Americans. It would also prove beneficial for the exploration of groups that share the same language (e.g., African and European Americans) but have different speech codes (Orbe & Harris, 2001). We can compare communication styles within groups as well as across groups.

The idea of a speech community is central to the ethnography of communication. A group of people is considered to be a speech community when they share goals and styles of communication in ways not like those outside of the group (Philipsen, 1998; Saville-Troike, 1989). There are four assumptions that ground the ethnography of communication (Philipsen. 1998). One is that meaning is created and shared among members of cultural communities. The differences in groups can be defined by geography and language and also by less visible boundaries such as class. Second, because speech codes are guided by a system or some order, those in a cultural group need to coordinate their actions, that is members of a group must share an understanding of what behavior means. Third, individual groups have particular meanings and actions, and fourth, the assignment of meaning is determined by each cultural groups' distinct resources.

Work by Philipsen (1975) and Carbaugh (1998) demonstrated these assumptions by showing how cultural orientations relate to living. For instance, Carbaugh (1998) found that silence in Blackfoot culture is considered to be a listener-active mode of nonverbal presence important for "communicating with animals and spirits." Silence allows one to maintain interconnectedness, a valued event in Blackfoot culture, while public speaking threatens to disrupt the harmony and is, therefore, considered risky. Philipsen's work in a community he called Teamsterville also demonstrated the importance of examining cultural meaning about the value and importance of talk from the participant's point of view. He found that a sense of place in terms of "marking a place for speech" was different from many other communities; front porches and street comers represented proper places for people to interact. "In Teamsterville it is the presence of such identity-matched personae in a location traditionally set aside for sociability among them, to the exclusion of others, that marks a place for speaking" (p. 224).

When we look at the four assumptions posited by Philipsen (1998), we can see how misunderstanding may arise, particularly when individuals fail to recognize that what they consider to be appropriate use of language or what people should and should not say may not be considered the same in another speech community. For instance, Carbaugh's (1993) analysis of a series of 1987 Phil Donahue talk shows from the former Soviet Union demonstrated that public discussion of sexual matters was not preferable. According to Carbaugh, Donahue brought a private, matter to a public forum when he discussed sex in a rational, technical, and individual way. However, in Russian culture public talk with outsiders should be reserved, while private talk shows a greater expressiveness among insiders. This is in contrast to the values expressed in the United States, particularly on television talk shows.

The end result of the ethnography of communication are descriptions of how diverse communities use speech and other channels of communication. Hymes (1974) wrote that "One needs fresh lands of data, one needs to investigate directly the use of language in contexts of situation, so to discern patterns of proper speech activity" (p. 3). The methods of inquiry include the ethnographic tradition of participant observation where a researcher spends extended periods of time observing and studying a community. What researchers strive to accomplish is a holistic picture of communication behavior in the context of the community or network, "so that any use of channel and code takes it place as part of the resources upon which the members draw" (Hymes, 1974, p. 4).

The idea here is to examine all facets of life that may impact communication behavior such as social institutions, roles and responsibilities, cultural values and beliefs, and the history of a community. "The starting point is the ethnographic analysis of the communicative conduct of a community" (Hymes, 1974, p. 9). This includes paying attention to the participants, the topics of conversation, the setting, and the event.

One goal of the ethnography of communication is communicative competence, skills that a speaker needs to know in order to communicate appropriately within a given speech community (Saville-Troike, 1989). To be successful an individual needs to know the rules of interaction, as well as the cultural rules that dictate the content and context of interaction. That is, what should be said to whom, when, and how. One simple question that a researcher can ask is, "What is being communicated" (Saville-Troike, 1989)? The ethnography of communication makes an important contribution in its focus on what a person needs to know to communicate appropriately in various contexts and the sanctions that may occur for violations of communicative competence in a speech community.

Summary

Intercultural communication is a complex interaction of codes, conversations, and communities. Cultures operate in layers or levels, which may be described as personal layers, enacted layers, relational layers, and communal layers. These four layers can work individually or in pairs, or in any combination. These layers can also be interpenetrating—meaning that they may be found within each other.

With respect to the personal layer, individualism/collectivism and gender are key variables that shape this layer. The relational layer focuses on relationships between different elements of a culture, and how the relationships between people are defined. In this layer co-cultures or sub-cultures exist that are part of the dominant culture, but exist independently of the dominant culture. The dialectical approach is also an aspect of the relational layer of cultures, and it examines how opposing tensions or dialectics affect individuals within these cultures. The enacted layer is an examination of how culture is expressed by behavior or more specifically, how it is communicated to members of the dominant culture and co-culture. Finally, the communal layer of a culture refers to the groups that share a common culture, and is most likely what people think of when they hear the word culture.

In the study of human communication no other variable has probably received more attention than interpersonal communication. The interest in the dynamics of two people communicating began slowly in communication research, but now is one of the most significant areas of research which the next chapter introduces.

Questions For Discussion

1. Why do the authors of this chapter say that culture is composed of many layers?
2. What is an example of individualism/collectivism in the U.S.?
3. Why has gender been neglected as a cultural dimension?
4. What are co-cultures? In which co-culture do you exist?
5. How has the theory of relational dialectics been applied to culture?

References

Anderson, P. A. (1985). Nonverbal immediacy in interpersonal communication. In A. W. Siegman & S. Feldstein (Eds.), *Multichannel integrations of nonverbal behavior* (pp. 1–36). Hillsdale, NJ: Lawrence Erlbaum Associates, Inc.

Baldwin, J. R., & Hecht, M. L. (1995). The layered perspective of cultural (in)tolerance(s): The roots of a multidisciplinary approach. In R. Wiseman (Ed.), *Intercultural communication theory* (pp. 59–91). Thousand Oaks, CA: Sage.

Baldwin, J. R., & Hecht, M. L. (2000). *The social construction of race. Studies in International Relations,* 20, 85–115.

Bateson, G. (1972). *Steps to an ecology of mind.* New York: Ballantine.

Baxter, L. A., & Montgomery, B. M. (1996). *Relating: Dialogues and dialectics.* New York: Guilford.

Bellah, R., Madsen, R., Sullivan, W., Swidler, A., & Tipson, S. (1985). *Habits of the heart: Individualism and commitment in American life.* Berkeley: University of California Press.

Borman, E. (1983). Symbolic convergence: Organizational communication and culture. In L. Putnam & M. Pacanowsky (Eds.), *Communication and organizations: An interpretive approach* (pp. 99–122). Newbury Park, CA: Sage.

Buck, R. (1984). *The communication of emotion.* New York: Guilford.

Carbaugh, D. (1985). Culture communication and organizing. *International and Intercultural Communication Annual,* 8, 30–47.

Carbaugh, D. (1989). *Talking American: Cultural discourses on Donahue.* Norwood, NJ: Ablex.

Carbaugh, D. (1993). "Soul" and "self: Soviet and American cultures in conversation. *Quarterly Journal of Speech*, 79, 182–200.

Carbaugh, D. (1998). "I can't do that! But I can actually see around corners": American Indian students and the study of "public communication." In J. N. Martin, T. K. Nakayama, & L. A. Flores (Eds.), *Readings in cultural contexts* (p. 160–172). Mountain View, CA: Mayfield.

Collier, M. J., Ribeau, S. A., & Hecht, M. L. (1986). Intracultural communication rules and outcomes within three domestic cultural groups. *International Journal of Intercultural Relations*, 10, 439–457.

Condon, J. C, & Yousef, F. (1983). *An introduction to intercultural communication*. Indianapolis, IN: Bobbs-Merrill.

Fiske, J. (1992). Cultural studies and the culture of everyday life. In L. Grossberg, C. Nelson, & P. Treichler (Eds.), *Cultural studies* (pp. 154–173). New York: Routledge.

Fitch, K. L. (1998). *Speaking relationally: Culture, communication, and interpersonal communication*. New York: Guilford.

Gaines, S. O., Jr., & Ickes, W. (1997). Perspectives on interracial relationships. In S. Duck (Ed.), *Handbook of personal relationships* (2nd ed., pp. 197–220). Chichester, England: Wiley.

Gaines, S. O., Jr., Rios, D. L, Granrose, C, Bledsoe, K., Farris, K., Page, M. S., et al. (1996, January). *Romanticism and resource exchange among interethnic/interracial couples*. Paper presented at the annual meeting of the Social Psychologists in Texas, Arlington.

Geertz, C. (1973). *The interpretation of cultures*. New York: Basic Books.

Giles, H., & Coupland, N. (1991). *Language: Contexts and consequences*. Pacific Grove, CA: Brooks/Cole.

Gudykunst, W. B., & Kim, Y. Y. (1992). *Communicating with strangers: An approach to intercultural communication*. New York: McGraw Hill.

Gudykunst, W. B., Matsumoto, Y, Ting-Toomey, S., Nishida, T., Kim, K., & Heyman, S. (1996). Influence of cultural individualism-collectivism, self-construals, and individual values on communication styles across cultures. *Human Communication Research*, 22, 510–543.

Hall, E. T. (1984). *The dance of life: The other dimension of time*. Garden City, NY: Anchor.

Hall, E. T., & Hall, M. R. (1989). *Understanding cultural differences*. Yarmouth, ME: Intercultural Press.

Hall, S. (1986). Gramsci's relevance for the study of race and ethnicity. *Journal of Communication Inquiry*, 10, 5–27.

Hecht, M. L. (1993). 2002: A research odyssey Toward the development of a communication theory of identity. *Communication Monographs,* 60, 76–82.

Hecht, M. L. (1998). *Communicating prejudice*. Thousand Oaks, CA: Sage.

Hecht, M. L., & Baldwin, J. R. (1998). Layers and holograms: A new look at prejudice. In M. L. Hecht (Ed.), *Communicating prejudice* (pp. 57–84). Thousand Oaks, CA: Sage.

Hecht, M. L., Jackson, R. L., & Ribeau, S. (2003). *African American communication: Exploring identity and culture* (2nd ed.). Mahwah NJ: Lawrence Erlbaum Associates.

Hecht, M. L., & Ribeau, S. (1984). Ethnic communication: A comparative analysis of satisfying communication. *International Journal of Intercultural Relations*, 8, 135–151.

Hecht, M. L., Ribeau, S., & Sedano, M. V. (1990). A Mexican American perspective on interethnic communication. *International Journal of Intercultural Relations, 14*, 31–55.

Hecht, M., Jackson, R. L., Lindsley, S., Strauss, S., & Johnson, K.E. (2001). A layered approach to ethnicity, language and communication. In H. Giles & W. P. Robinson (Eds.), *Handbook of language and social psychology* (pp. 429–450). New York: Wiley.

Hofstede, G. (1984/1990). Culture's consequences. Beverly Hills, CA: Sage. Hofstede, G. (1991). *Cultures and organizations.* London: McGraw-Hill.

Hofstede, G. (1998). Masculinity/femininity as a dimension of culture. In G. Hofstede (Ed.), *Masculinity and femininity: The taboo dimension of national cultures,* (pp. 3–28). Thousand Oaks, CA: Sage.

Hymes, D. (1974). *Foundations in sociolinguistics: An ethnographic approach.* Philadelphia: University of Pennsylvania.

Ickes, W. (1993). Traditional gender roles: Do they make, and then break, our relationships? *Journal of Social Issues, 49*, 71–83.

Inman, C. (1996). Friendships among men: Closeness in the doing. In J. T. Wood (Ed.), *Gendered relationships* (pp. 95–110). Mountain View, CA: Mayfield.

Jackson, R. L. (1997). Black "manhood" as xenophobe: An ontological exploration of the Heglian dialectic. *Journal of Black Studies, 27*, 731–750.

Jackson, R. L. (1999). *The negotiation of cultural identity: Perceptions of European Americans and African Americans.* Westport, CT: Praeger.

Jackson, R. L., & Dangerfield, C. (in press). Defining black masculinity as cultural property: An identity negotiation paradigm. In L. Samovar & R. Porter (Eds.), *Intercultural communication: A reader* (10th ed., pp. 120–131). Belmont, CA: Wadsworth.

Jones, G. P., & Dembo, M. H. (1989). Age and sex role differences in intimate friendships during childhood and adolescence. *Merrill-Palmer Quarterly, 35*, 445–462.

Kim, U. (1994). Individualism and collectivism: Conceptual clarification and elaboration. In U. Kim, H. C. Triandis, K. Cigdem, C. Sang-Chin., & G. Yoon, (Eds.), *Individualism and collectivism: Theory, methods, and applications* (pp. 19–40). Thousand Oaks, CA: Sage.

Kochman, T. (1981). *Black and White styles in conflict.* Chicago: University of Chicago Press.

Linton, R. (1955). *The tree of culture.* New York: Alfred. A. Knopf.

Lobel, T. E., Mashraki-Pedhatzur, S., Mantzur, A., & Libby, S. (2000). *Gender discrimination as a function of stereo-typic and counterstereotypic behavior: A cross-cultural study. Sex Roles, 43,* 395–406.

Martin, J. N., Nakayama, T. K., & Flores, L. A. (1998). A dialectical approach to intercultural communication. In J. N. Martin, T. K. Nakayama, & L. A. Flores (Eds.), *Readings in cultural contexts* (pp. 5–15). Mountain View, CA: Mayfield.

Milner, L. M., & Collins, J. M. (2000). Sex-role portrayals and the gender of nations. *Journal of Advertising, 29*, 67–79.

Murphy, R. F. (1986). *Cultural and social anthropology: An overview.* Englewood Cliff's, NJ: Prentice-Hall.

Orbe, M. P. (1996). Laying the foundation for co-cultural communication theory: An inductive approach to studying "non-dominant" communication strategies and the factors that influence them. *Communication Studies, 47*, 157–176.

Orbe, M. P. (1998a). From the standpoint of traditionally muted groups: Explicating a *co-cultural communication theoretical model. Communication Theory*, 8, 1–26.

Orbe, M. P. (1998b). An outsider within perspective to organizational communication: Explicating the communicative practices of co-cultural group members. *Management Communication Quarterly*, 12, 230–279.

Orbe, M. P., & Harris, T. M. (2001). *Interracial communication: Theory into practice.* Belmont, CA: Wadsworth.

Philipsen, G. (1975). Speaking like a man in teamsterville: Culture patterns of role enactment in an urban neighborhood. *Quarterly Journal of Speech,* 61, 13–22.

Philipsen, G. (1987). The prospect for cultural communication. In L. Kinckaid (Ed.), *Communication theory: Eastern and Western perspectives* (pp. 245–253). New York: Academic.

Philipsen, G. (1998). Places for speaking in teamsterville. In J. N. Martin, T. K. Nakayama, & L. A. Flores (Eds.), *Readings in cultural contexts* (pp. 217–226). Mountain View, CA: Mayfield.

Quackenbush, R. L. (1990). Sex roles and social-sexual effectiveness. *Social Behavior and Personality,* 18, 35–39.

Rawlins, W. K. (1992). *Friendship matters: Communication, dialectics, and the life course.* New York: Aldine de Gruyter.

Saville-Troike, M. (1989). *The ethnography of communication: An introduction.* New York: Basil Blackwell.

Schmidt, D. E. (1983). Personal control and crowding stress: A test of similarity in two cultures. *Journal of Cross-Cultural Psychology,* 14, 221–239.

Singelis, T. M. (1996). The context of intergroup communication. *Journal of Language and Social Psychology,* 15, 360–371.

Tajfel, H. (Ed.). (1981), *Human categories and social groups.* Cambridge, England: Cambridge University Press.

Tajfel, H., & Turner, J. C. (1986). The social identity theory of intergroup relations. In S. Worchel & W. Austin (Eds.), *The social psychology of intergroup relations* (pp. 33–47). Monterey, CA: Brooks/Cole.

Tomkins, S. S. (1984). Affect theory. In K. R. Scherer & P Ekman (Eds.), *Approaches to emotion* (pp. 163–195). Hillsdale, NJ: Lawrence Erlbaum Associates, Inc.

Tocqueville, A. D. (1945). *Democracy in America* (Vol. 1, Bradley, Trans.). New York: Random House.

Triandis, H. C. (1990). Theoretical concepts that are applicable to the analysis of ethnocentrism. In R. W. Brislin (Ed.), *Applied cross-cultural psychology* (pp. 34–55). Newbury Park, CA: Sage.

Triandis. H. C. (1994). Theoretical and methodological approaches to the study of individualism and collectivism. In U. Kim, H. C. Triandis, K. Cigdem, C. Sang-Chin., & G. Yoon, (Eds.), *Individualism and collectivism: Theory, methods, and applications* (pp. 41–51). Thousand Oaks, CA: Sage.

Werner, C. M., & Baxter, L. A. (1994). Temporal qualities of relationships: Organismic, transactional, and dialectical views. In M. L. Knapp & G. R. Miller (Eds.), *Handbook of interpersonal communication* (2nd ed., pp. 323–379). Newbury Park, CA: Sage.

Winkelman, M. (1993). *Ethnic relations in the U.S.* St Paul, MN: West.

Chapter 8

Interpersonal Communication

Charles R. Berger

Interpersonal communication is what builds relationships and allows human beings to form identities. Research in interpersonal communication has grown from a small area of study in the 1960s to one of the more dominant areas of research in human communication. With mediated social interaction now part of interpersonal communication research, the future of research in this area takes on even more significance in trying to understand what happens when two people communicate with each other.

Learning Objectives For This Chapter

- Explain why interpersonal communication is seen as a process of mutual influence
- Identify the key areas of study of interpersonal communication
- Discuss the process of uncertainty reduction
- Explain how interpersonal adaption is used in social interaction
- Describe the key areas of influence of message production
- Discuss the progression of relational development theories
- Identify two areas of inquiry in deceptive communication
- Identify the key differences between interpersonal communication in face-to-face encounters and computer mediated communication

Interpersonal communication concerns the study of social interaction between people. Interpersonal communication theory and research seeks to illuminate how individuals use verbal discourse and nonverbal actions, as well as written discourse, to achieve a variety of instrumental and communication goals such as informing, persuading and providing emotional support to others. Interpersonal communication traditionally has been conceived of as a process that occurs between people encountering each other face-to-face. Increasingly, social interaction is being accomplished through the use of such communication technologies as computers and mobile telephones, thus adding another dimension to this area of communication inquiry. However, technologically mediated social interaction is hardly new, having been possible since land-line telephone technology came into widespread use during the early decades of the 20th century. This older form of mediated interpersonal communication has been examined by communication researchers (Hopper, 1992).

Alternative Perspectives on Interpersonal Communication

An early and pervasive approach to defining interpersonal communication simply asserted that it is face-to-face communication between two people (King, 1979; Smith & Williamson, 1977). By contrast, face-to-face interaction involving from three to some relatively small number of people was defined as small group communication. Although this numerical distinction between interpersonal and small-group communication held sway for some time, Miller and Steinberg (1975) and Berger and Bradac (1982) questioned its utility. These researchers argued that in contrast to the number of individuals involved in an interaction, a more useful attribute for defining interpersonal communication is the kinds of knowledge people employ to make predictions about each other during their interactions.

Miller and Steinberg (1975) labeled social interactions based primarily on knowledge of cultural conventions noninterpersonal communication, since interactions depending upon the use of such conventions fail to individuate people. In these interactions, people are interchangeable members of ostensibly homogenous cultural or ethnic collectives and do not have unique, individual identities. Further, they proposed that social interaction based on what they called "sociological-level" information concerning individuals' demographic attributes such as sex, age, and socio-economic status also failed to provide a basis for interpersonal communication, although such information might provide somewhat more detail about individuals than cultural-level knowledge. Miller and Steinberg argued that interpersonal communication occurs when knowledge of individuals' beliefs, attitudes, and personalities, or what they termed "psychological-level" information, is used by cointerlocutors to make predictions about each others' beliefs, attitudes, and potential actions. When social interaction is based primarily on psychological-level information, messages are tailored to people as unique individuals rather than as members of apparently homogeneous cultural or sociological groupings. Miller and Steinberg recognized that in a large majority of social interactions, all three levels of knowledge are consulted; however, the increasing prominence of psychological-level knowledge in the prediction-making process was posited to be the sine qua non of interpersonal communication.

Cappella (1987) objected to this levels-of-knowledge approach to conceptualizing interpersonal communication on the grounds that people participating in the impersonal, role-defined relationships that Miller and Steinberg (1975) labeled "non-interpersonal relationships" still employ communication to carry out their roles. He observed that many impersonal interactions are nevertheless important in people's everyday lives, for example, transactions occurring in commercial or educational contexts. As an alternative to the knowledge-based approach to defining interpersonal communication, Cappella (1987) proposed that interpersonal communication occurs when an individual's behaviors affect the probability of another's subsequent behaviors with respect to the other's baseline rate of the behavior. When such behavioral influences are mutual, that is, when people alter each other's behaviors such that they deviate from their individual baselines, the preconditions for interpersonal communication have been met.

These two approaches to defining interpersonal communication are not necessarily incompatible. If the mutual influence postulate is granted, it is still possible to ask whether variations in message content (verbal and nonverbal) that are exchanged between people influence their psychological states and actions. Mutual influence may occur when an individual asks a store clerk for a pack of chewing gum or when the same individual requests a paramour's hand in marriage; however, the relationship consequences of these mutually influencing exchanges are radically different. Consequently, it is reasonable to assume that interpersonal communication rests on a foundation of mutual influence, and, further, the degree to which the mutually influencing messages exchanged are personal or impersonal is both constitutive and diagnostic of the type of relationship people have with each other (Bell, Buerkel-Rothfuss, & Gore, 1987; Bell & Healey, 1992). One implication of this perspective is that the concepts of interpersonal communication and interpersonal relationship are distinct. Interpersonal communication affects interpersonal relationships, and relationship states act to shape the communicative activity of those experiencing them.

Historical Antecedents of Interpersonal Communication Inquiry

The study of interpersonal communication developed during the years following World War II and grew out of two distinct areas of social-psychological research that appeared during and after the war (Delia, 1987). The more dominant area of the two concerned the role communication plays in the exercise of persuasion and social influence, while the other area, known as group dynamics, focused on social interaction within small groups. Group dynamics sought to illuminate how group interaction processes influence conformity to group norms, group cohesion, the exercise of social power, and group decision making (Cartwright & Zander, 1968). Although some group-dynamics-inspired interpersonal communication research appeared in this early period, during the 1960s most interpersonal communication research concerned the role that various source, message, channel and receiver factors play in changing audience members' attitudes and behavior; although studies of speech anxiety and communication apprehension also appeared in the interpersonal communication literature of that era.

For the most part, the vast majority of the communication and persuasion research appearing during this period did not examine social influence during the give-and-take of ongoing social interaction. Rather, experimental studies that systematically varied source and message factors were used to investigate the effects of persuasive messages on recipients' attitudes and opinions. Experimental studies of attitude change, inspired by the Yale group's communication and persuasion research program (Hovland & Janis, 1959; Hovland, Janis, & Kelley, 1953; Hovland & Rosenberg, 1960; Sherif & Hovland, 1961) and by balance (Heider, 1958; Newcomb, 1953), congruity (Osgood & Tannenbaum, 1955), dissonance (Brehm & Cohen, 1962; Festinger, 1957, 1964), reactance (Brehm, 1966), and social judgment theories (Sherif & Hovland, 1961; Sherif, Sherif, & Nebergall, 1965) dominated the interpersonal communication literature of that time. As elegant as this experimental approach to the study of persuasion was, unfortunately it did not encourage researchers to investigate reciprocal influence processes in face-to-face interaction (Berger & Burgoon, 1995; Miller, 1987). During face-to-face encounters, social influence is not a one-way street; individuals who enter such encounters with the goal of persuading their cointerlocutors may instead encounter resistance or find themselves being influenced by their partners.

Beginning in the late 1960s and early 1970s, the scope of interpersonal communication research expanded well beyond the narrow confines of the experimentally oriented, communication and persuasion paradigm to include the role social interaction plays in the development, maintenance, and deterioration of personal relationships. Much of this work was inspired by social penetration theory (Altman & Taylor, 1973) and filter theory (Duck, 1973). At the same time, relationships between interpersonal communication and interpersonal attraction began to become a focal point of study, much of this research being motivated by Byrne's studies of interpersonal attraction (Byrne, 1971) and Newcomb's (1961) earlier studies of the acquaintance process. At the same time, interpersonal communication researchers became interested in the study of self-disclosure (Jourard, 1964, 1971), an area that continues to be a research focus (Petronio, 2000, 2002). This period was also marked by a significant increase in attention to the study of nonverbal communication (Knapp, 1972; Mehrabian, 1971), and during the latter part of the 1970s, interpersonal communication research began to reflect increasing concern for understanding the cognitive structures and processes that underlie social interaction with respect to both message production and message comprehension and interpretation (Delia, 1977; Hewes & Planalp, 1987). Deceptive communication was another research focus that emerged during this period (Knapp & Comadena, 1979; Knapp, Hart, & Dennis, 1974). In the ensuing decades, each of these research traditions has continued to attract considerable research attention.

During the 1970s, communication researchers in general and the interpersonal communication researchers in particular expressed considerable frustration over the lack of original theories expressly developed to explain various interpersonal communication phenomena. As a consequence, beginning in this decade, interpersonal communication scholars engaged in debates concerning alternative meta-theoretical perspectives from which to develop communication theory (Benson & Pearce, 1977). Since that time, interpersonal communication researchers have proposed a variety of theories concerned with explaining such phenomena as relationship development, nonverbal communication, message production, interaction adaptation, and deceptive communication.

As the theoretical and research trends set in motion in the 1970s continued to play out during the 1980s, interpersonal communication researchers became increasingly interested in illuminating the communication strategies individuals use to achieve a wide variety of goals (Daly & Wiemann, 1994). This outpouring of strategic communication research was partially set in motion by an inquiry concerned with the conditions under which individuals deploy different strategies to achieve compliance goals (Miller, Boster, Roloff, & Seibold, 1977); an inquiry based on Marwell and Schmidt's (1967) earlier research. This initial work was quickly followed by a spate of compliance-gaining studies (Boster, 1995; Cody, Canary, & Smith, 1994); moreover, during this period the purview of the strategic communication enterprise became rapidly more catholic by expanding the number of different goals studied to include acquiring information, making requests, comforting others, resisting compliance-gaining attempts, and seeking affinity (Daly & Wiemann, 1994). In conjunction with this focus on strategic social interaction, some interpersonal communication researchers developed theories and models of message production, for the purpose of explaining how such strategic interaction takes place (Berger, 1995, 1997a; Greene, 1984, 1997; Wilson, 1990, 1995). This theory development work continued through the 1990s and into the new millennium.

The interpersonal communication domain can be divided into at least six unique but related areas of study, each representing a relatively coherent body of theory and research. These six areas are concerned with (1) uncertainty; (2) interpersonal adaptation; (3) message production; (4) relationship development; (5) deceptive communication; and (6) mediated social interaction. In addition to these theoretically articulated domains, interpersonal communication researchers have addressed such specific topic areas as interpersonal conflict, bargaining, and negotiation and emotion; some of these topics will be addressed as each of the six research areas is considered below.

Uncertainty in Interpersonal Communication

Although individuals enter social interactions with funds of cultural, sociological, and psychological knowledge regarding their interaction partners (Miller & Steinberg, 1975), they cannot be completely certain of their conversational partners' current emotional states, beliefs, attitudes, and future actions, even when their interaction partners are familiar and perhaps even well known to them (Berger, 1997b). That is, it is impossible to predict accurately all of these internal states and potential future actions at any given point in time. Consequently, when individuals engage in social interaction they do so under conditions of more or less uncertainty, but uncertainty is never completely absent. Moreover, because individuals and social relationships are dynamic, and sometimes highly so, relative certainty at one point in time may be replaced by substantial uncertainty at another. Individuals who are now apparently "well known" may later become "strangers."

In addition, because individuals harbor uncertainties about cointerlocutors, they must, by necessity, have uncertainties about how they should act toward their partners; consequently, individuals experience uncertainty with respect both to themselves and others. These uncertainties are maximal when strangers meet, but uncertainties can also arise in close relationships of long duration (Planalp & Honeycutt, 1985; Planalp, Rutherford, & Honeycutt, 1988). Uncertainty Reduction Theory (URT) (Berger & Calabrese, 1975; Berger & Gudykunst, 1991) proposes that individuals must reduce their uncertainties to some degree in order to be able to fashion verbal discourse and actions that will allow them to achieve their interaction goals. The theory's propositions describe relationships between verbal and nonverbal communication and information seeking, self-disclosure and interpersonal attraction.

Berger (1979) identified three general classes of strategies for reducing uncertainty. Passive strategies do not entail social interaction between parties; rather, they involve the unobtrusive observation of others for the purpose of acquiring information about them. Active strategies also do not involve face-to-face social interaction between information seekers and their targets. Acquiring information from third parties about a target person falls into this category. Finally, interactive strategies such as asking questions, disclosing information about one's self and relaxing the target may be used to acquire information when interaction occurs. These strategies vary with respect to their efficiency and social appropriateness. For example, acquiring personal information from another by asking questions might be an efficient strategy but it could become socially inappropriate if too many questions or excessively personal questions were to be asked. Conversely, relaxing the target person might be perceived to be highly appropriate socially but, at the same time, might be relatively inefficient for acquiring specific pieces of information from the target. A person who is more comfortable might say more than one who is less so but still not reveal the desired information. Studies have also examined the strategies individuals use to resist revealing information about themselves to highly inquisitive cointerlocutors (Berger & Kellermann, 1994). URT has been found to have some purchase in explaining social interaction in intercultural (Gudykunst, 1995, 2005) and organizational (Kramer, 2004) communication contexts.

Social actors may not only harbor uncertainties about themselves and others as individuals, they may also experience uncertainty with respect to their relationship with each other or relational uncertainty (Knobloch, 2005, 2006; Knobloch, & Carpenter-Theune, 2004; Knobloch & Solomon, 2002, 2005). The relational turbulence model posits that changes in intimacy within romantic relationships potentiate relational uncertainty, defined as questions or doubts about the nature of involvement in a relationship (Solomon & Knobloch, 2004). Relational uncertainty tends to polarize emotional, cognitive, and communicative reactions to various relationship events; however, reducing uncertainty and managing such events may promote intimacy between relationship partners.

Some researchers have argued that individuals may not necessarily be motivated to reduce their uncertainty when they anticipate experiencing negative outcomes by so doing (Afifi & Weiner, 2004; Babrow, 1992, 2001; Brashers, 2001). For example, individuals who have their blood tested for HIV because they suspect that they may be HIV positive may chose not to obtain their test results; presumably because they are fearful of an HIV positive outcome. They may elect to maintain their uncertainty in order to avoid hearing bad news. Similarly, married individuals who suspect their spouses are cheating on them may avoid reducing their uncertainty in this regard because of projected negative consequences that might accrue from such knowledge. According to this perspective, then, uncertainty is something to be managed rather than necessarily reduced. Although there are situations in which some people might avoid reducing their uncertainty, the degree to which these avoidance maneuvers portend optimal adaptation to the environment is open to question. In the long run, ignorance may not necessarily be bliss (Berger, 2005a).

Interpersonal Adaptation

Students of social interaction have long recognized that when individuals converse, they show strong proclivities to reciprocate each other's verbal and nonverbal behaviors. The norm of reciprocity, which states that in the conduct of social intercourse people are obligated to help and not harm those who help them, provides a potential explanation for the ubiquity of reciprocal social interaction (Gouldner, 1960). However, behavioral reciprocity has been observed between very young infants and their caregivers, suggesting a biological basis for such behavior (Burgoon, Stern, & Dillman, 1995). Evidence for the operation of the norm of reciprocity was found in early studies of self-disclosure and was labeled the "dyadic effect" (Cozby, 1973; Jourard, 1964, 1971). When individuals disclose information about themselves at a particular intimacy level, their cointerlocutors are likely to disclose information about themselves at a similar intimacy level. Moreover, as individuals increase or decrease the intimacy level of their self-disclosures, cointerlocutors tend to follow suite (Cozby, 1973). It is not that individuals reciprocate the same information about themselves; rather, individuals tend to match the intimacy level of their disclosures. In addition to reciprocity at the level of message content, early studies demonstrated reciprocity of nonverbal behaviors in interview situations. As interviewers purposively increased or decreased their speech rate or the number of pauses in their speech, interviewees were observed to respond by adjusting their speech or pause rate to match those of the interviewers (Matarazzo, Wiens, & Saslow, 1965).

Although there are pronounced tendencies for reciprocity in social interaction, there are conditions under which interacting individuals will show compensation in response to each other's behaviors. Compensation occurs when a behavior displayed by one person is responded to with an "opposite" behavior from another. For example, a smile by one person might be responded to by another's frown or an attempt to begin a conversation by moving closer to an individual might be met with eye-gaze aversion, potentially signaling an unwillingness to converse. In the smile-frown case, compensation occurs within the same nonverbal communication channel, facial expressions; in the second case, the compensatory behavior is expressed in a channel different from the initiating behavior.

A number of alternative theories have been devised to illuminate the conditions under which reciprocity and compensation are likely to occur during social interactions, especially with respect to nonverbal behaviors. Although Expectancy Violations Theory (Burgoon, 1993), Arousal Labeling Theory (Patterson, 1983), Discrepancy-Arousal Theory (Cappella & Greene, 1982, 1984), and Cognitive Valence Theory (Andersen & Guerrero, 1998a, 1998b) differ in terms of their explanations for reciprocity/compensation, they share the assumptions that (1) individuals have expectations for each other's nonverbal behaviors and (2) when the expectations for nonverbal behavior are violated, individuals tend to experience arousal. For instance, when people who try to converse at inappropriately close conversational distances or stare at conversational partners for inordinate lengths of time, they are likely to create arousal in their cointerlocutors. Arousal Labeling and Discrepancy Arousal theories suggest that when the experience of this arousal is pleasant, reciprocity is likely to occur; however, when this arousal is experienced negatively, compensation is likely to follow. Research comparing these theories has been inconclusive and has prompted the development of Interaction Adaptation Theory (IAT) (Burgoon et al., 1995). This theory argues that when an individual's interaction position matches a cointerlocutor's behavior, reciprocity or matching is likely to occur, but when an individual's interaction position is discrepant from the other's behavior, compensation is likely to occur. Interaction position is determined by the individual's basic drives and needs, their cognitive expectations concerning social norms and behavior and their goals and preferences. Although IAT proposes a potentially more comprehensive explanation of interaction adaptation than do the other theories, its scope may be ambitious to the point that it is difficult to evaluate.

While not invoking arousal-based explanations, Speech Accommodation Theory (Giles & Powesland, 1975) argues that individuals will become more similar with respect to their dialects and accents or converge to the extent that they desire to experience solidarity in their relationships. By contrast, individuals will show dialectical and accent divergence when they wish to assert a unique identity. These speech adjustments may be accomplished consciously, however, many times they occur outside of the conscious awareness of those involved in interactions. The notions of convergence and divergence are roughly similar to the concepts of reciprocity and compensation, respectively. This theory, which later morphed into Communication Accommodation Theory, extended this analytic framework to speech parameters beyond dialect and accent (Giles,

Coupland, & Coupland, 1991; Giles, Mulac, Bradac, & Johnson, 1987; Shepard, Giles, & Le Poire, 2001).

Message Production

The notion that language is a tool or an instrument for attaining everyday goals has enjoyed long acceptance among students of language and communication (Clark, 1994; Wittgenstein, 1953). Given the noncontroversial nature of this proposition, it is but a small step to contend that social interaction, like language, is a tool or an instrument for goal achievement (Berger 2003; Dillard, Anderson, & Knobloch, 2002; Wilson & Sabee, 2003). Consistent with this proposition, beginning in the 1970s and continuing through the 1990s, constructivist researchers (Delia, O'Keefe, & O'Keefe, 1982) endeavored to determine the characteristics of messages deemed to be effective for achieving a variety of goals, most of them concerned with persuasion (Clark & Delia, 1977; Delia, Kline, & Burleson, 1979); although, a parallel line of research concerned with the provision of emotional support developed within this tradition (Burleson, 2003). A robust finding from this line of research is that when given the task of devising messages to achieve such goals, individuals with high levels of cognitive complexity tend to generate messages showing greater evidence of social perspective taking than do their less cognitively complex counterparts (Applegate, 1990). Within this research perspective, cognitive complexity is indexed by the number of psychological constructs individuals typically use to construe other persons (cognitive differentiation) and the degree to which the constructs they use are abstract (construct abstractness). Greater numbers of highly abstract constructs contribute to higher cognitive complexity levels. Because highly differentiated individuals' messages take into account their cointerlocutors' goals, emotional states, and potential responses to their messages, their messages are, as a result, potentially more effective than the less socio-centric messages generated by their less cognitively complex counterparts.

Beginning in the 1980s, a more comprehensive and abstract message production theory labeled Action Assembly Theory (Greene, 1984, 1997) was developed to explain how individuals produce actions and discourse, and during the same period theories featuring such knowledge structures as scripts, plans, and Memory Organization Packets (MOPS) were devised (Berger, 1995, 1997a; Kellermann, 1995). In the case of these latter theories, sometimes referred to as Goal-Plan-Action (GPA) theories (Dillard, Anderson, & Knobloch, 2002), scripts, plans, and MOPS are conceived of as hierarchically organized knowledge structures representing action sequences aimed at bringing about goal attainment. Once goals and knowledge structures are activated, the knowledge structures guide actions toward goal achievement. Knowledge structures vary with respect to their abstractness and level of detail, and they can be made more complex by including contingencies that anticipate points at which projected actions in them might fail. Individuals who plan ahead during conversations, anticipate their cointerlocutor's future conversational moves, and develop plan contingencies to meet these future actions are more likely to attain their social interaction goals than are individuals who do not engage in such planning activity while they converse (Waldron, 1997). However, online planning must be flexible enough to deal with uncertainties that surround message production during social interactions (Berger, 1997b).

A potential shortcoming of GPA theories is that they do not provide a detailed account of how goals arise in the first place; that is, they begin with the assumption that social actors have a goal or goals to pursue. However, there are at least two examples of attempts to formulate and test theoretical explanations for how goals arise during social interaction (Meyer, 1997; Wilson, 1990, 1995; Wilson & Sabee, 2003). Because much of everyday social interaction is aimed at satisfying recurring goals, much of everyday conversational interaction is routine (Coulmas, 1981; Wray & Perkins, 2000). Moreover, efforts to routinize service interactions are common in commercial contexts (Ford, 1999; Leidner, 1993). Nonetheless, important questions can be asked about the conditions under which specific goals are activated and the consequences that follow from the disruption of these routines once they are undertaken. Interference with the completion of these routines should provoke annoyance and other negative emotions because it prevents the efficient achievement of recurring goals (Srull & Wyer, 1986); however, there may be circumstances under which the disruption of social interaction routines provides relief from boredom or from an undesirable situation such as a routine conflict with another person.

People sometimes imagine social interactions with others. These imagined interactions may occur before an encounter, as when employees imagine what they might say to their bosses, but imagined interactions can also take place after a particular encounter has ended. Under certain conditions, imagining what one might say to another person before an interaction with them takes place can reduce the amount of apprehension that the person who has imagined the interaction shows during the actual encounter. Moreover, imagining interactions may help those who imagine them cope with negative emotions they have experienced in their relationship with the person or persons with whom they imagine conversing (Honeycutt, 2003). However, imagining interactions before they take place may have the effect of encouraging individuals to commit themselves prematurely to a particular plan for the impending interaction and, as a result, render them less inclined to recognize potential problems that arise during the actual conversation and consider contingent actions that might be undertaken to deal with these problems (Berger, 1997a, 1997b).

Relationship Development

The idea that interpersonal communication plays a critical role in the development, maintenance, and deterioration of social and personal relationships is one that has gained widespread acceptance during the past 40 years. Although a great bulk of research attention has been paid to the development of romantic relationships, probably because college students, who are frequently used as research participants, are likely to be involved in such relationships, researchers have also investigated communication between friends, spouses, and family members.

A central question researchers have sought to answer is why some relationships become closer over time while others grow distant and perhaps end. Social exchange theories have frequently been invoked to explain why relationship growth and deterioration occur (Roloff, 1981, 1987; Roloff & Campion, 1985; Thibaut & Kelley, 1959). In general, these theories suggest that individuals experience both rewards and costs for being in relationships, and individuals not only assess their own rewards and costs, they also estimate their partners' levels of rewards and costs. Rewards may be material (wealth) or emotional (emotional support) and costs may be similarly material (lack of money) or emotional (undesirable personality). Each individual puts these reward and cost estimates into ratio form (rewards/costs) and compares the two ratios (self: rewards/costs versus partner: rewards/costs). Individuals will feel equity in their relationship to the degree that the reward/cost ratios match; however, if the self's ratio is less favorable than the partner's, the individual will feel inequity and thus dissatisfaction with the relationship. Dissatisfaction arising from felt inequity is sometimes expressed verbally when people say, "I am putting more into this relationship than I am getting out of it." In general, these theories suggest that favorable relative reward/cost ratios fuel relationship growth, whereas unfavorable ratios are associated with relationship deterioration. It is not the absolute levels of rewards and costs that determine equity but the degree to which the two ratios match.

Some have argued that social exchange theories and other relationship development perspectives make the processes of relationship development and deterioration appear to be much more continuous and linear than they actually are. These researchers contend that the development of relationships is fraught with dialectical tensions that pull individuals in opposite directions simultaneously (Baxter & Montgomery, 1996; Montgomery & Baxter, 1998). For example, individuals may at once desire both novelty and predictability with respect to their partners' behaviors, and because the tension between these polarities shifts over time, relationships are in a constant state of flux. Other dialectics such as openness-closeness and autonomy-connection may interact with each other through time. Given the dialectical nature of personal relationships and their dynamic interplay, proponents of this dialectical perspective contend that complete merger of relationship partners is not possible.

Although social exchange theories and the relational dialectics perspective provide explanations for the growth and deterioration of relationships, they do not centrally address the effects of messages exchanged between people. That is, in the case of social exchange theories, individuals' judgments about relative rewards and costs are presumed to be residues of verbal and nonverbal interactions; similarly, the dialectical contradictions that individuals retrospectively report experiencing in their relationships ostensibly arise from communicative exchanges with relationship partners; however, actual message exchanges between partners are generally not examined within this research tradition. However, although not necessarily strongly motivated by theory, there has been considerable research interest in interpersonal conflict in general and marital conflict in particular, much of it based on direct observations of partners engaged in social interaction (Roloff & Soule, 2002). Within the domain of marital interaction, studies have found that couples who display a demand-withdraw pattern of message exchanges when interacting with each other, such that one person makes a demand of the other and the other person responds by withdrawing, report lower levels of relational satisfaction than do couples who acknowledge and respond to each other's demands in a conciliatory way (Gottman & Leven-son, 1988; Gottman, Murray, Swanson, Tyson, & Swanson, 2002). The degree to which spouses reciprocate negative affect, or cross-complain, has also been found to potentiate reduced marital satisfaction (Gottman et al., 2002). Because the communication of emotion plays a vital role in many different types of relationships, there is increasing interest in how the regulation of emotions and emotional communication affect relationship development (Metts & Planalp, 2002; Planalp, 1998, 1999, 2003).

Deceptive Communication

Many interpersonal communication researchers subscribe to the view that deception is an integral part of social interaction (Goffman, 1959; G. R. Miller & Stiff, 1993; W.I. Miller, 2003). So-called "white lies" are commonplace in everyday social commerce. Some have gone so far as to argue that deception is an important lubricant that enables the smooth operation of the social interaction machine. Many times these lies are told to help cointerlocutors save face when potentially embarrassing circumstances arise in social situations (Brown & Levinson, 1978, 1987). For example, dinner guests might tell a host that the food they have just consumed was "wonderful" when, in fact, it was utterly horrible. Deception by commission occurs when proffered information is at variance with the "true" state of affairs, as in the previous examples; however, deception may also occur by omission; that is, individuals may intentionally withhold critical information so that others will draw erroneous inferences, as when a used car salesperson fails to reveal known mechanical defects present in a car to a prospective buyer. The customer is left to infer that the car is mechanically reliable.

Although interpersonal communication researchers have expended considerable research effort examining deceptive communication since the 1970s (Knapp & Comadena, 1979; Knapp et al., 1974), there are relatively few theories of deceptive social interaction. One of these, Information Manipulation Theory (McCornack, 1992), asserts that when individuals engage in deceptive communication, they may covertly flout one or more of Grice's (1989) four conversational maxims: quality, quantity, manner, and relevance. However, deception may also occur when verbal messages adhere to the four maxims but are delivered with nonverbal accompaniments that make them ambiguous, for example, sarcasm. Unfortunately, serious questions have been raised about the degree to which Information Manipulation Theory is falsifiable (Jacobs, Dawson, & Brashers, 1996). Interpersonal Deception Theory represents another attempt to explain the interaction between individuals' intentional attempts to deceive others and the degree to which those being deceived can detect the deceitful behavior (Buller & Burgoon, 1996). Although this theory presents 18 propositions, critics have observed that the propositions are not formulated in such a way that they address a central "why" question (DePaulo, Ainsfield, & Bell, 1996). Others have contended that some of the propositions are vague and non-falsifiable (Levine & McCornack, 1996; McCornack, 1997).

There are at least two enduring questions concerning deceptive communication that have attracted considerable research attention. One of these questions concerns the degree to which engaging in deception alters nonverbal behaviors; that is, do truth tellers' nonverbal behaviors differ systematically from those of individuals who are telling lies? The research germane to this question has focused on nonverbal behaviors because it is generally assumed that when people engage in deceptive communication, they can carefully monitor what they are saying but cannot necessarily control their nonverbal behaviors in ways that will make them appear to be telling the truth (Ekman & Friesen, 1969). In general, research findings suggest that no one nonverbal behavior, for example, eye gaze aversion, excessive leg movements, fast or slow speech rate, or changes in body posture can be used as a universal indicator of deceptive communication across all individuals (O'Sullivan, 2005; Vrig & Mann, 2005). That is, there appears to be no nonverbal indicator of deception equivalent to Pinocchio's fabled nose. However, some specific behaviors, for example, changes in leg and foot movements and the size of pupils and the degree to which one exhibits verbal and vocal immediacy and genuine smiles may differentiate some truth tellers from some liars in some situations (DePaulo, Lindsay, Malone, Muhlenbruck, Charlton, & Cooper, 2003).

Another enduring question investigated by deception researchers is the degree to which individuals are skilled at detecting deception as they interact with others. In this case research has generally shown that most individuals are not very adept at deception detection, even those whose professions frequently require them to ascertain whether people are lying or telling the truth; for example, judges, counselors, and law enforcement personnel (Buller & Burgoon, 1996; Vrig & Mann, 2005). One explanation for the apparent inability of most individuals to detect deception is the pervasiveness of the "truth bias." The truth bias arises from the fact that in the conduct of everyday social interaction, individuals must routinely assume that their conversational partners are telling the truth, as suggested by Grice's (1989) quality maxim. Consequently, because individuals generally assume others are telling the truth, it is difficult for them to detect deceit when it is being perpetrated. Failure to attend to potentially diagnostic cues and the use of various heuristics have also been proffered as explanations for low rates of deception detection accuracy; however, even though a the vast majority of people are poor deception detectors, approximately 1/1,000 people are deception detection "wizards" who are found in a wide array of occupations (O'Sullivan, 2005). These "wizards" achieve better than chance levels of deception detection accuracy.

Mediated Social Interaction

Increasingly, social interaction is being accomplished through such communication technologies as computers with e-mail and chat room capabilities and mobile telephones with text messaging and other communication features. Teleconferencing has become a commonplace in business communication. As the use of these technologies has become progressively more widespread, there has been a concomitant increase in research aimed at understanding their potential individual and social effects. However, as indicated earlier, technologically mediated social interaction is hardly a new phenomenon, having been possible on a wide scale since the advent of the land-line telephone.

In the wake of the introduction of such mass media as film, radio, and television, research was undertaken to investigate the potential deleterious effects of the then-new medium on those exposed to it. The voluminous Payne Fund studies of the late 1920s and early 1930s attempted to identify several potential negative impacts of film on youth (Charters, 1933), and not long after the widespread diffusion of television, similar research endeavors were undertaken (Schramm, Lyle, & Parker, 1961). More recently, such concerns have surfaced with respect to Internet use. Internet addiction (Griffiths, 1998) and increased social isolation and loneliness with increasing Internet use (Kraut, Lundmark et al., 1998) are among the purported toxic effects associated with Internet involvement; although, evidence for the latter association is both scant and equivocal (Kraut, Kiesler et al., 2002). An inherent difficulty in examining such effects is establishing directions of causal influence. Do people with "addictive personalities" find Internet use to be another activity to which to become addicted, or does heavy use of the Internet induce addictive behavior? Do high levels of Internet use induce people to feel socially isolated and lonely, or do people who are already socially isolated and lonely gravitate to the Internet to help them alleviate these unpleasant feelings? Yet another and perhaps more realistic possibility in each of these cases is that both causal directions interact with each other in a complex, reciprocal fashion.

Some researchers have observed that when individuals engage in anonymous Computer Mediated Communication (CMC), as they might in an Internet chat room or on e-mail, they are more likely to act in ways that they would not if they were interacting with others face-to-face (FtF) or if their identities were known to others in the CMC context. Researchers have postulated both positive and negative possibilities in this regard. On the positive side, anonymous individuals communicating with others by CMC might assume new identities, personalities, or both that could help them cope with personal problems (Turkle, 1995). For example, highly introverted and shy people who wish to overcome their social inhibitions might "try on" a highly extraverted and outgoing persona while engaging in CMC. The effect of this experimentation might be to move such individuals in the desired direction of becoming less shy and introverted in their FtF interactions. However, on the negative side, others have noted that this same cloak of anonymity may serve to embolden individuals to insult and attack others or to "flame" them, behaviors they would not normally display in most FtF interactions or in CMC if their identities were known to their cointerlocutors (Siegel, Dubrovsky, Kiesler, & McGuire, 1983).

Just as the advent of television prompted both considerable speculation and research aimed at comparing the medium's potential effects, especially with respect to its visual channel, with those of older media such as radio, so too the appearance of CMC has precipitated considerable research aimed at determining how CMC and FtF interaction differ with respect to various outcomes associated with their use (Walther & Parks, 2002). Because text-based CMC, as currently used in electronic mail (e-mail), news groups, and chat rooms, filters out many nonverbal cues typically available to people engaged in FtF interactions, it is presumed that communication via text-based CMC is more task focused than is FtF communication. Moreover, while relatively cue-deprived, text-based CMC venues may be quite useful for initially encountering and screening potential friends and romantic partners, they apparently do not afford sufficient information for developing most close relationships. Individuals who initially meet in the text-based CMC world usually elect to communicate with each other through other channels, for example, telephone and FtF encounters (Walther & Parks, 2002). These alternative communication channels afford their users potentially more rich and comprehensive samples of each other's behavior. Although the ability to send pictures and live video in the CMC context may overcome some of this cue loss in the visual realm, such nonverbal communication channels as touch, pheromones, body temperature and smell, that are at once both highly significant in most close romantic relationships and currently difficult or impossible to instantiate in CMC, probably necessitates FtF interaction for developing close relationships. In any case, for a variety of reasons a majority of relationships initially formed online fail to migrate successfully to off-line relationships (Baker, 2002).

Because text-based CMC may serve to filter out personal information that might be used to understand people as individuals rather than as group members, some researchers have suggested that when groups use CMC to communicate with each other, the lack of individuating information about group members may foster stronger in-group identity. Increased in-group loyalty may serve to "de-individuate" people to the point that they are willing to stereotype out-group members and behave negatively toward them. Although research has supported this possibility (Postmes, Spears, Lea, & Reicher, 2000), some have observed that these findings are limited to the domain of group-based CMC and may not apply in situations in which people are using CMC to interact with others on an individual basis (Walther & Parks, 2002). Beyond the CMC realm, under the aegis of Human Computer Interaction (HCI), considerable research evidence has been adduced to support the idea that people tend to treat computers and other communication technologies as if they are human agents, even when users know that they are interacting with a machine (Reeves & Nass, 1996). Apparently, technology users cannot help imputing human-like qualities to the communication technologies they encounter in their everyday lives.

Given the rapid rate at which new communication technologies that enable mediated social interaction between people are being made widely available to the public, understanding how the use of these technologies affect communication in these modes represents an opportunity to further understanding of FtF interaction processes. At the present time, FtF interaction is held as a kind of gold standard against which to compare mediated social interaction. However, prolonged use of communication technologies to enable mediated social interaction may alter the fundamental nature of FtF interaction; that is, communication conventions associated with CMC may insinuate themselves into FtF interaction over time (Berger, 2005b). This possibility represents a challenge to interpersonal communication researchers.

Other Research Areas

The six areas just considered do not exhaust the entire domain of interpersonal communication inquiry. In addition to these theoretically defined areas are specific concepts in which interpersonal communication researchers have had an enduring interest. Some of these concepts are briefly considered below.

Everyday experience suggests that some individuals are consistently better able than others to achieve their goals during their social interactions. Some people appear to be able to induce others to like them while others seem to be very effective at comforting those in distress. The skills associated with success in these and other social interaction domains can be subsumed under the notion of communication competence. Much has been written about the communication competence concept, but there remains considerable ambiguity concerning its meaning; moreover, there has yet to be a theory that elaborates the concept (Spitzburg & Cupach, 2002). Some have suggested that communication competence might profitably be viewed as a theoretical term or domain of study rather than a single theoretical construct (Wilson & Sabee, 2003).

There appears to be some agreement that communication competence refers to the degree to which individuals are able to reach their goals (effectiveness) and the extent to which goal achievement is accomplished in an appropriate manner (social appropriateness) (Parks, 1994). In addition, some have suggested that efficiency may be another component of competence; that is, how quickly individuals are able to achieve their goals (Berger, 2003). Another point of convergence is that communication competence is not a generalized skill but is specific to different kinds of communication goals and situations (Wilson & Sabee, 2003). The domain specificity of communication skills is clearly demonstrated in the vast array of chapters in a volume devoted to the topic (Greene & Burleson, 2003). This work's chapters ranged from nonverbal communication (Burgoon & Bacue, 2003), message production (Berger, 2003), and reception skills (Wyer & Adaval, 2003), to emotional support (Burleson, 2003), persuasion (Dillard & Marshall, 2003), negotiation (Roloff, Putnam, & Anastasiou, 2003), informing (Rowan, 2003), and arguing (Hample, 2003) skills. Thus, an individual might be very effective at offering social support and comfort to others but at the same time might be relatively ineffective at gaining compliance from them. Although most interpersonal communication researchers acknowledge that communication competence is goal and situation specific, as yet there is no typology of goals and situations that enables us to determine specific skill sets that are associated with various classes of goals and situations.

As noted previously, much of everyday social interaction is organized around recurring goals that arise in the course of everyday living. The routines associated with everyday family and work interactions and with daily transactions in business and commerce encourage the development of communication routines in order to reach these recurring goals effectively and efficiently. If people had to plan consciously how to reach each of these recurring goals every day, the pace of social life would slow to a crawl. Instead, communication is routinized and can be enacted automatically when the occasion arises. Routinization of language use is pervasive; it has been estimated that up to 70% of adult language is formulaic (Altenberg, 1990; Sinclair, 1991). The notion of communication routines may be related to communication competence. Competent communicators may be those who, in a given situation, have rapid access to communication routines that generally eventuate in goal achievement. Of course, the relationship between the availability and accessibility of communication routines and communication competence rests on the assumption that the routines accessed are both effective and socially appropriate. A given situation may be nonroutine and require conscious planning effort; thus, the discerning communicator must be able to differentiate between those social situations that are routine and those that are not. This requirement for astute social discernment suggests that competent communicative action involves more than the production of effective messages. Relatively accurate perception of others' current circumstances, moods, and emotional states is a vital prerequisite to competent social conduct.

With few exceptions, the individual has been the point of departure for much of the theory and research presented in this [selection]. Some have argued that this individually focused, psychological perspective on interpersonal communication must be augmented by a purview that takes into account the fact that individuals are embedded in a variety of social networks. The extensiveness and nature of these social networks has been shown to be consequential to the development and maintenance of specific personal relationships as well as health and well-being (Parks, 2007). Social network members may or may not provide support to particular relationships, thus affecting their outcomes, as when parents or relatives or both support or oppose the impending marriage of a child (Parks & Adelman, 1983). Clearly, the explanation of a large number of phenomena subsumed under the aegis of interpersonal communication requires that these social network influences be taken into account. After all, it is these social network ties that represent at least part of the "inter" in interpersonal communication.

Summary

Interpersonal communication research grew out of research in social influence and small group dynamics in the middle of the last century. One of the early tenets of interpersonal communication was that it is a process of mutual influence, and that belief still exists today. Research in interpersonal communication now examines a wide variety of communicative endeavors, including relationship development, nonverbal communication, message production, interaction adaptation, and deceptive communication. The new areas of research in computer mediated communication (CMC) with respect to interpersonal communication present endless new possibilities in research in this domain.

This chapter has examined six specific areas of interpersonal communication research beginning with uncertainty in interpersonal communication by examining how humans use interpersonal communication to reduce the amount of uncertainty in their environment. Interpersonal adaptation examines how individuals use communication to adapt to the world around them with specific focus on concepts of reciprocity and compensation. Message production is the analysis of interpersonal communication for the specific purpose of attaining one's goals, and has spawned such concepts as constructivism and action assembly theory.

Perhaps the most critical research in interpersonal communication has been on the analysis and understanding of how humans develop relationships. This has led to the development of many theories about this process, including social exchange, dialectical, and interpersonal conflict. Another aspect of research in this area has been an attempt to understand deceptive communication and how this can alter nonverbal behavior and an examination at people's ability to detect deceptive communication. Finally, mediated social interaction through CMC is a new and rich area of interest in interpersonal communication.

The next chapter focuses on interpersonal communication in relationships, and goes into more detail about some of the specific concepts of relational communication, including why we form relationships and strategies we use to maintain relationships.

Questions For Discussion

1. What are the most significant relationships in your life? What theory from this chapter would best explain how these relationships were formed?
2. How would uncertainty reduction explain what you would do when you enter a party and realize the only one you know if the person hosting the party?
3. Are you good at spotting interpersonal deception? Has this happened to you recently?
4. How has computer mediated communication affected relationships in which you are now engaged?
5. What is the most important aspect of interpersonal communication with respect to relationship development?

References

Afifi, W. A., & Weiner, J. L. (2004). Toward a theory of motivated information management. *Communication Theory*, 14(2), 167–190.

Altenberg, B. (1990). Speech as linear composition. In G. Caie, K. Haastrup, A. L. Jakobsen, J. Nielsen, Sevaldsen et al. (Eds.), *Proceedings from the Fourth Nordic Conference for English Studies* (Vol. 1, pp. 133–143). Copenhagen, Denmark: Department of English, University of Copenhagen.

Altman, I., & Taylor, D. A. (1973). *Social penetration: The development of interpersonal relationships*. New York: Holt, Rinehart, & Winston.

Andersen, P. A., & Guerrero, L. K. (1998a). The bright side of relational communication: Interpersonal warmth as a social emotion. In P. A. AAndersen & L. K. Guerrero (Eds.), *Handbook of communication and emotion: Research, theory, applications and contexts* (pp. 303–329). New York: Academic Press.

Andersen, P. A., & Guerrero, L. K. (1998b). Principles of communication and emotion in social interaction. In P. A. Andersen & L. K. Guerrero (Eds.), *Handbook of communication and emotion: Research, theory, applications and contexts* (pp. 49–96). New York: Academic Press.

Applegate, J. L. (1990). Constructs and communication: A pragmatic integration. In G. Neimeyer & R. Neimeyer (Eds.), *Advances in personal construct psychology* (Vol. 1, pp. 203–230). Greenwich, CT: JAL.

Babrow, A. S. (1992). Communication and problematic integration: Understanding diverging probability and value, ambiguity, ambivalence, and impossibility. *Communication Theory*, 2(2), 95–130.

Babrow, A. S. (2001). Uncertainty, value, communication, and problematic integration. *Journal of Communication*, 51, 553–573.

Baker, A. (2002). What makes an online relationship successful? Clues from couples who met in cyberspace. *CyberPsychology and Behavior*, 5, 363–375.

Baxter, L. A., & Montgomery, B. M. (1996). *Relating: Dialogues and dialectics*. New York: Guilford.

Bell, R. A., Buerkel-Rothfuss, N. L., & Gore, K. E. (1987). "Did you bring the yarmulke for the Cabbage Patch Kid?" The idiomatic communication of young lovers. *Human Communication Research*, 14, 47–67.

Bell, R. A., & Healy, J. G. (1992). Idiomatic communication and interpersonal solidarity in friends' relational cultures. *Human Communication Research*, 18, 307–335.

Benson, T. W., & Pearce, W. B. (Eds.). (1977). Alternative theoretical bases for the study of human communication: A symposium. *Communication Quarterly*, 25, 3–73.

Berger, C. R. (1979). Beyond initial interaction: Uncertainty, understanding and the development of interpersonal relationships. In H. Giles & R. St. Clair (Eds.), *Language and social psychology* (pp. 122–144). Oxford: Blackwell.

Berger, C. R. (1995). A plan-based approach to strategic communication. In D. E. Hewes (Ed.), *The cognitive bases of interpersonal communication* (pp. 141–179). Hillsdale, NJ: Erlbaum.

Berger, C. R. (1997a). Planning strategic interaction: *Attaining goals through communicative action*. Mahwah, NJ: Erlbaum.

Berger, C. R. (1997b). Producing messages under uncertainty. In J. Greene (Ed.), *Message production: Advances in communication theory* (pp. 221–244). Mahwah, NJ: Erlbaum.

Berger, C. R. (2003). Message production skill in social interaction. In J. O. Greene & B. R. Burleson (Eds.), *Handbook of communication and social interaction skills* (pp. 257–289). Mahwah, NJ: Erlbaum.

Berger, C. R. (2005a). Interpersonal communication: Theoretical perspectives, future prospects. *Journal of Communication*, 55, 415–447.

Berger, C. R. (2005b). Effects of interactive technology involvement on face-to-face interaction: Benign enablement or insidious insinuation? *Asian Communication Research, 2*, 5–22.

Berger, C. R., & Bradac, J. J. (1982). *Language and social knowledge: Uncertainty in interpersonal relations*. London: Edward Arnold.

Berger, C. R., & Burgoon, M. (1995). Preface. In C. R. Berger & M. Burgoon (Eds.), *Communication and social influence processes* (pp. ix–xii). East Lansing, MI: Michigan State University Press.

Berger, C. R., & Calabrese, R. J. (1975). Some explorations in initial interaction and beyond: Toward a developmental theory of interpersonal communication. *Human Communication Research, 1*, 99–112.

Berger, C. R., & Gudykunst, W. B. (1991). Uncertainty and communication. In B. Dervin & M. Voight (Eds.), *Progress in communication sciences* (pp. 21–66). Norwood, NJ: Ablex.

Berger, C. R., & Kellermann K. (1994). Acquiring social information. In J. A. Daly & J. M. Wiemann (Eds.), *Strategic interpersonal communication* (pp. 1–31). Hillsdale, NJ: Erlbaum.

Boster, F. J. (1995). Commentary on compliance-gaining message behavior research. In C. R. Berger & M. Burgoon (Eds.), *Communication and social influence processes* (pp. 91–113). East Lansing, MI: Michigan State University Press.

Brashers, D. E. (2001). Communication and uncertainty management. *Journal of Communication, 51*(3), 477–497.

Brehm, J. (1966). *A theory of psychological reactance*. New York: Academic Press.

Brehm, J., & Cohen, A. R. (1962). *Explorations in cognitive dissonance*. New York: Wiley.

Brown, P., & Levinson, S. (1978). Universals in language use: Politeness phenomena. In E. Goody (Ed.), *Questions and politeness* (pp. 56–289). Cambridge, UK: Cambridge University Press.

Brown, P., & Levinson, S. (1987). *Politeness: Some universals in language use*. Cambridge, UK: Cambridge University Press.

Buller, D. B., & Burgoon, J. K. (1996). Interpersonal deception theory. *Communication Theory, 6*, 203–242.

Burgoon, J. K. (1993). Interpersonal expectations, expectancy violations, and emotional communication. *Journal of Language and Social Psychology, 12*, 13–21.

Burgoon, J. K., & Bacue, A. E. (2003). Nonverbal communication skills. In J. O. Greene & B. R. Burleson (Eds.), *Handbook of communication and social interaction skills* (pp. 179–219). Mahwah, NJ: Erlbaum.

Burgoon, J. K., Stern, L. A., & Dillman, L. (1995). *Interpersonal adaptation: Dyadic interaction patterns*. New York: Cambridge University Press.

Burleson, B. R. (2003). Emotional support skills. In J. O. Greene & B. R. Burleson (Eds.), *Handbook of communication and social interaction skills* (pp. 551–594). Mahwah, NJ: Erlbaum.

Byrne, D. (1971). *The attraction paradigm.* New York: Academic Press.

Cappella, J. N. (1987). Interpersonal communication: Definitions and fundamental questions. In C. R. Berger & S. H. Chaffee (Eds.), *Handbook of communication science* (pp. 184–238). Newbury Park, CA: Sage.

Cappella, J. N., & Greene, J. O. (1982). A discrepancy-arousal explanation of mutual influence in expressive behavior for adult and infant–adult interaction. *Communication Monographs, 49,* 89–114.

Cappella, J. N., & Greene, J. O. (1984). The effects of distance and individual differences in arousability on nonverbal involvement: A test of discrepancy-arousal theory. *Journal of Nonverbal Behavior, 8,* 259–286.

Cartwright, D., & Zander, A. (1968). *Group dynamics: Theory and practice* (3rd ed.). New York: Harper Row.

Charters, W. W. (1933). *Motion pictures and youth: A summary.* New York: Macmillan.

Clark, H. H. (1994). Discourse in production. In M. A. Gernsbacher (Ed.), *Handbook of psycho-linguis-tics* (pp. 985–1021). San Diego, CA: Academic Press.

Clark, R. A., & Delia, J. G. (1977). Cognitive complexity, social perspective-taking, and persuasion skills in second- to ninth-grade children. *Human Communication Research, 3,* 128–134.

Cody, M. J., Canary, D. J., & Smith, S. W. (1994). Compliance-gaining goals: An inductive analysis of actors' and goal types, strategies, and successes. In J. A. Daly & J. M. Wiemann (Eds.), *Strategic interpersonal communication* (pp. 33–90). Hillsdale, NJ: Erlbaum.

Coulmas, F. (1981). Introduction: Conversational routine. In P. Coulmas (Ed.), Conversational routines: *Explorations in standardized communication situations and prepatterned speech* (pp. 1–17). Hague, Netherlands: Mouton.

Cozby, P. C. (1973). Self-disclosure: A literature review. *Psychological Bulletin, 79,* 73–91.

Daly, J. A., & Wiemann, J. M. (Eds.). (1994). *Strategic interpersonal communication.* Hillsdale, NJ: Erlbaum.

Delia, J. G. (1977). Constructivism and the study of human communication. *Quarterly Journal of Speech, 63,* 66–83.

Delia, J. G. (1987). Communication research: A history. In C. R. Berger & S. H. Chaffee (Eds.), *Handbook of communication science* (pp. 20–98). Beverly Hills, CA: Sage.

Delia, J. G., Kline, S. L., & Burleson, B. R. (1979). The development of persuasive communication strategies in kindergartners through twelfth-graders. *Communication Monographs, 46,* 241–225.

Delia, J. G, O'Keefe, B. J., & O'Keefe, D. J. (1982). The constructivist approach to communication. In F. E. X. Dance (Ed.), *Human communication theory: Comparative essays* (pp. 147–191). New York: Harper & Row.

DePaulo, B. M., Ainsfield, M. E., & Bell, K. L. (1996). Theories about deception and paradigms for studying it: A critical appraisal of Buller and Burgoon's interpersonal deception theory and research. *Communication Theory, 6,* 297–310.

DePaulo, B. M., Lindsay, J. J. Malone, B. E., Muhlenbruck, L. Charlton, K., & Cooper, H. (2003). Cues to deception. *Psychological Bulletin, 129,* 74–118.

Dillard, J. P., Anderson, J. W., & Knobloch, L. K. (2002). Interpersonal influence. In M. L. Knapp & J. A. Daly (Eds.), *Handbook of interpersonal communication* (3rd ed., pp. 425–474). Thousand Oaks, CA: Sage.

Dillard, J. P., & Marshall, L. J. (2003). Persuasion as a social skill. In J. O. Greene & B. R. Burleson (Eds.), Handbook of communication and social interaction skills (pp. 479–513). Mahwah, NJ: Erlbaum.

Duck, S. W. (1973). *Personal relationships and personal constructs: A study of friendship formation.* New York: Wiley.

Ekman, P., & Friesen, W. V. (1969). Nonverbal leakage cues to deception. *Psychiatry, 32,* 88–105.

Festinger, L. (1957). *A theory of cognitive dissonance.* Stanford, CA: Stanford University Press.

Festinger, L. (1964). *Conflict, decision, and dissonance.* Stanford, CA: Stanford University Press.

Ford, W. S. Z. (1999). Communication and customer service. In M. E. Roloff (Ed.), *Communication yearbook,* (Vol. 22, pp. 341–375). Thousand Oaks, CA: Sage.

Giles, H., Coupland, N., & Coupland, J. (1991). Accommodation theory: Communication, contexts and consequences. In H. Giles, N. Coupland, & J. Coupland (Eds.), Context of accommodation: *Developments in applied linguistics* (pp. 1–68). Cambridge, UK: Cambridge University Press.

Giles, H., Mulac, A., Bradac, J. J., & Johnson, P. (1987). Speech accommodation theory: The next decade. In M. McLaughlin (Ed.), *Communication yearbook,* (Vol. 11, pp. 13–48). Newbury Park, CA: Sage.

Giles, H., & Powesland, P. (1975). *Speech style and social evaluation.* London: Academic Press.

Goffman, E. (1959). *The presentation of self in everyday life.* Garden City, NY: Doubleday.

Gottman, J. M., & Levenson, R. W. (1988). The social psychophysiology of marriage. In P. Noller & M. A. Fitzpatrick (Eds.), *Perspectives on marital interaction* (pp. 182–200). Clevedon, UK: Multilingual Matters.

Gottman, J. M., Murray, J. D., Swanson, C. C., Tyson, R., & Swanson, K. R. (2002). *The mathematics of marriage: Dynamic nonlinear models.* Cambridge, MA: MIT Press.

Gouldner, A. W. (1960). The norm of reciprocity: A preliminary statement. *American Sociological Review, 25,* 161–178.

Greene, J. O. (1984). A cognitive approach to human communication: An action assembly theory. *Communication Monographs, 51,* 289–306.

Greene, J. O. (1997). A second generation action assembly theory. In J. O. Greene (Ed.), *Message production: Advances in communication theory* (pp. 151–170). Mahwah, NJ: Erlbaum.

Greene, J. O., & Burleson, B. R. (Eds.). (2003). *Handbook of communication and social interaction skills.* Mahwah, NJ: Erlbaum.

Grice, H. P. (1989). *Studies in the ways of words.* Cambridge, MA: Harvard University Press.

Griffiths, M. (1998). Internet addiction: Does it really exist? In J. Gakenbach (Ed.), *Psychology and the Internet: Intrapersonal, interpersonal, and transpersonal implications* (pp. 61–75). London: Academic Press.

Gudykunst, W. B. (1995). Anxiety/uncertainty management (AUM) theory. In R. L. Wiseman (Ed.), *Intercultural communication theory* (pp. 8–58). Thousand Oaks, CA: Sage.

Gudykunst, W. B. (2005). An anxiety/uncertainty management (AUM) theory of effective communication. In W. B. Gudykunst (Ed.), *Theorizing about intercultural communication* (pp. 281–322). Thousand Oaks, CA: Sage.

Hample, D. (2003). Arguing skill. In J. O. Greene & B. R. Burleson (Eds.), *Handbook of communication and social interaction skills* (pp. 439–477). Mahwah, NJ: Erlbaum.

Heider, F. (1958). *The psychology of interpersonal relations.* New York: Wiley.

Hewes, D. E., & Planalp, S. (1987). The individual's place in communication science, In C. R. Berger & S. H. Chaffee (Eds.), *Handbook of communication science* (pp. 146–183). Newbury Park, CA: Sage.

Honeycutt, J. M. (2003). *Imagined interactions: Daydreaming about communication.* Cresskill, NJ: Hampton.

Hopper, R. (1992). *Telephone communication.* Bloomington, IN: Indiana University Press.

Hovland, C. I., & Janis, I. L. (1959). *Personality and persuasibility.* New Haven, CT: Yale University Press.

Hovland, C. I., Janis, I. L., & Kelley, H. H. (1953). *Communication and persuasion: Psychological studies of opinion change.* New Haven, CT: Yale University Press.

Hovland, C. I., & Rosenberg, M. J. (1960). *Attitude organization and change: An analysis of consistency among attitude components.* New Haven, CT: Yale University Press.

Jacobs, S., Dawson, E. J., & Brashers, D. (1996). Information manipulation theory: A replication and assessment. *Communication Monographs, 63,* 70–82.

Jourard, S. M. (1964). *The transparent self: Self-disclosure and well-being.* Princeton, NJ: Van Nostrand.

Jourard, S. M. (1971). *Self-disclosure: An experimental analysis of the transparent self.* New York: Wiley-Interscience.

Kellermann, K. (1995). The conversation MOP: A model of patterned and pliable behavior. In D. E. Hewes (Ed.), *The cognitive bases of interpersonal communication* (pp. 181–221). Hillsdale, NJ: Erlbaum.

King, R. G. (1979). *Fundamentals of human communication.* New York: Macmillan.

Knapp, M. L. (1972). *Nonverbal communication in human interaction.* New York: Holt, Rinehart, & Winston.

Knapp, M. L., & Comadena, M. E. (1979). Telling it like it isn't: A review of theory and research on deceptive communication. *Human Communication Research, 5,* 270–285.

Knapp, M. L, Hart, R. R., & Dennis, H. S. (1974). An exploration of deception as a communication construct. *Human Communication Research, 7,* 15–29.

Knobloch, L. K. (2005). Evaluating a contextual model of responses to relational uncertainty increasing events: The role of intimacy, appraisals, and emotions. *Human Communication Research, 31*(1), 60–101.

Knobloch, L. K. (2006). Relational uncertainty and message production within courtship: Features of date request messages. *Human Communication Research, 32,* 244–273.

Knobloch, L. K., & Carpenter-Theune, K. E. (2004). Topic avoidance in developing romantic relationships: Associations with intimacy and relational uncertainty. *Communication Research, 31,* 173–205.

Knobloch, L. K., & Solomon, D. H. (2002). Information seeking beyond initial interaction: Negotiating relational uncertainty within close relationships. *Human Communication Research,* 28, 243–257.

Knobloch, L. K., & Solomon, D. H. (2005). Relational uncertainty and relational information processing: Questions without answers? *Communication Research,* 32, 349–388.

Kramer, M. W. (2004). *Managing uncertainty in organizational communication.* Mahwah, NJ: Erlbaum.

Kraut, R., Kiesler, S., Boneva, B., Cummings, J., Helgeson, V., & Crawford, A. (2002). Internet paradox revisited. *Journal of Social Issues,* 58, 49–74.

Kraut, R., Lundmark, V., Patterson, M., Kiesler, S. Mukopadhyay, T., & Scherlis, W. (1998). Internet paradox: A social technology that reduces social involvement and psychological well-being? *American Psychologist,* 53, 1017–1031.

Leidner, R. (1993). *Fast food, fast talk: Service work and the routinization of everyday life.* Berkeley: University of California Press.

Levine, T. R., & McCornack, S. A. (1996). Can BAE explain the probing effect? *Human Communication Research,* 22, 604–613.

Marwell, G., & Schmidt, D. R. (1967). Dimensions of compliance-gaining behavior: An empirical analysis. *Sociometry,* 30, 350–364.

Matarazzo, J. D., Wiens, A. N., & Saslow, G. (1965). Studies in interview speech behavior. In L. Krasner & L. P. Ullmann (Eds.), *Research in behavior modification: New developments and implications* (pp. 179–210). New York: Holt, Rinehart & Winston.

McCornack, S. A. (1992). Information manipulation theory. *Communication Monographs,* 59, 1–16.

McCornack, S. A. (1997). The generation of deceptive messages: Laying the groundwork for a viable theory of interpersonal deception. In J. O. Greene (Ed.), *Message production: Advances in communication theory* (pp. 91–126). Mahwah, NJ: Erlbaum.

Mehrabian, A. (1971). *Silent messages.* Belmont, CA: Wadsworth.

Metts, S., & Planalp, S. (2002). Emotional communication. In M. L. Knapp & J. A. Daly (Eds.), *Handbook of interpersonal communication* (3rd ed., pp. 339–373). Thousand Oaks, CA: Sage.

Meyer, J. R. (1997). Cognitive influences on the ability to address interaction goals. In J. O. Greene (Ed.), *Message production: Advances in communication theory* (pp. 71–90). Mahwah, NJ: Erlbaum.

Miller, G. R. (1987). Persuasion. In C. R. Berger & S. H. Chaffee (Eds.), *Handbook of communication science* (pp. 446–483). Newbury Park, CA: Sage.

Miller, G. R., & Steinberg, M. (1975). Between people: *A new analysis of interpersonal communication.* Chicago: Science Research Associates.

Miller, G. R., & Stiff, J. B. (1993). *Deceptive communication.* Newbury Park, CA: Sage.

Miller, G. R., Boster, F. J., Roloff, M. E., & Seibold, D. R. (1977). Compliance-gaining message strategies: A typology and some findings concerning effects of situational differences. *Communication Monographs,* 44, 37–51.

Miller, W. I. (2003). *Faking it.* Cambridge, UK: Cambridge University Press.

Montgomery, B. M., & Baxter, L. A. (Eds.). (1998). *Dialectical approaches to the study of relationships.* Mahwah, NJ: Lawrence Erlbaum.

Newcomb, T. M. (1953). An approach to the study of communicative acts. *Psychological Review,* 60, 393–404.

Newcomb, T. M. (1961). *The acquaintance process.* New York: Holt, Rinehart, & Winston.

Osgood, C. E., & Tannenbaum, P. H. (1955). The principle of congruity in the prediction of attitude change. *Psychological Review, 62,* 42–55.

O'Sullivan, M. (2005). Emotional intelligence and deception detection: Why most people can't "read" others, but a few can. In R. E. Riggio & R. S. Feldman (Eds.), *Applications of nonverbal communication* (pp. 215–253). Mahwah, NJ: Erlbaum.

Parks, M. R. (1994). Communicative competence and interpersonal control. In M. L. Knapp & G. R. Miller (Eds.), *Handbook of interpersonal communication* (2nd ed., pp. 589–618). Thousand Oaks, CA: Sage.

Parks, M. R. (2007). *Personal relationships and personal networks.* Mahwah, NJ: Erlbaum.

Parks, M. R., & Adelman, M. B. (1983). Communication networks and the development of romantic relationships: An expansion of uncertainty reduction theory. *Human Communication Research,* 10, 55–79.

Patterson, M. L. (1983). *Nonverbal behavior: A functional perspective.* New York: Springer-Verlag.

Petronio, S. (Ed.). (2000). Balancing the secrets of private disclosures. Mahwah, NJ: Erlbaum.

Petronio, S. (2002). *Boundaries of privacy: Dialectics of disclosure.* Albany: State University of New York Press.

Planalp, S. (1998). Communicating emotion in everyday life: Cues, channels, and processes. In P. A. Andersen & L. K. Guerrero (Eds.), *Handbook of communication and emotion* (pp. 29–48). New York: Academic Press.

Planalp, S. (1999). *Communicating emotions: Social, moral, and cultural processes.* New York: Cambridge University Press.

Planalp, S. (2003). The unacknowledged role of emotion in theories of close relationships: How do theories feel? *Communication Theory,* 13, 78–99.

Planalp, S., & Honeycutt, J. (1985). Events that increase uncertainty in relationships. *Human Communication Research,* 11, 593–604.

Planalp, S., Rutherford, D. K., & Honeycutt, J. M. (1988). Events that increase uncertainty in personal relationships II: Replication and extension. *Human Communication Research,* 14(4), 516–547.

Postmes, T., Spears, R., Lea, M., & Reicher, S. D. (Eds.). (2000). *SIDE issues centre stage: Recent developments in studies of deindividuation of groups.* Amsterdam: Royal Netherlands Academy of Arts and Sciences.

Reeves, B., & Nass, C. I. (1996). *The media equation: How people treat computers, television and new media like real people and places.* New York: Cambridge University Press.

Roloff, M. E. (1981). *Interpersonal communication: The social exchange approach.* Beverly Hills, CA: Sage.

Roloff, M. E. (1987). Communication and reciprocity within intimate relationships. In M. E. Roloff & G. R. Miller (Eds.), *Interpersonal processes: New directions in communication research* (pp. 11–38). Beverly Hills, CA: Sage.

Rololff, M. E., & Campion, D. B. (1985). Conversational profit–seeking: Interaction as social exchange. In L. Street & J. N. Cappella (Eds.), *Sequence and pattern in communication behavior* (pp. 161–189). London: Edward Arnold.

Roloff, M. E., Putnam, L. L, & Anastasiou, L. (2003). Negotiation skills. In J. O. Greene & B. R. Burleson (Eds.), *Handbook of communication and social interaction skills* (pp. 801–833). Mahwah, NJ: Erlbaum.

Roloff, M. E., & Soule, K. P. (2002). Interpersonal conflict: A review. In M. L. Knapp & J. A. Daly (Eds.), *Handbook of interpersonal communication* (3rd ed., pp. 475–528). Thousand Oaks, CA: Sage.

Rowan, K. E. (2003). Informing and explaining skills: Theory and research on informative communication. In J. O. Greene & B. R. Burleson (Eds.), *Handbook of communication and social interaction skills* (pp. 403–438). Mahwah, NJ: Erlbaum.

Schramm, W. L., Lyle, J., & Parker, E. B. (1961). *Television in the lives of our children.* Stanford, CA: Stanford University Press.

Shepard, C. A. Giles, H., & Le Poire, B. A. (2001). Communication accommodation theory. In W. Robinson & H. Giles (Eds.), *The new handbook of language and social psychology* (pp. 33–56). Chichester, UK: Wiley.

Sherif, C. W., Sherif, M., & Nebergall, R. E. (1965). *Attitude and attitude change: The social judgment-involvement approach.* Philadelphia, PA: Saunders.

Sherif, M., & Hovland, C. I. (1961). *Social judgment: Assimilation and contrast effects in attitude change.* New Haven, CT: Yale University Press.

Siegel, J., Dubrovsky, V., Kiesler, S., & McGuire, T. (1983). Group processes in computer-mediated communication. *Organizational Behavior and Human Decision Processes, 37,* 694–710.

Sinclair, J. (1991). Corpus, concordance, collocation. Oxford, UK: Oxford University Press.

Smith, D. R., & Williamson, L. K. (1977). *Interpersonal communication: Roles, rules, strategies and games.* Dubuque, IA: W. C. Brown.

Solomon, D. H., & Knobloch, L. K. (2004). A model of relational turbulence: The role of intimacy, relational uncertainty, and interference from partners in appraisals of irritations. *Journal of Social and Personal Relationships, 21,* 795–816.

Spitzberg, B. H., & Cupach, W. R. (2002). Interpersonal skills. In M. L. Knapp & J. A. Daly (Eds.), *Handbook of interpersonal communication* (3rd ed., pp. 564–611). Thousand Oaks, CA: Sage.

Srull, T. K., & Wyer, R. S. (1986). The role of chronic and temporary goals in social information processing. In R. Sorrentino & E. T. Higgins (Eds.), *Handbook of motivation and cognition* (pp. 503–549). New York: Guilford.

Stafford, L. (2005). Maintaining long-distance and cross-residential relationships. Mahwah, NJ: Erlbaum Thibaut, J., & Kelley, H. H. (1959). *The social psychology of groups.* New York: Wiley.

Turkle, S. (1995). *Life on the screen: Identity in the age of the Internet.* New York: Touchstone.

Vrig, A., & Mann, S. (2005). Police use of nonverbal behavior as indicators of deception. In R. E. Riggio & R. S. Feldman (Eds.), *Applications of nonverbal communication* (pp. 63–94). Mahwah, NJ: Erlbaum.

Waldron, V. R. (1997). Toward a theory of interactive conversational planning. In J. O. Greene (Ed.), *Message production: Advances in communication theory* (pp. 195–220). Mahwah, NJ: Erlbaum,

Walther, J. B., & Parks, M. R. (2002). Cues filtered out, cues filtered in: Computer-mediated communication and relationships. In M. L. Knapp & J. A. Daly (Eds.), *Handbook of interpersonal communication* (3rd ed., pp. 529–563). Thousand Oaks, CA: Sage.

Wilson, S. R. (1990). Development and test of a cognitive rules model of interaction goals. *Communication Monographs, 57,* 81–103.

Wilson, S. R. (1995). Elaborating the cognitive rules model of interaction goals: The problem of accounting for individual differences in goal formation. In B. R. Burleson (Ed.), *Communication yearbook* (Vol. 18, pp. 3–25). Thousand Oaks, CA: Sage.

Wilson, S. R., & Sabee, C. M. (2003). Explicating communicative competence as a theoretical term. In J. O. Greene & B. R. Burleson (Eds.), *Handbook of communication and social interaction skills* (pp. 3–50). Mahwah, NJ: Erlbaum.

Wittgenstein, L. (1953). *Philosophical investigations.* Oxford, UK: Blackwell.

Wray, A., & Perkins, M. K. (2000). The functions of formulaic language: An integrated model. *Language and Communication, 20,* 1–28.

Wyer, R. S., Jr., & Adaval, R. (2003). Message reception skills in social communication. In J. O. Greene & B. R. Burleson (Eds.), *Handbook of communication and social interaction skills* (pp. 291–355). Mahwah, NJ: Erlbaum.

Chapter 9

Dynamics of Interpersonal Relationships

Ronald B. Adler, Lawrence B. Rosenfeld, and Russell F. Proctor II

The most significant aspects of our lives lie in the relationships we form with others. The reasons we form relationships is just as important, and most people define themselves in light of their relationships: wife, friend, mother, grandfather. In order to better understand these relationships, it is necessary to grasp the dynamics of human relationships—why we form them and how we maintain them.

Learning Objectives For This Chapter

- Describe the reasons humans form relationships
- Identify the different aspects of intimacy in communication
- Discuss the developmental models of interpersonal relationships
- Explain the dialectical perspective of relational dynamics
- Describe how communication is used to maintain relationships
- Explain the strategies used for repairing damaged relationships

I'm looking for a meaningful relationship."
"Our relationship has changed lately."
"The relationship is good for both of us."
"This relationship isn't working."

Relationship is one of those words that people use all the time but have trouble defining. Even scholars who have devoted their careers to studying relationships don't agree on what the term means (Guerrero et al., 2007). Their definitions include words like "closeness," "influence," "commitment," and "intimacy"—but coming up with a single definition can be (as the old adage goes) like nailing Jell-O to a wall.

One useful way to distinguish interpersonal relationships from less personal ones is to look for the characteristics: uniqueness, irreplaceability, interdependence, disclosure, and rewards. Even the closest relationships don't always reflect all of these qualities, but, taken together, they are a good measure of where a relationship fits on the impersonal-interpersonal spectrum.

This chapter will explore some of the dynamics that characterize interpersonal relationships and the communication that occurs within them. After reading it, you will see that relationships aren't fixed or unchanging. Rather, they can, and often do, change over time. In other words, a relationship is less a *thing* than a *process*. We'll look at why we form relationships, the dynamics of those relationships, and how to maintain them.

Why We Form Relationships

Why do we form relationships with some people and not with others? Sometimes we have no choice: Children can't select their parents, and most workers aren't able to choose their colleagues. In many other cases, however, we seek out some people and actively avoid others. In this section, we'll look at reasons we form relationships: interpersonal attraction, a desire for intimacy, and a quest for commitment.

Attraction

Social scientists have collected an impressive body of research on interpersonal attraction (e.g., Byrne, 1997; Tadinac & Hromatko, 2004). The following are some of the factors they have identified that influence our choice of relational partners.

Appearance. Most people claim that we should judge others on the basis of how they act, not how they look. However, the reality is quite the opposite (Mehrabian & Blum, 2003; Swami & Furnham, 2008). Appearance is especially important in the early stages of a relationship. In one study, a group of over 700 men and women were matched as blind dates, allegedly for a "computer dance." After the party was over, they were asked whether or not they would like to date their partners again. The result? The more physically attractive the person (as judged in advance by independent raters), the more likely he or she was seen as desirable. Other factors—social skills and intelligence, for example—didn't seem to affect the decision (Walster et al., 1966).

Although we might assume that attractive people are radically different from those who are less attractive, the truth is that we view the familiar as beautiful. Langlois and Roggman (1990) presented raters with two types of photos: Some were images of people from North European, Asian, and Latino backgrounds, while others were computer-generated images that combined the characteristics of several individuals. Surprisingly, the judges consistently preferred the composite photos of both men and women. When the features of eight individuals were combined into one image, viewers rated the picture as more attractive than the features of a single person or of a smaller combination of people. Thus, we seem to be drawn to people who represent the most average qualities of ourselves and those people we know. In other words, beautiful people aren't different from the rest of us. Rather, they're "radically similar."

Even if your appearance isn't beautiful by societal standards, consider these encouraging facts: First, after initial impressions have passed, ordinary-looking people with pleasing personalities are likely to be judged as attractive (Berscheid & Walster, 1978), and perceived beauty can be influenced by traits such as liking, respect, familiarity, and social interaction (Albada et al., 2002; Kniffin & Wilson, 2004). Second, physical factors become less important as a relationship progresses. As Don Hamachek (1982, p. 59) puts it, "Attractive features may open doors, but apparently, it takes more than physical beauty to keep them open."

Similarity. It's comforting to know someone who likes the same things you like, has similar values, and may even be of the same race, economic class, or educational standing. The basis for this sort of relationship, commonly known as the *similarity thesis,* is the most frequently discussed and strongly supported determinant of relationship formation (Buss, 1985; Yun, 2002). For example, the more similar a married couple's personalities are, the more likely they are to report being happy and satisfied in their marriage (Luo & Klohnen, 2005). Friends in middle and high school report being similar to each other in many ways, including having mutual friends, enjoying the same sports, liking the same social activities, and using (or not using) alcohol and cigarettes to the same degree (Aboud & Mendelson, 1998; Urberg et al., 1998). For adults, similarity is more important to relational happiness than even communication ability:

Friends who have similarly low levels of communication skills are just as satisfied with their relationships as are friends having high levels of skills (Burleson & Samter, 1996).

There are several reasons why similarity is a strong foundation for relationships. First, similarities can be validating. The fact that another person shares your beliefs, tastes, and values can be a form of ego support. One study described the lengths to which "implicit egotism" may unconsciously affect perceptions of attractiveness (Jones et al., 2004). Results showed that people are disproportionately likely to marry others whose first or last names resemble their own, and they're also attracted to those with similar birthdays and even jersey numbers.

Second, when someone is similar to you, you can make fairly accurate predictions—whether the person will want to eat at the Mexican restaurant or hear the concert you're so excited about. This ability to make confident predictions reduces uncertainty and anxiety (Duck & Barnes, 1992).

There's a third explanation for the similarity thesis. It may be that when we learn that other people are similar to us, we assume they'll probably like us, so we in turn like them. The self-fulfilling prophecy creeps into the picture again.

Similarity turns from attraction to dislike when we encounter people who are like us in many ways but who behave in a strange or socially offensive manner (Cooper & Jones, 1969; Taylor & Metre, 1971). For instance, you have probably disliked people others have said were "just like you" but who talked too much, were complainers, or had some other unappealing characteristic. In fact, there is a tendency to have stronger dislike for similar but offensive people than for those who are offensive but different. One likely reason is that such people threaten our self-esteem, causing us to fear that we may be as unappealing as they are. In such circumstances, the reaction is often to put as much distance as possible between ourselves and this threat to our ideal self-image.

Complementarity. The old saying "opposites attract" seems to contradict the principle of similarity we just described. In truth, though, both are valid. Differences strengthen a relationship when they are *complementary*—when each partner's characteristics satisfy the other's needs. Research suggests that attraction to partners who have complementary temperaments might be rooted in biology (Fisher, 2007). In addition, some studies show that couples are more likely to be attracted to each other when one partner is dominant and the other passive (Nowicki & Manheim, 1991; Swami & Furnham, 2008). Relationships also work well when the partners agree that one will exercise control in certain areas ("You make the final decisions about money") and the other will take the lead in different ones ("I'll decide how we ought to decorate the place"). Strains occur when control issues are disputed.

Studies that have examined successful and unsuccessful couples over a 20-year period show the interaction between similarities and differences (Klohnen & Luo, 2003). When partners are radically different, the dissimilar qualities that at first appear intriguing later become cause for relational breakups (Amodio & Showers, 2005; Felmlee, 2001). Partners in successful marriages were similar enough to satisfy each other physically and mentally, but were different enough to meet each other's needs and keep the relationship interesting. The successful couples found ways to keep a balance between their similarities and differences while adjusting to the changes that occurred over the years.

Rewards. Some relationships are based on an economic model called *exchange theory* (Jeffries, 2002; Thibaut & Kelley, 1959). This approach suggests that we often seek out people who can give us rewards that are greater than or equal to the costs we encounter in dealing with them. Social exchange theorists define rewards as any outcomes we desire. They may be tangible (a nice place to live, a high paying job) or intangible (prestige, emotional support, companionship). Costs are undesirable outcomes: unpleasant work, emotional pain, and so on. A simple formula captures the social exchange explanation for why we form and maintain relationships:

Rewards – Costs = Outcome

According to social exchange theorists, we use this formula (often unconsciously) to calculate whether a relationship is a "good deal" or "not worth the effort," based on whether the outcome is positive or negative.

At its most blatant level, an exchange approach seems cold and calculating, but in some types of relationships it seems quite appropriate. A healthy business relationship is based on how well the parties help one another, and some friendships are based on an informal kind of barter: "I don't mind listening to the ups and downs of your love life because you rescue me when the house needs repairs." Even close relationships have an element of exchange. Friends and lovers often tolerate each other's quirks because the comfort and enjoyment they get make the less-than-pleasant times worth accepting. However, when one partner feels "underbenefited," it often leads to relational disruption or termination (DeMaris, 2007).

Costs and rewards don't exist in isolation: We define them by comparing a certain situation with alternatives. For example, consider a hypothetical woman, Gloria, who is struggling to decide whether to remain in a relationship with Raymond, her longtime boyfriend. Raymond does love Gloria, but he's not perfect: He has a hair-trigger temper, and he has become verbally abusive from time to time. Also, Gloria knows that Raymond was unfaithful to her at least once. In deciding whether or not to stay with Raymond, Gloria will use two standards.

The first standard is her **comparison level (CL)**—her minimum standard of what behavior is acceptable. If Gloria believes that relational partners have an obligation to be faithful and treat one another respectfully at all times, then Raymond's behavior will fall below her comparison level. This will be especially true if Gloria has had positive romantic relationships in the past (Merolla et al., 2004). On the other hand, if Gloria adopts a nobody's perfect" standard, she is more likely to view Raymond's behavior as meeting or exceeding her comparison level.

Gloria also will rate Raymond according to her **comparison level of alternatives (CL_{alt})**. This standard refers to a comparison between the rewards she is receiving in her present situation and those she could expect to receive in others (Overall & Sibley, 2008). If, for example, Gloria doesn't want to be alone and she thinks, "If I don't have Raymond I won't have anyone," then her CL_{alt} would be lower than her present situation; but if she is confident that she could find a kinder partner, her CL_{alt} would be higher than the status quo.

Social exchange theorists suggest that communicators unconsciously use this calculus to decide whether to form and stay in relationships. At first this information seems to offer little comfort to communicators who are in unsatisfying relationships, such as when the partner's behavior is below the CL and there are no foreseeable alternatives (CL_{alt}). But there are other choices than being stuck in situations where the costs outweigh the rewards. First, you might make sure that you are judging your present relationship against a realistic comparison level. Expecting a situation to be perfect can be a recipe for unhappiness. If you decide that your present situation truly falls below your comparison level, you might explore whether there are other alternatives you haven't considered.

And finally, the skills introduced throughout this book may help you negotiate a better relationship with the other person.

Competency. We like to be around talented people, probably because we hope their skills and abilities will rub off on us. On the other hand, we are uncomfortable around those who are too competent—probably because we look bad by comparison. Elliot Aronson and his associates (1966) demonstrated how competence and imperfection combine to affect attraction by having subjects evaluate tape recordings of candidates for a quiz program. One was a "perfect" candidate who answered almost all the questions correctly and modestly admitted that he was an honor student, athlete, and college yearbook editor. The "average" candidate answered fewer questions correctly, had average grades, was a less successful athlete, and was a low-level member of the yearbook staff. Toward the end of half the tapes, the candidates committed a blunder, spilling coffee all over themselves. The remaining half of the tapes contained no such blunder. These, then, were the four experimental conditions: (1) a person with superior ability who blundered; (2) a person with superior ability who did not blunder; (3) an average person who blundered; and (4) an average person who did not blunder. The students who rated the attractiveness of these four types of people revealed an interesting and important principle of interpersonal attraction. The most attractive person was the superior candidate who blundered. Next was the superior person who did not blunder. Third was the average person who did not blunder. The least attractive person was the average person who committed the blunder.

Aronson's conclusion was that we like people who are somewhat flawed because they remind us of ourselves. However, there are some qualifications to this principle. People with especially positive or negative self-esteem find "perfect" people more attractive than those who are competent but flawed (Helmreich et al., 1970). Furthermore, women tend to be more impressed by uniformly superior people, whereas men find desirable but "human" subjects especially attractive (Deaux, 1972). On the whole, though, the principle stands: The best way to gain the liking of others is to be good at what you do but also to admit your mistakes.

Proximity. As common sense suggests, we are likely to develop relationships with people with whom we interact frequently (Flora, 2005). In many cases, proximity leads to liking. For instance, we're more likely to develop friendships with close neighbors—whether near where we live or in adjacent seats in our classrooms (Back et al., 2008)—than with distant ones. Chances are also good that we'll choose a mate with whom we cross paths often. Proximity even has a role in computer-mediated communication, where sharing a portion of cyberspace—a chat room, or instant messaging connection, for example—constitutes virtual proximity (Levine, 2000). Facts like these are understandable when we consider that proximity allows us to get more information about other people and benefit from a relationship with them. Also, people in close proximity may be more similar to us than those not close—for example, if we live in the same neighborhood, odds are we share the same socioeconomic status.

Familiarity, on the other hand, can breed contempt. Evidence to support this fact comes from police blotters as well as university laboratories. Thieves frequently prey on nearby victims, even though the risk of being recognized is greater. Most aggravated assaults occur within the family or among close neighbors. The same principle holds in more routine contexts: You are likely to develop strong personal feelings, either positive or negative, toward others you encounter frequently.

Disclosure. Sometimes the basis of this attraction comes from learning about ways we are similar, either in experiences ("I broke off an engagement myself) or in attitudes ("I feel nervous with strangers, too"). Self-disclosure also increases liking because it indicates regard. Sharing private information is a form of respect and trust—a kind of liking that we've already seen increases attractiveness.

Not all disclosure leads to liking. Research shows that the key to satisfying self-disclosure is *reciprocity:* getting back an amount and kind of information equivalent to that which you reveal (Dindia, 2000a). A second important ingredient in successful self-disclosure is *timing.* It's probably unwise to talk about your sexual insecurities with a new acquaintance or express your pet peeves to a friend at your birthday party. The information you reveal ought to be appropriate for the setting and stage of the relationship (Archer & Berg, 1978; Wortman et al, 1976). (See the Dark Side box on this page for other concerns about self-disclosing too quickly in a relationship.)

Intimacy

The musical group Three Dog Night said it well: One *can* be the loneliest number. For most of us, the desire to connect with others is a powerful force that leads us to seek out and form relationships. Strong attachments with others not only make us happier, they also can make us healthier and help us live longer.

In their book *Intimacy: Strategies for Successful Relationships;* C. Edward Crowther and Gayle Stone (1986) offer a reminder of just how important close relationships can be. As part of a study of people who were dying in hospices and hospitals in the United States and England, Crowther and Stone asked each person what mattered most in his or her life. Fully 90 percent of these terminally ill patients put intimate relationships at the top of the list. Similarly, Christopher Peterson (2006) summarizes research showing that close relationships "may be the *single most important* source of life satisfaction and emotional well-being, across different ages and cultures" (p. 261). With this in mind, let's take a closer look at what it means to have intimate relationships with others.

Dimensions of Intimacy. When researchers asked several hundred college students to identify their "closest, deepest, most involved, and most intimate relationship" (Berscheid et al., 1989), the answers were varied. Roughly half (47 percent) identified a romantic partner. About a third (36 percent) chose a friendship. Most of the rest (14 percent) cited a family member.

Intimacy comes in many forms (Laurenceau &, Kleinman, 2006; Lippert & Prager, 2001). One type is *emotional:* sharing important information and feelings. These kinds of self-disclosures in detail. Sometimes emotional intimacy comes from talking about feelings, such as acknowledging when you're hurt and embarrassed or saying "I love you." In other cases, emotional intimacy develops as a result of topics that are discussed—personal information, secrets, or delicate subjects. One such subject can be money, which has led some self-help authors to use the term *financial intimacy* to describe how couples need to be open, honest, and in sync on this important topic (Hayes, 2006; Orman, 2005).

Another form of intimacy is *physical* Even before birth, the developing fetus experiences a kind of physical closeness with its mother that will never happen again: "Floating in a warm fluid, curling inside a total embrace, swaying to the undulations of the moving body and hearing the beat of the pulsing heart" (Morris, 1973, p. 7). As they grow up, fortunate children are continually nourished by physical intimacy: being rocked, fed, hugged, and held. As we grow older, the opportunities for physical intimacy are less regular, but still possible and important. Some physical intimacy is sexual, but this category also can include affectionate hugs, kisses, and even struggles. Companions who have endured physical challenges together—for example, in athletics or during emergencies—form a bond that can last a lifetime.

In other cases, intimacy comes from *intellectual* sharing (Cowan & Mills, 2004; Schaefer & Olson, 1981). Not every exchange of ideas counts as intimacy, of course. Talking about next week's midterm with your professor or classmates isn't likely to forge strong relational bonds. But when you engage another person in an exchange of important ideas, a kind of closeness develops that can be powerful and exciting.

Shared activities can provide a fourth way to emotional closeness (Wood & Inman, 1993). Not all shared activities lead to intimacy. You might work with a colleague for years without feeling any sort of emotional connection. But some shared experiences—struggling together against obstacles or living together as housemates are good examples—can create strong bonds. Play is one valuable form of shared activity. Leslie Baxter (1992) found that both same-sex friendships and opposite-sex romantic relationships were characterized by several forms of play. Partners invented private codes, fooled around by acting like other people, teased one another, and played games—everything from having punning contests to arm wrestling.

The amount and type of intimacy can vary from one relationship to another (Speicher, 1999). Some intimate relationships exhibit all four qualities: emotional disclosure, physical intimacy, intellectual exchanges, and shared activities. Other intimate relationships exhibit only one or two. Of course, some relationships aren't intimate in any way. Acquaintances, roommates, and coworkers may never become intimate. In some cases, even family members develop smooth but relatively impersonal relationships.

Not even the closest relationships always operate at the highest level of intimacy. At some times, you might share all of your thoughts or feelings with a friend, family member, or lover; at other times, you might withdraw. You might freely share your feelings about one topic and stay more distant regarding another one. The same principle holds for physical intimacy, which waxes and wanes in most relationships.

Despite the fact that no relationship is *always* intimate, living without *any* sort of intimacy is hardly desirable. For example, people who fear intimacy in dating relationships anticipate less satisfaction in a long-term relationship and report feeling more distant from even longtime dating partners. A great deal of evidence supports the conclusion that fear of intimacy can cause major problems in both creating relationships and sustaining them (Greenberg & Goldman, 2008; Vangelisti & Beck, 2007).

Gender and Intimacy. Until recently, most social scientists believed that women were more concerned with and better than men at developing and maintaining intimate relationships (Impett & Peplau, 2006). Most research *does* show that women (taken as a group, of course) are more interested than men in achieving emotional intimacy (Cross & Madson, 1997; Eldridge & Christensen, 2002), more willing to make emotional commitments (Rusbult & Van Lange, 1996), and somewhat more willing to share their most personal thoughts and feelings (Dindia & Allen, 1992; Stafford et al., 2000), although the differences aren't as dramatic as most people believe (Dindia, 2000b, 2002). In some settings, such as therapist-patient, there appear to be no differences at all (Roe, 2001).

Many social scientists who explored the relationship between biological sex, gender, and communication interpreted the relatively lower rate of male self-disclosure as a sign that men were unwilling or unable to develop close relationships. Some (e.g., Weiss & Lowenthal, 1975) argued that the female trait of disclosing personal information and feelings made them more "emotionally mature" and "interpersonally competent" than men. The title of one book captured this attitude of female superiority and male deficiency: *The Inexpressive Male: A Tragedy of American Society* (Balswick, 1988). Personal growth programs and self-help books urged men to achieve closeness by learning to open up and share their feelings.

But more recent scholarship has begun to show that emotional expression isn't the *only* way to develop close relationships (Floyd, 1996; Zorn & Gregory, 2005). Whereas women place a somewhat higher value on talking about personal matters as a measure of closeness, men are more likely to create and express closeness by doing things together—often in groups rather than in one-on-one interactions (Baumeister, 2005). In one study, more than 75 percent of the men surveyed said that their most meaningful experiences with friends came from shared activities (Swain, 1989). They reported that through shared activities they "grew on one another," developed feelings of interdependence, showed appreciation for one another, and demonstrated mutual liking. Likewise, men regarded practical help as a measure of caring. Findings like these show that, for many men, closeness grows from activities that don't always depend heavily on disclosure: A friend is a person who does things *for* you and *with* you. Of course, it's important not to assume that all men who value shared activities are reluctant to share feelings, or that doing things together isn't important to women. Recent scholarship offers convincing evidence that, in many respects, the meaning of intimacy is more similar than different for men and women (Goldsmith & Fulfs, 1999; Radmacher & Azmitia, 2006).

Whatever differences do exist between male and female styles of intimacy help explain some of the stresses and misunderstandings that can arise between the sexes. For example, a woman who looks for emotional disclosure as a measure of affection may overlook an inexpressive man's efforts to show he cares by doing favors or spending time with her. Fixing a leaky faucet or taking a hike may look like ways to avoid getting close, but to the man who proposes them, they may be measures of affection and bids for intimacy. Likewise, differing ideas about the timing and meaning of sex can lead to misunderstandings. Whereas many women think of sex as a way to *express* an intimacy that has already developed, men are more likely to see it as a way to *create* that intimacy (Reissman, 1990). In this sense, the man who encourages sex early in a relationship or after a fight may not just be a testosterone-crazed lecher: He may view the shared activity as a way to build closeness. By contrast, the woman who views personal talk as the pathway to intimacy may resist the idea of physical closeness before the emotional side of the relationship has been discussed.

As with all research looking at women's and men's communication, it's important to realize that no generalization applies to every person. Furthermore, stereotypes are changing. For example, an analysis of prime-time television sitcoms revealed that male characters who disclose personal information generally receive favorable responses from other characters (Good et al., 2002).

In addition, researchers Mark Morman and Kory Floyd (2002) note that a cultural shift is occurring in the U.S. in which fathers are becoming more affectionate with their sons than they were in previous generations—although some of that affection is still expressed through shared activities.

Culture and Intimacy. Historically, the notions of public and private behavior have changed dramatically (Adamopoulos, 1991; Gadlin, 1977). What would be considered intimate behavior today was quite public at times in the past. For example, in 16th-century Germany, the new husband and wife were expected to consummate their marriage upon a bed carried by witnesses who would validate the marriage! Conversely, in England as well as in colonial America, the customary level of communication between spouses was once rather formal—not much different from the way acquaintances or neighbors spoke to one another.

Today, the notion of intimacy varies from one culture to another (Adams et al., 2004; Marshall, 2008). In one study, researchers asked residents of Great Britain, Japan, Hong Kong, and Italy to describe their use of 33 rules that regulated interaction in social relationships (Argyle & Henderson, 1985). The rules governed a wide range of communication behaviors: everything from the use of humor, to handshaking, to the management of money. The results showed that the greatest differences between Asian and European cultures involved the rules for dealing with intimacy, including showing emotions, expressing affection in public, engaging in sexual activity, and respecting privacy.

While some of these distinctions continue to hold true, cultural differences in intimacy are becoming less prominent as the world becomes more connected through the media, travel, and technology. For instance, romance and passionate love were once seen as particularly "American" concepts of intimacy. However, recent evidence shows that men and women in a variety of cultures—individualist and collectivist, urban and rural, rich and poverty-stricken—may be every bit as romantic as Americans (Hatfield & Rapson, 2006). These studies suggest that the large differences that once existed between Western and Eastern cultures may be fast disappearing.

A principle to keep in mind when communicating with people from different cultures is that it's important to consider their norms for appropriate intimacy. On one hand, don't mistakenly judge them according to your own standards. Likewise, be sensitive about honoring their standards when talking about yourself. In this sense, choosing the proper level of intimacy isn't too different from choosing the appropriate way of dressing or eating when encountering members of a different culture: What seems familiar and correct at home may not be suitable with strangers.

Computer-Mediated Communication and Intimacy. A few decades ago, it would have been hard to conceive that the words *computer* and *intimacy* could be positively linked. Computers were viewed as impersonal machines that couldn't transmit important features of human communication, such as facial expression, tone of voice, and touch. However, researchers now know that computer-mediated communication (CMC) can be just as personal as face-to-face (FtF) interaction. In fact, studies show that relational intimacy may develop more quickly through CMC than in FtF communication (Hian et al., 2004) and that CMC enhances verbal, emotional, and social intimacy in friendships (Hu et al., 2004).

Your own experience probably supports these claims. The relative anonymity of chat rooms, blogs, and online dating services fosters a freedom of expression that might not occur in FtF meetings (Ben-Ze'ev, 2003), giving relationships a chance to get started. In addition, instant messaging, e-mailing, and text messaging offer more constant contact with friends, family, and partners than might otherwise be possible (Boase et al., 2006). The potential for developing and maintaining intimate relationships via computer is captured well by one user's comment (which has a fun double meaning): "I've never clicked this much with anyone in my life" (Henderson & Gilding, 2004, p. 505).

This doesn't mean that all cyber-relationships are (or will become) intimate. Just as in face-to-face relationships, communicators choose varying levels of self-disclosure with their cyberpartners. Some online relationships are relatively impersonal; others are highly interpersonal. In any case, CMC is an important component in creating and maintaining intimacy in contemporary relationships.

The Limits of Intimacy. It's impossible to have a close relationship with everyone you know—nor is that necessarily desirable. Social psychologist Roy Baumeister (2005) makes a compelling case that, on average, most people want four to six close, important relationships in their lives at any given time. While fewer than four such relationships can lead to a sense of social deprivation, more than six leads to diminishing returns. "It is possible," notes Baumeister, "that people simply do not have the time or energy to pursue emotional closeness with more than a half dozen people" (p. 113).

Even if we could seek intimacy with everyone we encounter, few of us would want that much closeness. Consider the range of everyday contacts that don't require any sort of intimacy. Some are based on economic exchange (the people at work or the shopkeeper you visit several times a week), some are based on group membership (church or school), some on physical proximity (neighbors, carpooling), and some grow out of third-party connections (mutual friends, child care). Simply engaging in conversational give-and-take with both strangers and acquaintances can be enjoyable.

Some scholars have pointed out that an *obsession* with intimacy can lead to *less* satisfying relationships (Bellah et al., 1985; Parks, 1982). People who consider intimate communication as the only kind worth pursuing place little value on relationships that don't meet this standard. This can lead them to regard interaction with strangers and casual acquaintances as superficial, or at best as the groundwork for deeper relationships. When you consider the pleasure that can come from polite but distant communication, the limitations of this view become clear. Intimacy is definitely rewarding, but it isn't the only way of relating to others.

Commitment

How important is the role of commitment in personal relationships? Sentiments like the following suggest an answer: "I'm looking for a committed relationship." "Our relationship didn't work because my partner wasn't committed." "I'm just not ready for commitment."

Relational commitment involves a promise—sometimes implied and sometimes explicit—to remain in a relationship and to make that relationship successful. Commitment is important in every type of interpersonal relationship, whether it's a friendship ("Friends for life!"), family ("We're always here for you"), a close-knit working team ("I've got you covered"), or a romantic relationship ("Till death do us part").

As these examples suggest, commitment is both formed and reinforced through communication. Table 9.1 spells out commitment indicators in romantic relationships. You can probably imagine how similar indicators of commitment would operate in other sorts of close relationships.

As Table 9.1 indicates, words alone aren't a surefire measure of true commitment. Deeds are also important. Simply saying "You can count on me" doesn't guarantee loyalty. But without language, commitment may not be clear. For this reason, ceremonies formalizing relationships are an important way to recognize and cement commitment. We'll discuss such ceremonies more in the discussion of bonding on pages 292–293.

Communication and Relational Dynamics

Even the most stable relationships vary from day to day and over longer periods of time. Communication scholars have attempted to describe and explain how communication creates and reflects the changing dynamics of relational interaction. The following pages describe two very different characterizations of relational development and interaction.

Table 9.1: Major Indicators of a Committed Romantic Relationship

- Providing affection
- Providing support
- Maintaining integrity
- Sharing companionship
- Making an effort to communicate regularly
- Showing respect
- Creating a relational future
- Creating a positive relational atmosphere
- Working on relationship problems together
- Reassuring one's commitment

Developmental Models of Interpersonal Relationships

One of the best-known models of relational stages was developed by Mark Knapp (Knapp & Vangelisti, 2006; see also Avtgis et al, 1998; Welch & Rubin, 2002), who broke the waxing and waning of relationships into 10 steps. Other researchers have suggested that in addition to coming together and coming apart, any model of relational communication ought to contain a third area, **relational maintenance**—communication aimed at keeping relationships operating smoothly and satisfactorily (we'll discuss relational maintenance in more detail later in this chapter). Figure 9.1 shows how Knapp's 10 stages fit into this three-part view of relational communication. This model seems most appropriate for describing communication between romantic partners, but in some cases it can depict other types of close relationships. As you read the following section, consider how the stages could describe a long-term friendship (Johnson et al., 2004), a couple in love, or even business partners.

Initiating. The goals in the **initiating** stage are to show that you are interested in making contact and to demonstrate that you are a person worth talking to. Communication during this stage is usually brief, and it generally follows conventional formulas: handshakes, remarks about innocuous subjects such as the weather, and friendly expressions. Such behavior may seem superficial and meaningless, but it is a way of signaling that you're interested in building some kind of relationship with the other person. It allows us to say, without saying, "I'm a friendly person, and I'd like to get to know you."

Initiating relationships—especially romantic ones—can be particularly difficult for people who are shy. Computer-mediated communication can make it easier for reticent people to strike up a relationship (Sheeks & Birchmeier, 2007). One study of an online

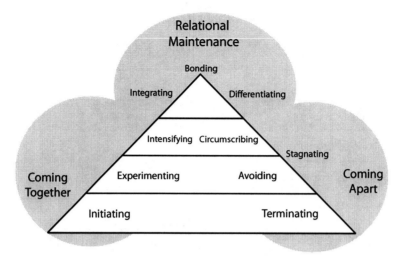

Figure 9.1: Stages of Relationship Development

dating service found that participants who identified themselves as shy expressed a greater appreciation for the system's anonymous, non-threatening environment than did non-shy users (Scharlott & Christ, 1995). The researchers found that many shy users employed the online service specifically to help them overcome their inhibitions about initiating relationships in face-to-face settings.

Experimenting. After making contact with a new person, we generally begin the search for common ground. This search usually starts with the basics: "Where are you from? What's your major?" From there we look for other similarities: "You're a runner too? How many miles do you run a week?"

It usually doesn't take long for communicators who are interested in one another to move from initiating to **experimenting.** The shift seems to occur even more rapidly in cyberspace than in person (Pratt et al., 1999; Tidwell & Walther, 2002). People who develop relationships via e-mail begin asking questions about attitudes, opinions, and preferences more quickly than those in face-to-face contact. It probably helps that e-mailers can't see each others' nonverbal reactions—they don't have to worry about blushing, stammering, or looking away if they realize that they asked for too much information too quickly.

The hallmark of experimenting is small talk. We tolerate the ordeal of small talk because it serves several functions. First, it is a useful way to find out what interests we share with the other person. It also provides a way to "audition" the other person—to help us decide whether a relationship is worth pursuing. In addition, small talk is a safe way to ease into a relationship. You haven't risked much as you decide whether to proceed further. Finally, small talk does provide some kind of link to others. It's often better than being alone.

The kind of information we look for during the experimentation stage depends on the nature of the relationship we are seeking (Miller, 1998; Stewart et al, 2000). For example, both men and women who are seeking short-term relationships look for someone with an exciting personality and a good sense of humor. Qualities of being trustworthy and romantic become more important when people seek long-term relationships.

Intensifying. In friendships, intensifying often includes participating in shared activities, hanging out with mutual friends, or taking trips together (Johnson et al., 2004). Dating couples use a wide range of strategies to communicate that their relationship is intensifying (Tolhuizen, 1989). About a quarter of the time they express their feelings directly to discuss the state of the relationship, such as saying "I love you" (Brantley et al., 2002; Owen, 1987). More often they use less direct methods of communication: spending an increasing amount of time together, asking for support from one another, doing favors for the partner, giving tokens of affection, hinting and flirting, expressing feelings nonverbally, getting to know the partner's friends and family, and trying to look more physically attractive (Richmond et al., 1987).

The intensifying stage is usually a time of relational excitement and even euphoria. For romantic partners, it's often filled with starstruck gazes, goose bumps, and daydreaming. As a result, it's a stage that's regularly depicted in movies and romance novels—after all, we love to watch lovers in love. The problem, of course, is that the stage doesn't last forever. Sometimes romantic partners who stop feeling goose bumps begin to question whether they're still in love. While it's possible that they're not, it also could be that they've simply moved on to a different stage in their relationship—such as integrating.

Integrating. As the relationship strengthens, the individuals enter an **integrating** stage. They begin to take on an identity as a social unit. Invitations begin to come addressed to a couple. Social circles merge. The partners share each other's commitments: "Sure, we'll spend Thanksgiving with your family." Common property may begin to be designated—our apartment, our car, our song (Baxter, 1987). Partners develop their own personal idioms (Bell & Healey, 1992) and forms of play (Baxter, 1992). They develop routines and rituals that reinforce their identity as a couple—jogging together, eating at a favorite restaurant, expressing affection with a goodnight kiss, and worshipping together (Afifi & Johnson, 1999; Bruess & Pearson, 1997). As these examples illustrate, the stage of integrating is a time when we give up some characteristics of our former selves and become different people.

As we become more integrated with others, our sense of obligation to them grows (Roloff et al., 1988). We feel obliged to provide a variety of resources, such as class notes and money, whether or not the other person asks for them. When intimates do make requests of one another, they are relatively straightforward. Gone are the elaborate explanations, inducements, and apologies. In short, partners in an integrated relationship expect more from one another than they do in less intimate associations.

As integration increases and as we become more intimate, uncertainty about our relationship decreases: We become clearer about relationship norms, and about what behaviors are appropriate and inappropriate. In addition, our ability to influence each other's daily activities increases, such as the amount of time spent with friends and doing schoolwork (Solomon & Knobloch, 2001). Reducing uncertainty about our partner and the relationship enhances attraction and feelings of closeness (Knobloch & Solomon, 2002).

Bonding. During the **bonding** stage, partners make symbolic public gestures to show the world that their relationship exists. These gestures can take the form of a contract between business partners or a license to be married. Bonding typically generates social support for the relationship. Custom and law impose certain obligations on partners who have officially bonded.

What constitutes a bonded, committed relationship is not always easy to define (Foster, 2008). Terms such as *common-law, cohabitation,* and *life partners* have been used to describe relationships that don't have the full support of custom and law but still involve an implicit or explicit bond. Nonetheless, given the importance of bonding in validating relationships and taking them to another level, it's not surprising that the gay and lesbian communities are striving to have legally sanctioned and recognized marriages.

For our purposes here, we'll define bonded relationships as those involving a significant measure of public commitment. These can include engagement or marriage, sharing a residence, a public ceremony, or a written or verbal pledge. The key is that bonding is the culmination of a developed relationship—the "officializing" of a couple's integration.

Relationships don't have to be romantic to achieve bonding. Consider, for instance, authors contracting to write a book together or a student being initiated into a sorority. As Lillian Rubin (1985) notes, in some cultures there are rituals for friends to mark their bonded status through a public commitment:

> Some Western cultures have rituals to mark the progress of a friendship and to give it public legitimacy and form. In Germany, for example, there's a small ceremony called *Duzen,* the name itself signifying the transformation in the relationship. The ritual calls for the two friends, each holding a glass of wine or beer, to entwine arms, thus bringing each other physically close, and to drink up after making a promise of eternal brotherhood with the word *Bruderschaft.* When it's over, the friends will have passed from a relationship that requires the formal *Sie* mode of address to the familiar *du.*

Bonding usually marks an important turning point in relationships. Up to now the relationship may have developed at a steady pace: Experimenting gradually moved into intensifying and then into integrating. Now, however, there is a spurt of commitment. The public display and declaration of exclusivity make this a critical period in the relationship.

Differentiating. Now that the two people have formed this commonality, they need to reestablish individual identities. How are we different? How am I unique? **Differentiating** often occurs when a relationship begins to experience the first, inevitable feelings of stress. This often shows up in a couple's pronoun usage. Instead of talking about "our" weekend plans, differentiating conversations focus on what "I" want to do. Relational issues that were once agreed upon (such as "You'll be the breadwinner and I'll manage the home") now become points of contention: "Why am I stuck at home when I have better career

Source: Weigel, D. J. (2008). Mutuality and the communication of commitment in romantic relationships. *Southern Communication Journal, 73,* 24–41.

potential than *you?*" The root of the term *differentiating* is the word *different*, suggesting that change plays an important role in this stage.

Differentiation also can be positive, for people need to be individuals as well as part of a relationship. And as the model on page 290 shows, differentiating is often a part of normal relational maintenance, in which partners manage the inevitable challenges that come their way. The key to successful differentiation is maintaining commitment to a relationship while creating the space for being individuals as well (well describe this later in the chapter as the connection-autonomy dialectic).

Circumscribing. So far, we have been looking at the growth of relationships. Although some reach a plateau of development, going on successfully for as long as a lifetime, others pass through several stages of decline and dissolution., In the **circumscribing** stage, communication between members decreases in quantity and quality (Duck, 1987). Subtle hints of dissatisfaction grow more evident. Working later at the office, seeking less and less romance, and more and more arguing begin to form a pattern that is hard to ignore (Kellermann et al., 1991). Ironically, both partners in a circumscribed relationship still cooperate in one way: suppressing the true status of the relationship. They hide its decline from others and even from themselves (Vaughn, 1987). Restrictions and restraints characterize this stage, and dynamic communication becomes static. Rather than discuss a disagreement (which requires some degree of energy on both parts), members opt for withdrawal: either mental (silence or daydreaming and fantasizing) or physical (where people spend less time together). Circumscribing doesn't involve total avoidance, which comes later. Rather, it entails a shrinking of interest and commitment.

Stagnating. If circumscribing continues, the relationship begins to stagnate. Members behave toward each other in old, familiar ways without much feeling. No growth occurs. The **stagnating** relationship is a hollow shell of its former self. We see stagnation in many workers who have lost enthusiasm for their job yet continue to go through the motions for years. The same sad event occurs for some couples who unenthusiastically have the same conversations, see the same people, and follow the same routines without any sense of joy or novelty.

Avoiding. When stagnation becomes too unpleasant, people in a relationship begin to create distance between each other by **avoiding**. Sometimes they do it under the guise of excuses ("I've been sick lately and can't see you") and sometimes directly ("Please don't call me; I don't want to see you now"). In either case, by this point the handwriting is on the wall about the relationship's future.

Research by Jon Hess (2000) reveals that there are several ways we gain distance. One way is *expressing detachment,* such as avoiding the other person altogether, or zoning out. A second way is *avoiding involvement,* such as leaving the room, ignoring the person's questions, steering clear of touching, and being superficially polite. *Showing antagonism* is a third technique, which includes behaving in a hostile way and treating the other person as a lesser person. A fourth strategy is to *mentally dissociate* from the other person, such as by thinking about the other person as less capable, or as unimportant. A vicious cycle gets started when avoiding the other person: the more one person avoids the other, the greater the odds the other will reciprocate. And the more topics that are avoided, the less satisfactory is the relationship (Sargent, 2002).

Terminating. Not all relationships end: Many partnerships, friendships, and marriages last for a lifetime once they're established. But many do deteriorate and reach the final stage of **terminating**. The process of terminating has its own distinguishable pattern (Battaglia et al., 1998; Conlan, 2008). Characteristics of this stage include summary dialogues of where the relationship has gone and the desire to dissociate. The relationship may end with a cordial dinner, a note left on the kitchen table, a phone call, or a legal document stating the dissolution. Depending on each person's feelings, this terminating stage can be quite short or it may be drawn out over time, with bitter jabs at each other. In either case, termination doesn't have to be totally negative. Understanding each other's investments in the relationship and needs for personal growth may dilute the hard feelings.

How do the individuals deal with each other after a romantic relationship has ended? The best predictor of whether the individuals will become friends after the relationship is terminated is whether they were friends before their romantic involvement (Metts et al., 1989). The way the couple splits up also makes a difference. It's no surprise to find that friendships are most possible when communication during the breakup was positive: expressions that there were no regrets for time spent together and other attempts to minimize hard feelings. When communication during termination is negative (manipulative, complaining to third parties), friendships are less likely.

Terminating a relationship is, for many people, a learning experience. Ty Tashiro and Patricia Frazier (2003) asked college students who recently had a romantic relationship breakup to describe the positive things they learned that might help them in future romantic relationships. Responses fell into four categories: "person positives," such as gaining self-confidence and that it's all right to cry; "other positives," such as learning more about what is desired in a partner; "relational positives," such as how to communicate better and how not to jump into a relationship too quickly; and "environment positives," such as learning to rely more on friends and how to better balance relationships and school work.

Limits of Developmental Models. While Knapp's model offers insights into relational stages, it doesn't describe the ebb and flow of communication in every relationship. For instance, many relationships don't progress from one stage to another in a predictable manner as they develop and deteriorate. One study found that some terminated friendships did indeed follow a pattern similar to the one described by Knapp and pictured in Pattern One of Figure 9.2 (Johnson et al., 2004). However, several other patterns of development and deterioration were also identified, as seen in Patterns Two through Five.

Knapp's model suggests that a relationship exhibits only the most dominant traits of just one of the 10 stages at any given time. Despite this fact, elements of other stages are usually present. For example, two lovers deep in the throes of integrating may still do their share of experimenting ("Wow, I never knew that about you!") and have differentiating disagreements ("I need a weekend to myself). Likewise, family members who spend most of their energy avoiding each other may have an occasional good spell in which their former closeness briefly intensifies. The notion that relationships can experience features

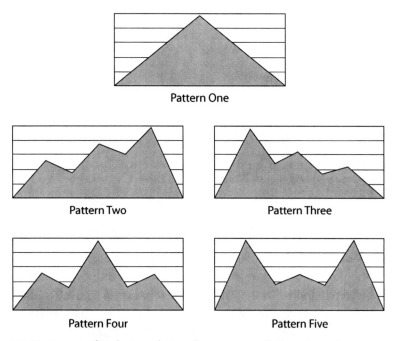

Figure 9.2: Patterns of Relational Development and Deterioration

Adapted from Johnson, A., Wittenberg, E., Haigh, M., Wigley, S., Becker, J., Brown, K., & Craig, E. (2004). The process of relationship development and deterioration: Turning points in friendships that have terminated. *Communication Quarterly, 52,* 54–67.

of both "coming together" and "coming apart" at the same time is explored in the following section, on relational dialectics.

Dialectical Perspectives on Relational Dynamics

Not all theorists agree that relational stages are the best way to explain interaction in relationships. Some suggest that communicators grapple with the same kinds of challenges whether a relationship is brand new or has lasted decades. Their focus, then, is on the ongoing maintenance of relationships (Lee, 1998). They argue that communicators seek important but apparently incompatible goals. The struggle to achieve these goals creates **dialectical tensions:** conflicts that arise when two opposing or incompatible forces exist simultaneously.

Communication scholars such as Leslie Baxter and Barbara Montgomery (1996) and William Rawlins (1992) have identified several dialectical forces that make successful communication challenging. They suggest that the struggle to manage these dialectical tensions creates the most powerful dynamics in relational communication. In the following pages we will discuss three influential dialectical tensions, which are summarized in Table 9.2. As the table shows, we experience dialectical challenges both *internally,* that is, within the relationship, and *externally* as we and our relational partners face other people whose desires clash with our own.

Table 9.2: Dialectical Tensions

	Dialectic of Integration-Separation	Dialectic of Stability-Change	Dialectic of Expression-Privacy
Internal Manifestations	Connection-Autonomy	Predicatability-Novelty	Openness-Closedness
External Manifestations	Inclusion-Seclusion	Conventionality-Uniqueness	Revelation-Concealment

From Baxter, L. A. (1994). A dialogic approach to relationship maintenance. In D. J. Canary & L. Stafford (Eds.)., *Communication and relational maintenance* (p. 240). San Diego, CA: Academic Press.

Integration versus Separation. No one is an island. Recognizing this fact, we seek out involvement with others. But, at the same time, we are unwilling to sacrifice our entire identity to even the most satisfying relationship. The conflicting desires for connection and independence are embodied in the **integration-separation dialectic**. This set of apparently contradictory needs creates communication challenges that can show up both within a relationship and when relational partners face the world.

Internally, the struggle shows up in the **connection-autonomy dialectic**. We want to be close to others, but at the same time we seek independence. Sociolinguist Deborah Tannen (1986) captures the insoluble integration-separation dialectic nicely by evoking the image of two porcupines trying to get through a cold winter:

> They huddle together for warmth, but their sharp quills prick each other, so they pull away. But then they get cold. They have to keep adjusting their closeness and distance to keep from freezing and from getting pricked by their fellow porcupines—the source of both comfort and pain.
> We need to get close to each other to have a sense of community, to feel we're not alone in the world. But we need to keep our distance from each other to preserve our independence, so others don't impose on or engulf us. This duality reflects the human condition. We are individual and social creatures. We need other people to survive, but we want to survive as individuals.

Baxter (1994) describes the consequences for relational partners who can't successfully manage the conflicting needs for connection and autonomy. Some of the most common reasons for relational breakups involve failure of partners to satisfy one another's needs for connection: "We barely spent any time together"; "My partner wasn't committed to the relationship"; "We had different needs." But other relational complaints involve excessive demands for connection: "I was feeling trapped"; "I needed freedom." Perhaps not surprisingly, research suggests that in heterosexual romantic relationships, men often want more autonomy and women typically want more connection and commitment (Buunk, 2005; Feeney, 1999).

In accounts of relational turning points, both men and women in heterosexual romantic pairs cited the connection-autonomy dialectic as one of the most significant factors affecting their relationship (Baxter & Erbert, 1999). This dialectical tension was crucial in negotiating turning points related to commitment, conflict, disengagement, and reconciliation. Research also shows that managing the dialectical tension between connection and autonomy is as important during divorce as it is at the beginning of a marriage, as partners seek ways to salvage and reconcile the unbreakable bonds of their personal history (including finances, children, and friends) with their new independence (Pam & Pearson, 1998).

Parents and children must deal constantly with the conflicting tugs of connection and autonomy. These struggles don't end when children grow up and leave home. Parents experience the mixed feelings of relief at their new freedom and longings to stay connected to their adult children. Likewise, grown children typically feel excitement at being on their own, and yet miss the bonds that had been taken for granted since the beginning of their lives (Blacker, 1999; Fulmer, 1999).

The tension between integration and separation also operates externally, when people within a relationship struggle to meet the competing needs of the inclusion-seclusion dialectic. They struggle to reconcile a desire for involvement with the "outside world" with the desire to live their own lives, free of what can feel like interference from others. For example, when the end of a busy week comes, does a couple accept the invitation to a party (and sacrifice the chance to spend quality time with one another), or do they decline the invitation (and risk losing contact with valued friends)? Does a close-knit nuclear family choose to take a much anticipated vacation together (disappointing their relatives), or do they attend a family reunion (losing precious time to enjoy one another without any distractions)?

Stability versus Change. Stability is an important need in relationships, but too much of it can lead to feelings of staleness. **The stability-change dialectic** operates both between partners and when they face others outside the relationship. Within a relationship, the **predictability-novelty dialectic** captures another set of tensions. While nobody wants a completely unpredictable relational partner ("You're not the person I married!"), humorist Dave Barry (1990, p. 47) exaggerates only slightly when he talks about the boredom that can come when husbands and wives know each other too well:

> After a decade or so of marriage, you know *everything* about your spouse, every habit and opinion and twitch and tic and minor skin growth. You could write a seventeen-pound book solely about the way your spouse eats. This kind of intimate knowledge can be very handy in certain situations—such as when you're on a TV quiz show where the object is to identify your spouse from the sound of his or her chewing—but it tends to lower the passion level of a relationship.

At an external level, the **conventionality-uniqueness dialectic** captures the challenges that people in a relationship face when trying to meet others' expectations as well as their own. On one hand, stable patterns of behavior do emerge that enable others to make useful judgments like "happy family" or "dependable organization." But those blanket characterizations can stifle people in relationships, who may sometimes want to break away from the expectations others hold of them. For example, playing the conventional role of "happy family" or "perfect couple" during a time of conflict can be a burden, when the couple feels the need to behave in less stereotypical ways.

Expression versus Privacy. Disclosure is one characteristic of interpersonal relationships. Yet, along with the drive for intimacy, we have an equally important need to maintain some space between ourselves and others. These sometimes conflicting drives create the **expression-privacy dialectic.**

The internal struggle between expression and privacy shows up in the **openness-closedness dialectic.** What do you do in an intimate relationship when a person you care about asks an important question that you don't want to answer? "Do you think I'm attractive?" "Are you having a good time?" Your commitment to the relationship may compel you toward honesty, but your concern for the other person's feelings and a desire for privacy may lead you to be less than completely honest. Partners use a variety of strategies to gain privacy from each other (Burgoon et al., 1989; Petronio, 2000). For example, they may confront the other person directly and explain that they don't want to continue a discussion, or they may be less direct and offer nonverbal cues, change the topic, or leave the room. There are both benefits and risks in self-disclosing.

The same conflicts between openness and privacy operate externally in the **revelation-concealment dialectic.** If you and a longtime fellow worker haven't been getting along, do you answer the boss's question "How's it going?" honestly, or do you keep your disagreement to yourselves? If your family has had a run of bad (or good) financial luck and a friend asks to borrow (or lend) money, do you share your situation or keep quiet? If you're part of a lesbian couple but you're not sure your relationship will be endorsed by others, when and how do you go "public" with that information? (Suter et al., 2006; Suter & Daas, 2007). All of these questions speak to tensions related to concealing versus revealing.

For many couples, the revelation-concealment dialectic centers on decisions about how much news to share about their relationship. "Should we tell our friends that we're dating?" or "Is it time for you to meet my family?" are questions they might ask about sharing positive relational information with others. For some couples, however, the concealed news isn't so pleasant. Lara Dieckmann (2000) looked into the world of battered women and found that most of them wrestle with the dialectic of staying private or going public about the abuse in their relationships. A word that Dieckmann used to describe the women's experience is balance—the need to constantly juggle the competing demands of privacy and publicity, secrecy and disclosure, safety and danger. Telling others about partner abuse can be the first step in disengaging from a violent relationship, but it can also threaten a woman's self-esteem, security, and very life.

Although all of the dialectical tensions play an important role in managing relationships, some occur more frequently than others. In one study (Paw-lowski, 1998), young married couples reported that connection-autonomy was the most frequent tension (30.8 percent of all reported contradictions). Predictability-novelty was second (occurring 21.7 percent of the time), and inclusion-seclusion was third (21.4 percent). Less common were tensions between openness-closedness (12.7 percent), conventionality-uniqueness (7.5 percent), and revelation-concealment (6 percent). Of all the dialectical tensions, connection-autonomy and openness-closedness seem to be the most important ones to manage, at least in romantic relationships (Baxter & Erbert 1999; Erbert, 2000).

Strategies for Managing Dialectical Tensions. Managing the dialectical tensions outlined in these pages presents communication challenges. There are at least eight ways these challenges can be managed (Baxter & Braith-waite, 2006).

- **Denial**. In the strategy of denial, communicators respond to one end of the dialectical spectrum and ignore the other. For example, a couple caught between the conflicting desires for stability and novelty might find their struggle for change too difficult to manage and choose to follow predictable, if unexciting patterns of relating to one another.
- **Disorientation**. In this mode, communicators feel so overwhelmed and helpless that they are unable to confront their problems. In the face of dialectical tensions they might fight, freeze, or even leave the relationship. A couple who discovers soon after the honeymoon that living a "happily ever after "conflict-free life is impossible might become so terrified that they would come to view their marriage as a mistake.
- **Alternation.** Communicators who use this strategy choose one end of the dialectical spectrum at some times, and the other end on different occasions. Friends, for example, might manage the connection-autonomy dialectic by alternating between times when they spend a large amount of time together and other periods when they live independent lives.
- **Segmentation.** Partners who use this tactic compartmentalize different areas of their relationship. For example, a couple might manage the openness-closedness dialectic by sharing almost all their feelings about mutual friends with one another, but keeping certain parts of their past romantic histories private.
- **Balance.** Communicators who try to balance dialectical tensions recognize that both forces are legitimate and try to manage them through compromise. Compromise is inherently a situation in which everybody loses at least a little of what he or she wants. A couple caught between the conflicting desires for predictability and novelty might seek balance by compromising with a lifestyle that is neither as predictable as one wants nor as surprise-filled as the other seeks—not an ideal outcome.
- **Integration.** With this approach, communicators simultaneously accept opposing forces without trying to diminish them. Barbara Montgomery (1993) describes a

couple who accept both the needs for predictability and novelty by devising a "pre-dictably novel" approach: Once a week they would do something together that they had never done before. Similarly, Dawn Braithwaite and her colleagues (1998) found that stepfamilies often manage the tension between the "old family" and the "new family" by adapting and blending their family rituals.

- **Recalibration**. Communicators can respond to dialectical challenges by reframing them so that the apparent contradiction disappears. Consider how a couple who felt hurt by one another's unwillingness to share parts of their past might redefine the secrets as creating an attractive aura of mystery instead of being a problem to be solved. The desire for privacy would still remain, but it would no longer compete with a need for openness about every aspect of the past.
- **Reaffirmation**. This approach acknowledges that dialectical tensions will never disappear. Instead of trying to make them go away, reaffirming communicators accept—or even embrace—the challenges they present. The metaphorical view of relational life as a kind of roller-coaster reflects this orientation, and communicators who use reaffirmation view dialectical tensions as part of the ride.

Which of these strategies do you use to manage the dialectical tensions your life? How successful is each one? Which strategies might serve your communication better? Since dialectical tensions are a part of life, choosing how to communicate about them can make a tremendous difference in the quality of your relationships.

Maintaining Relationships through Communication

Just as gardens need tending, cars need tune-ups, and bodies need exercise, relationships need ongoing maintenance to keep them successful and satisfying. Maintenance-related communication aims to sustain the features that make the relationship successful and satisfying: enjoyment, love, commitment, trust, and so forth (Canary & Stafford, 1992; Sahlstein, 2004). The communication involved in maintaining relationships may not always be exciting, but handling it effectively accounts for as much as 80 percent of the difference between satisfying and unsatisfying relationships (Weigel & Ballard-Reisch, 1999). In this section well look at how we communicate about relationships, some strategies for maintaining relationships, and some tips for repairing damaged relationships.

Communicating About Relationships

By now it is clear that relationships are complex, dynamic, and important. How do communicators address relational issues with one another?

Content and Relational Messages. Every message has a *content* and a *relational* dimension. The most obvious component of most messages is their content—the subject being discussed. The content of statements like "It's your turn to do the dishes" or "I'm busy Saturday night" is obvious.

Content messages aren't the only information being exchanged when two people communicate. In addition, every message—both verbal and nonverbal—also has a second, relational dimension, which makes statements about how the communicators feel toward one another (Dillard et al., 1999; Knobloch & Solomon, 2003; Watzlawick et al., 1967). These relational messages deal with one or more social needs: intimacy, affinity, respect, and control. Consider the two examples we just mentioned:

- Imagine two ways of saying "It's your turn to do the dishes," one that is demanding and another that is matter-of-fact. Notice how the different nonverbal messages make statements about how the sender views control in this part of the relationship. The demanding tone says, in effect, "I have a right to tell you what to do around the house," whereas the matter-of-fact one suggests, "I'm just reminding you of something you might have overlooked."
- You can easily imagine two ways to deliver the statement "I'm busy Saturday night," one with little affection and the other with much liking.

Like these messages, every statement we make goes beyond discussing the subject at hand and says something about the way the speaker feels about the recipient. You can prove this fact by listening for the relational messages implicit in your own statements to others and theirs to you.

Most of the time we are unaware of the relational messages that bombard us every day. Sometimes these messages don't capture our awareness because they match our belief about the amount of control, liking, or intimacy that is appropriate in a relationship. For example, you probably won't be offended if your boss tells you to drop everything and tackle a certain job, because you agree that supervisors have the right to direct employees. However, if your boss delivered the order in a condescending, sarcastic, or abusive tone of voice, you would probably be offended. Your complaint wouldn't be with the order itself, but with the way it was delivered. "I may work for this company," you might think, "but I'm not a slave or an idiot. I deserve to be treated like a human being."

Expression of Relational Messages. Exactly how are relational messages communicated? As the boss-employee example suggests, they are usually expressed nonverbally. To test this fact for yourself, imagine how you could act while saying "Can you help me for a minute?" in a way that communicates each of the following relationships:

superiority
helplessness
friendliness
aloofness
sexual desire
irritation

Although nonverbal behaviors are a good source of relational messages, remember that they are ambiguous. The sharp tone you take as a personal insult might be due to fatigue, and the interruption you take as an attempt to ignore your ideas might be a sign of pressure that has nothing to do with you. Before you jump to conclusions about relational clues, it is a good idea to verify the accuracy of your interpretation with the other person: "When you cut me off, I got the idea you're angry at me. Is that right?"

Not all relational messages are nonverbal. Social scientists use the term **metacommunication** to describe messages that refer to other messages (Dindia & Baxter, 1987; Tracy, 2004). In other words, metacommunication is communication about communication. Whenever we discuss a relationship with others, we are metacommunicating: "I wish we could stop arguing so much," or "I appreciate how honest you've been with me." Verbal metacommunication is an essential ingredient in successful relationships and relational repair (Becker et al., 2008). Sooner or later, there are times when it becomes necessary to talk about what is going on between you and the other person. The ability to focus on the kinds of issues described in this chapter can be the tool for keeping your relationship on track.

Despite its importance, overt metacommunication isn't a common feature of most relationships (Fogel & Branco, 1997; Wilmot, 1987). In fact, there seems to be an aversion to it, even among many intimates. When 90 people were asked to identify the taboo subjects in their personal relationships, the most frequent topics involved meta-communication (Baxter & Wilmot, 1985). For example, people were reluctant to discuss the state of their current relationships and the norms ("rules") that governed their lives together. Other studies suggest that when metacommunication does occur, it sometimes threatens the recipient and provokes conflict (Hocker & Wilmot, 1997). See the Focus on Research boxes "Friends with Benefits" (p. 286) and "Honest but Hurtful Messages" (p. 324) for examples of couples' tendencies to avoid metacommunicating—even when it could probably benefit them.

Relational Maintenance Strategies

Stafford and Canary (1991) identified five strategies for maintaining romantic relationships:

- *Positivity:* Keeping things pleasant by being polite, cheerful, and upbeat and also by avoiding criticism.
- *Openness:* Talking directly about the nature of the relationship and disclosing your personal needs and concerns.
- *Assurances:* Letting the other person know that he or she matters to you.
- *Sharing tasks:* Helping one another take care of life's chores and obligations.
- *Social networks:* Relying on friends and family to provide support and relief that helps relational partners understand and appreciate one another, as well as giving them other sources of companionship that take some load off of the relationship.

These maintenance strategies can also be used in nonromantic relationships. One study (Johnson et al., 2008) analyzed college students' e-mail to see which strategies they employed in messages to their family members, friends, and romantic partners. With family and friends, two strategies were used most: *openness* ("Things have been a little crazy for me lately") and *social networks* ("How are you and Sam? Hopefully good"). With romantic partners, however, *assurances* ("This is just a little e-mail to say I love you") was the most-used maintenance device. The study shows not only that different relationships call for different types of maintenance but that e-mail can be a helpful tool for maintaining interpersonal relationships.

In successful relationships it's important for both partners to use relational maintenance strategies (Canary & Wahba, 2006). Both men and women do a roughly equal amount of relational maintenance work. Women contribute somewhat more effort in joint tasks—especially household chores—and they share personal thoughts and feelings more than men (Aylor & Dainton, 2004). As in most relational matters, the *perception* that both partners are working equally hard at maintaining the relationship is perhaps more important than the reality. When one partner feels like the other isn't doing his or her share, the relationship is headed for trouble (Canary & Stafford, 2001).

Repairing Damaged Relationships

Sooner or later, even the strongest relationships hit a bumpy patch. Some Problems arise from outside forces: work, finances, competing relationships, and so on. At other times, problems arise from differences and disagreements within the relationship.

Table 9.3: Some Types of Relational Transgressions

Lack of Commitment
    Failure to honor important obligations (e.g., financial, emotional, task-related)
    Self-serving dishonesty
    Unfaithfulness

Distance
    Physical separation (beyond what is necessary)
    Psychological separation (avoidance, ignoring)

Disrespect   Criticism (especially in front of third parties)

Problematic Emotions
    Jealousy
    Unjustified Suspicion
    Rage

Aggression
    Verbal hostility
    Physical violence

A third type of relational problem comes from **relational transgressions**, when one partner violates the explicit or implicit terms of the relationship, letting the other one down in some important way.

Types of Relational Transgressions

Table 9.3 lists some types of relational transgressons. Violations like these fall into different categories (Emmers-Sommer, 2003).

Minor Versus Significant. Some of the items listed in Table 9.3 aren't inherently transgressions, and in small doses they can actually aid relationships. For instance, a *little* distance can make the heart grow fonder, a jealousy can be a sign of affection, and a *little* anger can start the process of resolving a gripe. In large and regular doses, however, these acts become serious transgressions that can damage personal relationships.

Social Versus Relational. Some transgressions violate *social rules* shared by society at large. For example, almost everyone would agree that ridiculing or humiliating a friend or family member in public is a violation of a fundamental social rule regarding saving others' face. Other rules are *relational* in nature—unique norms constructed by the parties involved. For instance, some families have a rule stating "If I'm going to be more than a little bit late, I'll let you know so that you don't worry." Once such a rule exists, failure to honor it feels like a violation, even though outsiders might not view it as such.

Deliberate Versus Unintentional. Some transgressions are unintentional. You might reveal something about a friend's past without realizing that this disclosure would be embarrassing. Other violations, though, are intentional. In a fit of anger, you might purposely lash out with a cruel comment, knowing that it will hurt the other person's feelings.

One-Time Versus Incremental. The most obvious transgressions occur in a single episode: an act of betrayal, a verbal assault, or walking out in anger. But more subtle transgressions can occur over time. Consider emotional withdrawal: Everybody has times when they retreat into themselves, and we usually give one another the space to do just that. But if the withdrawal slowly becomes pervasive, it becomes a violation of the fundamental rule in most relationships that partners should be available to one another.

Strategies for Relational Repair. Research confirms the commonsense notion that a first step to repairing a transgression is to talk about the violation (Dindia & Baxter, 1987). ("I was really embarrassed when you yelled at me in front of everybody last night"). In other cases, you might be responsible for the transgression and want to raise it for discussion:

"What did I do that you found so hurtful?" "Why was my behavior a problem for you?" Asking questions like these—and listening nondefensively to the answers—can be an enormous challenge.

Not surprisingly, some transgressions are harder to repair than others. One study of dating partners found that sexual infidelity and breaking up with the partner were the two least forgivable offenses (Bachman & Guerrero, 2006). For the best chance of repairing a seriously damaged relationship, an apology needs to be offered—ideally containing these three elements (Kelley & Waldron, 2005):

- An explicit acknowledgement that the transgression was wrong: "I acted like a selfish jerk."
- A sincere apology: "I'm really sorry. I feel awful for letting you down."
- Some type of compensation: "No matter what happens, I'll never do anything like that again."

An apology will be convincing only if the speaker's nonverbal behaviors match his or her words. Even then, it may be unrealistic to expect immediate forgiveness. Sometimes, especially with severe transgressions, expressions of regret and promises of new behavior will only be accepted conditionally, with a need for them to be demonstrated over time before the aggrieved party regards them as genuine (Merolla, 2008).

Given the challenges and possible humiliation involved in apologizing, is it worth the effort? Research suggests yes. Participants in one study consistently reported that they had more remorse over apologies they *didn't* offer than about those they did (Exline et al., 2007).

Forgiving Transgressions. Many people think of forgiveness as a topic for theologians and philosophers. However, social scientists have found that forgiving others has both personal and relational benefits. On a personal level, forgiveness has been shown to reduce emotional distress and aggression (Eaton & Struthers, 2006; Orcutt, 2006) as well as to improve cardiovascular functioning (Lawler et al., 2003). Interpersonally, extending forgiveness to lovers, friends, and family can help restore damaged relationships (Waldron & Kelley, 2005). Moreover, research shows that transgressors who have been forgiven are less likely to repeat their offenses than those who have not received forgiveness (Wallace et al, 2008).

Even when a sincere apology is offered, forgiving others can be difficult. Research shows that one way to improve your ability to forgive is to recall times when you have mistreated or hurt others in the past—in other words, to remember that you, too, have wronged others and needed their forgiveness (Exline et al, 2008; Takaku, 2001). Given that it's in our own best interest to be forgiving, communication researcher Douglas Kelley (1998) encourages us to remember these words from R. P. Walters: "When we have been hurt we have two alternatives: be destroyed by resentment, or forgive. Resentment is death; forgiving leads to healing and life" (p. 324).

Granting forgiveness to others can sometimes be done through nonverbal displays, such as replacing frowns with smiles or physical affection. More serious cases might require discussion and negotiation or even an explicit statement of forgiveness. The Self-Assessment on page 309 can help you recognize how you typically express forgiveness to others.

Summary

The dynamics of human relationships, more specifically why we form relationships, the development, and finally the maintenance of these relationships has been the focus of this chapter. In order to deal more effectively if our relationships with others, it is necessary to have some knowledge of these variables in our relationships.

Human being form relationships for very specific reasons: we are attracted to others, we desire intimacy, and we seek commitment from others. We are attracted to others for many reasons, but we generally seek out others whose interaction we find rewarding in some way. We also are more apt to develop relationships with individuals in our general proximity who we find attractive and similar to ourselves. We also seek intimacy in relationships, and in fact humans rank intimate relationships as one of the most important dimensions of their lives. Finally, we seek commitment in relationships; we do not seek relationships that will only be a part of our lives for a short period of time.

The developmental models of human relationships present the idea that relationships operate in two dimensions: either coming together or coming apart. The dialectical perspective takes an alternate view of relationships. It does not see relationships occurring in set stages, rather relationships are seen as a constant management of dialectical tensions that operate as two individuals struggle to have their own needs met without ignoring the needs of the other relational partner.

Humans communicate about their relationships in many ways, known as metacommunication, and have many different types of message they share with others which determine to a great extent the success of their relationships. Research has shown that relational maintenance strategies individuals use can include behaviors that seek to focus on the positive aspects of their relationships, open talk about their relationships, assurances of the importance of the relationship, sharing of tasks, and the development of social networks that help manage the relationship. Finally, this chapter presented strategies that humans use to repair damaged relationships—from a willingness to admit doing wrong in a relationship to offering the other person some type of compensation for their transgression.

In Chapter Ten we begin the study of small group communication which is an analysis of how and why humans form groups for a variety of reasons, followed by a chapter on the best ways to ensure success in small group decision making and problem-solving.

Questions For Discussion

1. For what reasons do human enter relationships?
2. What is the difference between the developmental and dialectical perspective with respect to relationship development?

3. What type of relational repair strategy have you used when a relationship of yours needed "fixing"?
4. Though most research has shown that in selecting relational partners opposites do not attract—do you think it is better to find someone different from yourself to avoid boredom in a relationship?
5. Do you believe that relationships pass through distinct phases in linear progression?

References

Aboud, F. E., &Mendelson, M.J. (1998). Determinants of friendship selection and quality: Developmental perspectives. In W. M. Bukowski &A. F. Newcomb (Eds.), *The company they keep: Friendship in childhood and adolescence* (pp. 87–112). New York: Cambridge University Press.

Adamopoulos,J. (1991). The emergence of interpersonal behavior: Diachronic and cross-cultural processes in the evolution of intimacy. In S. Ting-Toomey & F. Korzenny (Eds.), *Cross-cultural interpersonal communication* (pp. 155–170). Newbury Park, CA: Sage.

Adams, G., Anderson, S. L., & Adonu,]. K. (2004). The cultural grounding of closeness and intimacy. In D. Mashek & A. Aron (Eds.), *The handbook of closeness and intimacy* (pp. 321–339). Mahwah. NT: Erlbaum.

Afifi, W. A., &Johnson, M. L. (1999). The use and interpretation of tie signs in a public setting: Relationship and sex differences. *Journal of Social and Personal Relationships, 16,* 9–38.

Albada, K. F., Knapp, M. L., & Theune, K. E. (2002). Interaction Appearance Theory: Changing perceptions of physical attractiveness through social interaction. *Communication Theory, 12,* 8–40.

Amodio, D. M., & Showers, C.]. (2005). "Similarity breeds liking" revisited: The moderating role of commitment. *Journal of Social and Personal Relationships, 22,* 817–836.

Archer, R., &Berg,]. (1978, November). To encourage intimacy, don't force it. *Psychology Today, 12,* 39–40.

Argyle, M., &Henderson, M. (1985). The rules of relationships. In S. Duck &D. Perlman (Eds.), *Understanding personal relationships: An interdisciplinary approach* (pp. 63–84). Beverly Hills, CA: Sage.

Aronson, E., Willerman, B., & Floyd, J. (1966). The effect of a pratfall on increasing interpersonal attractiveness. *Psychonomic Science, 4,* 227–228.

Avtgis, T. A., West, D. V., &Anderson, T. L. (1998). Relationship stages: An inductive analysis identifYing cognitive, affective, and behavioral dimensions of Knapp's relational stages model. *Communication Research Reports, 15,* 28D-287.

Aylor, B., & Dainton, M. (2004). Biological sex and psychological gender as predictors of routine and strategic relational maintenance. *Sex Roles, SO,* 689–697.

Bachman, G. F., & Guerrero, L. K. (2006). Forgiveness, apology, and communicative responses to hurtful event. *Communication Reports, 19,* 45–56.

Back, M. D., Schmukle, S. C., & Egloff, B. (2008). Becoming friends by chance. *Psychological Science, 19,* 439–440.

Balswick, J.O. (1988). *The inexpressive male: A tragedy of American society.* Lexington, MA: Lexington Books.

Barry, D. (1990). *Dave Barry turns 40.* New York: Fawcett Columbine.

Battaglia, D. M., Richard, F. D., Datteri, D. L., & Lord, C. G. (1998). Breaking up is (relatively) easy to do: A script for the dissolution of close relationships. *Journal of Social and Personal Relationships, 15,* 829–845.

Baumeister, R. F. (2005). *The cultural animal· Human nature, meaning, and social lift.* New York: Oxford University Press.

Baxter, L. A. (1987). Symbols of relationship identity in relationship culture. *Journal of Social and Personal Relationships, 4,* 261–280.

Baxter, L.A. (1992). Forms and functions of intimate play in personal relationships. *Human Communication Research, 18,* 336–363.

Baxter, L.A. (1994). A dialogic approach to relationship maintenance. In D. J. Canary & L. Stafford (Eds.), *Communication and relational maintenance* (pp. 233–254). San Diego: Academic Press.

Baxter, L.A., & Erbert, L.A. (1999). Perceptions of dialectical contradictions in turning Points of development in heterosexual romantic relationships. *Journal of Social and Personal Relationships, 16,* 547–569.

Baxter, L.A., & Wilmot, W. W. (1985). Taboo topics in close relationships. *Journal of Social and Personal Relationships, 2,* 253–269.

Becker, J.A.H., Ellevold, B., & Stamp, G. H. (2008) The creation of defensiveness in social interaction II: A model of defensive communication among romantic couples. *Communication Monographs, 75,* 86–110.

Bell, R. A., &Healey,]. G. (1992). Idiomatic communication and interpersonal solidarity in friends' relational cultures. *Human Communication Research, 18,* 307–335.

Bellah, R.N., Madsen, R., Sullivan, W. M., Swidler, A., & Tipton, S.M. (1985). *Habits of the heart: Individualism and commitment in American life.* Berkeley: University of California Press.

Ben-Ze'ev, A. (2003). Privacy, emotional closeness, and openness in cyberspace. *Computers in Human Behavior, 19,* 451–467.

Berscheid, E., Schneider, M., & Omoto, A.M. (1989). Issues in studying close relationships: Conceptualizing and measuring closeness. In C. Hendrick (Ed.), *Close relationships* (pp. 63–91). Newbury Park, CA: Sage.

Berscheid, E., & Walster, E. H. (1978). *Interpersonal attraction* (2nd ed.). Reading, MA: Addison-Wesley.

Blacker, L. (1999). The launching phase of the life cycle. In B. Carter &M. McGoldnck (Eds.), *The expanded family life cycle: Individual, family, and social perspectives* (3rd ed., pp. 287–306). Boston: Allyn &Bacon.

Boase,]., Horrigan, J. B., Wellman, B., & Rainie, L. (2006). The strength ofInternet ttes. *Pew Internet & American Life Project.* Available at: http://www.pewinternet.org/pdfs/PIP _Internet_ ties. pdf.

Braithwaite, D. 0., Baxter, L.A., & Harper, A. M. (1998). The role of rituals in the management of the dialectical tension of "old" and "new" in blended families. *Communication Studies, 49,* 101–120.

Brantley, A., Knox, D., & Zusman, M. E. (2002). When and why gender differences in saying "I love you" among college students. *College Student Journal, 36,* 614–615.

Bruess, C. J. S., & Pearson,}. C. (1997). Interpersonal rituals in marriage and adult friendship. *Communication Monographs, 64,* 25–46.

Burgoon, J. K., Parrott, R., Le Poire, B. A., Kelley, D. L., Walther, J. B., & Perry, D. (1989). Maintaining and restoring privacy through different types of relationships. *Journal of Social and Personal Relationships, 6,* 131–158.

Burleson, B. R., &Samter, W. (1985). Individual differences in the perception of comforting messages: An exploratory investigation. *Central States Speech Journal, 36,* 39–50.

Buss, D. M. (1985,January-February). Human mate selection. *American Scientist, 73, 47–51.*

Buunk, A. P. (2005). How do people respond to others with high commitment or autonomy in their relationships? *Journal if Social and Personal Relationships, 22,* 653–672.

Byrne, D. (1997). An overview (and underview) of research and theory within the attraction paradigm. *Journal if Social and Personal Relationships, 14,* 417–431.

Canary, D. J., & Stafford, L. (1992). Relational maintenance strategies and equity in marriage. *Communication Monographs, 59,* 243–267.

Canary, D. J., & Stafford, L. (2001). Equity in maintaining personal relationships. In J. H. Harvey &A. E. Wenzel (Eds.), *Close romantic relationships: Maintenance and enhancement* (pp. 133–150). Mahwah, NJ: Erlbaum.

Canary, D. J., & Wahba, J. (2006). Do women work harder than men at maintaining relationships? In K. Dindia & D. J. Canary (Eds.), *Sex dijftrences and similarities in communication* (2nd ed.). Mahwah, NJ: Erlbaum.

Conlan, S. K. (2008). Romantic relationship termination. *DAL* 68(7–B), 4884.

Cooper,]., &Jones, E. E. (1969). Opinion divergence as a strategy to avoid being miscast. *Journal of Personality and Social Psychology, 13,* 23–30.

Cowan, G., &Mills, R. D. (2004). Personal inadequacy and intimacy predictors of men's hostility toward women. *Sex Roles, 51,* 67–78.

Cross, S. E., &Madson, L. (1997). Models of the self: Self-construals and gender. *Psychological Bulletin, 122,* 5–37.

Crowther, C. E., & Stone, G. (1986). *Intimacy: Strategies for successful relationships.* Santa Barbara, CA: Capra Press.

Deaux, K. (1972). To err is humanizing: But sex makes a difference. *Representative Research in Social Psychology, 3,* 20–28.

DeMaris, A. (2007). The role of relationship inequity in marital disruption. *Journal of Social and Personal Relationships, 24,* 177–195.

Derlega, V. J., Metts, S., Petronio, S., & Margulis, S. T. (1993). *Self-disclosure.* Newbury Park, CA: Sage.

Dieckmann, L. E. (2000). Private secrets and public disclosures: The case of battered women. InS. Petronio (Ed.), *Balancing the secrets of private disclosures* (pp. 275–286). Mahwah, NJ: Erlbaum.

Dillard, J. P., Solomon, D. H., & Palmer, M. T. (1999). Structuring the concept of relational communication. *Communication Monographs, 66,* 49–65.

Dindia, K. (2000a). Self-disclosure research: Advances through meta-analysis. In M. A Allen, R. W. Preiss, B. M. Gayle, & N. Burrell (Eds.), *Interpersonal communication: Advances through meta-analysis.* Mahwah, NJ: Erlbaum.

Dindia, K. (2000b). Sex differences in self-disclosure, reciprocity of self-disclosure, and self-disclosure and liking: Three meta-analyses reviewed. InS. Petronio (Ed.), *Balancing the secrets of private disclosures* (pp. 21–35). Mahwah, NJ: Erlbaum.

Dindia, K. (2002). Self-disclosure research: Knowledge through meta-analysis. In M. Allen & R. W. Preiss (Eds.), *Interpersonal communication research: Advances through metaanalysis* (pp. 169–185). Mahwah, NJ: Erlbaum.

Dindia, K., & Allen, M. (1992). Sex differences in self-disclosure: A meta-analysis. *Psychological Bulletin, 112,* 106–124.

Dindia, K., & Baxter, L.A. (1987). Strategies for maintaining and repairing marital relationships. *Journal of Social and Personal Relationships, 4,* 143–158.

Duck, S. (1987). How to lose friends without influencing people. In M. E. Roloff & G. R. Miller (Eds.), *Interpersonal processes: New directions in communication research* (pp. 278–298). Beverly Hills, CA: Sage.

Duck, S., & Barnes, M. K. (1992). Disagreeing about agreement: Reconciling differences about similarity. *Communication Monographs, 59,* 199–208.

Eaton, J., & Struthers, C. W. (2006). The reduction of psychological aggression across varied interpersonal contexts through repentance and forgiveness. *Aggressive Behavior, 32,* 195–206.

Eldridge, K. A., & Christensen, A. (2002). Demand-withdraw communication during couple conflict: A review and analysis. In P. Noller&J. A. Feeney (Eds.), *Understanding marriage: Developments in the study of couple interaction* (pp. 289–322). New York: Cambridge University Press.

Erbert, L. A. (2000). Conflict and dialectics: Perceptions of dialectical contradictions in marital conflict. *Journal of Social and Personal Relationships, 17,* 638–659.

Evans, G. W., & Wener, R. E. (2007). Crowding and personal space invasion on the train: Please don't make me sit in the middle. *Journal of Environmental Psychology, 27*(1), 90–94.

Exline, J. J., Baumeister, R. F., & Zell, L (2008). Not so innocent: Does seeing one's own capability for wrongdoing predict forgiveness? *Journal of Personality and Social Psychology, 94,* 495–515.

Feeney, J. A. (1999). Issues of closeness and distance in dating relationships: Effects of sex and attachment style. *Journal of Social and Personal Relationships, 16,* 571–590.

Felmlee, D. H. (2001). From appealing to appalling: Disenchantment with a romantic partner. *Sociological Perspectives, 44,* 263–280.

Fisher, H. (2007, May!June). The laws of chemistry. *Psychology Today, 40,* 76–81.

Flora, C. (2005, Jan-Feb). Close quarters. *Psychology Today, 37,* 15–16.

Floyd, K. (1996). Communicating closeness among siblings: An application of the gendered closeness perspective. *Communication Research Reports, 13,* 27–34.

Fogel, A., & Branco, A. U. (1997). Metacommunication as a source of indeterminism in relationship development. In A. Fogel, M. C. D.P. Lyra, &J. Valsiner (Eds.), *Dynamics and indeterminism in developmental and social processes* (pp. 65–92). Hillsdale, NJ: Erlbaum.

Foster, E. (2008). Commitment, communication, and contending with heteronormativity: An invitation to greater reflexivity in interpersonal research. *Southern Communication Journal, 73,* 84–101.

Fulmer, R. (1999). Becoming an adult: Leaving home and staying connected. In B. Carter & M. McGoldrick (Eds.), *The expanded family life cycle: Individual, family, and social perspectives* (3rd ed., pp. 215–230). Boston: Allyn &Bacon.

Gadlin, H. (1977). Private lives and public order: A critical view of the history of intimate relations in the United States. In G. Levinger & H. L. Raush (Eds.), *Close relationships: Perspectives on the meaning of intimacy* (pp. 33–72). Amherst, MA: University of Massachusetts Press.

Goldsmith, D. J., & Fulfs, P. A. (1999). "You just don't have the evidence": An analysis of claims and evidence in Deborah Tannen's *You just don't understand.* In M. E. Roloff (Ed.), *Communication yearbook 22* (pp. 1–49). Thousand Oaks, *CA:* Sage.

Good, G. E., Porter, M. *J.,* & Dillon, M. G. (2002). When men divulge: Men's selfdisclosure on prime time situation comedies. *Sex Roles, 46,* 419–427.

Greenberg, L. S., & Goldman, R.N. (2008). Fear in couples therapy. In L. S. Greenberg & R. N. Goldman (Eds.), *Emotion-focused couples therapy: The dynamics of emotion, love, and power* (pp. 283–313). Washington, *DC:* American Psychological Association.

Hatfield, E., & Rapson, R. L. (2006). Passionate love, sexual desire, and mate selection: Cross-cultural and historical perspectives. In P. Noller &J. A. Feeney (Eds.), *Close relationships: Functions, forms and processes* (pp. 227–243). Hove, England: Psychology Press/Taylor & Francis.

Hayes, H. (2006). "Don't worry about a thing, dear": Why women need financial intimacy. San Mateo, CA: Primelife.

Helmreich, R., Aronson, E., & Lefan,]. (1970). To err is humanizing-sometimes: Effects of self-esteem, competence, and a pratfall on interpersonal attraction. *Journal of Personality and Social Psychology, 16,* 259–264.

Henderson, S., & Gilding, M. (2004). "I've never clicked this much with anyone in my life": Trust and hyperpersonal communication in online friendships. *New Media & Society, 6,* 487–506.

Hess, J. A. (2000). Maintaining nonvoluntary relationships with disliked partners: An investigation into the use of distancing behaviors. *Human Communication Research, 26,* 458–488.

Hian, L. B., Chuan, S. L., Trevor, T. M. K., & Detenber, B. H. (2004). Getting to know you: Exploring the development of relational intimacy in computer-mediated communication. *Journal of Computer-Mediated Communication, 9*(3). Available at: http://jcmc.indiana.edu/vol9/issue3/detenber.html.

Hocker, J. L., & Wilmot, W. W. (1997). *Interpersonal conflict* (5th ed.). New York: McGraw-Hill.

Hu, Y., Wood, J. F., Smith, V., & Westbrook, N. (2004). Friendships through IM: Examining the relationship between instant messaging and intimacy. *Journal of Computer-Mediated Communication 10(1)*. Available at: http://jcmc.indiana.edu/voll 0/issue 1/hu.html.

Impett, E. A., & Peplau, L. A. (2006). "His" and "her" relationships? A review of the empirical evidence. In A. Vangelisti & D. Perlman (Eds.), *The Cambridge handbook o/personal relationships*. New York: Cambridge University Press.

Jeffries, V. (2002). The structure and dynamics of love: Toward a theory of marital quality and stability. *Humboldt Journal if" Social Relations, 27(1)*, 42–72.

Johnson, A.J., Haigh, M. M., Becker,J. A. H., Craig, E. A., & Wigley, S. (2008). College students' use of relational management strategies in email in long-distance and geogn.phically close relationships. *Journal o/Computer-MEdiated Communication, 13*, 381–404.

Johnson, A.J., Wittenberg, E., Haigh, M., Wigley, S., Becker, J., Brown, K., & Craig, E. (2004). The process of relationship development and deterioration: Turning points in friendships that have terminated. *Communication Quarterly, 52*, 54–67.

Jones,J. T., Pelham, B. W., & Carvallo, M. (2004). How do I love thee? Let me count the Js: Implicit egotism and interpersonal attraction. *Journal o/Personality and Social Psychology, 87*, 665–683.

Kellermann, K., Reynolds, R., & Chen, J. B. (1991). Strategies of conversational retreat: When parting is not sweet sorrow. *Communication Monographs, 58*, 362–383.

Kelley, D. (1998). The communication of forgiveness. *Communication Studies, 49, 255–272.*

Klohnen, E. C., &Luo, S. (2003). Interpersonal attraction and personality: What is attractive-self similarity, ideal similarity, complementarity or attachment security? *Journal of Personality and Social Psychology, 85*, 709–722.

Knapp, M. L., & Vangelisti, A. (2006). *Interpersonal communication and human relationships* (6th ed.). Boston: Allyn & Bacon.

Kniffin, K. M., & Wilson, D. S. (2004). The effect of nonphysical traits on the perception of physical attractiveness: Three naturalistic studies. *Evolution and Human Behavior, 25(2)*, 88–101.

Knobloch, L. K., & Solomon, D. H. (2002). Information seeking beyond initial interaction: Negotiating relational uncertainty within close relationships. *Human Communication Research, 28*, 243–257.

Knobloch, L. K., & Solomon, D. H. (2003). Manifestations of relationship conception in conversation. *Human Communication Research, 29*, 482–515.

Langlois, J. H., & Roggman, L.A. (1990). Attractive faces are only average. *Psychological Science, 1,* 115–121.

Laurenceau,J. P., & Kleinman, B. M. (2006). Intimacy in personal relationships. In A. Vangelisti & D. Perlman (Eds.), *The Cambridge handbook of personal relationships*. New York: Cambridge University Press.

Lawler, K. A., Younger,J. W., Piferi, R. L., Billington, E., Jobe, R., Edmondson, K., & Jones, W. H. (2003). A change of heart: Cardiovascular correlates of forgiveness in response to interpersonal conflict. *Journal of Behavioral Medicine, 26*, 373–393.

Lee, J. (1998). Effective maintenance communication in superior-subordinate relationships. *WesternJournalof-Communication, 62*, 181–208.

Levine, D. (2000). Virtual attraction: What rocks your boat. *CyberPsychology and Behavior, 3*, 565–573.

Lippert, T., & Prager, K. J. (2001). Daily experiences of intimacy: A study of couples. *Personal Relationships, 8*, 283–298.

Luo, S., & Klohnen, E. (2005). Assortive mating and marital quality in newlyweds; A couple-centered approach. *Journal of Personality and Social Psychology, 88*, 304–326.

Mehrabian, A., &Blum,]. S. (2003). Physical appearance, attractiveness, and the mediating role of emotions. In N.J. Pallone (Ed.), *Love, romance, sexual interaction: Research perspectives from current psychology* (pp. 1–29). New Brunswick, NJ: Transaction.

Merolla, *A.].,* Weber, K. D., Myers, S. A., & Booth-Butterfield, M. (2004). The impact of past dating relationship solidarity on commitment, satisfaction, and investment in current relationships. *Communication Quarterly, 52,* 251–264.

Metts, S., Cupach, W. R., & Bejllovec, R. A. (1989). "I love you too much to ever start liking you": Redefining romantic relationships. *Journal of Social and Personal Relationships, 6,* 259–274.

Miller, G. F. (1998). How mate choice shaped human nature: A review of sexual selection and human evolution. In C. B. Crawford & D. L. Krebs, *Handbook of evolutionary psychology: Ideas, issues, and applications* (pp. 87–129). Mahwah, NJ: Erlbaum.

Morman, M. T., & Floyd, K. (2002). A "changing culture of fatherhood": Effects of affectionate communication, closeness, and satisfaction in men's relationships with their fathers and their sons. *Western Journal of Communication, 66,* 395–411.

Morris, D. (1973). *Intimate behavior.* New York: Bantam.

Nowicki, S., & Manheim, S. (1991). Interpersonal complementarity and time of interaction in female relationships. *Journal of Research in Personality, 25,* 322–333.

Orcutt, H. K. (2006). The prospective relationship of interpersonal forgiveness and psychological distress symptoms among college women. *Journal of Counseling Psychology, 53,* 35G-361.

Orman, S. (2005). *The money book for the young, fabulous, and broke.* New York: Riverhead.

Overall, N.C., & Sibley, C. G. (2008). Attachment and attraction toward romantic partners versus relevant alternatives within daily interactions. *Personality and Individual Differences, 44,* 1126–113 7.

Owen, W. F. (1987). The verbal expression of love by women and men as a critical communication event in personal relationships. *Women's Studies in Communication, 10,* 15–24.

Pam, A., & Pearson, J. (1998). *Splitting up: Enmeshment and estrangement in the process of divorce.* New York: Guilford Press.

Parks, M. R. (1982). Ideology in interpersonal communication: Off the couch and into the world. In M. Burgoon (Ed.), *Communication yearbook 5* (pp. 79–107). New Brunswick, NJ: Transaction.

Peterson, C. (2006). *A primer in positive psychology.* New York: Oxford University Press.

Petronio. S. (2000). The boundaries of privacy: Praxis of everyday life. In S. Petronio (Ed.), *Balancing the secrets of private disclosures* (pp. 37–49). Mahwah, NJ: Erlbaum.

Pratt, L., Wiseman, R. L., Cody, M. J., & Wendt, P. F. (1999). Interrogative strategies and information exchange in computer-mediated communication. *Communication Quarterly, 47,* 46--66.

Radmacher, K., &Azmitia, M. (2006). Are there gendered pathways to intimacy in early adolescents' and emerging adults' friendships? *Journal of Adolescent Research, 21,* 415–448.

Rawlins, W. K. (1992). *Friendship matters: Communication, dialectics, and the lifo course.* New York: Aldine De Gruyter.

Reissman, C. K. (1990). *Divorce talk: Women and men make sense of personal relationships.* New Brunswick, NJ: Rutgers University Press.

Richmond, V., Gorham, J. S., & Furio, B. J. (1987). Affinity-seeking communication in collegiate female-male relationships. *Communication Quarterly, 35,* 334–348.

Roe, D. (2001). Differences in self-disclosure in psychotherapy between American and Israeli patients. *Psychological Reports, 88,* 611–624.

Roloff, M. E., Janiszewski, C. A., McGrath, M.A., Burns, C. S., &Manrai, L.A. (1988). Acquiring resources from intimates: When obligation substitutes for persuasion. *Human Communication Research, 14,* 364–396.

Rubin, L. (1985). *Just friends: The role qf.friendship in our lives.* New York: Harper & Row.

Rusbult, C. E., & Van Lange, P. A.M. (1996). Interdependence processes. In E. T. Higgins & A. W. Kruglanski (Eds.), *Social psychology: Handbook of basic principles* (pp. 564–596). New York: Guilford Press.

Sahlstein, E. (2004). Relational maintenance research: A review of reviews. *PsycCRITIQUES,* 49(Suppl.14), np. Available at http://www.apa.org.

Sargent, J. (2002). Topic avoidance: Is this the way to a more satisfying relationship? *Communication Research Reports, 19,* 175–182.

Schaefer, M. T., & Olson, D. H. (1981). Assessing intimacy: The PAIR Inventory. *Journal q[Marital and Family Therapy, 7,* 47–60.

Scharlott, B. W., & Christ, W. G. (1995). Overcoming relationship-initiation barriers: The impact of a computer-dating system on sex role, shyness, and appearance inhibitions. *Computers in Human Behavior, 11,* 191–204.

Sheeks, M. S., & Birchmeier, Z. P. (2007). Shyness, sociability, and the use of computermediated communication in relationship development. *CyberPsychology & Behavior, 10,* 64–70.

Solomon, D. H., & Knobloch, L. K. (2001). Relationship uncertainty, partner interference, and intimacy within dating relationships. *Journal of Social and Personal Relationships, 8,* 804–820.

Speicher, H. (1999). Development and validation of intimacy capability and intimacy motivation measures. *Dissertation Abstracts International, 59,* 5172.

Stafford L., & Canary, D. J. (1991). Maintenance strategies and romantic relationship type, gender, and relational characteristics. *Journal of Social and Personal Relationships, 8,* 217–242.

Stafford, L., Dainton, M., & Haas, S. (2000). Measuring routine and strategic relational maintenance. *Communication Monographs, 67,* 306–323.

Stewart, S., Stinnett, H., & Rosenfeld, L.B. (2000). Sex differences in desired characteristics of short-term and long-term relationship partners. *Journal of Personal and Social Relationships, 17,* 843–853.

Suter, E. A., Bergen, K. M., Daas, K. L., & Durham, W. T (2006). Lesbian couples' management of public-private dialectical contradictions. *Journal of Social & Personal Relationships, 23,* 349–365.

Suter, E. A., & Daas, K. L. (2007). Negotiating heteronormativity dialectically: Lesbian couples' display of symbols in culture. *Western Journal of Communication, 71,* 177–195.

Swain, S. (1989). Covert intimacy in men's friendships: Closeness in men's friendships. In B. J. Risman & P. Schwartz (Eds.), *Gender in intimate relationships: A microstructural approach* (pp. 71–86). Belmont, CA: Wadsworth.

Swami, V., & Furnham, A. (2008). *The psychology of physical attraction.* New York: Routledge/ Taylor & Francis.

Tadinac, M., & Hromatko, I. (2004). Sex differences in mate preferences: Testing some predictions from evolutionary theory. *Review of Psychology, 11,* 45–51.

Takaku, S., Weiner, B., & Ohbuchi, K (2001). A cross-cultural examination of the effects of apology and perspective-taking on forgiveness. *Journal of Language & Social Psychology, 20,* 144–167.

Tannen, D. (1986). *That's not what I meant! How conversational style makes or breaks your relations with others.* New York: William Morrow.

Tashiro, T., & Frazier, P. (2003). "I'll never be in a relationship like that again": Personal growth following romantic relationship breakups. *Personal Relationships, 10,* 113–128.

Taylor, S., & Mette, D. (1971). When similarity breeds contempt. *Journal of Personality and Social Psychology, 20,* 75–81.

Thibaut,]. W., & Kelley, H. H. (1959). *The social psychology of groups.* New York: Wiley.

Tidwell, L. C., & Walther, J. B. (2002). Computer-mediated communication effects on disclosure, impressions, and interpersonal evaluations: Getting to know one another a bit at a time. *Human Communication Research, 28,* 317–348.

Tolhuizen,]. H. (1989). Communication strategies for intensifying dating relationships: Identification, use and structure. *Journal of Social and Personal Relationships, 6,* 413–434.

Tracy, S. J. (2004). Dialectic, contradiction, or double bind? Analyzing and theorizing employee reactions to organizational tension. *Journal of Applied Communication Research, 32,* 119–146.

Urberg, K. A., Degirmencioglu, S. M., & Tolson, J. M. (1998). Adolescent friendship selection and termination: The role of similarity. *Journal of Social and Personal Relationships, 15,* 703–710.

Vangelisti, A. L., & Beck, G. (2007). Intimacy and fear of intimacy. In L. L'Abate (Ed.), *Low-cost approaches to promote physical and mental health: Theory, research, and practice* (pp. 395–414). New York: Springer Science+ Business Media.

Vaughn, D. (1987, July). The long goodbye. *Psychology Today, 21,* 37–42.

Waldron, V. R., & Kelley, D. L (2005). Forgiving communication as a response to relational transgressions. *Journal of Social and Personal Relationships, 22,* 723–742.

Wallace, H. M., Exline, J. J., & Baumeister, R. F. (2008). Interpersonal consequences of forgiveness: Does forgiveness deter or encourage repeat offenses? *Journal of Experimental Social Psychology, 44,* 453–460.

Walster, E., Aronson, E., Abrahams, D., & Rottmann, L. (1966). Importance of physical attractiveness in dating behavior. *Journal of Personality and Social Psychology, 4,* 508–516.

Watzlawick, P., Beavin, J., &Jackson, D. (1967). *Pragmatics of human communication: A study of interactional patterns, pathologies, and paradoxes.* New York: Norton.

Weigel, D. J., & Ballard-Reisch, D. S. (1999). Using paired data to test models of relational mainte-nance and marital quality. *Journal of Social and Personal Relationships, 16,* 175–191.

Weiss, L., & Lowenthal, M. F. (1975). Life-course perspectives on friendship. In M. F. Lowenthal, M. Thurnher, & D. Chiriboga (Eds.), *Four stages of life: A comparative study of women and men focing transitions* (pp. 48–61). San Francisco: Jossey-Bass.

Welch, S. A., & Rubin, R. B. (2002). Development of relationship stage measures. *Communication Quarterly, 50,* 24–40.

Wilmot, W. W. (1987). *Dyadic communication* (3rd ed.). New York: Random House.

Wood,]. T., & Inman, C. C. (1993). In a different mode: Masculine styles of communicating close-ness. *Journal of Applied Communication Research, 21,* 279–295.

Wortman, C. B., Adosman, P., Herman, E., &Greenberg, R. (1976). Self-disclosure: An attribu-tional perspective. *Journal of Personality and Social Psychology, 33,* 184–191.

Yun, K. A. (2002). Similarity and attraction. In M. Allen, N. Burrell, B. M. Eayle, & R. W. Preiss (Eds.), *Interpersonal communication research: Advances through metaanalysis* (pp. 145–168). Mahwah, NJ: Erlbaum.

Zorn, T. E., & Gregory, K. W. (2005). Learning the ropes together: Assimilation and friendship development among first-year male medical students. *Health Communication, 17,* 211–231.

Chapter 10

Small Group Communication

Joseph A. Bonito, Gwen M. Wittenbaum, and Randy Y. Hirokawa

The study of small group communication began in the 1950s, and has been a vibrant aspect of communication research ever since. Much of the literature on group communication has examined how people in groups interact, and the search for the best interaction patterns to maximize group performance. Most recently, the effects of technology on group outcomes has been introduced to the study of group performance.

Learning Objectives For This Chapter

- Discuss the progression of group interaction theories
- Identify the key group discussion methods
- Describe the relationship between communication variables and group decision-making outcomes
- Explain the relationship between group communication and group performance
- Identify how group performance affects group outcomes
- Discuss the significance of group participation with respect to group performance
- Describe the significant differences between zero-history and bona fide groups
- Identify the role that technology can play in group communication

The study of small group communication focuses on the exchange of messages among three or more mutually interacting individuals.[2] The origins of this research subfield are amorphous and traverse many cognate disciplines (Gouran, 1999). Early interest in small group communication emerged from the pioneering work of sociologists like Kurt Lewin (1947,

1951) and Robert Freed Bales (1950), as well as psychologists like Raymond Cattell (1948, 1951a, 1951b). Lewin's work on group dynamics, for example, paved the way for decades of small group communication research that focused on the influence of group participation and interaction on member's attitudes and behaviors (Hirokawa et al., 1996a). Bales' development of the method of interaction analysis provided small group communication researchers with a reliable and systematic tool for empirically studying communication processes in small group settings (Gouran, 1999). Cattell's work on group synergy called to our attention the need for small group communication scholars to focus not only on the task dimensions of group communication, but also on the social aspects of it, in understanding productivity and performance of groups (Salazar, 1995).

This [selection] provides a general overview of small group communication research as it emerged and developed in the field of communication. As such, it is not an exhaustive review of all group communication research.

In the Beginning

Within the field of communication, the study of small group communication first emerged as a topic of research in the 1950s. The first published study of group *communication* is credited to Edwin Black (1955), who examined interaction sequences in decision-making discussions to determine the causes of breakdowns in group deliberation. Other early works included Crow-ell, Katcher, and Miyamoto's (1955) investigation of the relationship between group members' confidence in their communication skills as it affected their performance in group discussions; Barnlund's (1955) research on the effects of leadership training on group participation in decision-making groups; and Scheidel, Crowell, and Shepherd's (1958) study of the effects of group members' personality characteristics on their group discussion behaviors.

It was not until the 1960s that study of group communication began to appear regularly in communication journals. Group communication research in the 1960s was largely concerned with identifying the content and structural characteristics of group communication, as well as identifying the most effective manner of engaging in group discussion (Gouran, 1999). Research by Pyron and Sharp (1963), Pyron (1964), and Sharp and Milliken (1964) examined the effectiveness of a group discussion agenda based on Dewey's (1910) method of "reflective thinking." In 1964, Thomas Scheidel and Laura Crowell published a study of idea development in group discussions. Their investigation utilized the innovative interaction analysis method proposed by Bales (1950) to analyze the role of communication in idea development in group deliberation. This was followed by research examining feedback sequences (Scheidel & Crowell, 1964), communicative traits of leaders (Geier, 1967), and thematic development of ideas in group discussion (Berg, 1967).

The study of small group communication began to hit its full stride in the 1970s. Between 1970 and 1978 alone, a total of 114 studies dealing with groups were published in communication journals (Cragan & Wright, 1980). That number increased by an additional 89 articles by 1990 (Cragan & Wright, 1990). Five basic questions guided small group communication research between 1970 and 1990s:

1. Is group communication characterized by recognizable and predictable patterns of interaction?
2. Are certain discussion methods better than others?
3. Is group communication associated with group outcomes like consensus and group satisfaction?
4. Is group communication associated with effective group performance?
5. Is group communication associated with group leadership?

Group Interaction Structure

One major line of research emerging in the 1970s examined the interactional and developmental structure of group communication. Researchers focusing on the interactional structure of group communication sought to determine whether group discussion is characterized by discernible structure (or patterns) of communication acts and, if so, how those structures become patterned over time (Baird, 1974; Fisher & Hawes, 1971; Gouran & Baird, 1972; Saine & Bock, 1973; Saine, Schulman, & Emerson, 1974). In general, these various investigations found that the utterances of group members tend to follow each other in predictable patterns such that it is often possible to anticipate what a group member will say if we know what another has said previously.

In contrast, investigations of the developmental structure of group communication were concerned with understanding whether group communication displays qualitatively different "phases" or stages of group interaction during which certain types of communication behaviors appear more or less frequently than other phases of interaction. Fisher (1970), for instance, studied the developmental nature of group discussion leading to consensus group decisions. His research provided evidence suggesting that decision-making groups go through a four-phase process in reaching consensus. He labeled these stages orientation, conflict, emergence, and reinforcement. In the orientation phase, utterances asking for, and providing, clarification were at their peak; in the conflict phase, evaluative comments and comments expressing disagreements tended to dominate the discussion; in the emergence phase, disagreements dropped off dramatically and comments providing support for particular ideas increased in frequency; and in the reinforcement phase, comments providing support and reinforcement of ideas dominated the discussion. Other researchers (Cheseboro, Cragan, & McCullough, 1973; Ellis & Fisher, 1975; Mabry, 1975a, 1975b) utilized different sets of communication variables to investigate the developmental nature of group interaction. The findings of these descriptive studies formed the corpus of a theoretical model of group interaction development referred to as the "unitary sequence model" (Poole, 1981). In essence, this model posited that all groups display the same phases (or stages) of discussion development as they move toward completion of their task.

In the early 1980s, Poole and his colleagues provided empirical evidence challenging the unitary sequence model's notion that all groups move through the same phases of development in the same sequential order (Poole, 1981, 1983; Poole & Roth, 1989a, 1989b). To the contrary, Poole's research revealed that groups will not necessarily proceed through the same phases of development in the same sequential order, because each group responds to existing contingencies and exigencies in unique ways. On the basis of their research, Poole and his colleagues (Poole, 1983; Poole & Doelger, 1986; Poole & Roth, 1989a, 1989b) described the group process as consisting of a complex set of group communication activities characterized by "extreme variability of phases and phase sequences" (Poole, 1983, p. 325). Poole and his colleagues (Poole & Doelger, 1986; Poole & Roth, 1989b) subsequently outlined the features of the developmental theory of group interaction that posited that task characteristics (e.g., novelty, goal clarity, time requirements) and group structural characteristics (e.g., conflict history, group size) influence the development of the decision in three ways: (1) the nature of the "path" (i.e., sequence of decision activities) that a group employs in reaching a decision; (2) the complexity of the path that the group employs in reaching a decision; and (3) the degree of disorganization during group interaction.

Group Discussion Methods

A second major line of research beginning in the 1970s centered on the study of effective group discussion methods. Among the discussion techniques examined were brainstorming (Jablin, Seibold, & Sorenson, 1977; Jablin, Sorenson, & Seibold, 1978; Philipsen, Mulac, & Dietrich, 1979), Delphi method (Delbecq, Van de Ven, & Gustafson, 1975), PERT (Applbaum & Anatol, 1971; Phillips, 1966), reflective thinking (Bayless, 1967; Brilhart & Jochem, 1964; Larson, 1969), and T-groups (Larson & Gratz, 1970). The central concern of these studies was to identify the most effective discussion procedures.

The findings of these studies, bolstered by the results of more recent investigations (Burleson, Levine, & Samter, 1984; Comadena, 1984; Hiltz, Johnson, & Turoff, 1986; Hirokawa, 1985; Jablin, 1981; Jarboe, 1988), suggest strongly that the discussion procedures used by a group in problem solving or decision making are not necessarily a determinant to effective group performance. Hirokawa (1985), for example, compared four different discussion formats (reflective thinking, single question, ideal solution, and free discussion) and found no difference among them in terms of their association with high-quality decisions. Similarly, Jarboe (1988) compared the reflective thinking format to the nominal group technique to determine which better facilitated group decision making. She found that the nominal group technique led to a greater number of ideas than the reflective thinking procedure, but that the two procedures did not differ in terms of the uniqueness or quality of the ideas it produced. Hiltz et al. (1986) compared computerized conferences and face-to-face discussion procedures. They found that both discussion formats produced equally good decisions, although group members found it more difficult to reach consensus in a computerized conference.

Group Communication and
Group Outcomes

Another important line of research in the 1970s examined the relationship between communication variables and group decision-making outcomes. Gouran (1969) focused on the relationship between communication characteristics and a group's ability to reach consensus (unanimous agreement). He found that the communication variable most closely related to consensus decision making is orientation. That is, groups that reached consensus, as contrasted with those that did not, made more statements that attempted to clarify and familiarize members with the group task, goals, procedures, and the like. Gouran's findings stimulated a series of investigation focusing on the relationship between orientation and group consensus (e.g., Kline, 1972; Kline & Hullinger, 1973; Knutson, 1972; Knutson & Holdridge, 1975; Knutson & Kowitz, 1977).

Group consensus research continued to receive attention in the 1980s. DeStephen (1983), for example, found that there were communication characteristics which differentiated high and low consensus groups. She, along with Hirokawa (DeStephen & Hirokawa, 1988), also developed an instrument to measure the degree of consensus in decision-making groups. Further, Canary, Brossman, and Seibold (1987) found that groups arriving at consensus tended to use a greater percentage of convergent arguments than groups that did not arrive at consensus. Beatty (1989), meanwhile, examined the effect of group members' "decision rule orientation" on consensus formation. He found that groups composed of members with similar criteria for making a decision among a set of alternatives (similar decision rule orientation), arrived at consensus decisions with greater frequency than groups whose members were dissimilar in their selection criteria.

Group Communication and
Group Performance

The 1970s also brought the emergence of research focusing on the relationship between group communication and group performance. Leathers (1972) found that groups characterized by high quality communication also tended to make high quality decisions. That is, groups experiencing good feedback (e.g., high quality, positive, task-oriented when necessary and maintenance-oriented when necessary) also tended to make good decisions. This line of research continued and increased in the 1980s with the development and testing of the functional perspective of communication and group decision-making effectiveness (Gouran & Hirokawa, 1983; Hirokawa & Scheerhorn, 1983). This theory posited that communication influences group performance by affecting the satisfaction of a group's particular task requirements. These "functional requisites" include assessment of the problematic situation, identification of goals, identification of viable choices, and evaluation of choices (Gouran & Hirokawa, 1983; Hirokawa & McLeod, 1993). Central to the functional perspective is the notion that communication can function to promote or inhibit the effective facilitation of the four requisite functions (Gouran & Hirokawa, 1986).

On the basis of this theory, Hirokawa (1983) developed an interaction coding system that focused on the task-relevant group communication; that is, communication that attends to the functional requisites of the task in question. Using this new system, Hirokawa found that groups which displayed utterances that fulfilled the functional requisites of a group's task tended to arrive at higher quality decisions than those that did not (Hirokawa, 1988). Further, as suggested earlier, the order in which the requisites were fulfilled did not appear to make a difference, nor did the particular format used by the group in fulfilling those requisites appear to matter (Burleson et al., 1984). Rather, what appeared to make the greatest difference for group performance was the number of functional requisites satisfied by a group during the course of its deliberation (Hirokawa, 1985). In short, in the 1980s, the functional perspective dominated research focusing on the relationship between group communication and group decision-making performance.

Communication and Group Leadership Research

Finally, the 1970s marked the emergence of research focused on the communicative aspects of group leadership. A number of studies focused on the communication characteristics of emergent group leaders. Investigations that exemplify this research interest included those by Geier (1967), which focused on the communicative traits of emergent group leader communication traits; Morris and Hackman (1969), which focused on the relationship between talkativeness and leader emergence; Schultz (1982), which focused on the effects of argumentativeness on emergent group leadership; and Smith and Powell (1988), which focused on the relationship between humor and leadership emergence. Other researchers sought to obtain a clearer understanding of the effects of different communication styles of group leadership on various socioemotional and task outputs in groups (Downs & Pickett, 1977; Rosenfeld & Fowler, 1976; Rosenfeld & Plax, 1975; Sargent & Miller, 1971; Wood, 1977; Yerby, 1975).

Contemporary Research

Research directions that emerged in the 1970s, and reached their peak in the 1980s, continued into the 1990s. At the same time, important developments beginning in the 1990s infused renewed energy and excitement in the study of small group communication. Around 1997, group communication scholars acquired enough support to form their own division in the National Communication Association (NCA). This division serves as an important source of identity and community for group communication scholars, allowing its members to discuss research at the annual NCA convention and recognize top work in the field. Also during this period, group communication scholars began to forge new connections with scholars who study groups in other disciplines, such as psychology and information systems (see Wittenbaum, Keyton, & Weingart, 2006). These connections are reflected in the research trends that have emerged since the mid-1990s.

With few exceptions, group communication research since 1996 falls into four main areas: (1) performance, (2) participation, (3) bona fide groups, and (4) technology. *Performance* research is concerned with predicting group outcomes, such as decisions, from knowing relevant features of the group (e.g., its task and members) and communication between members. *Participation* research focuses on understanding the frequency, content, and patterning of communication in groups. Research in the *bona fide group* perspective examines ongoing, natural groups that are interdependent with their context. The newest trend in group communication research, *technology,* focuses on the influence of and processes within communication technologies and the Internet. These areas reflect not only distinct research trends, but also particular theoretical perspectives and methodological tendencies. We will review these four research areas, demonstrating the main theoretical and empirical themes within each.

Performance

Group communication scholars have long been interested in understanding how communication impacts performance on group decision-making and problem-solving tasks. Much of the work in the performance area comes from a functional perspective where the quality of a group's output is a function of inputs (e.g., group size, leader style) and communication processes (Gouran & Hirokawa, 1983; Wittenbaum et al., 2004). Salazar (1995) proposed that group outputs are the function of interactions between inputs and communication processes. In his ambiguity model, he argued that communication processes and performance are more strongly related under conditions of high rather than low ambiguity, where features of the group's situation (task, diversity of information, and preference) interact with individual differences between members to impact the level of ambiguity. Given its long tradition of study, it should not be surprising that work designed to understand the relation between group communication and performance has continued and grown in recent years. A few studies continued classic lines of work on group polarization (Henningsen & Henningsen, 2004), and groupthink (Henningsen, Henningsen, Eden, & Cruz, 2006). But by far, the recent work in this area examines processes that are new to the study of group communication: information sharing, remembering, and resource sharing. What is not new, however, are the methods used to understand group performance. Nearly all of the research in this area is experimental and conducted using ad hoc student groups in a laboratory.

Information Sharing

Since the mid-1990s, group communication research has exploded with interest in information processing in groups. Much of this work was inspired by psychological research on information sharing in decision-making groups, originally conducted by Stasser and Titus (1985, 1987) but later replicated and extended by scholars across many fields (see Wittenbaum, Hollingshead, & Botero, 2004 for a review). Stasser and Titus originally expected that unique and novel arguments would be particularly persuasive in decision-making groups as predicted by persuasive arguments theory (see Stasser & Titus, 2003). Instead, they found that *unshared* information, which is uniquely known by a single group member, was less likely to appear in group discussions and impact group decisions compared to *shared* information that all members knew (Gigone & Hastie, 1993). This *collective information sharing bias* would not be a problem if it were not for the fact that it can impair group decision quality when thorough pooling of unshared information is essential for determining the best decision alternative—a condition called a *hidden profile*. Much of the research since Stasser and Titus's (1985) original study has sought to understand the conditions that increase the likelihood of groups discussing unshared information and thus making a better decision.

It should not be surprising why this line of work caught on in the field of communication. It fits a functional perspective well, examining how various input factors influence the communication of shared and unshared information during group discussion to impact the group output or decision quality. The hidden profile task, which involves giving all group members shared information that supports an inferior decision alternative and each group member unshared information that supports the optimal decision alternative, makes it easy to examine the relation between quality of communication and group decision. In the past decade, group communication scholars have published at least ten research articles using a hidden profile task to examine information exchange in decision making in groups (Cruz, Boster, & Rodriguez, 1997; Cruz, Henningsen, & Smith, 1999; Cruz, Henningsen, & Williams, 2000; Henningsen & Henningsen, 2003; Henningsen, Henningsen, Jakobsen, & Borton, 2004; Hollingshead, 1996; Reimer, Kuendig, Hoffrage, Park, & Hinsz, 2007; Savadori, Van Swol, & Sniezek, 2001; Van Swol & Ludutsky, 2007; Van Swol, Savadori, & Sniezek, 2003). From these works, we have learned that information exchange and group decisions suffer when members choose one decision alternative rather than rank them all (Hollingshead, 1996a,b), when the group leader tries to influence the group to select his or her poor quality preference (Cruz, Henningsen, & Smith, 1999), and when members emphasize shared information through repetition (Van Swol, Savadori, & Sniezek, 2003). Composing groups of equal status members (Hollingshead, 1996) and being able to compare each decision alternative on common dimensions (Reimer et al., 2007) improves members' performance on a hidden profile task.

Although the hidden profile task provides an interesting group decision making case, overreliance on this task can be problematic. Wittenbaum et al. (2004) argued that the hidden profile paradigm carries with it assumptions that may not reflect the processes in natural decision-making groups, namely that members are cooperative communicators and unshared information is more important than shared information. To the contrary, members may hold competitive goals, motivating them to withhold unshared information from fellow group members or communicate it in goal-congruent ways (Wittenbaum, Hollingshead, & Bowman, 2003).

Interesting information sharing processes may be seen in decision-making groups that do not work on a hidden profile. For example, Wittenbaum (1998, 2000) showed that the bias toward shared information holds for high rather than low status members when deciding between equally attractive decision alternatives. When information is given to members so that they can communicate either shared or unshared information, those who communicate shared information are judged as more task capable (Wittenbaum, Hubbell, & Zuckerman, 1999). This mutual enhancement effect may occur because communicated shared information is judged as more important than communicated unshared information (Van Swol & Ludutsky, 2007). Shared information is not always favored, however. Sometimes, one group member (i.e., the judge) makes the decision for the group upon hearing information and advice from "advisors." In such a Judge-Advisor System (JAS), judges solicit more information from the advisor who knows a lot of unshared information compared to the advisor who knows a lot of shared information. In a JAS, judges probably associate the role of advisor with communicating novel information, which is why they may favor such advisors. Although assessing group decision quality was not paramount in these studies, they highlight the value of examining information sharing processes under various group decision making conditions.

Remembering

Several information sharing studies have examined group members' retrieval of shared and unshared information using a free recall or recognition task. This focus on remembering represents another new direction for group communication research. Research shows that group members recall shared information better than unshared information (Reimer et al., 2007; Savadori et al., 2001), an effect that replicates even when just considering information that supports the optimal decision alternative (Henningsen et al., 2006). And, the unshared information of high status members is better recognized than that of low status members (Wittenbaum, 2000). These studies highlight the added challenge of getting decision-making groups to use unshared information: members are less likely to recall it, particularly when mentioned by members with low regard.

Group memory was highlighted in a colloquy published in a 2003 issue of *Human Communication Research*. Remembering often occurs collaboratively in small groups—a phenomenon examined by Pavitt (2003). He lamented that group members do not reap the potential benefits of collective remembering, and, instead, they fall short of the recall performance of those remembering alone—a problem exacerbated by a large group size. Group discussion has the potential to help members recall more collectively than alone, but process losses during discussion (e.g., difficulty coordinating or reduced motivation) prevent this from happening. One potential criticism of Pavitt's work was that he did not examine communication processes directly, linking only inputs (e.g., group size) with outputs (recall performance) (Wittenbaum, 2003). Likewise, Hollingshead and Brandon (2003) argued that examining how encoding, storage, and retrieval of information occur via communication in transactive memory systems can demonstrate the central role of communication processes in producing collective recall output that exceeds the potential output of individual members. When communication has been examined in group memory research, it tends to be operationalized in overly simplistic ways (Propp, 2003). The recent interest of group communication scholars in collective memory shows great promise in uncovering ways that communication processes help or hinder the encoding, storage, and retrieval of information.

Resource Sharing

Finally, a new line of work examines communication processes in the context of resource dilemmas and highlights the potential contributions that group communication scholars can make to understanding pressing social problems. Social dilemma research provides an analogue to the "tragedy of the commons"—the tendency for group members to act selfishly by hoarding a scarce resource, depleting it for others and eventually for themselves in the long run (Komorita & Parks, 1994). Despite years of research on the topic by scholars in psychology, economics, and environmental sciences, Pavitt and colleagues were the first to link it with communication processes (Pavitt, McFeeters, Towey, & Zingerman, 2005; Pavitt, Zingerman, Towey, & McFeeters, 2006). In these experiments, students played a game in small groups where they consumed a resource that replenished itself at a higher or lower rate. Results showed that groups with a higher replenishment rate performed better (harvested more of the resource) and contributed more maintenance and procedural comments during group discussion compared to groups with a lower replenishment rate. This research nicely fits the input-process-output framework of the functional perspective, showing that a higher replenishment rate facilitates communication that is conducive to cooperation, which helped groups to harvest more of the resource. As the depletion of clean water and oil become more widespread problems on Earth, it will be important for communication scholars to aid the understanding of how people share resources in groups.

Participation

One of the first sustained lines of theory and research on small group communication was on participation. Bales, Strodtbeck, Mill, and Roseborough (1951) and Stephan and Mishler (1952) were among the first to document the problem and outline some of its characteristics. It has proved to be an important problem because it is not uncommon for participation to influence discussion and outcomes, and it is also an attractive problem because it lends itself to sophisticated statistical modeling techniques (for reviews see Bonito & Hollingshead, 1997; Stasser & Vaughan, 1996).

The scope of participation research depends, in part, on one's conceptualization of the problem. The narrow view is that the phenomenon consists of just the number of behaviors, irrespective of variation in content, substance, or function. This is bolstered by research that reveals the amount of participation predicts influence on group outcomes, with some qualifications (Bottger, 1984; Sorrentino & Boutillier, 1975). The broad view, and the one adopted here, is that participation is an umbrella term for studies that (1) categorize contributions in theoretically relevant ways; (2) look for patterns in such contributions; or (3) model the conditions under which contributions are produced during discussion. In general, the evaluation of group outcomes and its relation to participation is of secondary importance, if at all (cf. Gouran, 1990). Thus, the broad view includes areas such as argumentation, coherence and relevance, and deliberation.

There are three theoretical issues that drive participation research from a communication perspective. First is a concern with the nature of participation itself. This is important, because, as Wilson (2002) noted, the typology one uses to describe contributions is inextricably bound to the explanations for the process of participation. A second theoretical objective is to explain the co-occurrence of different types of contributions. Co-occurrence can be defined in many ways, including simple correlation (within and across groups) to lag-sequential analyses (e.g., Jackson & Poole, 2003). A third theoretical problem is to explain the influence of exogenous (to discussion) factors on participation. Here researchers run into an important issue. Some research assumes (often implicitly) a "mediated" view, which characterizes communication as a conduit through which individual differences are made manifest (Hirokawa, Erbert, & Hurst, 1996). Communication features do not otherwise figure in the process of participation. Others assume a "constitutive" view in which the process of participation itself creates opportunities for participation that individual differences or contextual features cannot predict. The truth is that participation is a function of both mediation and constitutive processes, but issues are not often framed that way.

Bonito's Participation Model

Bonito's (2007) local model of participation adopts a constitutive role for the process of participation. The model has three components. First, participants make judgments regarding the relative abilities of their colleagues to contribute usefully to discussion. Members perceived as more able are provided with and take more speaking turns than those who are judged as less able. Second, substantive participation occurs only if members possess active (i.e., available in short term memory) relevant information at certain points during the discussion. Third, discussion influences both the activation of information and the development of participator judgments. Findings from this line of work indicate support for the model. Information resources are associated with participation (Bonito, 2001, 2003a) but there is some evidence that colleagues' information resources also influence one's participation (Bonito & Lambert, 2005). Participator judgments are related to interaction (Bonito, 2003b; Bonito, DeCamp, Coffman, & Fleming,

2006) such that the more one participates substantively the more favorably colleagues perceive him or her. Finally, participation is an interdependent phenomenon such that one's participation is affected by other members' behavior and cognitions, including the extent to which information is shared (Bonito, 2001), the degree to which members share expectations regarding the purpose of discussion (Bonito, 2004), and satisfaction with discussion (Bonito, 2000). Criticisms of this work include a fairly rudimentary typology of participation types and vague or ill-specified features of temporal change of participator judgments within discussions.

Argument in Small Groups

The study of argument is central to the communication discipline, and several scholars, most notably Meyers, Seibold, and their associates, have examined the occurrence and patterning of argument in small groups (for a review, see Seibold & Meyers, 2007). Coding schemes for argument have been in development for some time (Meyers & Brashers, 1998a), with scholars focusing on the quality and type of arguments produced during discussion. The work is often framed within a structuration account of group processes, with arguments assumed to be the function of the intersection of micro (e.g., individual abilities in arguing) and macro (e.g., interaction patterns) processes. Fundamentally, interaction is viewed as constitutive to both the production of argument as well as its effects.

Meyers and Brashers (1998b) explicated a process model of argument in which disagreement generates argument within groups, and that different argument types, especially their distribution within groups, is associated with group outcomes. In general, studies of argument have evaluated distributions of argument types across members and within context. For example, Meyers, Brashers, and Hanner (2000) noted that majorities and minorities (in terms of the number of persons advocating a particular solution) differed in the number and type of arguments produced during discussion. For example, "winning" majorities produced more arguables (e.g., assertions and elaborations), disagreements, and delimiters (e.g., framing and securing common ground) than did losing majorities. In addition, losing minorities contributed more disagreement than did winning minorities. Finally, across all subgroups, winning teams produced more convergence statements than did losing teams. Sex differences also influence the distribution of arguments to some degree, as women are more likely to state agreement and provide propositions than is expected given their overall contributions, whereas men provided fewer of those comments (Meyers, Brashers, Winston, & Grob, 1997). However, men issued more challenges and asked more context-framing questions, given the number of their overall contributions, than did women.

Coherence

Several group communication scholars have addressed Hewes's (1996) challenge to look for coherence in terms of the connections among contributions to discussion that are unambiguously a function of interaction processes rather than preexisting individual differences or contextual constraints. Two types of coherence, *local* and *global,* characterize group discussion (Pavitt & Johnson, 1999). Local refers to connections among contiguous contributions whereas global describes coherence over larger stretches of the interaction. Pavitt and Johnson (1999) investigated features of local coherence in their study of proposal sequencing during problem solving discussion. They found that proposals were sequenced contiguously; any given proposal was likely to be followed by a comment relevant to that proposal. Pavitt and Johnson (Pavitt & Johnson, 2001, 2002) also evaluated more global aspects of coherence, including spirals (in which a proposal made early in discussion is evaluated later), finding that groups vary in the extent to which spiraling occurs. In addition, spiraling is less common in groups with a linear process orientation than those with a "reach-testing" (i.e., interested in trying a new idea then dropping them in favor of others) one. In an ambitious study, Corman and Kuhn (2005) asked participants to rate the coherence of computer-generated egocentric discussion transcripts (i.e., ones in which the sequence of contributions were randomly assembled by a computer) and actual group discussions. (Participants were asked to evaluate two transcripts, and were told in advance that the transcript might be from actual discussions or computer-generated.) Unexpectedly, participants were unable to distinguish between the two types of transcripts. Additional analyses revealed that the ability to distinguish among transcripts was aided (or made worse) by focusing on such attributes as clarity, reasoning, or depth. Thus, although participants in general could not tell computer-generated from actual discussion, there are cases when, using the appropriate evaluation orientation, such distinctions could reliably be made.

Deliberation

Research on deliberation has focused on jury groups, but it is not limited to those groups. Instead, deliberation refers to face-to-face discussions involving political or policy issues; the decisions have the potential to affect many people, not just group members (Burkhalter, Gastil, & Kelshaw 2002). Theoretical accounts are found in Burkhalter, Gastil, and Kelshaw, and Sunwolf and Sei-bold (1998), the central focus of which is understanding the conditions under which people contribute to deliberative discussions. Moy and Gastil (2006) tested a model in which network size, network heterogeneity, and media exposure predicted willingness to deliberate. Results varied across the two samples, one of which consisted of well-educated, politically aware participants, and the other a group of adult literacy students. One consistency in the findings was the network effect—the more persons with whom one discusses political events influences the extent to which he or she is willing to engage in deliberation. Gastil, Burkhalter, and Black (2007) asked if juries deliberate, and, if so, what are the antecedents to deliberation. Self-reports from actual jurors indicated that juries do indeed deliberate, and the vast majority indicated that they had ample opportunities to express themselves. Antecedents, including political knowledge, partisanship, and political self-confidence were associated with features of deliberation. However, uneven distribution with juries of some of these antecedents (e.g., political knowledge) seemed to inhibit, or at least reduce, levels of deliberation. Finally, Sager and Gastil (2002) noted that agreeableness (from the so-called Big 5 personality factors inventory) was correlated with perceived confirming interaction (i.e., the extent to which one feels confirmed or validated by other group members), and that confirming interaction was associated with perceptions of democratic decision making. Although not tested, the implication is that confirming interaction moderates member agreeableness with perceived democratic deliberations.

Bona Fide Groups

Scholars have long been interested in the communication practices of existing or "real world" groups. There are two reasons for this. First is a general dissatisfaction with the limitations of zero-history or experimental groups. Although laboratory studies provide useful information regarding input, process, and output characteristics of small groups, such groups are divorced from, or are rarely forced to encounter, exigencies that most real world groups encounter. Second, existing groups provide research contexts that are either unanticipated by the researcher or impossible to recreate validly in the laboratory. For example, Sigman (1984) detailed how members of a nursing home admissions board were responsible for certain types of information (e.g., knowing the number of available beds) and the conditions under which leaders structured discussion such that relevant information was contributed as needed. Laboratory groups rarely work on tasks with such important implications for the group, the organization, and the environment (i.e., those who are admitted and those who are not).

Much of that context-based research prior to the 1990s was theoretically fragmented, with no real unifying theme or perspective that allowed for comparisons of communicative behavior across contexts. The *bona fide perspective* (Putnam & Stohl, 1990) is a recent attempt to provide unity by making context a central feature of theory and research. A central feature of the bona fide perspective is to characterize "a group as a social system linked to its context, shaped by fluid boundaries, and altering its environment" (Putnam & Stohl, 1996, p. 148). There are two main assumptions (Frey, 2003b). The first is the notion that boundaries are permeable and fluid. A boundary is typically thought of in one of several ways, for example, as a physical space that delineates the group from other entities (e.g., a meeting room), a set of member characteristics that separate the group from others (e.g., faculty members), or a job or set of responsibilities that differentiate the group from other groups (e.g., a faculty search committee). These features are certainly important and at least function to provide the group with a "nominal" basis for starting and maintaining their collective work. The bona fide perspective, however, assumes a social constructionist approach to boundaries such that whatever defines a group is brought about by or is a function of a group's interactions, both internal and external (Stohl & Putnam, 2003). The second element of the bona fide perspective is interdependence with immediate context. Features of group processes, as well as outcomes, affect and are affected by a group's working environment. This includes, but is not limited to, historical context, anticipated outcomes, economics, location, and technological resources and support (Frey, 2003b). Intergroup communication is an integral component, as perceived support at a variety of levels depends on the extent to which the group successfully interacts with other groups with an interest in the outcome.

As one might imagine, given the scope of the bona fide perspective, there is no one "correct" set of methods and analyses; research is not "methodologically determinant" (Stohl & Putnam, 2003, p. 401). Thus, one finds many different types of investigations, including ethnographies, participant observations, textual analyses, and field and laboratory experiments. As Stohl and Putnam noted, the type of method is inconsequential as long as the starting point for the research questions involves interdependence between the group and its contexts. An advantage to this approach is a description of group processes of unparalleled depth and breadth, whereas disadvantages include comparability of results across studies and, in some cases, the inability to generalize to a larger population of groups and group members.

Researchers working from the bona fide perspective have examined groups in a wide variety of natural settings. The bulk of the work is collected in the edited volume by Frey (2003a), although a fair number of studies have appeared in peer-reviewed journals. Not surprisingly, the research might be usefully grouped into themes based on the extent to which studies investigate issues related to membership or interaction with immediate contexts. Some studies examine both boundaries and interaction with context, the notable case being Lammers and Krikorian (1997) who not only endeavored to apply virtually every aspect of the bona fide perspective extant in the contemporary literature to surgical teams, but added several constructs to the mix. Most studies have been more modest in their reach, examining a few issues in some detail.

Two recent examples of research from the bona fide perspective are Kramer's (2005) examination of a fund raising group (that raised funds by soliciting sponsorships for a charity marathon), and Sunwolf and Leets's (2004) study of adolescent and child peer groups. Kramer (a member of the group at the time of the study) used ethnographic methods to document, among other things, the role of communication in the formation of the group, as well as its relationship to external contexts. In terms of group formation, members used communication to develop both a sense of joint activities (although not every member participated in each activity) and a group identity. Members engaged external contexts in order to solicit sponsorships, and people external to the group provided valuable support to members while they (members) trained for the marathon. The findings, Kramer argued, are important for understanding how volunteer groups form and work together. Sunwolf and Leets used surveys and interviews to examine how children form groups, with emphasis on the development of boundaries. Children use a variety of communication methods, including ignoring, disqualifying, insulting, and blaming, to prevent outsiders from joining. In addition, the authors evaluated "rejection stress," the negative emotional impact of being denied access to groups. They argue that such experiences likely have consequences for attitudes toward working in more traditional groups.

Technology

With the advent of communication technologies and the Internet, group members no longer need to be co-present in space and time to collaborate and socialize. These technological advancements have opened up a new area of investigation for group communication scholars. Without a doubt, the newest explosion of research has examined groups whose members use computer-mediated communication (CMC). The initial research in this area, not surprisingly, compared the differences in process and performance between groups whose members communicate faceto-face (FTF) versus those who communicate via computer (e.g., see Baltes, Dickson, Sherman, Bauer, & LaGanke, 2002 for a review of work in group decision making). FTF and CMC groups often differ in member anonymity (awareness of one another's identities), familiarity with the communication medium, degree of synchrony of communication, and social collocation. These differences highlight a major theme in group technology research: understanding the effects of member identification. We will address this theme in addition to issues of stability of effects over time, status equalization, and online communities.

Most of the group technology work has centered on issues of group member identity and the processing of social information about the self and fellow members. The most prevalent theory in this area, the Social Identity Model of Deindividuation Effects (SIDE) predicts that the anonymity of CMC heightens social identity and leads to a loss of individual identity of the self (i.e., deindividuation) (Reicher, Spears, & Postmes, 1995). Because CMC often does not permit the communication of social cues that would be salient in FTF settings (e.g., attractiveness, sex, race), members are less likely to think of themselves in terms of their individuating characteristics. Instead, membership in the CMC group takes precedence over one's individual identity, which leads members to conform to in-group norms more readily (Postmes, Spears, & Lea, 1998) and increasingly over the course of interaction (Postmes, Spears, & Lea, 2000). However, conformity to group norms is reduced when personal dimensions of the self are made salient (Lee, 2004). Not all forms of anonymity were created equally, as Scott (1999) showed with groups using Group Decision Support Systems (GDSS). In his research, discursive anonymity (whether member messages were preceded by the member's name or not) influenced identification and communication outcomes more than physical anonymity (whether members were physically co-present or not).

One thing to keep in mind is that deindividuation effects in CMC groups may attenuate over time. Once members become familiar with the new communication medium, differences between CMC and FTF groups tend to dissipate (Hollingshead, 2001). Walther (1992) made a similar claim in his Social Information Processing Theory (SIPT), arguing that members of CMC groups will exchange social information to get to know one another personally, but it just takes more time than in FTF groups. Most of the SIDE research examines identification in short-lived groups, so its predictions for deindividuation may not hold over time in CMC groups.

Because cues indicating member status are less salient in CMC groups, some have argued that participation should be more equal across members in CMC than in FTF groups (DeSanctis & Gallupe, 1987). Despite some effects to the contrary (e.g., Peña, Walther, & Hancock, 2007), a meta-analysis of 44 different experiments showed that CMC groups demonstrated greater equality of participation and member influence and lower member dominance compared to those meeting FTF (Raines, 2005). Admittedly, there are probably several factors that moderate this status equalizing effect (Hollingshead, 2001). Nevertheless, the desire for fair and equal participation among members is apparent, especially among female members of mixed-sex groups who probably realize their potential low status vis-á-vis men (Flanagin, Tiyaamornwong, O'Connor, & Seibold, 2002). Such women may exploit the anonymity benefits of CMC by misrepresenting their sex to fellow members (Flanagin et al., 2002). Dissatisfaction with the group process is seen more generally, however, for both sexes working in CMC groups as participation rates become more unequal across members (Flanagin, Park, & Seibold, 2004).

Research on technology and groups can be characterized as using a wide variety of research methods. Although much of the research (particularly that in the SIDE tradition) uses experimental designs with student participants, many of the studies examine groups that interact over several weeks in the field rather than in a laboratory hour (e.g., Contractor, Seibold, & Heller, 1996; Flanagin, Park, & Seibold, 2004). In this regard, research on CMC groups reflects the processes of natural groups more than research in the group performance tradition. Increasingly, scholars are bringing more of a bona fide groups' perspective to the study of online groups. As an example, Matei and Ball-Rokeach (2005) described how WELL (Whole Earth Lectronic Link) navigated the ideological tensions experienced by being one of the first virtual communities by analyzing the discourse in their postings regarding being a virtual community. Research on technology and groups will likely continue to thrive with the use of experiments and surveys, content and discourse analysis, and laboratory and field methods. Because this research area has exploded so quickly, it can be criticized, however, for lacking theoretical integration and unity (Hollingshead, 2001). Future efforts may address this problem.

Sample Study

It is impossible to describe a sample study that touches all of the possible research questions suggested by our review of the group communication literature. It seems reasonable, however, to limit our discussion to quantitative social science research because (1) it is our area of methodological expertise, and (2) the majority of the work reviewed here is of that type. Rather than focus on just one area of the typical input-process-output model of group communication, we provide general guidelines regarding all three areas.

Input

Inputs are features of the group that are exogenous to discussion and precede or are antecedents of group interaction. Typically, but not always, the researcher manipulates inputs along theoretically important lines hoping that such manipulations have predicted effects on processes, outputs, or on both. As noted, an important research question concerns the conditions under which information is mentioned during discussion. This often entails that the researcher distributes the information to groups (usually of the zero-history, laboratory kind) such that some is shared and the rest unique (assuming a hidden profile design). Doing so often creates a set of initial solution preferences that are incorrect or at least suboptimal. (And this assumes the task has a correct or optimal answer, and that the researcher has identified in advance which information is important for correctly solving the problem.) The researcher will often manipulate other inputs (e.g., status of role of participants, communication channel) that he or she thinks will influence information sharing in groups. Other researchers have taken a different approach by using judgmental tasks (i.e., ones without correct answers) and measuring information units generated by participants (e.g., Bonito, 2001). Researchers must also identify the nature and measurement of the criterion variables, including characteristics of discussion, affective or perceptual issues (e.g., satisfaction), or nature of group outcomes, where appropriate.

Process

Researchers interested in process generally conceptualize and measure features of discussion, and are generally interested in the relation among discussion features. There is no correct way to categorize messages but one might, if not careful, generate inappropriate typologies (O'Keefe, 2003); one's choices depend on the research question of interest and, to some extent, on the properties of observed communication practices. Thus, for example, a scheme that is sensitive to variations in group argument is unlikely to be of much use for examining idea generation or information exchange. This type of research often occurs without manipulation of input variables, and often without concern for any inputs at all. Process research is reliant on recording and transcribing group interactions. Transcriptions must be reliably unitized (divided into smaller units that are of analytical interest) and then reliably coded, typically not by the researchers (because of the possibility of bias) but by "naïve" (to the study's purpose and hypotheses, if any) research assistants. Analysis of process data is often complex because of the interdependent (or nonindependent) nature of the data—it is often the case that one's contributions to discussion are influenced by those of others. Bonito (2001, 2006), for example, used multilevel models to analyze process; such models "nest" individuals within groups, and that allows for evaluation of (among other things) the extent to which behaviors are correlated within groups.

Outcomes

Group research is replete with a host of outcomes at a variety of levels of analysis (for a review, see Bonito & Hollingshead, 1997). In some cases, the outcomes are categorical in nature and determined by the researcher before the fact, as when groups are asked to choose from among three "candidates" for a hypothetical faculty position (Larson, Foster-Fishman, & Keys, 1994). Or they consist of range of choices that reflect an ordinal level of measurement, as in the case of the choice dilemma often used in studies of argumentation (e.g., Meyers & Brashers, 1998a). In other cases, outcomes take the form of self-reports that, for example, indicate affective reactions to discussion (e.g., satisfaction) or toward one's colleagues (e.g., credibility, perceptions of competence or ability). These outcomes are often evaluated against features of process (e.g., if the use of certain types of argument predicts a group's choice) or certain types of inputs, for example if distributions of information are related to perceptions of one's colleagues (Wittenbaum et al., 1999).

Summary

Beginning in the 1950s, the study of small group communication has been a vibrant aspect of research in the field of human communication. Key areas of interest have been analysis of the patterns of interactions in small groups, the best discussion methods, the association of group communication with group outcomes, the affects of group communication on group performance, and the interaction of group communication and leadership.

Probably one of the most analyzed aspect of group communication has been an attempt to find out if group communication follows specific patterns of interaction or phases. Also of concern of group researchers were determining the most effective group discussion methods along with the outcomes of these discussion methods. Another focus of early research on group communication was examining the relationship between group communication and group performance. Finally, another concern of research in this realm was the effect of communication on group leadership—in other words were there specific traits that could be associated with effective leadership?

Based on the above mentioned research, the following areas have been the focus on group research in the last several decades: performance, participation, bona fide groups, and the effects of technology on group performance. The key foci on group performance studies concluded that the group outputs or decisions were based on specific group inputs including group size, leadership style, and the communication patterns within the group. Participation research has attempted to understand the effects of the frequency, content and patterns of communication on group outcomes. Research into bona fide groups has focused attention on ongoing versus zero history groups. The research on the effects of technology on group performance with respect to computer mediated communication and the Internet.

With this chapter as an introduction to the study of small group communication, the next chapter takes research into this realm and identifies successful group decision making and problem solving techniques to maximize efficiency when individuals have to participate in group tasks.

Questions For Discussion

1. What has been your worst group experience? How did you manage this experience?
2. It is often said that a camel is a horse invented by a group. Do you agree with this?
3. How has computer mediated communication affected your participation in a group?
4. Have you ever had a group member who did not participate in the group's discussion? Did anyone try to get this individual to participate?
5. What is the difference between group input and group outcomes?

Notes

1. Portions of this [selection] are excerpted from an earlier version of this [reading] written by Randy Y. Hirokawa, Abran J. Salazar, Larry Erbert, and Richard J. Ice.
2. The number of people involved for their communication to count as "small group communication" is rather arbitrary. Most definitions identify small group communication as involving between 3 and 12 individuals.

References

Applbaum, R. L., & Anatol, K. (1971). PERT: A tool for communication research planning. *Journal of Communication, 21,* 368–380.

Baird, J. E., Jr. (1974). A comparison of distributional and sequential structure in cooperative and competitive group discussion. *Speech Monographs, 41,* 226–232.

Bales, R. F. (1950). *Interaction process analysis: A method for the study of small groups.* Cambridge, MA: Addison-Wesley.

Bales, R. F., Strodtbeck, F. L., Mills, T. M., & Roseborough, M. E. (1951). Channels of communication in small groups. *American Sociological Review, 16,* 461–468.

Baltes, B. B., Dickson, M. W., Sherman, M. P., Bauer, C. C., & LaGanke, J. (2002). Computer-mediated communication and group decision making: A meta-analysis. *Organizational Behavior and Human Decision Processes, 57*(1), 156–179.

Barnlund, D. C. (1955). Experiments in leadership training for decision-making discussion groups. *Speech Monographs, 22,* 1–14.

Bayless, O. (1967). An alternate pattern for problem-solving discussion. *Journal of Communication,* 17,188–198.

Beatty, M. J. (1989). Group members' decision rule orientations and consensus. *Human Communication Research, 16,* 279–296.

Berg, D. M. (1967). A descriptive analysis of the distribution and duration of themes discussed by small groups. *Speech Monographs, 34,* 172–175.

Black, E. B. (1955). A consideration of the rhetorical causes of breakdown in discussion. *Speech Monographs, 22,* 15–19.

Bonito, J. A. (2000). The effect of contributing substantively on perceptions of participation. *Small Group Research, 31*(5), 528–553.

Bonito, J. A. (2001). An information-processing approach to participation in small groups. *Communication Research, 28*(3), 275–303.

Bonito, J. A. (2003a). Information processing and exchange in mediated groups: Interdependence and interaction. *Human Communication Research, 29*(4), 533–559.

Bonito, J. A. (2003b). A social relations analysis of participation in small groups. *Communication Monographs, 70*(2), 83–97.

Bonito, J. A. (2004). Shared cognition and participation in small groups: Similarity of member prototypes. *Communication Research, 31,* 704–730.

Bonito, J. A. (2006). A longitudinal social relations analysis of participation in small groups. *Human Communication Research, 32*(3), 302–321.

Bonito, J. A. (2007). A local model of information sharing in small groups. *Communication Theory, 17*(3), *252–280.*

Bonito, J. A., DeCamp, M. H., Coffman, M., & Fleming, S. (2006). Participation, information, and control in small groups: An actor-partner interdependence model. *Group Dynamics: Theory, Research, and Practice, 10*(1), 16–28.

Bonito, J. A., & Hollingshead, A. B. (1997). Participation in small groups. In B. R. Burleson (Ed.), *Communication yearbook* (Vol. 20, pp. 227–261). Newbury Park, CA: Sage.

Bonito, J. A., & Lambert, B. L. (2005). Information similarity as a moderator of the effect of gender on participation in small groups: A multilevel analysis. *Small Group Research, 36*(2), 139–165.

Bottger, P. C. (1984). Expertise and air time as bases of actual and perceived influence in problem-solving groups. *Journal of Applied Psychology, 69*(2), 214–221.

Brilhart, J. K., & Jochem, L. M. (1964). Effects of different patterns on outcomes of problem-solving discussion. *Journal of Applied Psychology, 48,* 175–79.

Burkhalter, S., Gastil, J., & Kelshaw, T. (2002). A conceptual definition and theoretical model of public deliberation in small face-to-face groups. *Communication Theory, 12*(4), 398–422.

Burleson, B. R., Levine, B. J., & Samter, W. (1984). Decision-making procedure and decision quality. Human *Communication Research, 10,* 557–574.

Canary, D. J., Brossman, B. G., & Seibold, D. R. (1987). Argument structures in decision-making groups. *Southern States Communication Journal, 53,* 18–37.

Cattell, R. B. (1948). Concepts and methods in the measurement of group syntality. *Psychological Monographs, 55,* 48–63.

Cattell, R. B. (1951a). Determining syntality dimension as a basis for morale and leadership measurement. In H. Guetzkow (Ed.), *Groups, leadership, and men* (pp. 16–27). Pittsburgh, PA: Carnegie Press.

Cattell, R. B. (1951b). New concepts for measuring leadership in terms of group syntality. *Human Relations, 4,* 161–184.

Cheseboro. J. W., Cragan, J. E., & McCullough, P. (1973). The small group techniques of the radical revolutionary: A synthetic study of consciousness-raising. *Communication Monographs, 40,* 136–146.

Comadena, M. E. (1984). Brainstorming groups: Ambiguity tolerance, communication apprehension, task attraction, and individual productivity. *Small Group Behavior, 15,* 251–254.

Contractor, N. S., Seibold, D. R., & Heller, M. A. (1996). Interactional influence in the structuring of media use in groups: Influence in members' perceptions of group decision support system use. *Human Communication Research, 22*(4), 451–481.

Corman, S. R., & Kuhn, T. (2005). The detectability of socio-egocentric group speech: A quasi-turing test. *Communication Monographs, 72*(2), 117–143.

Cragan, J. F., & Wright, D. W. (1980). Small group communication of the 1970s: A synthesis and critique of the field. *Central States Speech Journal, 31,*197–213.

Cragan, J. F., & Wright, D. W. (1990). Small group communication of the 1980s: A synthesis and critique of the field. *Communication Studies, 41,* 212–236.

Crowell, L., Katcher, A., & Miyamoto, S. F. (1955). Self-concepts of communication skill and performance in small group discussions. *Speech Monographs, 22,* 20–27.

Cruz, M. G., Boster, F. J., & Rodriguez, J. I. (1997). The impact of group size and proportion of shared information on the exchange and integration of information in groups. *Communication Research, 24*(3), 291–313.

Cruz, M. G., Henningsen, D. D., & Smith, B. A. (1999). The impact of directive leadership on group information sampling, decisions and perceptions of the leader. *Communication Research, 26*(3), 349–369.

Cruz, M. G., Henningsen, D. D., & Williams, M. L. M. (2000). The presence of norms in the absence of groups? the impact of normative influence under hidden-profile conditions. *Human Communication Research, 26*(1), 104–124.

Delbecq, A. L., Van de Ven, A. H., & Gustafson, D. H. (1975). *Group techniques for program planning: A guide to nominal group and delphi process.* Glenview, IL: Scott, Foresman.

DeSanctis, G., & Gallupe, R. B. (1987). A foundation for the study of group decision support systems. *Management Science, 33*(5), 589–609.

DeStephen, R. S. (1983). High and low consensus groups: A content and relational interaction analysis. *Small Group Behavior, 14,* 143–162.

DeStephen, R. S., & Hirokawa, R. Y. (1988). Small group consensus: Stability of group support of the decision, task process, and group relationship. *Small Group Behavior, 19,* 227–239.

Dewey, J. (1910). *How we think.* Boston: D. C. Heath.

Downs C. W., & Pickett, T. (1977). Analysis of the effects of nine leadership-group compatibility contingencies upon productivity and member satisfaction. *Communication Monographs, 44,* 220–230.

Ellis. D. G., & Fisher, B. A. (1975). Phases of conflict in small group development: A Markov analysis. *Human Communication Research, 1,* 195–212.

Fisher, B. A. (1970). Decision emergence: Phases in group decision-making. *Speech Monographs, 37,* 53–66.

Fisher, B. A., & Hawes, L. (1971). An interact system model: Generating a grounded theory of small groups. *Quarterly Journal of Speech, 57,* 444–453.

Flanagin, A. J., Park, H. S., & Seibold, D. R. (2004). Group performance and collaborative technology: A longitudinal and multilevel analysis of information quality, contribution equity, and members' satisfaction in computer-mediated groups. *Communication Monographs, 71*(3), 352–372.

Flanagin, A. J., Tiyaamornwong, V., O'Connor, J., & Seibold, D. R. (2002). Computer-mediated group work: The interaction of member sex and anonymity. *Communication Research, 29*(1), 66–93.

Frey, L. R. (Ed.). (2003a). *Group communication in context: Studies of bona fide groups* (2nd ed.). Mahwah, NJ: Erlbaum.

Frey, L. R. (2003b). Group communication in context: Studying bona fide groups. In L. R. Frey (Ed.), *Group communication in context: Studies of bona fide groups* (2nd ed., pp. 1–20). Mahwah, NJ: Erlbaum.

Gastil, J., Burkhalter, S., & Black, L. W. (2007). Do juries deliberate? A study of deliberation, individual difference, and group member satisfaction at a municipal courthouse. *Small Group Research, 38*(3), 337–359.

Geier, J. G. (1967). A trait approach to the study of leadership in small groups. *Journal of Communication, 17,* 316–323.

Gigone, D., & Hastie, R. (1993). The common knowledge effect: Information sharing and group judgment. *Journal of Personality & Social Psychology, 65*(5), 959–974.

Gouran, D. S. (1969). Variables related to consensus in group discussion of questions of policy. *Speech Monographs, 36,* 387–391.

Gouran, D. S. (1990). Exploiting the predictive potential of structuration theory. In J. A. Anderson (Ed.), *Communication yearbook* (Vol. 13, pp. 313–322). Newbury Park, CA: Sage.

Gouran, D. S. (1999). Communication in groups: The emergence and evolution of a field of study. In L. R. Frey, D. S. Gouran, & M. S. Poole (Eds.), *The handbook of group communication theory and research* (pp. 3–36). Thousand Oaks, CA; Sage.

Gouran, D. S., & Baird, J. E., Jr. (1972). An analysis of distributional and sequential structure in problem-solving and informal group discussions. *Speech Monographs, 39,* 18–22.

Gouran, D. S., & Hirokawa, R. Y. (1983). The role of communication in decision-making groups: A functional perspective. In M. S. Mander (Ed.), *Communications in transition* (pp. 168–185). New York: Praeger.

Gouran, D. S., & Hirokawa, R. Y. (1986). Counteractive functions of communication in effective group decision-making. In R. Y. Hirokawa & M. S. Poole. (Eds.), *Communication and group decision making* (pp. 81–90). Beverly Hills, CA: Sage.

Henningsen, D. D., & Henningsen, M. L. M. (2003). Examining social influence in information-sharing contexts. *Small Group Research, 34*(4), 391–412.

Henningsen, D. D., & Henningsen, M. L. M. (2004). The effect of individual difference variables on information sharing in decision-making groups. *Human Communication Research, 30*(4), 540–555.

Henningsen, D. D., Henningsen, M. L. M., Eden, J., & Cruz, M. G. (2006). Examining the symptoms of groupthink and retrospective sensemaking. *Small Group Research, 37*(1), 36–64.

Henningsen, D. D., Henningsen, M. L. M., Jakobsen, L., & Borton, I. (2004). It's good to be leader: The influence of randomly and systematically selected leaders on decision-making groups. *Group Dynamics: Theory, Research, and Practice, 5*(1), 62–76.

Hewes, D. E. (1996). Small group communication may not influence decision making: An amplification of socio-egocentric theory. In R. Y. Hirokawa & M. S. Poole (Eds.), *Communication and group decision making* (2nd ed., pp. 179–212). Thousand Oaks, CA: Sage.

Hiltz, S. R., Johnson, K., & Turoff, M. (1986). Experiments in group decision-making: Communication process and outcome in face-to-face versus computerized conferences. *Human Communication Research, 13,* 225–252.

Hirokawa, R. Y. (1983). Group communication and problem-solving effectiveness: An investigation of procedural functions. *Western Journal of Speech Communication, 47,* 59–74.

Hirokawa, R. Y. (1985). Discussion procedures and decision performance. Human Communication Research, 12, 203–224.

Hirokawa, R. Y., & Scheerhorn, D. R. (1986). Communication and Faulty Group Decision-Making. In R. Y. Hirokawa & M. S. Poole (Eds.), *Communication and group decision-making* (pp. 63–80). Beverly Hills, CA: Sage.

Hirokawa, R. Y., & McLeod, P. L. (1993, November). *Communication, decision development, and decision quality in small groups: An integration of two approaches.* Paper presented at the annual meeting of the Speech Communication Association, Miami Beach.

Hirokawa, R. Y., Erbert, L., & Hurst, A. (1996a). Communication and group decision-making effectiveness. In R. Y. Hirokawa & M. S. Poole (Eds.), *Communication and group decision making* (pp. 269–300). Thousand Oaks, CA: Sage.

Hollingshead, A. B. (1996a). Information suppression and status persistence in group decision making: The effects of communication media. *Human Communication Research, 23*(2), 193–219.

Hollingshead, A. B. (1996b). The rank-order effect in group decision making. *Organizational Behavior & Human Decision Processes, 65*(3), 181–193.

Hollingshead, A. B. (2001). Communication technologies, the internet, and group research. In M. A. Hogg & R. S. Tindale (Eds.), *Blackwell handbook of social psychology: Group processes* (pp. 557–573). Malden, MA: Blackwell.

Hollingshead, A. B., & Brandon, D. P. (2003). Potential benefits of communication in transactive memory systems. *Human Communication Research, 29*(4), 607–615.

Jablin, F. M. (1981). Cultivating imagination: Factors that enhance and inhibit creativity in brainstorming groups. *Human Communication Research, 7,* 245–258.

Jablin, F. M., Seibold. D. R., & Sorenson, R. (1977). Potential inhibitory effects of group participation on brainstorming performance. *Central States Speech Journal, 25,* 113–121.

Jablin, F. M., Sorenson, R., & Seibold, D. R. (1978). Interpersonal perception and group brainstorming performance. *Communication Quarterly, 26,* 36–44.

Jackson, M. H., & Poole, M. S. (2003). Idea-generation in naturally occurring contexts: Complex appropriation of a simple group procedure. *Human Communication Research,* 29(4), 560–591.

Jarboe, S. (1988). A comparison of input-output, process-output, and input-process-output models of small group problem-solving effectiveness. *Communication Monographs, 55,* 121–142.

Kline, J. A. (1972). Orientation and group consensus. *Central States Speech Journal, 23,* 44–47.

Kline, J. A., & Hullinger, J. L. (1973). Redundancy, self-orientation, and group consensus. *Speech Monographs, 40,* 72–74.

Knutson, T. J. (1972). An experimental study of the effects of orientation behavior on small group consensus. *Speech Monographs, 39,* 159–165.

Knutson, T. J., & Holdridge, W. E. (1975). Orientation behavior, leadership, and consensus: A possible functional relationship. *Speech Monographs, 42,* 107–114.

Knutson, T. J., & Kowitz, A. C. (1977). Effects of information type and level of orientation on consensus achievement in substantive and affective small-group conflict. *Central States Speech Journal, 28,* 54–63.

Komorita, S. S., & Parks, C. D. (1994). *Social dilemmas.* Madison, WI: Brown & Benchmark.

Kramer, M. W. (2005). Communication in a fund-raising marathon group. *Journal of Communication,* 55(2), 257–276.

Lammers, J. C., & Krikorian, D. H. (1997). Theoretical extension and operationalization of the bona fide group construct with an application to surgical teams. *Journal of Applied Communication Research, 25,* 17–38.

Larson, C. E. (1969). Forms of analysis and small group problem-solving. *Speech Monographs, 36,* 452–455.

Larson, J. R., Foster-Fishman, P. G., & Keys, C. B. (1994). Discussion of shared and unshared information in decision-making groups. *Journal of Personality and Social Psychology,* 67(3), 446–461.

Larson, C. E., & Gratz, R. D. (1970). Problem-solving discussion training and T-group training: An experimental comparison. *Speech Teacher, 19,* 54–57.

Leathers, D. G. (1972). Quality of group communication as a determinant of group product. *Speech Monographs, 39,* 166–173.

Lee, E. (2004). Effects of visual representation on social influence in computer-mediated communication: Experimental tests of the social identity model of deindividuation effects. *Human Communication Research,* 30(2), 234–259.

Lewin, K. (1947). Frontiers in group dynamics. *Human Relations, 1,* 5–41.

Lewin, K. (1951). *Field theory in social science: Selected theoretical papers* (D. Cartwright, Ed.). New York: Harper & Row.

Mabry, E. A. (1975a). Exploratory analysis of a developmental model for task-oriented small groups. *Human Communication Research, 2,* 66–74.

Mabry, E. A. (1975b). An instrument for assessing content themes in group interaction. *Communication Monographs, 42,* 291–297.

Matei, S. A., & Ball-Rokeach, S. (2005). Watts, the 1965 Los Angeles riots, and the communicative construction of the fear epicenter of Los Angeles. *Communication Monographs, 72*(3), 301–323.

Meyers, R. A., & Brashers, D. E. (1998a). Argument in group decision making: Explicating a process model and investigating the argument-outcome link. *Communication Monographs, 65*(4), 261–281.

Meyers, R. A., & Brashers, D. E. (1998b). Argument in group decision making: Explicating a process model and investigating the argument-outcome link. *Communication Monographs, 65*(4), 261–281.

Meyers, R. A., Brashers, D. E., & Hanner, J. (2000). Majority-minority influence: Identifying argumentative patterns and predicting argument-outcome links. *Journal of Communication, 50*(4), 3–30.

Meyers, R. A., Brashers, D. E., Winston, L., & Grob, L. (1997). Sex differences and group argument: A theoretical. *Communication Studies, 45*(1), 19.

Morris, C. G., & Hackman, J. R. (1969). Behavioral correlates of perceived leadership. *Journal of Personality and Social Psychology, 13,* 350–361.

Moy, P., & Gastil, J. (2006). Predicting deliberative conversation: The impact of discussion networks, media use, and political cognitions. *Political Communication, 23*(4), 443–460.

O'Keefe, D. J. (2003). Message properties, mediating states, and manipulation checks: Claims, evidence, and data analysis in experimental persuasive message effects research. *Communication Theory, 13*(3), 251–274.

Pavitt, C. (2003). Colloquy: Do interacting groups perform better than aggregates of individuals? Why we have to be reductionists about group memory. *Human Communication Research, 29*(4), 592.

Pavitt, C., & Johnson, K. K. (1999). An examination of the coherence of group discussions. *Communication Research, 26*(3), 303–321.

Pavitt, C., & Johnson, K. K. (2001). The association between group procedural MOPs and group discussion procedure. *Small Group Research, 32*(5), 595–624.

Pavitt, C., & Johnson, K. K. (2002). Scheidel and Crowell revisited: A descriptive study of group proposal sequencing. *Communication Monographs, 69*(1), 19–32.

Pavitt, C., McFeeters, C., Towey, E., & Zingerman, V. (2005). Communication during resource dilemmas: 1. Effects of different replenishment rates. *Communication Monographs, 72*(3), 345–363.

Pavitt, C., Zingerman, V., Towey, E., & McFeeters, C. (2006). Group communication during resource dilemmas: 2. Effects of harvest limit and reward asymmetry. *Communication Research, 33*(1), 64–91.

Peña, J., Walther, J. B., & Hancock, J. T. (2007). Effects of geographic distribution on dominance perceptions in computer-mediated groups. *Communication Research, 34*(3), 313–331.

Philipsen, G., Mulac, A., & Dietrich, D. (1979). The effects of social interaction on group idea generation. *Communication Monographs, 46,*119–125.

Phillips, G. M. (1966). *Communication and the small group.* Indianapolis: Bobbs-Merrill.

Poole, M. S. (1981). Decision development in small groups I: A comparison of two models. *Communication Monographs, 45,* 1–24.

Poole, M. S. (1983). Decision development in small groups III: A multiple sequence model of group decision development. *Communication Monographs, 50,* 321–341.

Poole, M. S., & Doelger, J. A. (1986). Developmental processes in group decision-making. In R. Y. Hirokawa & M. S. Poole (Eds.), *Communication and group decision making* (pp. 35–61). Beverly Hills, CA: Sage.

Poole, M. S., & Roth, J. (1989a). Decision development in small groups IV: A typology of group decision paths. *Human Communication Research, 15,* 323–356.

Poole. M. S., & Roth, J. (1989b). Decision development in small groups V: Test of a contingency model. *Human Communication Research, 15,* 549–589.

Postmes, T., Spears, R., & Lea, M. (1998). Breaching or building social boundaries? SIDE-effects of computer-mediated communication. *Communication Research, 25*(6), 689–715.

Postmes, T., Spears, R., & Lea, M. (2000). The formation of group norms in computer-mediated communication. *Communication Research, 26*(3), 341–371.

Propp, K. M. (2003). In search of the assembly bonus effect: Continued exploration of communication's role in group memory. *Human Communication Research, 29*(4), 600–606.

Putnam, L. L., & Stohl, C. (1990). Bona fide groups: A reconceptualization of groups in context. *Communication Studies, 41,* 248–265.

Putnam, L. L., & Stohl, C. (1996). In Hirokawa R. Y. & Poole M. S. (Eds.), *Bona fide groups: An alternative perspective for communication and small group decision making.* Thousand Oaks, CA: Sage.

Pyron, H. C. (1964). An experimental study of the role of reflective thinking in business and professional conferences and discussions. *Speech Monographs, 31,* 157–161.

Pyron, H. C., & Sharp, H., Jr. (1963). A quantitative study of reflective thinking and performance in problem-solving discussion. *Journal of Communication, 13,* 46–53.

Raines, S. (2005). Leveling the organizational playing field–virtually: A meta-analysis of experimental research assessing the impact of group support system use on member influence behaviors. *Communication Research, 32,* 193–234.

Reicher, S., Spears, R., & Postmes, T. (1995). A social identity model of deindividuation phenomena. *European Review of Social Psychology, 6,* 161–198.

Reimer, T., Kuendig, S., Hoffrage, U., Park, E., & Hinsz, V. (2007). Effects of the information environment on group discussions and decisions in the hidden-profile paradigm. *Communication Monographs, 74*(1), 1–28.

Rosenfeld, L. B., & Fowler, G. D. (1976). Personality, sex and leadership style. *Communication Monographs, 43,* 320–324.

Rosenfeld, L. B., & Plax, T. G. (1975). Personality determinants of autocratic and democratic leadership. *Speech Monographs, 42,* 203–208.

Sager, K. L., & Gastil, J. (2002). Exploring the psychological foundations of democratic group deliberation: Personality factors, confirming interaction, and democratic decision making. *Communication Research Reports, 19*(1), 56–65.

Saine, T. J., & Bock, D. G. (1973). A comparison of the distributional and sequential structures of interaction in high and low consensus groups. *Central States Speech Journal, 24,* 125–130.

Saine, T. J., Schulman, L. S., & Emerson, L. C. (1974). The effects of group size on the structure of interaction in problem-solving groups. *Southern Speech Communication Journal, 39,* 333–345.

Salazar, A. J. (1995). Understanding the synergistic effects of communication in small groups: Making the most out of group members' abilities. *Small Group Research, 26,* 169–199.

Sargent, J. F., & Miller, G. R. (1971). Some differences in certain communication behaviors of autocratic and democratic leaders. *Journal of Communication, 21,* 233–252.

Savadori, L., Van Swol, L. M., & Sniezek, J. A. (2001). Information sampling and confidence within groups and judge advisor systems. *Communication Research, 25*(6), 737–771.

Scheidel, T. M., & Crowell, L. (1964). Idea development in small discussion groups. *Quarterly Journal of Speech, 50,* 140–145.

Scheidel, T. M., Crowell, L., & Shepherd, J. R. (1958). Personality and discussion behavior: A study of possible relationships. *Speech Monographs, 25,* 261–267.

Schultz. B. (1982). Argumenativeness: Its effect in group decision-making and its role in leadership perception. *Communication Quarterly, 30,* 368–475.

Scott, C. R. (1999). Communication technology and group communication. In L. R. Frey, D. Gouran, & M. S. Poole (Eds.), *Handbook of group communication and research* (pp. 432–472). Thousand Oaks, CA: Sage.

Seibold, D. R., & Meyers, R. A. (2007). Group argument: A structuration perspective and research program. *Small Group Research, 35*(3), 312–336.

Sharp, H., Jr., & Milliken, J. (1964). The reflective thinking ability and the product of problem-solving discussion. *Speech Monographs, 31,* 124–127.

Sigman, S. J. (1984). Talk and interaction strategy in a task-oriented group. *Small Group Research, 15*(1), 33–51.

Smith, C. M., & Powell, L. (1988). The use of disparaging humor by group leaders. *Southern Speech Communication Journal, 53,* 279–292.

Sorrentino, R. M., & Boutillier, R. G. (1975). The effect of quantity and quality of verbal interaction on ratings of leadership ability. *Journal of Experimental Social Psychology, 11*(5), 403–411.

Stasser, G., & Titus, W. (1985). Pooling of unshared information in group decision making: Biased information sampling during discussion. *Journal of Personality and Social Psychology, 45*(6), 1467–1478.

Stasser, G., & Titus, W. (1987). Effects of information load and percentage of shared information on the dissemination of unshared information during group discussion. *Journal of Personality and Social Psychology, 53,* 81–93.

Stasser, G., & Titus, W. (2003). Hidden profiles: A brief history. *Psychological Inquiry, 14*(3), 304–313.

Stasser, G., & Vaughan, S. I. (1996). Models of participation during face-to-face unstructured discussion. In E. H. Witte & J. H. Davis (Eds.), *Understanding group behavior* (pp. 165–192). Mahwah, NJ: Erlbaum.

Stephan, F. F., & Mishler, E. G. (1952). The distribution of participation in small groups: An exponential approximation. *American Sociological Review, 17,* 598–608.

Stohl, C., & Putnam, L. L. (2003). Communication in bona fide groups: A retrospective and prospective account. In L. R. Frey (Ed.), *Group communication in context: Studies of bona fide groups* (2nd ed., pp. 399–414). Mahwah, NJ: Erlbaum.

Sunwolf, & Leets, L. (2004). Being left out: Rejecting outsiders and communicating group boundaries in childhood and adolescent peer groups. *Journal of Applied Communication Research, 32*(3), 195–223.

Sunwolf, & Seibold, D. R. (1998). Jurors' intuitive rules for deliberation: A structurational approach to communication in jury decision making. *Communication Monographs, 65*(4), 282–307.

Van Swol, L. M., & Ludutsky, C. L. (2007). Tell me something I don't know. *Communication Research, 34*(3), 297–312.

Van Swol, L. M., Savadori, L., & Sniezek, J. A. (2003). Factors that may affect the difficulty of uncovering hidden profiles. *Group Processes & Intergroup Relations, 6*(3), 285–304.

Walther, J. B. (1992). Interpersonal effects in computer-mediated interaction: A relational perspective. *Communication Research, 19*(1), 52–90.

Wilson, S. R. (2002). *Seeking and resisting compliance: Why people say what they do when trying to influence others.* Thousand Oaks, CA: Sage.

Wittenbaum, G. M. (1998). Information sampling in decision-making groups: The impact of members' task-relevant status. *Small Group Research, 29*(1), 57–84.

Wittenbaum, G. M. (2000). The bias toward discussing shared information: Why are high-status group members immune? *Communication Research, 27*(3), 379–400.

Wittenbaum, G. M. (2003). Putting communication into the study of group memory. *Human Communication Research, 29*(4), 616.

Wittenbaum, G. M., Bowman, J. M., & Hollingshead, A. B. (2003, November). *Strategic information sharing in mixed-motive decision-making groups.* Paper presented at the annual meeting of the National Communication Association, Miami Beach, FL.

Wittenbaum, G. M., Hollingshead, A. B., & Botero, I. C. (2004). From cooperative to motivated information sharing in groups: Moving beyond the hidden profile paradigm. *Communication Monographs, 71*(3), 286–310.

Wittenbaum, G. M., Hollingshead, A. B., Paulus, P. B., Hirokawa, R. Y., Ancona, D. G., Peterson, R. S., et al. (2004). The functional perspective as a lens for understanding groups. *Small Group Research, 35*(1), 17–43.

Wittenbaum, G. M., Hubbell, A. P., & Zuckerman, C. (1999). Mutual enhancement: Toward an understanding of the collective preference for shared information. *Journal of Personality and Social Psychology, 77*(5), 967–978.

Wittenbaum, G. M., Keyton, J., & Weingart, L. R. (2006). A new era for group research: The formation of INGRoup. *Small Group Research, 37,* 1–7.

Wood, J. T. (1977). Leading in purposive discussions: A study of adaptive behavior. *Communication Monographs, 44,* 152–165.

Yerby, J. (1975). Attitude, task and sex composition as variables affecting female leadership in small problem-solving groups. *Speech Monographs, 42,* 160–168.

Chapter 11

Solving Problems and Making Decisions

Joann Keyton

Everyone probably has a nightmare about working in groups. The central theme of the popular cartoon "Dilbert" is that group work is a waste of time and there are more effective ways for employees to spend their time. However, groups can be efficient, effective, and successful at problem solving and decision-making if members understand how to work effectively in groups. This chapter explains how that can be achieved.

Learning Objectives For This Chapter

- Identify the three key decision making skills that group members need to possess
- Describe why group decision making is seen as a circular as opposed to a liner process
- Explain why groups are better at making decision than individuals working alone
- Discuss the basic functions that a group needs to satisfy
- Explain the problems that can be created if a group does not follow a procedure for decision making
- Identify the steps in the standard agenda
- Describe the procedures that can be employed to help groups reach decisions
- Explain some problems that can arise when groups follow set procedures

Decision making in groups is fundamental to many different types of groups. Family groups make decisions about where to spend their vacation or how to organize a garage sale. Groups of friends make decisions about where they are going on Friday night or how to surprise one member with a birthday party. At work, groups and teams make decisions in developing new products and enhancing customer service. Some of these decisions are more straightforward than others. Still, for any of these decisions, a group needs to engage in two processes: problem solving and decision making. Problem solving represents the group's attempts to analyze a problem in detail so that good decisions can be made. This includes generating alternatives for the group to consider. Once these are developed, the group can turn to a decision-making procedure to make a choice between alternatives. Before we look at procedures groups can use in decision making, let's turn our attention to the skills group members need to effectively make decisions in groups.

Decision-Making Skills

Across the range of decisions that groups make, group members need task, relational, and procedural skills (Gouran, 2003). In fact, the quality of group members' contributions and a group's ability to make effective decisions depends on these skills. Different decision-making tasks place different demands on members and the group. Some decisions require a great deal of discussion and deliberation, and, as a result, require a higher degree of skill and a greater variety of skills. Simple decisions require little discussion and fewer skills, as group members make a choice from known alternatives, each of which is agreeable to them. Although we identified the skills college students used to describe an ideal group member, these three sets of skills are specific to group decision making.

Task Skills for Decison Making

Group members need task-related skills to manage the content or substance of the decisions made in the group. First, group members must have skills with **problem recognition and framing**. A group cannot make a decision if its members cannot identify the decision that needs to be made or if they frame a decision inaccurately or inappropriately. In other words, group members have to agree upon what the decision is really about. For example, the mayor and council members of one town debated vigorously through one entire meeting when to schedule subsequent city council meetings. The issue, of course, wasn't really about scheduling meetings, but about who had the power to control what the council did (Barge & Keyton, 1994). Clearly this group misframed the problem as one of scheduling. The council failed to recognize the problem as one of authority. The group needed to make a decision about who had authority to set council meetings. This example demonstrates how difficult it can be for group members to recognize or articulate the issue before the group.

Inference drawing is another task-related decision-making skill. As group members solve problems or make decisions, they will be required to use analysis and reasoning and then communicate that analysis and reasoning as judgments or claims that go beyond the available information. Inferences can be drawn by using analogy or cause-to-effect reasoning. For example, a human resources task force draws a conclusion about the effectiveness of a sexual harassment policy they are ready to submit to the employees' union because the discrimination policy they submitted earlier was well received. Inferences drawn using analogy are based on the similarities of different objects or situations that are believed to have the same qualities. Members of the task force also draw inferences with cause-to-effect reasoning as they argue that having a discrimination policy in place (the cause) will influence employees to behave more respectfully (the immediate effect) and thereby decrease the number of complaints (a longer-term effect).

The third task-related decision-making skill is **idea generation**. To make effective decisions, groups must have adequate alternatives from which to select. When groups limit themselves to a few obvious choices, they unnecessarily restrict their opportunity to make an effective decision. For example, a policy team was created for the purpose of generating ideas for stimulating regional economic growth. As soon as introductions were completed, Charles, a member with high status in the community and a vice-president of a large organization, went to the podium and began a slide presentation that described his idea. The group, whose members had not worked together before, were impressed with his preparation. When he was finished, group members asked Charles questions for about an hour; then they took a vote to pursue his idea. The problem: All of the group members were high-status members of the community and had the potential to generate a number of useful ideas for economic development. While Charles's idea was sound, the policy team did not consider other alternatives that may have proven to be better than the only idea discussed. Brainstorming, a group technique for generating ideas, could have helped this group create additional proposals to consider; it will be described in detail later in this chapter.

The fourth task-related decision-making skill is **argument**. Group members need to be capable of generating and presenting reasons for a position they support or reject. Novel arguments, or arguments not considered by group members prior to discussion, can be especially influential in decision making (Meyers & Brashers, 1999). In the policy team example earlier, Charles was skilled at presenting arguments with sufficient evidence, which influenced the group. Moreover, his arguments were novel, as the other group members could not have possibly considered them before the meeting since they had no idea what Charles would propose. Although in the minority, Charles skillfully used argument to convince the majority of the group into accepting his proposal. The obvious tension between the policy group's failure to generate other ideas and Charles's skill in presenting arguments demonstrates why multiple skills are required when groups make decisions.

Relational Skills for Decision Making

While problem recognition and framing, inference drawing, idea generation, and argument are required for group decision making to occur, relational skills—or skills that focus on members rather than the task—can enhance decision-making effectiveness.

Leadership is a skill that can counteract the cognitive, affiliative, and egocentric constraints that can arise in group interaction (Gouran & Hirokawa, 1996; Janis, 1989).

Cognitive constraints, or difficulties and inadequacies in processing information, occur when there is little information available or limited time for making a decision, or when the decision is more difficult than group members can comfortably or normally handle. When decision making occurs under these conditions, group members believe they have limited capacity or motivation to make an effective decision.

The second type of constraint is **affiliative constraints**—those that are based on the relationships among members of the group. When relationships, or the fear that relationships will deteriorate, are the dominant concern, some group members exert undue influence on other group members.

The third type of decision-making constraint is **egocentric constraints**, which occur when one group member has a high need for control over the group or its activities or has a personal or hidden agenda.

A leader with effective communication skills can help group members reduce the impact of these constraints by refocusing the group's relational energy and shifting the group's focus back to decision making. Facilitating discussion among all group members, assisting the group in information gathering, helping members to verbalize unstated positions, and focusing conversation on the group's goal are three techniques anyone in the group can use to provide leadership for the group and minimize the negative influence of cognitive, affiliative, and egocentric constraints. Leadership is described in detail in Chapter 10.

The second relational skill needed for decision making is **climate building**. As described in Chapter 6, a positive or supportive climate develops when group members communicate with equality, spontaneity, and empathy, and avoid evaluation, control, and certainty. To help build a supportive climate for decision making, group members should be friendly with and respectful of others. Doing so helps group members to feel valued and that their input is welcomed. Climate building is as easy to accomplish as it is to overlook. Members of a project team who do not know each other well will meet each Friday until their marketing plan is developed. To help members become comfortable in the team, each meeting begins with members providing a brief update of what they accomplished during the week in their respective departments. By sharing this type of information, team members get to know one another better because they learn about the skills each member possesses, as well as getting a feel for how the team's output will influence activities across the organization. Most importantly, this opening procedure ensures that everyone has talked, which deemphasizes role and status differences among group members.

Conflict management is the third relational skill needed for decision making. It's not conflict per se that creates a problem for group decision making. Conflict about ideas can actually help groups make better decisions. But when conflict about issues is not managed or when conflict is focused on personal differences, then the struggle between group members takes precedence over the decision-making task. To help manage conflict, group members can steer the conversation from personal issues back to task issues and

Procedural Skills for Decision Making

Finally, there are two procedural skills, or skills that help the group move from discussion to decision making. The first procedural skill is **planning**. Members with this skill help the group by communicating what needs to be first, second, and so on, and by suggesting a decision-making procedure to use. Planning, of course, can only be based on a goal, so group members engaged in planning need to remind others about the goal and help them reach agreement on it. The second procedural decision-making skill is **process enactment**, or helping the group through the decision-making process. Even with the best planning, a decisionmaking group will have to address unforeseen circumstances. Thus members with process-enactment skills can help the group manage these difficulties and stay on track. A group member might set up procedures for the group (for example, concluding each meeting with a review of assignments or creating mechanisms to help the group track its work, like posting information on the group's website). These skills are not difficult; any group member can contribute to the group's decision making by using planning and process enactment skills.

While we consider decision making one type of group task or activity, effective decision making is only accomplished when skilled group members engage in a number of different tasks or activities throughout the decision-making process. The types of decisions that most groups make are either ones that are fairly complex (for example, managing a program for evicting drug dealers from rental property; see Keyton & Stallworth, 2003) or ones in which group members are personally involved (for example, an activist group developing plans for a protest; see Meyers & Brashers, 2003). Reviewing these task, relational, and procedural skills reminds us why some groups have difficulty with their decision making, but also how group members can use their skills to help their group through the decision process.

Decision-Making Principles

Regardless of the procedure or process your group uses, four principles seem to, fit most group problem-solving and decision-making situations (Hirokawa & Johnston, 1989). First, group decision making is an evolutionary process. The final decision of the group emerges over time as a result of the clarification, modification, and integration of ideas that group members express in their interaction. A student government group may know that it needs to make a decision about how to provide child care for university students, but the final decision results from the group bringing new information to meetings and other group members asking for clarification and development of proposed ideas. Thus, a group will have a general idea about a decision that needs to be made, but not necessarily its specifics.

Relatedly, the second principle is that group decision making is a circular rather than a linear process. Even when they try, it is difficult for group members to follow a step-by-step approach to group decision making. Group decision making is circular because group members seldom bring all the needed information into the group's discussion at the same time. Let's say that your group decides to hold the fund-raiser on June 3, close to the end of the spring semester. Your group needs to make this decision first to secure a date on your university's student activities calendar. Now that the date is settled, your group can concentrate on what type of fund-raiser might be best. But you have to take into consideration that it is late in the semester. Not only will students have limited time because of term papers and final exams, but their funds likely will be depleted. That information will affect the type of fund-raiser you will plan. But wait! At that, point in the semester, students really enjoy having coffee and doughnuts available in the early morning, after all-night study sessions. And your group can sell lots of coffee and doughnuts to many students for very little money. In this way, group members move information about the date and type of event back and forth to integrate into a final fund-raising decision.

The third principle is that many different types of influences affect a group's decision making. Group members' moods, motivations, competencies, and communication skills are individual-level variables that affect the group's final decision. These are individual-level variables because each member brings a unique set of influences to the group. The dynamics of the interpersonal relationships that result in group member cohesiveness and satisfaction also affect a group's decision making. Finally, the communication structure or network, developed in the group impacts information flows among group members. The quality of information exchanged by group members affects a group's decision outcomes. And forces outside a group also generate influences. An example of this type of external influence is the generally accepted societal rule about making decisions quickly and cost-efficiently.

The fourth principle of group decision making is that decisions are made within a system of external and internal constraints. Few groups have as much freedom of choice as they would like. Groups are constrained by external forces such as deadlines or budgets imposed by outsiders and the preferences of the people who will evaluate or use the group's decision. Internal constraints are the values, morals, and ethics that individual members bring to the group setting. These values guide what the group does and how it does it.

These four principles reveal that decision making may be part of a larger problem-solving process. Problem solving is the communication group members engage in when there is a need to address an unsatisfactory situation or overcome some obstacle. Decision making and problem solving are often used interchangeably, but they are different. Decision making involves a choice between alternatives; problem solving represents the group's attempts to analyze a problem in detail so that effective decisions can be made (Sunwolf & Seibold, 1999). Hence, this problem: Groups often make decisions without engaging in the analysis associated with problem solving. For anything but the simplest matters, groups are more likely to make faulty decisions when they do not take advantage of the problem-solving process to address the contextual details or do the thoughtful analysis good decisions require.

Why Groups Are Better at Making Decisions

Why are groups better at decision making than individuals? For complex decisions or problems, it is unlikely that any individual will possess or have access to all the knowledge and resources necessary to make a good decision. Second, groups generally bring a greater diversity of perspectives to the situation, so it is more difficult to become locked onto an idea that lacks merit. Third, and probably most importantly, when more people are involved in decision making, the group has the opportunity to check out ideas before one is selected and implemented. This opportunity to try out ideas allows groups to be more confident than individuals in making decisions (Sniezek, 1992).

Groups produce better decisions through communication. The quality of communication among and the full participation of group members are central to their ability to work together to select high-quality solutions (Mayer, 1998; Salazar, Hirokawa, Propp, Julian, & Leatham, 1994). Even when group members have high potential (are highly skilled or highly knowledgeable), communication is the process that allows the group to do its best. Groups that spend their time on goal-directed communication to evaluate task-relevant issues and generate ideas create superior group outcomes.

Decision making is a social process. The presence of others creates a context of social evaluation that motivates people to find the best possible solution (Kameda, 1996). For decisions that affect many individuals, involving them in the process increases their commitment to upholding the decision as it is implemented. To carry out some decisions, the cooperation of many people is needed. Including those people in the decision-making process helps to ensure their cooperation, as well as overall satisfaction with the decision. Moreover, involving them in the decision making increases their understanding of the solution so that they can perform better in the implementation stage.

To take advantage of their strengths, however, groups need some structure in the decision-making discussion (Van de Ven & Delbecq, 1971). Using a procedure to structure group discussion and decision making helps groups in three ways. First, the content of the discussion is more controlled and on task than when discussions are left unstructured. Second, group member participation in the discussion is more equal when some type of procedure is used. Alternative viewpoints from group members cannot help the group unless those viewpoints are revealed during discussion. Third, the emotional tone of a group's discussion is less likely to become negative or out of control. Think of a procedure as a map to follow or a guidebook to show you the way. You could get there from here—but it is easier with some help.

Before turning to specific procedures, let's examine the characteristics group decision-making procedures need to satisfy. Obviously, the goal of any group is to find the solution best suited to solving the problem or making the decision. To do that effectively, group members need to accomplish five functions: (a) thoroughly discuss the problem, (b) examine the criteria of an acceptable solution before discussing specific solutions, (c) propose a set of realistic alternative solutions, (d) assess the positive aspects of each proposed solution, and (e) assess the negative aspects of each proposed solution. According to functional theory, these are the five critical functions in decision-making and problem-solving activities (Gouran & Hirokawa, 1983; Hirokawa, 1982, 1983a, 1983b, 1988; Hirokawa & Pace, 1983; Hirokawa & Salazar, 1999; Hirokawa & Scheerhorn, 1986). A function is not just a step or a procedure, but an activity required for the group to make a decision. When the five functions are not addressed, a group diminishes its chances for identifying an effective solution or making a good decision. Your group can accomplish these functions by using one of the formal discussion procedures described later in the chapter.

First, group members need to achieve an understanding of the problem they are trying to solve. The group should deliberate until it believes all members understand the nature and seriousness of the problem, its possible causes, and the consequences that could develop if the problem is not dealt with effectively. For example, parking is generally a problem on most campuses. But a group of students, faculty, staff, and administrators addressing the parking problem without having an adequate understanding of the issue is likely to suggest solutions that will not really solve the problem. The parking problem on your campus may be that there are not enough parking spaces. Or it may be that there are not enough parking spaces where people want to park. Or perhaps the parking problem exists at only certain times of the day. Another type of parking problem exists when students do not want to pay for parking privileges and park their cars illegally on campus and in the surrounding community. Each parking problem is different and so requires different solutions. When group members address this function—understanding the nature of the problem before trying to solve it—their decision-making efforts result in higher-quality decisions (Hirokawa, 1983a).

Second, the group needs to develop an understanding of what constitutes an acceptable resolution of the problem. In this critical function, group members need to understand the objectives that must be achieved to remedy the problem or the specific standards that must be satisfied for the solution to be acceptable. This means that the group needs to develop criteria by which to evaluate each proposed alternative. Let's go back to the parking problem. In this step, group members need to consider how much students and employees will be willing to pay for parking. Group members also need to identify and discuss the type of solutions campus administrators and campus police will find acceptable. The group probably also should consider if the local police need to agree with its recommendation. In other words, the group has to decide on the objectives and standards that must be used in selecting an appropriate solution. Any evaluation of alternatives must be based on known and agreed-upon criteria (Graham, Papa, & McPherson, 1997).

Third, the group needs to seek and develop a set of realistic and acceptable alternatives. With respect to the parking problem, groups frequently stop generating alternatives when they generate a solution they like. Look at the following dialogue:

> Marty: Okay, I think we should think about building a parking garage.
> Lindsey: Where would it go?
> Marty: I don't know. But there's all kinds of empty lots around campus.
> Helen: What about parking in the church parking lots?
> Lindsey: That's an idea, but I like the idea of our own parking garage better.
> Todd: I like that, too. It would be good to know that whatever time I go to campus a parking spot would be waiting for me.
> Marty: Any other ideas, besides the parking garage?
> Lindsey: No, I can't think of any. I think we need to work on the parking garage idea.
> Todd: Me, too.
> Helen: Shouldn't we consider something else in case the parking garage idea falls through?
> Marty: Why? We all like the idea, don't we?

If a group gets stuck in generating alternatives, as our parking group does, a brainstorming session or nominal group technique (discussed later in the chapter) may help. A group cannot choose the best alternative if all the alternatives are not known.

Fourth, group members need to assess the positive qualities of each of the alternatives they find attractive. This step helps the group recognize the relative merits of each alternative. Once again, let's turn to the parking problem. Students and employees probably will cheer for a solution to the parking problem that does not cost them money. Certainly, no-cost or low-cost parking will be attractive to everyone. But if this is the only positive quality of an alternative, it is probably not the best choice. For example, to provide no-cost or low-cost parking, your recommendation is that during the daytime students park in the parking lots of churches and that at night they park in the parking lots of office buildings. Although the group has satisfied concerns about cost, it is doubtful that those who manage church and office building properties will find this alternative attractive. This leads us to the fifth function: Group members need to assess the negative qualities of alternative choices.

When group members communicate to fulfill these five functions, they increase the chance that their decision making will be effective. This is because group members have worked together to pool their information resources, avoid errors in individual judgment, and create opportunities to persuade other group members (Gouran, Hirokawa, Julian, & Leatham, 1993). For example, the members of the parking group bring different information to the discussion because they come to school at different times of the day.

Those who come early or late in the day have a harder time finding a place to park than those who come early in the afternoon. By pooling what each participant knows about the parking situation, the group avoids becoming biased or choosing a solution that will resolve only one type of parking problem.

In addition, as the group discusses the problem, members can identify and remedy errors in individual judgment. It is easy to think that parking is not a problem when you come in for one class in the early afternoon and leave immediately after. In your experience, the parking lot has some empty spaces because you come at a time when others have left for lunch. And when you leave 2 hours later, the lot is even emptier, making you wonder what the fuss is about in the first place!

Discussion also provides an opportunity to persuade others or to be persuaded. Discussion allows alternatives to be presented that might not occur to others and allows for reevaluation of alternatives that initially seem unattractive. Let's go back to the group discussing the parking problem:

> Marty: Okay, where are we?
> Helen: Well, I think we've pretty much discussed parking alternatives. I'm not sure.
> Lindsey: What about using the bus?
> Todd: You've got to be kidding.
> Lindsey: Why not? The bus line goes right by campus and the fare is only 50 cents.
> Marty: Well, it's an idea.
> Helen: Well, what if the bus doesn't have a route where I live?
> Lindsey: Well, that may be the case for you, Helen, but I bet many students and employees live on or near a bus line.
> Marty: I wonder how many?
> Lindsey: Why don't we call the bus company and get a copy of the entire routing system.
> Marty: Good idea, Lindsey. We were looking for parking alternatives and hadn't thought about other modes of transportation.

Groups that successfully achieve each of the five critical functions of decision making make higher-quality decisions than groups that do not (Hirokawa, 1988). However, the functional perspective is not a procedure for making decisions, because there is no prescribed order to the five functions. Rather, it is the failure of the group to perform one of the five functions that has a profound effect on the quality of the group's decision making. But do the five functions contribute equally to group decision-making effectiveness? An analysis across hundreds of groups indicates that the most important function is group members' assessment of the negative consequences of proposed alternatives. Next in importance were thorough discussion and analysis of the problem, and the establishment of criteria for evaluating proposals (Orlitzky & Hirokawa, 2001). The procedures described in the next section will help your group satisfy the five critical functions. But first, try "Identifying Decision-Making Functions" to get some practice in analyzing group decision making.

Using Decision-Making Procedures

You may think that it's natural for all groups to use some type of procedure or set of guidelines in making decisions. But many groups are unaware of procedures that can help them. Even when a group uses some procedure or structure as an aid to decision making, group members may not be aware of the rules their group uses (Johnson, 1991). Why should groups use procedures to help them generate ideas, make decisions, and solve problems? Procedures help guide a group through the process of decision making and help it overcome problems or limitations that routinely arise when groups make decisions. Without procedures, a group's conversation is more likely to result in problems like the following:

- The group has trouble staying focused on what it needs to accomplish.
- The group has difficulty sticking to the meeting agenda.
- The group performs superficial rather than detailed analyses of alternatives.
- The groups' members have little motivation for working on this decision, or the group has fallen into a rut.
- The group relies on the perceived expert or the person who seems to care the most about the problem.
- Group members consider one alternative and then drop it for discussion of the next alternative without comparing alternatives.
- Group members go straight to decision making without problem solving.
- The group accepts the first solution mentioned.
- The group fails to think of a complex decision as a series of smaller decisions.
- The group does not use its time wisely.
- Group members will make a choice without evaluating its merits.

When groups do not use procedures to help them manage the decision-making process, social or relational pressures can result in pressures to conform or unnecessary conflict. Why does this happen? Without procedures, some group members will not speak up or will not have the opportunity to contribute to the discussion, as the most talkative or high-status group members control the discussion. Simply, without process procedures, members have difficulty balancing the task and relational dimensions of their group (Sunwolf & Seibold, 1999).

The procedures described in the following sections—standard agenda, brainstorming, nominal group technique, consensus, voting, and ranking—vary widely in the amount of control and the type of help they provide to groups. Procedures can vary according to how group members participate in decision making (style) and according to how much group members participate (quantity). Procedures also differ according to whether participation is voluntary or forced. Some procedures are formal; others are more informal (Schweiger & Leana, 1986). Some procedures help structure a group's communication during decision making and problem solving. Other procedures provide an analytical function to help members to evaluate, question, and investigate their ideas. Some procedures help a group with its creativity. Finally, some procedures assist a group in managing conflict and developing agreement (Sunwolf & Seibold, 1998). Groups that use these procedures generally outperform groups that do not. Although the use of such procedures does not guarantee group effectiveness, using procedures maximizes opportunities for groups to achieve the results they desire. Actually, groups should be able to use a variety of decision-making procedures. Few complex decisions have a single right answer; thus groups may need to use several procedures to identify solutions and make the best decision.

Each of the procedures described in the following sections provides guidelines or ground rules for members to follow. One procedure that is not discussed here is parliamentary procedure, which is a highly formalized method to help larger groups (for example, parent-teacher organizations and community groups; Weitzel & Geist, 1998) structure their discussion, decision-making, and business activities. If you are an officer in an organization that uses parliamentary procedure, you will want to become familiar with its many protocols. However, small task groups or informal groups rarely follow these procedures. We will start with the standard agenda.

Standard Agenda

The standard agenda, also known as reflective thinking, is a strict linear process that groups follow in considering decision alternatives. A group using this procedure passes through a series of six steps—each focusing on different aspects of the problem-solving process. The six steps are (a) identifying the problem, (b) analyzing the problem, (c) identifying the minimal criteria for the solution, (d) generating solutions, (e) evaluating solutions and selecting one as best, and (f) implementing the solution. This step-by-step process creates a structure for group members to use in thoroughly analyzing the problem it is dealing with. Each step must be completed before going on to the next.

The first step in the standard agenda is problem identification. Here the group must clarify what it wants to do or what it is being asked to do. A good way to start is to ask this question: What exactly is the problem before the group? Too frequently, groups overlook this step. When this happens, each group member can have a different idea of what constitutes the problem and assume that other group members have the same problem in mind. For example, suppose a student group is seeking a solution to the lack of food services on the north campus. All of the food outlets are at least a mile away from this part of campus. So what precisely is the problem? Is it that students, faculty, and staff do not have access to food for lunch and dinner? To be sure, the group members canvass students to examine the problem from their point of view. This helps them be certain that they are on track before going ahead with the rest of the project. Before going on to the next step, each group member should be able to state the problem clearly and succinctly.

The second step is problem analysis. Here group members gather information, data, and even opinions to help them understand the history and causes of the problem. Group members need to decide how serious or widespread the problem is. Considering solutions that will resolve a problem for a few isolated people is quite different from considering solutions that will resolve a problem that affects many. Continuing with the previous example, the group surveys students for the type of food service they might prefer. Their next step is to contact the food services department on campus to discuss the types of services they could make available on north campus. With both sets of information, the group can compare the foods that are easily accessible from food services with the foods students want. And, although the general focus is on problems, group members also need to think about any hidden issues. One hidden issue—and the real reason food is not available on this part of campus—is that custodial staff is limited on this part of campus, meaning that there are not enough custodians to keep the food areas up to health department standards of sanitation.

The third step involves identifying the minimal criteria for the solution. In the food problem, the primary criterion is money. How much are students willing to spend for the convenience of eating near their classes? How much money can food services allot in their budget to establish food service on the north campus? How much money will be required for extra custodial help? In discussing these issues, the group finds other criteria that need to be considered. For example, where will these new food services be located? Who will give permission to install food outlets in classroom buildings? Because space is so tight, the only place that can reasonably hold a food outlet is the theatre department's ticket office. But the group does not pursue the issue of what will happen to the ticket office if it is moved to accommodate food outlets. The more criteria group members can think of for evaluating solutions, the more complete and the more useful their decisions will be.

In the fourth step, group members generate solutions. As you might guess, it is difficult to keep from doing this throughout the discussion generated in the first three steps. But groups that generate solutions too quickly can come to premature conclusions without fully investigating all potential solutions. For example, the group studying the problem of food on the north campus fails to generate other solutions such as independent food cart vendors, which do not require permanent space. It is a good idea to allow at least two meetings for idea generation. That way, group members have the opportunity to think about the problem individually before coming back to the group.

The fifth step is evaluating solutions and selecting one as best. If the group has followed the standard agenda, this step will be relatively easy because the group has access to all needed information. Using the criteria generated in the third step, the group should evaluate the advantages and disadvantages of each solution generated in the fourth step. What about our campus food group? Unfortunately, they get stuck early on in the process. That is, they become so focused on moving the ticket office and installing a fast food outlet that they have no other options to evaluate at this stage. As a result, they force themselves into recommending a solution that will not be approved.

The sixth step of the standard agenda is solution implementation. But follow-through can be a weak area for groups. Sometimes the charge of the group does not include implementation, so group members get little practice in this area. Other times the group has used all of its energy in making a decision and has little left over for implementing the decision. Thus they simply stop after selecting a solution. Because implementation is a common weakness for groups, we will explore this step in detail in the next chapter.

Using these six steps maximizes group effectiveness in decision making because it provides equal opportunity to all proposals, no matter who makes them. Highly cohesive groups benefit from using the standard agenda procedure because members of such groups can feel inhibited about criticizing an idea or proposal before the group (Pavitt, 1993). Following the steps of the standard agenda allows group members to question ideas and ask for clarification.

Although the standard agenda is often seen as the ideal procedure for most decision-making activities, it is not always practical (Jarboe, 1996). Some groups may find it difficult to follow the steps of the standard agenda. The sequence of steps structures the type of discussion the group has at each point in the process, and the procedure certainly takes time. However, this procedure satisfies the five critical functions that a group must perform to make effective decisions.

The other five decision-making procedures can be used in the various steps of the standard agenda. Each procedure can contribute to the group's decision making in different ways. In practice, groups may use several different procedures throughout their decision-making activity.

Brainstorming

Brainstorming is an idea generation technique designed to improve productivity and creativity (Osborn, 1963). Thus the brainstorming procedure helps a group to function creatively. In a brainstorming session, group members first state as many alternatives as possible to a given problem. Creative ideas are encouraged; ideas do not have to be traditional or unoriginal. Actually, the wilder and crazier the ideas, the better. But it's important that all ideas be accepted without criticism—verbal or nonverbal—from other group members. Next, ideas that have been presented can be improved upon or combined with other ideas. Finally, the group evaluates ideas after the idea generation phase is complete. The group should also record all ideas for future consideration, even those that are initially discarded. A group member can act as the facilitator of the brainstorming session, but research has shown that someone external to the group may be more effective in this role. The facilitator helps the group maintain momentum and helps members remain neutral by not stopping to criticize ideas (Kramer, Fleming, & Mannis, 2001).

This brainstorming procedure helps groups generate as many ideas as possible from which to select a solution. Generally, as the number of ideas increases, so does idea quality.

Members may experience periods of silence during idea generation, but research has shown that good ideas can come after moments of silence while members reflect and think individually (Ruback, Dabbs, & Hopper, 1984). So it may be premature to end idea generation the first time all members become quiet.

When should a group use brainstorming? Brainstorming is best used when the problem is specific rather than general. For example, brainstorming can be effective in identifying ways to attract minority employees to an organization. But the problem—what does a group hope to accomplish in the next 5 years—is too broad. Use a brainstorming session to break it down into subproblems, and then devote a further session to each one. Brainstorming works best with smaller rather than larger groups. Finally, members are more likely to generate a greater number of unique ideas if they write their ideas down before presenting them to the group (Mullen, Johnson, & Salas, 1991).

Brainstorming can help increase group cohesiveness because it encourages all members to participate. It also helps group members realize that they can work together productively (Pavitt, 1993). In addition, group members report that they like having an opportunity to be creative and to build upon one another's ideas (Kramer, Kuo, & Dailey, 1997), and they usually find brainstorming fun. However, groups do better if they have a chance to warm up or to practice the process (Firestien, 1990). The practice session should be unrelated to the subject of the actual brainstorming session. Practice sessions are beneficial because they reinforce the procedure and reassure participants that the idea generation and evaluation steps will not be integrated. Posting the five brainstorming steps so they are visible during the session helps remind participants of the procedure's rules.

To summarize, the brainstorming procedure should include the following steps:

1. State as many alternatives as possible.
2. Encourage creative ideas.
3. Examine ideas that have been presented to see if they can be improved upon or combined with other ideas.
4. Accept all ideas without criticism.
5. Evaluate ideas after the idea generation phase is complete.

Notice that brainstorming is a procedure for generating ideas, and not for making decisions. As a result, brainstorming by itself cannot satisfy the five critical functions of group decision making. However, it is especially effective in helping a group seek and develop a set of realistic and acceptable alternatives and in coming to an understanding of what constitutes an acceptable resolution, and moderately effective in helping group members achieve an understanding of the problem.

Nominal Group Technique

The same basic principles of brainstorming are also applied in the nominal group technique (NGT) except that group members work both independently as individuals and interdependently in the group. Thus the **nominal group technique** is an idea generation process in which individual group members generate ideas on their own before interacting as a group to discuss the ideas. The unique aspect of this procedure is that the group temporarily suspends interaction to take advantage of independent thinking and reflection (Delbecq, Van de Ven, & Gustafson, 1975). NGT is based on two principles: (a) Individuals think most creatively and generate more alternatives working alone, and (b) group discussion is best used for refining and clarifying alternatives.

NGT is a six-step linear process, with each step focusing on different aspects of the problem-solving process. In step 1, group members silently generate as many ideas as possible, writing down each idea. It's sensible to give members a few minutes after everyone appears to be finished, as some of our best ideas occur to us after we think we are finished.

In step 2, the ideas are recorded on a flip chart by a facilitator. Generally, it is best to invite someone outside the group to help facilitate the process so all group members can participate. Members take turns, giving one idea at a time to be written on the flip chart. Duplicate ideas do not need to be recorded, but ideas that are slightly different from those already posted should be listed. Ideas are not discussed during this step. The person recording the group's ideas on the flip chart should summarize and shorten lengthy ideas into a phrase. But first, this person should check with the member who originated the idea to make sure that editorializing did not occur. When a member runs out of ideas, he or she simply says "pass," and the facilitator moves on to the next person. When all members have passed, the recording step is over.

In step 3, group interaction resumes. Taking one idea at a time, group members discuss each idea for clarification. If an idea needs no clarification, then the group moves on to the next one. Rather than asking only the group member who contributed the idea to clarify it, the facilitator should ask if any group member has questions about the idea. By including everyone in the clarification process, group ownership of the idea increases.

In step 4, group members vote on the ideas they believe are most important. For instance, if your group generates 40 ideas, consider asking group members to vote for their top 5. By not narrowing the number of choices too severely or too quickly, group members have a chance to discuss the ideas they most prefer. If time permits, let group members come to the flip charts and select their most important ideas themselves. This helps ensure that members select the ideas that are important to them without the influence of peer pressure.

In step 5, the group discusses the vote just taken. Suppose that, from the 40 ideas presented, 11 receive two or more votes. Now is the time for group members to farther elaborate on each of these ideas. Direct the discussion according to the order of ideas as they appear on the flip chart, rather than starting with the idea that received the most votes. Beginning the discussion in a neutral or randomly selected place encourages discussion on each item, not just on the one that appears most popular at this point in the procedure.

With that discussion complete, step 6 requires that group members repeat steps 4 and 5. That is, once again, members vote on the importance of the remaining ideas. With 11 ideas left, you might ask members to select their top 3 choices. After members vote, the group discusses the three ideas that received the most votes. Now it is time for the final vote. This time, group members select the idea they most favor.

The greatest advantage of NGT is that the independent idea generation steps encourage equal participation of group members regardless of power or status. The views of more silent members are treated the same as the views of dominant members (Van de Ven & Delbecq, 1974). In fact, NGT groups develop more proposals and higher-quality proposals than groups using other procedures (Green, 1975; Kramer et al., 1997). Another advantage of NGT is that its specified structure helps bring a sense of closure and accomplishment to group problem solving (Van de Ven & Delbecq, 1974). When the meeting is finished, members have a firm grasp of what the group decided and a feeling of satisfaction because they helped the group reach that decision.

To summarize, NGT includes the following steps:

1. Individuals silently generate ideas, writing down each idea.
2. Have a facilitator record the ideas, one at a time, on a flip chart.
3. As a group, discuss each idea for clarification.
4. To narrow the number of ideas, vote on the ideas believed to be most important.
5. Discuss the ideas that receive the most votes.
6. Repeat steps 4 and 5 until only one idea remains.

When is it best to use NGT? Several group situations can be enhanced by the NGT process (Pavitt, 1993). NGT is most helpful when proposal generation is crucial. For example, suppose your softball team needs to find new and creative ways to raise funds. Your team has already tried most of the traditional approaches to raising money, and members' enthusiasm for selling door to door is low. NGT can help the team identify alternatives without group members surrendering to the ideas of the coach or the best players. NGT also can be very helpful for groups that are not very cohesive. When a group's culture is unhealthy and cohesiveness is low but the group's work must be done, NGT can help the group overcome its relationship problems and allow it to continue with its tasks. The minimized interaction in the idea generation phase of NGT gives everyone a chance to participate, increasing the likelihood that members will be satisfied with the group's final choice. Finally, NGT is particularly helpful when the problem facing the group is particularly volatile—for example, when organizational groups have to make difficult decisions about which items or projects to cut from the budget. The conflict that is likely to occur through more interactive procedures or unstructured processes can be destructive. The structured process of NGT helps group members focus on the task because turn taking is controlled.

With respect to the five critical functions of group decision making, NGT satisfies four. Because interaction is limited, especially in the idea generation phase, group members are not likely to achieve understanding of the problem. The discussion phase of NGT, however, should be effective in helping group members come to understand what constitutes an acceptable resolution to the problem, develop realistic and acceptable alternatives, and assess the positive and negative qualities of alternatives considered.

Consensus

Consensus means that each group member agrees with the decision or that group members' individual positions are close enough that they can support the group's decision (DeStephen & Hirokawa, 1988; Hoffman & Kleinman, 1994). In the latter case, even if members do not totally agree with the decision, they choose to support the group by supporting the decision. Consensus is achieved through discussion. Through members' interactions, alternatives emerge and are tested. In their interaction, group members consult with one another and weigh various alternatives. Eventually, one idea emerges as the decision that group members can support.

To the extent that group members feel they have participated in the decisionmaking process, they are satisfied with the group's interaction. That satisfaction is then extended to the consensus decision. Thus, when all group members can give verbal support, consensus has been achieved. To develop consensus, a group uses discussion to combine the best insights of all members to find a solution that incorporates all points of view. For example, juries that award damages in lawsuits must make consensus decisions—everyone must agree on the amount of money to be awarded.

Too frequently, consensus building is seen as a freewheeling discussion without any sort of process, plan, or procedure. But there are guidelines a group can use to achieve consensus. This procedure is especially useful for groups that must make highly subjective decisions (for example, a panel of judges deciding which contestant best represents the university, or the local United Way board of directors deciding how much money will be allocated to community service agencies) (Hare, 1982). Thus consensus is a procedure that helps a group reach agreement.

To develop consensus, the leader or another group member takes on the role of coordinator to facilitate the group's discussion. This coordinator does not express his or her opinions or argue for or against proposals suggested by the group. Rather, he or she uses ideas generated by members to formulate proposals acceptable to all members. Another group member can act as a recorder to document each of the proposals. Throughout the discussion, the recorder should read back statements that reflect the initial agreements of the group. This ensures that the agreement is real. When the group feels it has reached consensus, the recorder should read aloud this decision so members can give approval or modify the proposal.

To summarize, the steps for using consensus include the following:

1. Assign one group member to the role of coordinator to facilitate the discussion.

2. The coordinator uses ideas generated by members to formulate proposals acceptable to all members.
3. Assign another group member to record each of the proposals.
4. Throughout the discussion, the recorder reads back statements that reflect the agreements of the group.
5. The recorder reads aloud the final decision so members can give approval or modify the proposal.

In addition to following these steps, all group members need to be aware of a few basic discussion rules. First, the goal of the group's discussion is to find a solution that incorporates all points of view. Second, group members should not only give their opinions on the issue but also seek out the opinions of other members. The coordinator should make an extra effort to include less talkative members in the discussion. Third, group members should address their opinions and remarks to the group as a whole, and not to the coordinator. Finally, group members should avoid calling for a vote, which has the effect of stopping the discussion.

Consensus can only be reached through interaction. Although each group member should be encouraged to give his or her opinion, group members should avoid arguing for their personal ideas. It is better to state your ideas and give supporting reasons. Arguing about whose idea is better or whose idea is more correct will not help the group achieve consensus. If other group members express opinions that differ from yours, avoid confrontation and criticism. Rather, ask questions that can help you understand their points of view.

As the group works toward consensus, it can be tempting to change your mind just so the group can reach consensus and move on to other activities. Be careful! Changing your mind only to reach agreement will make you less satisfied with the process and the decision. If the group has trouble reaching consensus, it is better to postpone the decision until another meeting. Pressing for a solution because time is short will not help group members understand and commit to the decision. If a decision is postponed, assigning group members to gather more information can help the next discussion session.

How well does consensus achieve the five critical functions of decision making? As a decision procedure, it is very effective in helping group members achieve an understanding of the problem they are trying to resolve, identify what constitutes an acceptable resolution, and develop a set of realistic and acceptable alternatives. Discussion leading to consensus allows more viewpoints to be discussed, so members are made aware of issues and facts they did not previously know. As a result, group members become more knowledgeable about the problem. Consensus discussions involve everyone, which results in a high degree of integration as at least part of everyone's point of view is represented in the final decision. Thus consensus can help achieve the first three critical functions. However, it is less effective in helping groups assess the positive and negative qualities of the alternatives presented.

There are a few disadvantages to using consensus. First, this procedure takes time. When not enough time is allotted, some members may opt out of the discussion process, allowing the group to come to a **false consensus**—agreeing to a decision simply to be done with the task. Thus the extent to which consensus is effective depends on the voluntary and effective participation of group members. Second, consensus is usually not effective when controversial or complex decisions must be made. A group charged with making a decision that heightens emotional issues for members is likely to make a better decision with a more standardized approach that structures group inquiry. This is why the consensus procedure is not always effective in assessing the positive and negative qualities of the alternatives presented.

Voting

Voting, another decision-making procedure, is simply the process of casting written or verbal ballots in support of or against a specific proposal. Many organizational groups rely on the outcomes of majority voting to elect officers or pass resolutions. A group that votes needs to decide on three procedural issues before a vote is taken.

The first procedural issue centers on the discussion the group should have before members vote. Members do not simply walk into a meeting and vote. Voting should be on clear proposals, and only after substantial group discussion. Here is a suggested procedure to follow in voting (Hare, 1982). Members bring items to the attention of the group by making proposals in the form of motions. Let's say that your communication students' association is making decisions about its budget. Karen says, "I move that we set aside part of our budget for community activities." But subsequent discussion among group members reveals two ambiguities. What does Karen mean by "part of our budget": 20 percent? 40 percent? And what are "community activities"? Do they include teaching junior high students how to give speeches? With other members' help, Karen's proposal is made more specific: "I move that we set aside 20 percent of our budget for community intervention activities that help children appreciate the value of communicating effectively." Now, with a specific motion, Karen can argue for her proposal by stating its merits. Even with a specific proposal, she is going to receive some opposition or face more questions. That is okay because it helps all group members understand her motion more clearly. During this discussion, the group leader makes sure that all those who want to be heard get a chance to talk. However, the leader does not argue for or against any particular motion. To do so would put undue influence on the group. The group's secretary or recorder keeps track of the motions and identifies which ones receive approval from the group.

The second procedural issue is to decide how the vote will be taken. When sensitive issues are being voted on, it is better to use a written ballot. Similar ballots or pieces of paper are given to each group member. This way group members can vote their conscience and retain their anonymity. Two group members should count the votes and verify the decision before announcing it to the group.

A verbal vote, or a show of hands, is more efficient when it is necessary only to document the approval or disapproval apparent in the group's discussion. For example, suppose your communication students' association has several items of business to take care of at the next meeting. Specifically, the association needs to elect officers, approve the budget, and select a faculty member for the outstanding professor award. The budget was read to members at the last meeting and then discussed. Although members will ask some questions before the vote, the group basically needs to approve or disapprove the budget. Because there is nothing out of the ordinary about the budget and little controversy is expected, it is okay to use a show of hands in this case.

However, electing officers and voting for one professor to receive an award can bring up conflicting emotions among group members. Both of these matters are better handled with written ballots. This way group members can freely support the candidates and the professor they desire without fear of intimidation or retaliation.

The final procedural issue that needs to be agreed on before taking a vote is how many votes are needed to win or decide an issue. Most of the time, a simple majority vote (one more than half of the members) is satisfactory. However, if a group is changing its constitution or taking some type of legal action, a two-thirds or three-fourths majority may be preferable. Both the method of voting and the majority required for a decision need to be agreed upon before any voting takes place.

Voting can be efficient, but it can also arbitrarily limit a group's choices. Many times motions considered for a vote take on an either/or quality that limits the choice to two alternatives. And a decision made by voting is seen as final—groups seldom revote. This is why having an adequate discussion period before voting is necessary. As you can see, voting is not the best choice when complex decisions must be made.

To summarize, the procedures for voting include the following:

1. Hold discussions to generate a clear proposal.
2. Decide how the vote will be taken—written ballot, verbal vote, or show of hands.
3. Decide how many votes are needed to win or decide an issue.
4. Restate the proposal before voting.

How well a group develops the discussion before voting determines how well the group satisfies the five critical functions of group decision making. Although voting is often perceived as a way of providing a quick decision, inadequate time for group discussion can severely limit the appropriateness or effectiveness of the proposals to be voted on.

Ranking

Ranking is the process of assigning a numerical value to each decision alternative so that group members' preferences are revealed. Groups often use a ranking process when there are many viable alternatives from which to choose, but the group must select the preferred alternative or a set of preferred alternatives. There are two steps to the ranking process.

First, each member individually assigns a numerical value to each decision alternative. In effect, rankings position each alternative from highest to lowest, as well as relative to one another. Usually, 1 is assigned to the most valued choice, 2 to the next most valued choice, and so on. These rankings may be based on a set of criteria developed by the group (for instance. How well does this alternative fix the problem? Is the alternative possible within the time frame allotted the project?).

Second, after group members complete their individual rankings, the values for each alternative are summed and totaled. Now the group has a score for each alternative. The alternative with the lowest total is the group's first-ranked alternative. The alternative with the second-lowest score is the group's second-ranked alternative, and so on. This procedure, which helps group members come to agreement, can be done publicly so group members can see or hear the ranking of one another's alternatives, or the process can be done on paper so individual rankings are anonymous.

Just as with voting, the ranking procedure is most effective when the group has adequate time to develop and discuss the alternatives to be ranked. Compared to groups instructed to "choose the best alternative," groups that rank-order their alternatives do a better job, as all alternatives must be discussed for members to perform the ranking task (Hollingshead, 1996). Thus the extent to which this procedure satisfies the five critical functions of group decision making depends on the quality of the group's discussion.

To summarize, to use ranking effectively as a decision procedure, a group should take the following steps:

1. Hold adequate discussion that leads to clear proposals.
2. Have each member assign a numerical value to each decision alternative.
3. Sum individual rankings and total them for the group.
4. The alternative with the lowest total is the group's first-ranked alternative.

Although ranking decreases group members' feelings of personal involvement or participation, groups using this procedure report little negativity in decision making. Fewer arguments or conflicts are reported when ranking is used because it is more difficult for one or two individual members to alter a group's decision-making process. Each member gets to indicate his or her preference, and all preferences are treated equally. Thus group members report feeling satisfied with the outcome (Green & Taber, 1980). Group members usually prefer ranking to voting for making a decision when more than two alternatives exist.

Comparing Procedures

Procedures help groups by managing their discussions and decision-making processes. In turn, this enhances the quality of decision making in the group by coordinating members'

Table 7.1: The Ways in Which Various Procedures Satisfy Problem-Solving and Decision-Making Functions

	Understand the Problem	Understand What Constitutes Acceptable Resoloution	Develop Realistic and Acceptable Alternatives	Assess the Positive Qualities of Alternatives	Assess the Nagative Qualities of Alternatives
Standard Agenda	Yes	Yes	Yes	Yes	Yes
Brainstorming	Somewhat	Yes	Yes	No	No
NGT	No	Yes	Yes	Yes	Yes
Consensus	Yes	Yes	Yes	No	No
Voting	Depends on quality of group discussion *before* voting	Depends on quality of group discussion *before* voting	Depends on quality of group discussion *before* voting	Depends on quality of group discussion *before* voting	Depends on quality of group discussion *before* voting
Ranking	Depends on quality of group discussion *before* ranking	Depends on quality of group discussion *before* ranking	Depends on quality of group discussion *before* ranking	Depends on quality of group discussion *before* ranking	Depends on quality of group discussion *before* ranking

thinking and communication, providing a set of ground rules all members can and must follow, balancing member participation, managing conflicts, and improving group climate (Jarboe, 1996; Poole, 1991; Sunwolf & Seibold, 1999). Most importantly, procedures help groups avoid becoming solution-minded too quickly.

But which procedure is best? Sometimes the group leader or facilitator selects a procedure. Other times the group relies on familiarity—selecting the procedure it used last time regardless of its effectiveness. Rather than select a procedure arbitrarily, groups should select a procedure or a combination of procedures that best suits their needs and satisfies the five critical functions of group decision making. Table 7.1 summarizes the ways in which each procedure satisfies the five functions.

Thinking of each function as a unique type of decision task, we can see that the standard agenda fulfills all five functions and seems to be the most effective decision procedure. But we should be cautious in recommending it as the most effective procedure in all group decision-making tasks. Why? Although the standard agenda identifies which steps need to be completed, it does not ensure that all members will participate. Recall that the type and structure of communication among group members differs across these procedures. Groups need to select the procedure that best fits their communication needs.

Before you select a procedure, you should analyze the type of task before your group. If the task is easy—for example, the group has all of the necessary information to make effective choices—the type of procedure you select will have less influence on the group's ability to resolve the problem or reach a decision. However, if the group task or decision is difficult—for example, members' decisionmaking skills vary, the group needs to consult with people outside the group, or the decision has multiple parts—the decision procedure selected will have a greater impact on the group's decision-making abilities. Generally, in these situations, the procedure that encourages vigilant and systematic face-to-face interaction will result in higher-quality outcomes (Hirokawa et al., 1996).

Regardless of which procedure your group selects, all members must agree to using the procedure if any benefits are to be achieved. Also remember that the procedure itself does not ensure that all members will be motivated and willing to participate. Decision procedures cannot replace group cohesiveness. To help you distinguish among these procedures, see "Which Procedures Will Help Your Group?"

The Paradox of Using Procedures

Research has demonstrated that groups using formal discussion procedures generally develop higher member satisfaction and greater commitment to the decision. Although the standard agenda procedure helps groups pay greater attention to detail, NGT and brainstorming groups generally produce more ideas and higher-quality ideas, and voting and ranking can make decision outcomes clearer. Yet many groups try to avoid using procedures. This is because discussion and decision-making procedures take time, and groups must plan their meetings accordingly. Group members often are reluctant to use procedures because they are unaccustomed to using them or initially find them too restrictive. Group members may be more willing to try a procedure when they find out that one of the most frequent mistakes groups make is to plunge into their tasks without adequate discussion and thorough review of alternatives. Remember the student group trying to find a solution to the problem of food services not being available on the north campus?

It is often difficult for groups to stick with a procedure once it has been initiated. For example, members may find it difficult to refrain from nonverbal evaluation of ideas in brainstorming. Groups using NGT may believe they have found the best idea in the initial voting and discussion steps and so fail to pursue the rest of the process. Groups find that the standard agenda is difficult to stick with because it requires the diligence of all group members. One group member can successfully dislodge others from using the process. But it is exactly these difficulties that procedures guard against. In each case, the group avoids the procedure to move along more quickly, but efficiency is generally not a characteristic of effective groups.

Procedures help group members resist sloppy thinking and ineffective group habits (Poole, 1991). When procedures seem unnatural, it is often because group members have had little practice with them. If members have not used a particular procedure before, it is best to hold a practice session on a nonrelated topic. Practice can help demonstrate that the use of a procedure keeps groups from failing into traps of ineffectiveness or faulty thinking. Procedures also help groups manage their discussions and decision-making conversations and improve their effectiveness by providing a set of objective ground rules. When all group members know the procedure, it keeps the leader from assuming too much power and swaying the decision process. In addition, procedures help coordinate members' thinking and interaction, making it less likely that a group will go off topic. As member participation becomes more balanced, more voices are heard, and more ideas are deliberated.

To help your group gain experience with procedures, use these seven guidelines (Poole, 1991). First, motivate your group to use a procedure. For instance, provide positive feedback to group members when a procedure is used. Or look for discussion and decision-making problems that occur in your group, and then suggest a procedure to help the group overcome that difficulty. Second, champion the procedure process. For example, know and advocate the value of the procedure, remind the group to use it, and provide advice and help when the group does so. Also, train yourself in several procedures so you can help your group use them effectively. Third, help other group members learn the procedure. The more members who know and can use the procedure, the more likely the procedure is to be used.

Fourth, if needed, tailor the procedure to the group's needs. For example, perhaps your group works so fast at brainstorming that two facilitators are needed to write down members' ideas. This modification helps the group use the procedure more effectively. Tailoring a procedure to a group's particular needs gives the group ownership over the process. Fifth, suggest that your group spend time analyzing its discussion interaction with and without procedures. Getting members accustomed to talking about the group's strengths and weaknesses helps them realize that procedures can become a natural part of the group's activities. Sixth, when conflicts are high or cohesiveness is low, ask someone who is not a member of the group to act as the facilitator. Someone who is neutral, and not intrinsically interested in the group's outcomes, can ensure that a procedure is fairly administered. Finally, help the group set reasonable expectations with respect to using procedures. Using a procedure cannot solve all of a group's problems, but it can help a group discuss alternatives and make decisions more effectively. And make sure the procedure fits the group need. This will ensure that the group achieves greater success and will encourage group members to view the procedure as a tool, not as a panacea for all of the group's troubles.

Summary

Effective decision-making in small groups is not accident; it is based on competent membership and creative participation by all group members. In this chapter you learned the different procedures groups can use as they make a decision. The steps of the Standard Agenda were presented as a structured model of group decision-making and problem solving. The chapter also discussed the various group decision-making methods: brainstorming, nominal group technique, consensus, voting, ranking,

Decision making skills are not a personal trait; they can be learned by anyone. This chapter stressed the importance of groups using some type of procedure to follow when making decisions. If groups simply begin a free-for-all discussion, the chances of making a quality decision are greatly reduced. The basic skills that any group needs are task, relationship, and procedural skills. Groups need task kills to help them recognize the problem and the appropriate way to frame the problem. A key relational skill that every group needs is effective leadership—it is needed to keep the group on track and minimize the chances of problematic group behaviors and manage conflict. Finally, groups need procedural skills for planning and to help the group move through the decision making process

This chapter also explained why groups are better at making decisions than individuals working alone. The basic reasons for this conclusion is that (1) groups have greater access to knowledge through the expertise of the group members, (2) possess a greater diversity of perspectives on the problem they are discussing, and (3) a greater ability to analyze their decisions before one is implemented.

The next chapter presents the medium that has revolutionized communication since its introduction at the end of the Twentieth Century: the Internet. Whether or not the Internet will become the central gatekeeper of information is still up to debate, but there is no doubt that its influence will dramatically change the nature of communication as we know it.

Questions For Discussion

1. What are some of the most needed skills for group leaders? What can be some problems in group leadership?
2. Do you agree that groups follow a circular rather than a linear process?
3. What ways have you managed conflict in groups in which you have been a member?
4. Have you ever used the standard agenda before? Do you think it is a effective process for decision making?
5. Do you think that consensus or voting is the most effective way for a group to reach a decision?

References

Barge, J. K., & Keyton, J. (1994). Contextualizing power and social influence in groups. In L. R. Frey (Ed.), *Group communication in context: Studies of natural groups* (pp. 85–105). Hillsdale, NJ: Erlbaum.

Delbecq, A. L., Van de Ven, A. H., & Gustafson, D. H. (1975). *Group techniques for program planning: A guide to nominal group and delphi processes.* Glenview, IL: Scott, Foresman.

DeStephen, R. S., & Hirakawa, R. Y. (1988). Small group consensus: Stability of group support of the decision, task process, and group relationships. *Small Group Behavior, 19,* 227–239.

Firestien, R. L. (1990). Effects of creative problem solving training on communication behavior in small groups. *Small Group Research, 21,* 507–521.

Gouran, D. S. (2003). Communication skills for group decision making. InJ. 0. Greene & B. R. Burleson (Eds.), *Handbook of communication and social interaction skills* (pp. 83 5–870). Mahwah, NJ: Erlbaum.

Gouran, D. S., & Hirakawa, R. Y. (1983). The role of communication in decision making groups: A functional perspective. In M. S. Mander (Ed.), *Communications in transition* (pp. 168–185). New York: Praeger.

Gouran, D. S., & Hirakawa, R. Y. (1996). Functional theory and communication in decisionmaking and problem-solving groups. In R. Y. Hirokawa & M. S. Poole (Eds.), *Communication and group decision making* (pp. 55–80). Thousand Oaks, CA: Sage.

Gouran, D. S., Hirakawa, R. Y., Julian, K. M., & Leatham, G. B. (1993). The evolution and current status of the functional perspective on communication in decision-making and problem-solving groups. InS. A. Deetz (Ed.), *Communication yearbook 16* (pp. 573–600). Newbury Park, CA: Sage.

Graham, E. E., Papa, M. J., & McPherson, M. B. (1997). An applied test of the functional communication perspective of small group decision-making. *Southern Communication Journal, 62,* 269–279.

Green, S. G., & Taber, T. D. (1980). The effects of three social decision schemes on decision group process. *Organizational Behavior and Human Performance, 25,* 97–106.

Green, T. B. (197 5). An empirical analysis of nominal and interacting groups. *Academy of Management Journal, 18,* 63–73.

Hare, A. P. (1982). *Creativity in small groups.* Beverly Hills: Sage.

Hirokawa, R. Y. (1982). Group communication and problem-solving effectiveness I: A critical review of inconsistent findings. *Communication Quarterly, 30,* 134–141.

Hirokawa, R. Y. (1983a). Group communication and problem-solving effectiveness: An investigation of group phases. *Human Communication Research, 9,* 291–305.

Hirokawa, R. Y. (1983b). Group communication and problem-solving effectiveness II: An exploratory investigation of procedural functions. *Western Journal of Speech Communication, 47,* 59–74.

Hirokawa, R. Y., & Johnson, D. D. (1989). Toward a general theory of group decision making: Development of an integrated model. *Small Group Behavior, 20,* 500–523.

Hirokawa, R. Y., & Scheerhorn, D. R. (1986). Communication in faulty group decisionmaking. In R. Y. Hirokawa & M. S. Poole (Eds.), *Communication and group decision-making* (pp. 63–80). Beverly Hills: Sage.

Hoffman, L. R., & Kleinman, G. B. (1994). Individual and group in problem solving: The valence model redressed. *Human Communication Research, 21,* 36–59.

Hollingshead, A. B. (1996). The rank-order effect in group decision making. *Organizational Behavior and Human Decision Processes, 68,* 181–193.

Janis, I. L. (1989). *Crucial decisions: Leadership in policy making and crisis management.* New York: Free Press.

Jarboe, S. (1996). Procedures for enhancing group decision making. In R. Y. Hirokawa & M. S. Poole (Eds.), *Communication and group decision making* (pp. 345–383). Thousand Oaks, CA: Sage.

Johnson, V. (1991, June). Group decision making: "When trying to persuade others, knowledge is power. *Successful Meetings, 40,* 76–77.

Kramer, M. W, Kuo, C. L., & Dailey,}. C. (1997). The impact of brainstorming techniques on subsequent group processes: Beyond generating ideas. *Small Group Research, 28,* 218–242.

Kramer,T. J., Fleming, G. P., & Mannis, S.M. (2001). Improving face-to-face brainstorming through modeling and facilitation. *Small Group Research, 32,* 533–557.

Mullen, B., Johnson, C., & Salas, E. (1991). Productivity loss in brainstorming groups: A metaanalytical integration. *Basic and Applied Social Prychology, 12,* 3–2 3.

Orlitzky, M., & Hirakawa, R. Y. (2001). To err is human, to correct for it divine: A metaanalysis of research testing the functional theory of group decision-making effectiveness. *Small Group Research, 32,* 313–341.

Osborn, A. F. (1963). *Applied imagination* (3rd ed.). New York: Scribner.

Pavitt, C. (1993). What (little) we know about formal group discussion procedures: A review of relevant research. *Small Group Research, 24,* 217–235.

Poole, M. S. (1991). Procedures for managing meetings: Social and technological innovation. In R. A. Swanson & B. 0. Knapp (Eds.), *Innovative meeting management* (pp. 53–110). Austin: 3M Meeting Management Institute.

Ruback, R. B., Dabbs,). M., & Hopper, C. H. (1984). The process of brainstorming: An analysis with individual and group vocal parameters. *Journal of Personality and Social Psychology, 47,* 558–567.

Schweiger, D. M., & Leana, C. R. (1986). Participation in decision making. In E. A. Locke (Ed.), *Generalizing from laboratory to field settings: Research findings from industrial-organizational psychology, organizational behavior, and human resource management* (pp. 147–166). Lexington, MA: Lexington Books.

Sniezek, J. A. (1992). Groups under uncertainty: An examination of confidence in group decision making. *Organizational Behavior and Human Decision Processes, 52,* 124–155.

Sunwolf, & Seibold, D. R. (1998). Jurors' intuitive rules for deliberation: A structurational approach to communication in jury decision making. *Communication Monograph, 6 5,* 2 82–3 01.

Sunwolf, & Seibold, D. R. (1999). The impact of formal procedures on group processes, members, and task outcomes. In L. R. Frey, D. S. Gouran, & M.S. Poole (Eds.), *The handbook of group communication theory and research* (pp. 395–431). Thousand Oaks, CA: Sage.

Van de Ven, A. H., & Delbecq, A. L. (1971). Nominal versus interacting group processes for committee decision-making effectiveness. *Academy of Management Journal, 14,* 203–212.

Van de Ven, A. H., & Delbecq, A. L. (1974). The effectiveness of nominal, delphi, and interacting group decision-making processes. *Academy of Management Journal, 17,* 605–621.

Weitzel, A., & Geist, P. (1998). Parliamentary procedure in a community group: Communication and vigilant decision making. *Communication Monographs, 65,* 244–259.

Chapter 12

Internet Communication

Marcus Messner and Bruce Garrison

When the Internet was introduced near the end of the Twentieth Century, no one had any idea of the way it would change the nature of communication. From e-mail to web sites, the Internet is now deeply entrenched in the lives most people. This chapter examines the Internet with respect to its gate-keeping and agenda setting functions, and how these functions continue to evolve as does the Internet.

Learning Objectives For This Chapter

- Discuss the rapid growth of Internet use
- Understand the gate keeping function of the Internet
- Discuss how the Internet is used for agenda setting
- Explain how the intermedia concept applies to the Internet
- Discuss the significance of hyperlinking networks
- Explain how the Internet has revitalized the uses and gratification theory
- Identify the basic research methodologies that are used in Internet research

Since the World Wide Web made the Internet accessible for mass audiences in the early and mid-1990s, it has taken its place as the fourth type of mass medium besides print, television, and radio by matching penetration rates and audience sizes. Today, the Internet is omnipresent in people's lives. According to the Pew Internet and American Life Project, 73 percent of adults in the United States used the Internet in 2006, an increase from 66 percent only a year earlier. In the age groups of the 18- to 29-year-olds and 30- to 49-year-olds, the Internet penetration rate is well over 80 percent at this point. Already in the age group of 12- to 17-year-olds, 87 percent are Internet users (Madden, 2006). This development stresses the current and future importance of the medium. It is further enhanced by the increasing and widespread international adoption of high-speed and wireless Internet connections, which allow users to not only work faster, but also to access their online applications from anywhere. While 42 percent of adults in the United States had a high-speed connection at home, 34 percent of the users entered the Internet through a wireless connection in 2006 (Horrigan, 2006a, 2007). Many of the online activities have become routine tasks for the users. More than 40 percent of American Internet users utilize search engines on a daily basis and more than 50 percent send e-mails (Rainie & Shermak, 2005).

Most commonly, the Internet has developed into a mass medium for news and information. Online news has been growing ever since the first news organizations offered their services online in the early 1980s. In the last decade, Internet usage has drastically increased during major news events and, thereby, the Internet has become a part of the 24-hour news cycle first established by cable news. During the 2006

Congressional mid-term elections, 13 percent of all adults in the United States used the Internet on an average daily basis to retrieve political information (Horrigan, 2006b). While overall media ownership has concentrated on a few internationally operating corporations, new Internet news formats such as blogs with interactive, multilinked features have increased the overall news flow and enjoy high popularity especially with younger Internet users (Bucy, Gantz, & Wang, 2007; Klopfenstein, 2002). Burnett and Marshall (2003) pointed out that these new formats enable Internet users to retrieve information that has previously not been disseminated by the traditional media.

The emergence of the Internet as a mass medium has caused widespread interest in academia and has produced a constantly growing body of research. Tomasello (2001) was one of the first researchers to analyze the state of Internet research and found that between 1994 and 1999 only 4 percent of the articles published in leading communication journals focused on the Internet. However, Kim and Weaver (2002) found in an analysis of journal articles that the number of Internet-related studies increased from 2.3 percent in 1996 to 8.4 percent in 1999. In addition, Cho and Khang (2006) found in an analysis of 15 communication journals between 1994 and 2003 that 13.3 percent of the articles studied the Internet and its applications. Their study also revealed that only 14.5 percent of the Internet studies were theory-driven and concluded that Internet research "has not yet achieved an equivalent level of theoretical rigorousness" (p. 158) as other areas in communication research. Many studies were of an exploratory nature.

Internet research has not yet developed a distinct theory or theoretical base that would explain or predict certain online phenomena and behavior, but rather applies existing theories, many of which are discussed in other chapters of this book. This chapter, therefore, traces the most significant advancement of existing theories through the study of mass communication on the Internet, which includes changes in gatekeeping theory, intermedia agenda-setting, the concept of credibility, as well as the uses and gratifications model. In addition, the Internet specific concepts of interactivity and hyperlinking will be discussed.

Besides studying the diffusion of the Internet, researchers have especially focused on the gatekeeping and agenda setting dimensions of the Internet and its distinct news formats. Recent research has challenged the foundations of gatekeeping theory developed by White (1950), which established the central role of traditional news media editors in the news flow (Williams & Delli Carpini, 2000, 2004). This circumstance has also led a variety of researchers to analyze the credibility of online information.

The emergence of distinct Internet formats, such as the collaborative formats of blogs and wikis, which are generally referred to under the concept of the Web 2.0, has also led to a new focus in agenda-setting research, which was originally applied to mass communication by McCombs and Shaw (1972) in their much-cited Chapel Hill study. The new direction of agenda-setting research increasingly focuses on the impact of Internet sources and their intermedia influence on the traditional media agenda (Bucy, Gantz, & Wang, 2007; McCombs, 2005). Furthermore, social networking and uses and gratifications have been emergent fields of Internet research in recent years. The interactive nature of the Internet has led researchers to focus on the constantly emerging online social networks and their impact on communication (Barnett & Sung, 2005; Flew, 2005; McMillan, 2006). The concept of hyperlinking has established a new means to measure popularity of information and levels of influence (Tremayne, 2004). In addition, the application of the model of uses and gratifications, based on the assumption by Katz, Blumler, and Gurevitch (1974) that the news audience is active and that media compete with other sources to fulfill audience need gratifications, has also produced a growing body of Internet research that has contributed to explaining the Internet phenomenon in its initial stages (Bucy, Gantz, & Wang, 2007).

Cho and Khang (2006) view the application of these existing theories as the preceding step to the development of distinct theories that explain the Internet and its effects: "We not only need to apply more existing concepts and theories to comprehend general Internet phenomena, but should also strive to develop new concepts and theories for understanding new aspects of the Internet that might not be completely explained by the existing knowledge structure" (p. 158). This [selection], therefore, will help to lay the basis for much-needed Internet theory development.

Gatekeeping Challenges

The impact of the Internet is most profound in how it has changed the overall media environment and the channels through which news is disseminated. While gatekeeping research studied how information is filtered for publication, starting with White's (1950) "Mr. Gates," and had long established the central position of traditional media journalists in the news flow, the emergence of the Internet and its distinct formats has posed a challenge to the traditional news cycle. Even in the most advanced gatekeeping model by Shoemaker (1991), which accounted for individual, organizational, and social influences, the media gatekeepers made the ultimate decision on the news flow. There was no competition for the gatekeepers' media outlets. This started to change when the Internet became a mass medium in the mid-1990s and diversified the media environment. While at first, new media research focused on the changes caused by the Internet within the traditional media, it has gradually changed its focus towards the changes of the entire media environment. Through the diversification of news channels with newly developed Internet formats, the central gatekeeping position of the traditional news media editor has been challenged.

Singer (1997) was one of the first mass communication scholars to examine the changing gatekeeping roles within the traditional media and to conclude that the role of the editor had to be modified in the online environment. Based on interviews with reporters and editors of the printed and the online versions of newspapers, Singer found that traditional journalists still viewed themselves as the central gatekeepers in the news flow in 1995. The editors did not view the selection process itself as their most important task, but the protection of news quality.

However, only a few years later, Singer (2001) found gatekeeping modifications in news selection through a content analysis of print and online versions of newspapers. While at that point in time, the majority of the content was still duplicated from the printed versions, the study showed an increasing local focus in the online content. Singer concluded that the only way for newspapers to compete in the global news environment of the Internet was to stress the local news expertise online. However, in the early stages of traditional news media moving online, only little original information was produced for these websites (Matheson, 2004). While the format was changing, journalism was not. Even the adoption of the popular blog formats by traditional news outlets preserved the role of the journalistic gatekeeper. New media applications by major news outlets, thereby, mostly remained traditional media at the time.

In surveys of newspaper editors involved in the coverage of the 2000 and 2004 presidential elections, nevertheless, Singer (2003a, 2006) found that their gatekeeping roles were further evolving. The 2000 election exemplified that newspapers were starting to use their online versions to break news faster and report it in more detail as space restraints were abandoned online. In the 2004 election, however, the emphasis of the gatekeepers shifted toward using online news content to engage Internet users. While most editors were still focusing their central gatekeeping task on delivering credible information, they began to acknowledge the necessity to reconceptualize their gatekeeping roles to include newly developed, distinct formats of the Internet. Chats, forums, and blogs became important tools exclusively available online. User-generated content, which was not provided by journalists but by readers, became a much more important element. Singer (2006) concluded that an "evolution in online journalists' thinking" (p. 275) was occurring.

A survey of print and online newspaper journalists by Cassidy (2005) also stressed the development of different interpretations of gatekeeping roles. While print journalists perceived their traditional roles as interpreters and investigators most important, online journalists stressed the quick news delivery as their main concern. The online coverage of the Iraq War also showed that the websites of some newspapers moved beyond duplicating content of the printed versions. Dimitrova and Neznanski (2006) found in a content analysis of U.S. and international newspaper websites that multimedia content gained increasing importance in the online war coverage. Hoffman (2006), however, found that "online newspapers provide content that simply reinforces print content" (p. 69).

In addition to the modification of the gatekeeping roles within the traditional media, a significant challenge to the central gatekeeping position of journalists has occurred with the emergence of distinct online formats, most predominantly through blogs. Most scholars refer to the Clinton-Lewinsky scandal in 1998 as the first incident involving an online news outlet circumventing the traditional media gatekeepers. In their analysis of the scandal, Williams and Delli Carpini (2000, 2004) concluded that the authoritative gatekeeping role of traditional media had broken down when a national magazine halted a story on the president's affair with an intern and a blog decided to report the story and subsequently forced the traditional media, including the magazine to follow. The researchers concluded that traditional journalists had lost their central gatekeeping position, being unable to control or shape news events. This new media environment allowed individuals previously barred by gatekeepers to influence public discourse. Thereby online journalism evolved into another type of mass media, besides print, radio, and television.

As Kahn and Kellner (2004) pointed out, citizens equipped with laptops were now able to provide alternative news coverage and commentary. The resignation of U.S. Senate Majority Leader Trent Lott in 2002 over racist remarks, largely ignored by traditional media at first but propelled into public outrage by bloggers, demonstrated how significant the challenge to gatekeeping had become. Later, in the 2004 presidential election, weblogs reported exit poll results while the traditional media had decided to shield its readers from possibly unreliable facts based on problems in the previous election (Messner & Terilli, 2007).

Singer (2003b) pointed out that the rise of alternative news formats such as blogs blurred the line between professional and non-professional journalists. While the traditional gatekeeper sorted and limited the news flow in order to maintain quality, the challenge of this position increased the quantity of the information available to the public while at the same time decreasing the overall quality. Any person now had the ability to circumvent the traditional gatekeepers, shape the flow of news, and influence public discourse (Poor, 2006).

The war in Iraq has exemplified this new gatekeeping environment like no other news event over the course of several years. Wall (2005) analyzed blogs throughout the initial phase of the war in 2003 and found that in contrast to the neutral and detached tone of traditional media journalists bloggers are involved in their stories with a personalized and opinionated tone. While traditional news stories are aimed at giving the most complete and objective picture of an event, blog entries are fragmented, evolve over time, and are supplemented by reader comments. While Wall (2006) did not find a broadening of the discussion on the war as bloggers' opinions were linked to the prowar and anti-war sentiments in society overall, the researcher concluded that bloggers became "secondary war correspondents" (p. 122), critical of the traditional news media reporting. Deuze (2003) notes that this opportunity to provide alternative information on news events "challenges perceptions of the roles and functions of journalism as a whole" (p. 216). Kovach and Rosenstiel (2001) concluded that journalists do not determine the news flow anymore, but they help by sorting it for their audience.

The challenges to journalism gatekeepers, however, are not distinct in the new media environment. Alternative formats enabled by the Internet also challenge gatekeepers in other areas of information distribution. The collaborative wiki format for instance, mostly known through the development of the online encyclopedia Wikipedia, has challenged the elitist model of encyclopedia worldwide. Before Wikipedia was developed in 2001, Nobel and Pulitzer Prize winners among other experts acted as gatekeepers who defined encyclopedia entries. Today, as DiStaso, Messner, and Stacks (2007) pointed out, any individual can participate in the definition process using the wiki format.

Gaining Credibility

The challenge of the traditional gatekeepers is intensified by the high credibility of online information in general, despite the continuing proliferation of hoaxes and rumors on the Internet. While traditional media journalists have long questioned the credibility of alternative online sources (Ruggerio & Winch, 2004), online news sites have already overtaken print and broadcast sources in popularity and are steadily increasing their audiences.

In one of the first studies measuring the credibility of online information and comparing it to traditional media sources before and after the 1996 presidential election, Johnson and Kaye (1998) found that Internet users viewed political information online as more credible than in the traditional media counterparts. Nevertheless, in this survey, all media were ranked low on credibility. In a follow-up study, Johnson and Kaye (2000) confirmed that reliance on online media also influences their credibility ranking. The more often someone uses a medium, the higher will that individual rank the credibility of the medium. Thereby, the results of the study linked the credibility of online information to its growing popularity.

In the late 1990s, Internet users already viewed the credibility of general online information as being equal to that of television, magazines, and radio. A survey by Flanagin and Metzger (2000) found that only newspapers still had a credibility advantage over online information. The results were surprising because the researchers themselves viewed information on the Internet at the time as deriving from "the least critical medium" (p. 529). The Internet users surveyed, nevertheless, only rarely verified information found online with traditional media. The researchers excluded a direct transfer of traditional media credibility to online media, because newspapers ranked higher than their online counterparts.

By the 2000 presidential election, online information had gained significant credibility with Internet users in the four years since the 1996 campaign (Johnson & Kaye, 2002). Bucy (2003) found in an experiment in 2001 that students viewed television and online news as more credible than adults did. In addition, alternative Internet formats such as blogs were also gaining credibility. In a 2003 survey of blog readers, Johnson and Kaye (2004) found that blogs were ranked as more credible than traditional sources. While weblogs were rated as highly credible, traditional media information was rated as moderately credible. Only 3.5 percent of the respondents rated blogs as not credible. This high credibility rating was mainly based on the notion that blogs provide more depth and better analysis than other media outlets. The fact that blogs were not viewed as fair by the respondents but were still ranked credible constitutes another challenge to journalistic standards of fairness and objectivity. Abdulla, Garrison, Salwen, Driscoll, and Casey (2005) also found that online news in general is viewed as more biased than other media. Their survey, however, also established the higher credibility of online information over newspapers and television.

In their survey on the effects of audience participation on the perception of journalism, Lowrey and Anderson (2005) found that the definition of news is broadening. Two-thirds of the respondents used non-traditional news sources online to gather information. More than a quarter also personalized the news retrieved from the Internet. In addition, Choi, Watt, and Lynch (2006) analyzed the perceptions on credibility in regard to online information on the war in Iraq. They found that war opponents, who were in the minority in 2003, viewed online information as highly credible based on the greater diversity of information and the perception of less alignment with a pro-government position in comparison to traditional news media. Supporters of the war and people with neutral viewpoints gave online information lower credibility ratings. In conclusion, the researchers asked what balancing means in news reporting "when people can access a virtually limitless number of news sources."

Media Agenda Setters

Williams and Delli Carpini (2004), who had concluded that traditional media gate-keeping had broken down in the aftermath of the Clinton-Lewinsky scandal, were also the first scholars to claim the same for mass media agenda-setting. The researchers argued that traditional media journalists had not only lost their central gatekeeping position, but also their central position as agenda setters. "Traditional journalists are now one among many agenda setters and issue framers within the media…the new media environment with its multiple points of access and more continuous news cycle has increased the opportunities for less mainstream individuals and groups to influence public discourse" (p. 1225). While the news sites of the traditional media generally have similar editorial policies as their counterparts, independently developed Internet formats such as blogs are mostly responsible for the changes in gatekeeping and agenda setting. However, the readership of blogs has not reached levels that would allow conclusions on their effects on public opinion. Thirty-nine percent of Internet users in the United States read blogs in 2006 (Lenhart & Fox, 2006). Hargrove and Stempel (2007) came to the conclusion that blogs have not developed into a major source of news for the general public and are more of a media phenomenon.

Consequently, most research has focused on the intermedia agenda-setting effects of Internet formats. McCombs (2005) described the importance of research on the agenda-setting role of Internet formats as follows: "Blogs are part of the journalism landscape, but who sets whose agenda under what circumstances remains an open question. Intermedia agenda setting at both the first and second levels is likely to remain high on the journalism research agenda for a very long time" (p. 549).

The intermedia dimension of agenda-setting research developed in the late 1980s, most notably by Atwater, Fico, and Pizante (1987), Rogers and Dearing (1988), and Danielian and Reese (1989). In recent years this intermedia concept, which studies how the media influence themselves, has been applied to Internet-related research by a variety of scholars. Roberts, Wanta, and Dzwo (2002) were among the first scholars to analyze the effects of the traditional news media agenda on discussions on electronic bulletin boards during the 1996 presidential election. They found that *The New York Times,* The Associated Press, *Reuters, Time,* and *CNN* all had agenda-setting effects on the discussions, but also found that the impact of *The New York Times* was most significant, confirming previous findings that established the special influence of certain elite media. This approach was extended by Lee, Lancendorfer, and Lee (2005), who looked at intermedia agenda-setting effects in both directions. During the 2000 general election in South Korea, they documented agenda-setting effects of newspapers' agendas on the opinions posted on bulletin boards. They also established that discussions on bulletin boards had an influence on the newspapers' agenda. They concluded that traditional journalists use the Internet to gather a variety of opinions on issues and that the Internet has the power to shape public opinion by affecting the agendas of other media. This constituted a shift in Internet-related research towards a focus on the effects of the Internet rather than the effects of traditional media on online formats.

The growing influence of Internet-generated information on the traditional news media has led several scholars to analyze intermedia agenda-setting effects of Internet formats in political elections (Bichard, 2006; Davis, 2005; Verser & Wicks, 2006). Ku, Kaid, and Pfau (2003) found a strong influence of website campaigns on the traditional news agenda and public opinion. They studied the intermedia agenda-setting effects between the campaign websites and *The New York Times, The Washington Post,* ABC, CBS, and NBC in the 2000 presidential election and concluded that "Internet-based communication has established powerful new links between politicians and voters and created great impact on the information flow of the traditional news media" (p. 544).

With the emergence of blogs as a new influential Internet format during the last five years, most intermedia agenda-setting research has focused on the impact of these online journals on the traditional media agenda. Tremayne (2007) pointed out that this influence of blogs is greatest when they influence news events as a collective by creating a buzz. Lowrey (2006) also found that blogs derive their influence on the traditional media from a focus on partisan expression and stories that are based on alternative, non-elite sources and thereby become sources themselves. However, as Drezner and Farrell (2004) stressed, while the blogosphere is growing rapidly, only few blogs have agenda-setting power on the traditional media. Filter blogs serve as "focal points" (p. 35) that bring attention to less renowned blogs. The researchers also found that traditional media journalists tend to concentrate on the same filter weblogs. Through these filter blogs, it becomes easier and less time consuming for journalists to survey the blogosphere on a daily basis and select them as sources for stories.

Research on the agenda-setting power of blogs has mainly focused on the creation of buzz within the blogosphere, the increasing blogging during certain news events. Cornfield, Carson, Kalis, and Simon (2005) traced the buzz on filter blogs during the 2004 presidential campaign and compared it with the buzz in the traditional media, campaign statements, and Internet forums. They found that blogs had difficulties to influence other media when there was no advancement of the stories, such as results of an investigation. Overall, their study concluded that "blogger power, the capacity of blog operators to make buzz and influence decision makers, is circumstantial" (p. 2). However, they also found that bloggers served as guides for the traditional media to the discourse on the Internet. Schiffer (2006) also found in his analysis of blog buzz about the Downing Street Memo controversy during the 2004 presidential election that the issue was transferred into the traditional media, but was only covered there for a short time. The researcher concluded that activists have a better chance to influencing traditional media by targeting media agenda setters, e.g. politicians, rather than the traditional media themselves. However, hyperlinking within the blogosphere is the factor that makes blog buzz accessible to the traditional media. This has also led political campaigns to adopt the blog format for their information distribution purposes (Bichard, 2006; Trammell, Williams, Postelnicu, & Landreville, 2006; Williams, Trammell, Postelnicu, Landreville, & Martin, 2005).

Overall, the coverage of blogs in the traditional media has changed from a focus "on the sexy or 'hot' aspects of new media technology" (Perlmutter & McDaniel, 2005, p. 60) to the use of weblogs as sources in the reporting. Through the inherent agenda-setting power of news sources, blogs gain influence over the traditional media agenda. While Perlmutter and McDaniel (2005) found a sharp increase in mentioning of blogs in the traditional media between 1998 and 2005, Messner and DiStaso (2008) also analyzed the use of blogs as sources in *The New York Times* and *The Washington Post* from 2000 to 2005 and found steady increase of the overall number of articles. They found that the reporting on the weblog phenomenon did not increase as much as the use of weblogs as sources and the simple mentioning of weblogs in the articles. At the same time, however, blogs were also found to use traditional media 43 percent of the time as sources in the posts. Scott (2007) had similar findings with 49.5 percent of sources in blogs as traditional media in the 2004 presidential election.

While Lim (2006) found support for the notion of intermedia agenda-setting between online media and traditional media in South Korea, other scholars have also noted that it would be an oversimplification to state that online news sources set the agenda of the traditional media. Song (2007) studied the impact of online news services in South Korea on the traditional media reporting and argued that intermedia agenda-setting cannot only be studied by counting news stories and issues over time to build correlations, but that an in-depth analysis of the decision making process is necessary to fully understand the interaction of new and old media. This suggested approach would combine the gatekeeping and agenda-setting dimensions of the new media phenomenon.

Hyperlinking Networks

As mentioned above, the Internet is capable of creating a buzz, or intensive public discussion, on certain issues that consequently has the potential of influencing the traditional media agenda. The main characteristic that allows the creation of a buzz and that distinguishes Internet news formats from traditional media formats are interactivity and networking capabilities. Flew (2005) defined interactivity as a system "where each pattern of use leads the user down a distinctive 'pathway'" (p. 13). Hyperlinks make it possible to connect news websites with other websites and contribute to the creation of Internet networks. As the dominant search engine Google bases the rankings of its search results on the principles of interactivity, hyperlinking, and networking, success on the Internet is measured by the number of hyperlinks to a certain website. Therefore, "understanding interactivity is central to developing theory and research about new media," according to McMillan (2006, p. 205).

Tremayne (2004) was one of the first mass communication scholars to apply network theory to research on Internet news formats and has advanced this still developing research track the furthest to date. A content analysis of ten traditional news media websites between 1997 and 2001 found that the number of links associated with individual news stories increased sharply over time. The researcher concluded that the increase of hyperlinks will have a significant influence on the future of journalism: "If television news favors good pictures to hold an audience, we might expect Web editors to use links strategically to keep readers on their site" (p. 250). In addition, as hyperlinks allow editors to provide more context for the news stories, the news coverage on the Internet overall may become more driven by event reporting rather than contextual analysis.

Harp and Tremayne (2006) also applied network theory to the emerging blogosphere and detected through a discourse analysis that an inequality exists in the hyperlinking patterns of the blogosphere, which disadvantages female bloggers. While overall the blogosphere enables almost anybody to enter the public sphere, hyperlinking patterns give greater audience and thereby more power to certain websites and prevent others from gaining attention. As the scholars pointed out, ignored groups can increase their popularity on the Internet by creating their own hyperlinking network.

Further research into hyperlinking patterns of blogs drew the focus on the central opinion leaders within the blogosphere. Tremayne, Zheng, Lee, and Jeong (2006) identified several key blogs out of a sample of 70 blogs in the war blogosphere that connected the opposing sides, conservatives and liberals, in the discourse on the war in Iraq. The researchers concluded that blogs in a public limited to one issue—like the war—tend to link to blogs that support their viewpoints, but that there is space within the blogosphere for open discussion by utilizing these central blogs through hyperlinking. Trammell and Keshelashvili (2005) also examined 209 popular blogs and found that they reveal more about themselves and manage their impressions in their Internet presence than less popular blogs.

While the Internet and blogs in particular have certainly contributed to a more diverse media environment, the evolving research on online networks has shown that a hierarchy is developing within the new Internet formats. Thereby, some websites will gain more influence over the discourse on a certain issue than others. This is a concept similar to the structure of the traditional media. For this reason, Haas (2005) argued that the central filter blogs take on a role within the blogosphere similar to the one that elite media like *The New York Times, The Washington Post,* and the television networks play within the traditional media. Overall, however, research involving the concepts of interactivity and hyperlinking and their influence on the news flow is only emergent at this point. With the growing impact of Internet news formats and the transformation of the traditional media towards converged online news outlets, more research and scholarly attention will be necessary to explain this evolving phenomenon.

Revitalizing Uses and Gratifications

The increasing Internet penetration rate and the increasingly popular use of websites as sources of news has revitalized research utilizing the uses and gratifications model developed by Katz, Blumler, and Gurevitch (1974). Kaye and Johnson (2004) called it a "renaissance in the uses and gratifications tradition as scholars are increasingly interested in going beyond discovering who uses the Internet to examine why they use this new medium" (p. 197). The model has been criticized by mass communication scholars for being "too descriptive and insufficiently theoretical, and for relying too heavily on audiences for reporting their true motivations for media use" (Bucy, Gantz, &Wang, 2007, p. 150). However, an increasing number of scholars have employed the model for the study of Internet use (Flanagin & Metzger, 2001; LaRose & Eastin, 2004; Lin, 1999; Ogan & Cagiltay, 2006). Ruggerio (2000) even argued that the future development of mass communication theory inevitably must include a uses and gratifications dimension as it "has always provided a cutting-edge theoretical approach in the initial stages of each new mass communications medium: newspaper, radio and television, and now the Internet" (p. 3). Nevertheless, the researcher added that the traditional uses and gratifications approach must incorporate the concepts of interactivity and hypertextuality as well as demassification and asynchroneity to account for a greater media selection menu and the breakdown of a set time scheme under which news was delivered in the past, which gives the audience greater ability to choose its media use.

While only few studies have analyzed uses and gratifications aspects of the online news and information environment to date, an increasing number of studies has explored the adoption and use patterns on the Internet in general. Charney and Greenberg (2002) found eight gratifications dimensions related to Internet use in a 1996 survey: keeping informed, diversion/entertainment, peer identity, good feelings, communications, sights and sounds, career, and coolness. Nevertheless, the researchers pointed out that the gratification of keeping informed was so dominant "that it encompasses virtually all of the apparent uses" (p. 400). In two subsequent surveys during the 1996 and 2000 presidential elections, Kaye and Johnson (2002, 2004) found that online political information was primarily used for guidance, meaning that those interested in politics rely on the Internet for political information. In their second survey in 2000, the researchers also examined the motivations for using message boards and electronic mailing lists and found that guidance was a weaker indicator for use and entertainment/social utility, information seeking, and convenience were stronger indicators. Overall, the researchers found that convenience became a weaker motivator for Internet use, which they interpreted to be a result of maturing and more skilled users seeking specific information online.

In addition to studying motivations for Internet use, several scholars have conducted uses and gratifications research with a focus on how audiences differentiate in their use between online and traditional news formats. Tewksbury and Althaus (2000) explored in an experiment how the greater selection opportunities for online newspaper users impact the knowledge acquisition and found that online users of *The New York Times* read fewer international, national and political stories and were less likely to recall public affairs events. The researchers suggested that additional content online diverts readers' attention away from public affairs stories and that differences in the online layout reduce importance cues and have an effect on which stories are noticed and read by the readers. They warned that "with this increased opportunity to personalize the flow of news, fewer people may be exposed to politically important stories. As a consequence, online news providers may inadvertently develop a readership that is more poorly informed than traditional newspaper readers" (p. 459). The findings of Lin, Salwen, and Abdulla (2005), however, partially contradicted this assumption. Their survey showed that the information scanning gratification was stronger for online use than for traditional media use and they concluded that the Internet was the best tool for newspapers to compete with cable news networks in the 24-hour news cycle: "If newspapers are able to attract more users to their Web sites, they may be able to help stabilize existing users and readers" (p. 234). This was underlined by the findings of Dimmick, Chen, and Li (2004), who found that the Internet has a "competitive displacement effect on traditional news media in the daily news domain" (p. 19). Their survey showed that 33.7 percent of the broadcast television viewers and 28 percent of newspaper readers used these media less often after they started using the Internet for news. The researchers concluded that the new medium provides more contemporary solutions to gratify audiences' needs and thereby competes with the traditional media.

Methodologies

Internet-related studies have employed a variety of research methodologies, generally those that are common practice in communication and mass communication research. Nevertheless, Internet-related research still differs in its overall distribution of the applied methodologies from the broader discipline. While the communication field in general has a greater emphasis on quantitative than qualitative methods, this emerging field of research has had a greater emphasis on qualitative methods to date. Kim and Weaver (2002) found that between 1996 and 1999 only 26.7 percent of journal articles on Internet-related research used quantitative methods. Cho and Khang (2006) stated that between 1994 and 2003 the most used methods in communication research articles related to the Internet were critiques and essays (30.8 percent), surveys (19.3 percent), and content analyses (16 percent). They found experiments to have a stronger presence in advertising and marketing related research than in communication research overall. However, they also found a more evenly distributed use of quantitative and qualitative methods, with over 46 percent of Internet-related communication journal articles using quantitative methods.

Interestingly, the researchers also detected a methodological difference between leading communication journals and Internet-specific journals. The dominant method in the leading journals was survey (29.4 percent), while critiques and essays (39.6 percent) dominated the methodologies in the Internet-specific journals. This, on one hand, underlines the more rigorous review process of the leading journals, but on the other hand also stresses the need for exploratory research in an emerging field of mass communication research. Researchers report that 71.5 percent of the Internet-related research in communication journals was exploratory, 24.1 percent descriptive and only 4.3 percent explanatory. Overall, only 14.5 percent of all Internet-related journal articles used a theoretical framework, while 27.2 percent generated hypotheses. However, the researchers found an increase of theory-driven research when comparing the time frames of 1994 to 1998 (8.7 percent) and 1999 to 2003 (16.3 percent). Cho and Khang (2006) concluded "that Internet-related research is becoming more theoretically sound," but that "more explanatory research studies are needed" (p. 158).

Critiques and Essays

Many of the early studies on Internet-related communication took exploratory approaches through media critiques and essayist analysis that attempted to modify existing theories. Ruggerio (2000) for instance used a critical analysis of the historical development of the uses and gratifications model to justify its application in Internet research. From the application of uses and gratifications in the 1950s and the development of the model in the 1970s, the scholar developed theoretical modifications that allow researchers to apply the model to the contemporary media environment. Williams and Carpini (2000) also used a historical-critical approach to outline the changes to the gatekeeping environment in the late 1990s. They described media incidents, in which the traditional media gatekeepers were circumvented by new Internet formats. In a subsequent study, Williams and Delli Carpini (2004) extended their theoretical modification to agenda-setting theory, by closely examining media incidents, in which Internet formats influenced the traditional media news agenda. While these exploratory approaches were mostly dominant in the development stage of the Internet, they are still valued today within the discipline as new Internet formats continue to develop. Haas (2005), for instance, wrote an essay in which the development of blogs and their increasing influence are analyzed, also contributing to the developing model of intermedia agenda-setting within the blogosphere.

Surveys

An increasing number of research studies has used survey methodologies to describe and explain Internet communication. Johnson and Kaye (2002) used a Web-based survey technique to explore the credibility of online and traditional media. They used a convenience sample of politically interested Internet users, as a central registry of Internet users is not available. Before and after the 1996 presidential election, the survey was promoted for a total of one month on newsgroups, mailing lists as well as chat rooms and several websites also helped to promote participation through hyperlinks. This resulted in 442 responses. Johnson and Kaye (2004) used a similar technique when they analyzed the credibility of blogs. They used a Web-based survey that was posted online for one month in 2003 and established links from 131 blogs as well as bulletin boards and mailing lists to sample blog readers. Again, since a random sample of blog users is impossible to generate, they used a convenience sample, which resulted in 3,747 responses. Response rates cannot be assessed with these techniques. However, other researchers are still relying on the more traditional mail and telephone surveys, which generally allow the researcher to gain more control over sampling and responses than Web-based surveys. Abdulla et al. (2005) conducted a national telephone survey to assess online news credibility. They drew a probability sample from all states and completed 536 interviews, which constituted a response rate of 41 percent. Other researchers also use electronic mail to distribute surveys. In a study to analyze the gatekeeping role of online newspaper editors in 2004, Singer (2006) sampled the largest newspaper in each state and other daily newspapers with circulations over 250,000 and identified the news editors. Depending on the speed of responses, a total of one to four e-mails were sent to 77 editors. This resulted in 43 responses, a rate of 61 percent.

Content Analyses

Similar to the increase in survey research, quantitative content analyses are more frequently used in Internet-related studies in recent years. Especially when measuring the influence of new media formats on the traditional media, researchers rely on content analyses instruments to measure the degree of influence. Ku, Kaid, and Pfau (2003) studied the impact of campaign websites on traditional media during the 2000 presidential campaign. They sampled content from the *New York Times* and the *Washington Post* as well as the television networks ABC, CBS, and NBC and the news releases from the candidates' websites during three constructed weeks. In addition they drew secondary data from public opinion polls. The researchers developed rank orders of issues for the media, campaign and public agendas and used cross-lagged comparisons to determine correlations between the agendas. Lim (2006) used a similar approach when exploring intermedia agenda-setting effects among online news media in South Korea. However, as in most intermedia analysis, the researcher only conducted content analyses. A content sample was drawn from an online news agency and two online newspapers in two constructed weeks. The researcher also developed issue agendas from the sample content and analyzed correlations through cross-lagged comparisons to establish causal relationships between variables in different time periods. Content analysis is also utilized in studies that explore networks on the Internet. Trammell and Keshelashvili (2005) identified 209 single-authored blogs from a popularity ranking based on hyperlinks and examined their content on impression management tactics and self-presentation. Tremayne (2004), on the other hand, sampled ten traditional media websites and examined their hyperlinks over a five-year period.

Experiments

Experimental studies, which allow researchers to identify causal relationships, are still rare in research on the Internet as a news medium. This also explains the low rate of explanatory research to date. Tewksbury and Althaus (2000) conducted one of the few experiments to study differences in knowledge acquisition among readers of online and print versions of the *New York Times*. The researchers sampled student volunteers into three groups, one of them a control group, another one exposed to the online version of the newspaper, and the third exposed to the print version for five consecutive days. The posttest of the experiment tested the participants on how much knowledge they had acquired and revealed differences between reading the online or printed versions of the newspaper. Bucy (2003) also used an experimental design to analyze the synergy effects between on-air and online network news. Students and older adults were sampled into eight groups, which were exposed to television news online, online news online, television and online news, and no exposure and then completed media credibility questionnaires.

Future Research

While the field of Internet communication has already developed a broad body of research, the field in general is still emerging as a research discipline at this point. Research has explored the issues and uses of the Internet as a mass medium, but has only recently started to analyze the effects of Internet communication. More empirical research is needed to explain Internet phenomena and their consequences for society. This includes more frequent applications of existing theories, which also have to be further modified to suit this new media environment, as well as the development of Internet specific models and theories. Future research approaches should include the following five characteristics:

Collaborative Information

The concept of Web 2.0 so far has only been explored through research on the blogosphere. Only a few researchers have turned their attention to the wiki concept, which has become influential with Internet users through the growing popularity of the online encyclopedia Wikipedia, which changes the way information is generated. In addition, online portals such as YouTube, Facebook, MySpace, and Flickr have not been explored at all, but are likely to cause even greater changes to the overall media environment.

New Gatekeepers

Elitist gatekeepers are likely to be replaced by collective information gathering models. While blogs have already posed a challenge to traditional media gatekeepers, multimedia search portals such as Google will only intensify these challenges. The search rankings of Google and other search engines are most likely to determine which information is accessed by Internet users. As Google interlinks more news content of traditional and online media outlets, its strengthening gatekeeping position within the news flow needs much more scholarly attention.

Hyperlinking as Agenda Setting

Some researchers have focused their research on the concepts of interactivity and hyperlinking, but much more empirical research is needed to explore the gatekeeping and agenda-setting dimensions of hyperlinking on the Internet. Hyperlinking, on the one hand, can be used as a new way of gatekeeping, while on the other hand it can also be utilized as an intermedia agenda-setting device. Future research should engage with the question of which medium links to which medium, and with what effect.

Intermedia Sourcing

Some research has indicated that traditional media and online media increasingly use each other as sources in their reporting and editorializing. Research should explore whether Internet formats are used by the traditional media as a way to explore online buzz and opinion. In addition, research is needed to analyze under which conditions one medium becomes a source for the other.

Mainstreaming Internet Formats

Traditional media organizations are increasingly adopting the newly developed Internet formats such as blogs. Research should not only analyze the adoption rates, but also the evolution of these initially alternative formats into mainstream media applications.

Summary

When the Internet made its debut in the mid-1990s, it began a revolution in communication that continues to evolve. This chapter has discussed how the Internet now challenges the gatekeeping function of the traditional news media with its immediate dissemination of information and the increase in the number of bloggers. The rise in the credibility of online information has steadily increased, and online outlets now compete with the media giants for agenda setting. The intermedia concept—the way that media influences other media, has increased as a line of research as the Internet becomes more dominant with respect to its affect on other types of media.

The ability of the Internet to create intensive public discussion through hyperlinks—something that printed matter cannot accomplish. The Internet has revitalized research in the uses and gratification model, and has spawned a multitude of research in many diverse areas, surveys, content analysis, hyperlinking, etc.

While the Internet is still evolving as a field of scholarly inquiry, social media and social networking sites have made Marshall McLuhan's global village a reality in much shorter time than anyone could have imagined. Humans now connect in cyberspace through social media, and the implications of this are the focus of the next chapter.

Questions For Discussion

1. How has the Internet changed the role of the traditional gatekeepers? Who are the new gatekeepers?
2. As the amount of information available on the Internet has grown, how has the perception of that information changed?
3. How does a theory like Uses and Gratifications apply to the Internet?
4. Why does hyperlinking provide more information and a more complete view of information contained on the Internet?
5. What is the essence of the intermedia concept?

References

Abdulla, R. A., Garrison, B., Salwen, M. B., Driscoll, P. D., & Casey, D. (2005). Online news credibility. In M. B. Salwen, B. Garrison, & P. D. Driscoll (Eds.), *Online news and the public* (pp. 147–163). Mahwah, NJ: Erlbaum.

Atwater, T., Fico, F., & Pizante, G. (1987). Reporting on the state legislature: A case study of intermedia agenda-setting. *Newspaper Research Journal,* 8(2), 53–61.

Barnett, G. A., & Sung, E. (2005). Culture and structure of the international hyperlink network. Journal of *Computer-Mediated Communication,* 11(1), article 11. Retrieved June 5, 2007, from http://jcmc.indiana.edu/vol11/issue1/barnett.html.

Bichard, S. L. (2006). Building blogs: A multi-dimensional analysis of the distribution of frames on the 2004 presidential candidate web sites. *Journalism & Mass Communication Quarterly,* 83(2), 329–345.

Bucy, E. P. (2003). Media credibility reconsidered: Synergy effects between on-air and online news. *Journalism & Mass Communication Quarterly,* 80(2), 247–264.

Bucy, E. P., Gantz, W., & Wang, Z. (2007). Media technology and the 24-hour news cycle. In C. A. Lin & D. J. Atkin (Eds.), *Communication technology and social change: Theory and implications.* (pp. 143–166). Mahwah, NJ: Erlbaum.

Burnett, R., & Marshall, P. D. (2003). *Web theory: An introduction.* London: Routledge.

Cassidy, W. P. (2005). Web-only online sites more likely to post editorial policies than are daily paper sites. *Newspaper Research Journal,* 26(1), 53–58.

Charney, T., & Greenberg, B. S. (2002). Uses and gratifications of the Internet. In C. A. Lin & D. J. Atkin (Eds.), *Communication technology and society: Audience adoption and uses* (pp. 379–407). Cresskill, NJ: Hampton Press.

Cho, C. H., & Khang, H. K. (2006). The state of Internet-related research in communications, marketing, and advertising: 1994–2003. *Journal of Advertising,* 35(3), 143–163.

Choi, J. H., Watt, J. H., & Lynch, M. (2006). Perceptions of news credibility about the war in Iraq. Why war opponents perceived the internet as the most credible medium. *Journal of ComputerMediated Communication,* 12(1), article 11. Retrieved June 5, 2007, from http://jcmc. indiana.edu/vol12/issue1/choi.html.

Cornfield, M., Carson, J., Kalis, A., & Simon, E. (2005). *Buzz, blogs, and beyond: The Internet and the national discourse in the fall of 2004.* Pew Internet & American Life Project. Retrieved February 15, 2006, from http://www.pewinternet.org.

Danielian, L. H., & Reese, S. D. (1989). A closer look at intermedia influences on agenda setting: The cocaine issue of 1986. In P. Shoemaker (Ed.), *Communication campaigns about drugs: Government,media and the public* (pp. 47–66). Hillsdale, NJ: Erlbaum.

Davis, S. (2005). Presidential campaigns fine-tune online strategies. *Journalism Studies,* 6(2), 241–244.

Deuze, M. (2003). The web and its journalisms: Considering the consequences of different types of news media online. *New Media & Society,* 5(2), 203–230.

Dimitrova, D. V., & Neznanski, M. (2006). Online journalism and the war in cyberspace: A comparison between U.S. and international newspapers. *Journal of Computer-Mediated*

Communication, 12(1), article 11. Retrieved June 5, 2007, from http://jcmc.indiana.edu/vol12/issue1/dimitrova.html.

Dimmick, J., Chen, Y., & Li, Z. (2004). Competition between the Internet and traditional news media: The gratification-opportunities niche dimension. *The Journal of Media Economics, 17*(1), 19–33.

DiStaso, M. W., Messner, M., & Stacks, D. W. (2007). The wiki factor: A study of reputation management. In S. C. Duhé (Ed.), *New media & public relations* (pp. 121–133). New York: Peter Lang.

Drezner, D. W., & Farrell, H. (2004). Web of influence. *Foreign Policy, 145,* 32–40.

Flanagin, A. J., & Metzger, M. J. (2000). Perceptions of internet information credibility. *Journalism & Mass Communication Quarterly, 77*(3), 515–540.

Flanagin, A. J., & Metzger, M. J. (2001). Internet use in the contemporary media environment. *Human Communication Research, 27*(1), 153–181.

Flew, T. (2005). *New media: An introduction.* Victoria, Australia: Oxford University Press.

Haas, T. (2005). From "public journalism" to the "public's journalism"? Rhetoric and reality in the discourse on weblogs. *Journalism Studies, 6*(3), 387–396.

Hargrove, T., & Stempel, G. H., III. (2007). Use of blogs as a source of news presents little threat to mainline news media. *Newspaper Research Journal, 25*(1), 99–102.

Harp, D., & Tremayne, M. (2006). The gendered blogosphere: Examining inequality using network and feminist theory. *Journalism & Mass Communication Quarterly, 53*(2), 247–264.

Hoffman, L. H. (2006). Is internet content different after all? A content analysis of mobilizing information in online and print newspapers. *Journalism & Mass Communication Quarterly, 53*(1), 58–67.

Horrigan, J. B. (2006a). *Home broadband adoption* 2006. Pew Internet & American Life Project. Retrieved April 5, 2007, from http://www.pewinternet.org.

Horrigan, J. B. (2006b). Politics online. *Pew Internet & American Life Project.* Retrieved April 5, 2007, from http://www.pewinternet.org.

Horrigan, J. B. (2007). Wireless Internet access. *Pew Internet & American Life Project.* Retrieved April 5, 2007, from http://www.pewinternet.org.

Johnson, T. J., & Kaye, B. K. (1998). Cruising is believing? Comparing Internet and traditional sources on media credibility measures. *Journalism & Mass Communication Quarterly, 75*(2), 325–340.

Johnson, T. J., & Kaye, B. K. (2000). Using is believing: The influence of reliance on the credibility of online political information among politically interested internet users. *Journalism & Mass Communication Quarterly, 77*(4), 865–879.

Johnson, T. J., & Kaye, B. K. (2002). Webelievability: A path model examining how convenience and reliance predict online credibility. *Journalism & Mass Communication Quarterly, 79*(3), 619–642.

Johnson, T. J., & Kaye, B. K. (2004). Wag the blog: How reliance on traditional media and the internet influence credibility perceptions of weblogs among blog users. *Journalism & Mass Communication Quarterly, 51*(3), 622–642.

Kahn, R., & Kellner, D. (2004). New media and internet activism: From the "Battle of Seattle" to blogging. New Media & Society, 6(1), 87–95.

Katz, E., Blumler, J. G., & Gurevitch, M. (1974). The uses of mass communications: Current perspectives on gratifications research. Beverly Hills, CA: Sage.

Kaye, B. K., & Johnson, T. J. (2002). Online and in the know: Uses and gratifications of the web for political information. Journal of Broadcasting & Electronic Media, 46(1), 54–71.

Kaye, B. K., & Johnson, T. J. (2004). A web for all reasons: Uses and gratifications of Internet components for political information. Telematics and Informatics, 21, 197–223.

Kim, S. T., & Weaver, D. (2002). Communication research about the Internet: A thematic meta-analysis. New Media & Society, 4(4), 518–538.

Klopfenstein, B. (2002). The Internet and web as communication media. In C. A. Lin & D. J. Atkin (Eds.), Communication technology and society: Audience adoption and uses (pp. 353–378). Cresskill, NJ: Hampton Press.

Kovach, B., & Rosenstiel, T. (2001). The elements of journalism. New York: Three Rivers Press.

Ku, G., Kaid, L. L., & Pfau, M. (2003). The impact of web site campaigning on traditional news media and public information processing. Journalism & Mass Communication Quarterly, 80(3), 528–547.

LaRose, R., & Eastin, M. S. (2004). A social cognitive theory of Internet uses and gratifications: Toward a new model of media attendance. Journal of Broadcasting & Electronic Media, 48(3), 358–377.

Lee, B., Lancendorfer, K. M., & Lee, K. J. (2005). Agenda-setting and the Internet: The intermedia influence of Internet bulletin boards on newspaper coverage of the 2000 general election in South Korea. Asian Journal of Communication, 15(1), 57–71.

Lenhart, A., & Fox, S. (2006). Bloggers: A portrait of the internet's new storytellers. Pew Internet & American Life Project. Retrieved November 24, 2006, from http://www.pewinternet.org.

Lim, J. (2006). A cross-lagged analysis of agenda setting among online news media. Journalism & Mass Communication Quarterly, 83(2), 298–312.

Lin, C. (1999). Online-service adoption likelihood. Journal of Advertising Research. 39(2), 79–89.

Lin, C., & Salwen, M. B., & Abdulla, R. A. (2005). Uses and gratifications of online and offline news: New wine in an old bottle. In M. B. Salwen, B. Garrison, & P. D. Driscoll (Eds.), Online news and the public (pp. 221–236). Mahwah, NJ: Erlbaum.

Lowrey, W. (2006). Mapping the journalism-blogging relationship. Journalism, 7(4), 477–500.

Lowrey, W., & Anderson (2005). The journalists behind the curtain: Participatory functions of the internet and their impact on perceptions of the work of journalism. Journal of Computer-Mediated Communication, 12(1), article 11. Retrieved June 5, 2007, from http://jcmc.indiana.edu/vol10/is-sue3/lowrey.html.

Madden, M. (2006). Internet penetration and impact. Pew Internet & American Life Project. Retrieved April, 5, 2007, from http://www.pewinternet.org.

Matheson, D. (2004). Weblogs and the epistemology of the news: Some trends in online journalism. New Media & Society, 6(4), 443–468.

McCombs, M. (2005). A look at agenda-setting: Past, present and future. Journalism Studies, 6(4), 543–557.

McCombs, M., & Shaw, D. (1972). The agenda-setting function of the media. *Public Opinion Quarterly, 36,* 176–187.

McMillan, S. J. (2006). Exploring models of interactivity from multiple research traditions: Users, documents and systems. In L. A. Lievrouw & S. Livingstone (Eds.), *The handbook of new media* (pp. 162–182). London: Sage.

Messner, M., & DiStaso, M. W. (2008). The source cycle: How traditional media and weblogs use each other as sources. *Journalism Studies, 9*(3), 447–463.

Messner, M., & Terilli, S. (2007). Gates wide open: The impact of weblogs on the gatekeeping role of the traditional media in the 2004 presidential election. *Florida Communication Journal, 35*(1), 1–14.

Ogan, C. L., & Cagiltay, K. (2006). Confession, revelation and storytelling: Patterns of use on a popular Turkish website. *New Media & Society, 5*(5), 801–823.

Perlmutter, D. P., & McDaniel, M. (2005). The ascent of blogging. Nieman Reports, 59(3), 60–64.

Poor, N. (2006). Playing internet curveball with traditional media gatekeepers: Pitcher Curt Schilling and Boston Red Sox fans. *Convergence, 12*(1), 41–53.

Rainie, L., & Shermak, J. (2005). Search engine use. *Pew Internet & American Life Project.* Retrieved April 5, 2007, from http://www.pewinternet.org.

Roberts, M., Wanta, W., & Dzwo, T.-H. (2002). Agenda setting and issue salience online. *Communication Research, 29*(4), 452–465.

Rogers, E. M., & Dearing, J. W. (1988). Agenda-setting research: Where has it been, where is it going? *Communication Yearbook, 11,* 555–594.

Ruggerio, T. E. (2000). Uses and gratifications theory in the 21st century. *Mass Communication & Society, 3*(1), 3–37.

Ruggiero, T. E., & Winch, S. P. (2004). The media downing of Pierre Salinger: Journalistic mistrust of the internet as a news sources. *Journal of Computer-Mediated Communication, 10*(2), article 8 Retrieved June 5, 2007, from http://jcmc.indiana.edu/vol10/issue2/ruggiero.html.

Schiffer, A. J. (2006). Blogswarms and press norms: News coverage of the Downing Street Memo controversy. *Journalism & Mass Communication Quarterly, 53*(3), 494–510.

Scott, D. T. (2007). Pundits in muckrakers' clothing: Political blogs and the 2004 U.S. presidential election. In M. Tremayne (Ed.), *Blogging, citizenship, and the future of media* (pp. 39–57). New York: Routledge.

Shoemaker, P. J. (1991). *Gatekeeping.* Newbury Park, CA: Sage.

Singer, J. B. (1997). Still guarding the gate? The newspaper journalist's role in an on-line world. *Convergence, 3*(1), 72–89.

Singer, J. B. (2001). The metro wide web: Changes in newspapers' gatekeeping role online. *Journalism & Mass Communication Quarterly, 75*(1), 65–80.

Singer, J. B. (2003a). Campaign contributions: Online newspaper coverage of election 2000. *Journalism & Mass Communication Quarterly, 50*(1), 39–56.

Singer, J. B. (2003b). Who are these guys? The online challenge to the notion of journalistic professionalism. *Journalism, 4*(2), 139–163.

Singer, J. B. (2006). Stepping back from the gate: Online newspaper editors and the co-production of content in campaign 2004. *Journalism & Mass Communication Quarterly*, 53(2), 265–280.

Song, Y. (2007). Internet news media and issue development: A case study on the roles of independent online news services as agenda-builders for anti-US protests in South Korea. *New Media & Society*, 9(1), 71–92.

Tewksbury, D., & Althaus, S. L. (2000). Differences in knowledge acquisition among readers of the paper and online versions of a national newspaper. *Journalism & Mass Communication Quarterly*, 77(3), 457–479.

Tomasello, T. K. (2001). The status of Internet-based research in five leading communication journals, 1994–1999. *Journalism & Mass Communication Quarterly*, 78(4), 659–674.

Trammell, K. D., & Keshelashvili, A. (2005). Examining the new influencers: A self-presentation study of A-list blogs. *Journalism & Mass Communication Quarterly*, 82(4), 968–982.

Trammell, K. D., Williams, A. P., Postelnicu, M., & Landreville, K. D. (2006). Evolution of online campaigning: Increasing interactivity in candidate web sites and blogs through text and technical features. *Mass Communication & Society*, 9(1), 21–44.

Tremayne, M. (2004). The web of context: Applying network theory to the use of hyperlinks in journalism on the web. *Journalism & Mass Communication Quarterly*, 81(2), 237–253.

Tremayne, M. (2007). *Blogging, citizenship and the future of media.* New York: Routledge.

Tremayne, M., Zheng, N., Lee, J. K., Jeong, J. (2006). Issue politics on the Web: Applying network theory to the war blogosphere. *Journal of Computer-Mediated Communication*, 12(1), article 15. Retrieved June 5, 2007, from http://jcmc.indiana.edu/vol12/issue1/tremayne.html.

Verser, R., & Wicks, R. H. (2006). Managing voter impressions: The use of images on presidential candidate web sites during the 2000 campaign. *Journal of Communication*, 56, 178–197.

Wall, M. (2005). Blogs of war. *Journalism*, 6(2), 153–172.

Wall, M. (2006). Blogging Gulf War II. *Journalism Studies,* 7(1), 111–126.

White, D. M. (1950). The "gate keeper": A case study in the selection of news. *Journalism Quarterly*, 27, 383–390.

Williams, A. P., Trammell, K. D., Postelnicu, M., Landreville, K. D., & Martin, J. D. (2005). Blogging and hyperlinking: Use of the Web to enhance viability during the 2004 US campaign. *Journalism Studies*, 6(2), 177–186.

Williams, B. A., & Delli Carpini, M. X. (2000). Unchained reaction: The collapse of media gatekeeping and the Clinton-Lewinsky scandal. *Journalism*, 1(1), 61–85.

Williams, B. A., & Delli Carpini, M. X. (2004). Monica and Bill all the time and everywhere: the collapse of gatekeeping and agenda setting in the new media environment. *The American Behavioral Scientist,* 47(9), 1208–1230.

Chapter 13

Understanding Social Media from the Media Ecological Perspective

Susan B. Barnes

T he ability of the Internet to facilitate human relationships has grown to heights than no one could have expected in the early days of the Internet. Facebook has changed the way people socialize, and according to some, has led to the downfall of several Middle East dictators. The Media Ecological Perspective asserts that this change in human behavior will affect all other aspects of human communication and is the focus of this chapter.

Learning Objectives For This Chapter

- Explain the difference between mass media and digital media
- Identify the relationship between the media ecological perspective transactional view of communication
- Understand the differences between computer mediated communication and face-to-face communication
- Describe the types of communication that can be called social media
- Understand how the internet changes the way people interactively communicate across space
- Identify how peer-to-peer networks can be used to build social capital in online communities

In 1962, Marshall McLuhan envisioned a world in which electric media would extend the human embrace on a worldwide scale and create a new type of global village. Although his vision tends to be interpreted as a technological phenomenon, it is equally, if not more so, a human one. At a time when television and mass media messages dominated the media landscape, it was difficult to see the human communication aspect of media change—the use of media to facilitate human relationships. However, starting with the telegraph and telephone, media environments have gradually come to replace many face-to-face contexts in which interpersonal interactions occur. Utilizing a media ecological perspective, this [article] will describe how mediated contexts facilitate interpersonal human communication and how computers are now being used to initiate, support, and develop communication exchanges between people. Today, interpersonal communication takes place in mediated contexts and software developers are creating social computing tools to facilitate this process. The study of computer-mediated communication (CMC) explores how mediated environments support and extend the process of human communication and social computing examines the tools that facilitate this process.

The study of media is not only a technological endeavor. It also includes the human side of technological change (see Hickman, 1990; Postman, 1985 & 1992). Schroeder (1996) argued "technological and social change must be examined conjointly at several inter-related levels" (p. 137). On a basic level, understanding interpersonal communication in a mediated world requires awareness about how one person communicates with another using a communication medium. By focusing on how the interpersonal communication process is altered when moving from face-to-face to mediated contexts, the media ecological view can be utilized to study CMC and social media because it examines changes in communication patterns, such as the shift from broadcast mass media systems to interactive digital systems. What are the characteristic differences between these systems and how will the shift from one system to another alter the process of communication? In terms of interpersonal communication, what are the differences between communicating face-to-face and in a mediated context? How will these differences influence interpersonal communication and social activities? These are central questions asked in a basic media ecological analysis.

Interactivity is a key characteristic technological difference between mass media (television, radio) and digital media (computers, internet). With the introduction of digital communication, scholars are now developing interactive models to describe how human communication occurs in mediated space. An example is Rafaeli and Sudweeks' (1998) "One Way, Two Way, and Interactive Models of Communication." These models visualize the process of sending a one-way (mass) message, as well as interactive (interpersonal) exchanges between two people. Another visualization of this process is the one-to-one and many-to-many communication models, topics that were first discussed by computer scientists Licklider and Taylor (1968) (also see Barnes, 2003). Once a characteristic difference is discovered in a medium, the next question is how does the introduction of interactivity in mediated environments alter or change the process of communication? A simple answer is that interactivity enables two people to directly exchange personal messages in a mediated context.

A media ecological study of CMC also explores the similarities and differences between face-to-face and mediated communication contexts (Barnes, 2001; Rheingold, 1993; Turkle, 1995). For example, the primary form of communication in email is the exchange of written text instead of spoken language. Early CMC studies explored how this shift in linguistic codes influenced communication behaviors (Baym, 2000; Jones, 1995; Hiltz & Turoff, 1978; Murray, 1991; Rice & Love, 1987, Sproull & Kiesler, 1991; Walther, 1996; zuboff, 1988). For example, textual exchanges led to the development of exaggerated behaviors between communicators. Researchers speculated that CMC would lead to the sharing of impersonal messages due to the lack of facial and tonal cues.

Moreover an underlying assumption of interpersonal communication research tends to be the notion that interpersonal communication must take place in a face-to-face context, but for a number of years media scholars have been challenging this idea (Gumpert & Cathcart, 1986; Horton & Wohl, 1956/1986; Meyrowitz, 1985; Reeves & Nass, 1996). Ironically, an early description of the human communication process was based on telephone communication systems (a mediated context), but the telephone as an interpersonal communication context is often ignored in basic texts (Adler et al., 2005). In contrast, media ecologists (Barnes, Strate, Jacobs, Gibson) have been observing how mediated contexts have gradually been replacing face-to-face ones in the process of interpersonal communication.

The Media Ecological View

A number of writers have utilized the ecological metaphor to describe media in terms of perceptual and information space (Burnett, 2004; Davenport, 1997; Nardi & O'Day, 1999; Rennie & Mason, 2003). Although "ecology" is a popular metaphor for the study of information space, there is a theoretical perspective associated with the idea of media ecology. As a theoretical concept, the media ecological approach developed from the work of Marshall McLuhan (1964, 1962) and the Toronto School of Communication (Innis, 1951; Olson, 1994). Neil Postman and his various students (Barnes, 2001, 2003; Levinson, 1997, 1999; Meyrowitz, 1985; Strate, 1999) graduating from the Media Ecology Program at New York University further developed the concept in the United States. Media ecological principles include: all technological change is a Faustian bargain; technological change is not additive, it changes everything; the symbolic forms of technologies differ, leading to different intellectual and emotional biases; when the conditions in which we attend to media change, different media have social biases; and different technical and economic structures will contribute to media content biases. This is a systemic approach to communication that examines "the leading role that media play in influencing meanings and minds, ways of life and world views" (Barnes & Strate, 1996: 182). Media biases include space/time, sensory, intellectual, social, emotional, political, symbolic, and content biases.

From a media ecological point of view, introducing a new technology into a culture will alter the culture because the communication ecology of the social system will change. How that change will occur is dependent upon the culture. For example, television in American culture tends to take the form of entertainment because the United States is a capitalist country (Postman, 1985). Advertising is a central component of American television programming and entertainment programming attracts viewers who will be exposed to the commercial messages. Thus, commercial television in the United States tends to have a bias toward entertainment content. In contrast, Singapore is a dictatorship and the government edits and censors entertainment content to better conform to social ideals. Additionally, the government will often broadcast messages to further its political and social agendas. It is technology and society together that shape our communication environments.

Media ecologists contend that one change in a communication system will alter the entire environment. This reflects a systemic position and media ecology can ideologically be related to systems theory and cybernetics. Norbert Wiener (1954) created the concept of cybernetics, the science of communication and control. During World War II, feedback and control were applied to technology to foster the relationship between human and machine integration. Today, these ideas are applied to human-computer interaction (HCI), which describes human interaction with technology. A central idea of cybernetics and HCI is to help enable humans to be more efficient machine operators. In contrast, CMC tends to study the ways in which people exchange messages between themselves.

According to Postman (1979: 4), "Cybernetics is merely a synonym for ecology" because both examine how systems alter when a new element or change is introduced into the process. A media ecological view considers human-machine interactions to be included in the ecology of CMC environments because both humans and machines are part of the message system. The symbolic methods used in technology interaction can influence the interpersonal communication process. For instance, people need to have a computer and know how to use it before they have access to internet interpersonal communication.

Both the media ecological perspective and the transactional view of human communication examine systems and how systems alter interpersonal communication behaviors (see Greller & Barnes, 1993). In media ecology, the direction in which messages can flow or be exchanged is an important characteristic to be examined. Ong (1982: 176) states: "Human communication is never one-way. Always, it not only calls for a response but is shaped in its very form and content by anticipated response." The transactional or systems approach is a circular model that can include the communication environment along with personal and cultural experiences (see Adler et al., 2005). The media ecological approach looks at the total communication process. For example, mass media supports a one-directional message flow and the internet is multidirectional (interactive), which includes one-to-one (interpersonal communication); one-to-many (human and mass communication); and many-to-many (organizational communication). Media ecological writings about internet interpersonal communication include the works of Strate et al. (1996, 2003), Gibson and Oviedo (2000), and Barnes (2001).

In addition to a directional bias, media also have a sensory bias. According to McLuhan (1964), global networks extend the human nervous system. Making social connections through the internet exposes individuals to a wider variety of ideas and worldviews. Thus, people are exposed to many more ideas than they would be when situated in a single geographic location. The internet's sensory bias is one that extends the human nervous system and fosters the formation of a global village. Thus, an intellectual worldview shift can occur as people become more aware of global issues. McLuhan (1964: 19) says:

> Today, after more than a century of electric technology, we have extended our central nervous system itself in a global embrace, abolishing both space and time as far as our planet is concerned. Rapidly, we approach the final phase of the extension of man—technological simulation of consciousness, when the creative process of knowing will be collectively and corporately extended to the whole of human society, much as we have already extended our senses and our nerves by the various media.

The sensory bias of the internet extends human communication across time and space. This sensory extension fosters a new type of social bias—using technology to connect people together. Postman (1995: 193) stated: "Because of the conditions in which we attend to them, different technologies have different social biases." For instance, online or wireless communication does not require communicators to be co-present in the same physical location. Thus, conditions of attendance are different in face-to-face and online conversations because online communicators do not see the people they are talking to.

Additionally, online communicators can be dispersed spatially and temporally, which creates a time/space bias. The idea of a time/space bias in media is a key characteristic in any media ecological examination of communication technologies. Harold Innis (1951) argued that a communication medium tends to create a bias that emphasizes the idea of time or space. Carey (1989: 134) described Innis's idea in the following way:

> Innis divided communication and social control into two major types. Space-binding media, such as print and electricity, were connected with expansion and control over territory and favored the establishment of commercialism, empire and eventually technocracy. On the other hand, time-binding media, such as manuscript and human speech, favored relatively close communities, metaphysical speculation, and traditional authority.

The term "cyberspace" refers to the perceptual space created by computer networks, suggesting that networks have a spatial bias. However, computer networks also alter concepts of time, a characteristic that James gleick (1999/2000) describes in Faster: the Acceleration of Just About Everything. For instance, email creates a situation in which there is no shared physical space or sense of time. Email correspondents can be dispersed spatially and temporally. Time speeds up as we quickly send messages through the network and space dissolves.

In interpersonal communication, a central media ecological question facing research-ers utilizing this perspective is: How does the geographic separation of interpersonal correspondents influence the ways in which people communicate? When conditions of attendance change, how do communication messages change? One change is the lack of facial and tonal information, which can contribute to exaggerated communication, such as rude behavior and flaming.

Additionally the symbolic shift from face-to-face spoken to textual messages can blur the boundaries between reality and virtuality. For some correspondents, the virtual expe-rience is believed to be more socially desirable than in-person encounters (see Walther, 1996). Instead of seeing physical objects and contexts, people now experience virtual objects and perceptual spaces that are constructed in mediated environments. Thus, our symbolic notions of abstraction and representation are altered as virtual experiences begin to replace actual ones. For example, pilots learn to fly in simulators before they fly physical planes and doctors can practice medical procedures on virtual, rather than actual, patients. In online dating, individuals tend to add fantasy elements to online com-munication (see Barnes, 2003).

Although, CMC creates new types of communication environments for interaction to occur, communicating in a mediated context is different from sharing face-to-face experiences. The media environment alters the ways in which people attend to the communication. First, conditions of attendance in face-to-face communication require physical co-presence. In contrast, online communicators generally interact while being physically removed from each other. Second, the separation of people from their words, has numerous implications for the communication exchange and internet behavior pat-terns. Initially, researchers hypothesized that the lack of physical co-presence would lead to the exchange of impersonal and hostile messages, but, the opposite was discovered to be true. It has been observed that people will type their most intimate thoughts into the computer (Whittle, 1997). Sitting at home alone typing on a keyboard creates the illusion of privacy. In contrast, the words can be distributed around the globe. Once a message is sent out over the internet, the author loses control over his or her message. Digital text does not evaporate like the sounds of words in the air. We can share private thoughts, but the media environment is not a private place. Therefore, ideas of privacy change as private words can become public; this is the situation with teenagers posting private information on blogs (Kornblum, 2005).

Observations of a virtual community (Barnes, 2001) revealed four reasons why conditions of attendance in internet communities are conducive to personal relationship development. First, people can choose when to disclose information about their age, sex, and race. Second, people voluntarily communicate with each other and conversations can easily be terminated. Third, people can put their best foot forward by carefully editing their replies. Finally, people have the ability to hide defects, including physical handicaps and shyness. For instance, email is a wonderful communication tool for deaf teachers and students because hearing is not a requirement for CMC correspondence to occur.

However, conditions of attendance can also lead to misbehavior. Postman (1995: 192) reminds us "all technological change is a Faustian Bargain. For every advantage a new technology offers, there is always a corresponding disadvantage." Separating the physical body from the human communication process allows people to separate themselves from their actions (see Barnes, 1999). Its easier for people to write deceptive messages, flame each other, and act in socially unacceptable ways, such as spam, and identity theft. How can we protect ourselves from harmful remarks and actions when the identity of the perpetrator is unknown? This is one of the many ethical questions facing societies today. By focusing on symbolic shifts, time/space relationships, interactivity, sensory biases, and conditions of attendance, media ecology provides a framework for understanding how interpersonal communication is shifted from face-to-face to mediated contexts.

Historical Overview of the
Socialization of Media

A number of scholars have applied a media ecological framework to historical studies of communication technologies and their influences on culture. For example, Eisenstein (1979) examined the influence of the printing press on early-modern Europe and Ong (1982) studied the technologizing of the word in terms of a shift from oral to literate cultures.

A media ecological critique of social media would begin with a historical overview of how mass media have gradually been replacing interpersonal communication as a socializing force. Beniger (1987: 353) says, "Although intimate group relations remained important, increased attention to mass media ultimately came—because the individual's time and energy were limited—at the expense of interpersonal communication." Moreover, mass media themselves have increasingly become more personalized. Direct marketing addresses people by individual name and database marketing enables marketers to pinpoint individuals to target for products and services. Beniger called this social change the development of pseudo-community, a trend in mass media to speak in a more personal voice. Today, web programs can directly address the consumer and websites can be personalized for every user. Thus, mass and computer generated messages appear to be personal ones directed at individuals rather than groups.

In 1956, Horton and Wohl (1956/1986) observed that mass media—radio, television, and the movies—create the illusion of a face-to-face relationship with a performer. They called this new type of relationship a para-social one. The idea of media creating a sense of interpersonal communication was the subject of Gumpert and Cathcart's (1986: 24) book Inter/Media. They state: "A systems theory of human communication assumes that all message inputs—verbal, nonverbal, firsthand or mediated, and purposeful or accidental—affect the internal states of the individual and help shape the message outputs from the individual to others (interpersonal behaviors) as well as the messages one sends to oneself (intrapersonal behaviors)." Building on concepts presented in Inter/Media, Meyrowtiz (1985) further examined television usage in terms of Goffman's

(1959) dramaturgical model of social behavior. He argued that viewers consider television characters to be their media friends. Thus, Meyrowitz asserted that people develop a sense of having an interpersonal relationship with media content.

Presently, the internet has replaced the sense of an interpersonal relationship with a performer with the ability to conduct interpersonal relationships with other people. Digital media have now evolved to the point in which human-to-human exchanges are completely interactive. Senders and receivers exchange positions as if they were together in a face-toface encounter. Early research on CMC speculated that textual exchanges with cues filtered out would create a hostile communication environment (Hiltz & Turoff, 1978). However, contrary to this view, observations and studies of online exchanges later revealed that people form virtual or electronic communities when they regularly exchanged messages through the internet (Baym, 2000; Jones, 1995; Rheingold, 1993). Although some writers remain skeptical about the relationships built through cyberspace (Doheny-Farina, 1996; Slouka, 1995; Stoll, 1995), others have begun to embrace the idea that CMC is a new form of interpersonal communication (Barnes, 2001, 2003; Baym, 2000).

People need to connect with others and this is the driving force behind online relationships. For this reason, email and Instant Messenger are two very popular software applications that support the creation of interpersonal media environments. Communication technologies are transformed into media environments when people begin using the tools to support social practices, such as chatting with friends or co-workers in Instant Messenger. According to Postman (1985: 86), while "a technology…is merely a machine," it "becomes a medium as it employs a symbolic code, as it finds its place in a particular social setting." Thus, "a medium is the social and intellectual environment a machine creates." A new generation of software tools is emerging that are specifically designed to support social practices. This new technology sector is called "social media" or "social computing." Today, mediated contexts have developed from pseudo relationships to actual ones as people exchange messages through social software.

Social Media

Social media is an umbrella concept that describes social software and social networking. "Social software refers to various, loosely connected types of applications that allow individuals to communicate with one another, and to track discussions across the Web as they happen" (Tepper, 2003: 19). Simply stated, social media is software that enables people to interact with each other and build social networks that increase social capital. The term "social media" may be new; however, the idea of using media environments for socializing practices goes back to the telegraph and telephone. Since the early twentieth century, communication technologies have been used to create media environments that facilitate interpersonal communication (see Marvin, 1988).

In the pioneering stages of the internet, computer scientists transformed the technology into a media environment when they started exchanging email messages with each other. Interpersonal message exchange is a central aspect of the internet. The social bias of the computer enables anyone with access to an internet connection to connect with others. This social aspect of the computer's transformation into a media environment has been demonstrated through the formation of discussion groups, forums, bulletin boards, and newsgroups. Today's social media environments include: chat, instant messages, online role-play games, collaborative work tools, online education, and cell phones with internet access. Many of these environments are used to share interpersonal messages.

The idea of social media is a new organizing concept that has come to the public's attention through activities such as music and photo sharing, the social networking site meetup.com, the collaborative writing of Wikipedia, and numerous blogs available on the internet. Social software is already starting to change political, social, and personal communication patterns between individuals and organizations in the U.S.A. (see Crumlish, 2004). For instance, online learning environments provide distance education to people in remote regions. Computer-supported collaborative work environments support collaborative teams and the building of research communities. Examples include the concept of "outsourcing" American technical support jobs to India and data entry positions to Cambodia (see Friedman, 2005). Websites such as meetup.com and Match.com are altering the ways in which members of political parties organize and couples meet each other. From politics to romance, social media is influencing how people meet and make contact with each other. According to Friedman (2005), the use of social media tools has already had a profound influence on social, professional, and political life around the world.

Today, these tools are influencing the political process. In the United States, cyber-politics are a new type of political communication that is being used by many political candidates. Whillock (1997: 1208) states: "cyber-politics involve information dissemination, communication exchange, and the formation of electronic political coalitions across the internet." For instance, Sakkas (1993) provides a description of the use of discussion lists during the 1992 presidential campaign. A political bias associated with computer networks is the ability to organize people around a political or social cause. Similarly, Rheingold (2002) describes how people around the world are using cell phones to organize themselves to promote activism.

Social media is interpersonal media. It supports the sharing of personal exchanges in new and unique ways. It is not the relationship between humans and machines that makes social media powerful. In contrast, it is the relationship facilitated between people through the use of machines to foster the building of social networks and a new network society. Castells (1996/2000) describes the network society as a culture that is virtually constructed "by pervasive, interconnected, and diversified media system[s]." He continues by saying "this new form of social organization, in its pervasive globality, is diffusing throughout the world" (pp. 1–2). The network society is based on the idea of using CMC to build social capital, which is an informal social norm that promotes cooperation between two or more individuals. The norms can range from the reciprocity between two friends to the use of social networks to support community involvement and work activities.

Research in the area of social media includes the visual mapping of social networks (Turner et al., 2005); social networking in organizations (Quan-Haase, et al., 2005; Garton et al., 1997); distributed computing (Friedman, 2005; Holohan & Garg, 2005); peer-to-peer networks (Adar & Huberman 2000; Svensson & Bannister, 2004; Xu et al., 2005); mobile communications (cell phones and personal digital assistants) (Ito et al., 2005; Rheingold, 2002) and blogs (Crumlish, 2004; Hewitt, 2005; Kline & Burstein, 2005). Distributed computing primarily has economic and technological goals. "In Distributed Computing, a large computing problem is divided into small tasks that are assigned over the internet to be processed by individual users on their own computers" (Holohan & Garg, 2005: 1) An example of the use of distributed computing was the development of Linux, a current alternative to the Microsoft operating system (see Raymond, 1999/2001). It is a homegrown system that was constructed by thousands of programmers around the world, organizing themselves through the internet.

The geographic reach (space) and multidirectional (interactive) flow of message exchange available through the internet enabled programmers around the world to band together and create a computer program. By examining how the internet changes the way people interactively communicate (direction) across space, we can understand how the internet changes our notions of work and social collaboration. It was a networked group of thousands of programmers that began to challenge the hegemony of Microsoft's operating systems. This is an example of the potential social bias associated with social media. Individuals can organize themselves outside a corporate or government structure and their activities could challenge the hegemony of corporate and political systems. Friedman (2005) refers to this as the "flattening of the world," or the ability of individuals to easily communicate with each other across the globe to work, collaborate, and socialize with each other.

Social Media Analysis

Media ecology provides a framework in which to examine how social media tends to be used and how its media characteristics create new types of social challenge. The media characteristics being utilized in the following analysis are conditions of attendance, direction, time/space, social, and political biases. As previously stated, CMC introduces new conditions of attendance for communication partners—people no longer have to be physically co-present for communication to occur. Two issues introduced by this change are the issues of presence and trust.

People can now sit alone in their bedrooms and be part of a global conversation. According to Hillis (1999: 64): "When mediation inserts a 'psychic' distance, even among spatially proximate individuals, co-presence is superseded by telepresence." The idea of telepresence (Wood & Smith, 2001; Woolley, 1992) has evolved into presence research. Telepresence, a term created in the mid-1980s by nASA, originally referred to people controlling robots. A number of researchers have been examining how a sense of presence is created in electronic space (Biocca, 1997; giese, 1998; Liu, 1999; Lombard & Ditton, 1997; Lombard et al., 2000; Riva et al, 2003; Short et al., 1976).

Today's presence research conceptualizes the representation of self in mediated environments in a variety of ways. According to Lombard and Ditton (1997), there are six different conceptualizations of presence: presence as social richness (channels of communication) (Short et al., 1976); presence as visual realism (computer graphics) (Heeter, 1995); presence as transportation (traveling across space) (Biocca & Levy, 1995); presence as immersion (perceptual space) (Mantovani & Castelnuovo, 2003); presence as a social actor within a medium (avatars and actions) (Laurel, 1993); and presence as medium as social actor (anthropomorphism of technology) (Reeves and Nass, 1996). A number of different theories and approaches are emerging to describe the sense of self and others in perceptually mediated space.

Perceptual space is an amalgamation of the visual space created by the computer screen, the information space established through the network, and the social space experienced as people interact with each other (see Strate, 1999). Because communicators are separated by geographic space, establishing a sense of presence for the other to perceive oneself is a central issue in CMC. Presence replaces visual "first impressions" and compensates for the lack of visual information. Although, presence can compensate for visual information, it cannot verify identity and build trust because people are separated from their words and actions.

Trust is an issue that people need to establish between themselves, and programmers need to consider how to integrate trust in their software designs. For e-business and online dating, people need to be able to trust the person that they are corresponding with. Friedman et al. (2000: 40) state: "Perhaps the greatest difference between trust online and in other contexts is that when online, we have more difficulty (sometimes to the point of futility) of reasonably assessing the potential harm and good will of others." To address the issue of online trust, multidisciplinary researchers want to create technology that accounts for human values in the design process. A number of interface researchers have been addressing the issue of trust in the online experience (Cassell and Bickmore, 2000; Shneiderman, 2000). From the social perspective, Uslaner (2000: 63–64) observed:

> People who mistrust others fear the net as much as they accept all sorts of other conspiracy theories we might see on the X Files. They worry about their privacy generally and about the security of their medical records and the risk of downloading viruses in particular. Trusters view the Internet as more benign. Trusting people believe they can control the world and have faith that science will solve their problems and the net is another tool giving them leverage over their world.

His research revealed that the internet is very much like the physical world. "Children develop trust in others by learning from and emulating their parents, not from what they (don't) see on television or online" (Uslaner, 2000: 64). The idea of trust that we develop as children tends to determine how much we trust people in later life. People need to be able to connect with others and establish a feeling of trust before a reciprocal and meaningful relationship can be established. In mediated contexts, establishing methods for developing trust in relationships is both a technological and social concern.

The many directions in which messages flow in social media can support the building of meaningful relationships and collaboration. The multidirectional flow of messages contributes to collaborative work between people around the globe, such as the development of Linux and the outsourcing of global services. In addition to connecting people together around the world, various social computing tools focus on aspects of conditions of attendance in terms of local geographic space. Services, such as Face-book, Friendster, and MySpace enable people to connect locally or across distances. For instance, some college students use Facebook to organize parties on their campus, while others use it as a way to meet students on different campuses. "Students can also add their course schedules to their profiles, allowing them to browse the people in their classes" (Majmudar, 2005: E4). Thus, Facebook can be used to facilitate meeting people in a specific geographic location, which is why it is so popular with students on campuses. It is the one-to-one communication between people that is most appealing to individuals because that communication can be with someone next door or thousands of miles away.

Time and space biases are characteristics to be examined in social media contexts. Geographic location is a factor in social media design. For instance, technologies are being developed that place geographic locators in cell phones. When you are in the close proximity of a cell phone buddy, the phone will beep you and you can arrange to meet. Dodgeball and England's Playtxt are mobile social-networking services (called MoSoSos) that connect nearby people who have subscribed to the service. Playtxt connects people together based on similar interests. Dodgeball enables users to find old friends and meet new ones. Social media is not just computing; it includes cell phones, personal digital assistants, the development of peer-to-peer networking, and file sharing (see Ito et al., 2005; Rheingold, 2002).

The peer-to-peer sharing of information and mobilization of people illustrates a subversive aspect that is inherent in network design. The ability to easily share and distribute files and information is a new technological feature that could have profound political and social influences. For example, music file sharing impacts on the copyright laws in the United States. On a business level, peer-to-peer activities could alter social business practices (see Friedman, 2005). Eric Raymond (1999: 29) suggested that "Linux is subversive. Who would have thought even five years ago [1991] that a world-class operating system could coalesce as if by magic out of the part-time hacking of several thousand developers scattered all over the planet, connected only by the tenuous strands of the Internet?" Linux is an example of how distributed computing can be used to solve a problem. While participating in the project, social capital was also gained as people developed business contacts and interpersonal friendships with each other.

Peer-to-peer (P2P) networks enable people to communicate in multiple directions across time and space. In P2P networks, "the computer of each end user only connects to the computers of nearby peers, which themselves are connected to other computers, and so on, to form a dynamic, truly centreless network" (Svensson & Bannister, 2004: 2). P2P networking tends to foster the development of groups of individuals and the formation of online communities. Burnett (2004: 148) states:

Wireless P2P devices, such as PDAs and cellphones, are part of a growing movement that involves everything from text messaging to the transfer of photographs and video images. These devices will enhance another characteristic of P2P communities, which is the spontaneous desire to meet like-minded people and build communities while moving from one location to another.

Peer-to-peer networks help to build social capital and online communities in new and unique ways. "Much of what happens in the P2P world is unpredictable, which is part of its allure. The technology that comes close to the duplication of P2P networks is the telephone. Unlike telephones, P2P communications can spread, grow and redefine the meaning of community. In fact, I would make the claim the P2P is a disruptive technology" because it alters common assumptions about how technology is used (Burnett, 2004: 164). For instance a number of researchers (Adar & Huberman, 2000; Carmichael, 2003; Svensson & Bannister, 2004) have examined P2P networks and deviant behavior, such as illegal file sharing and network virus attacks. A political bias embedded in the technology is its ability to directly connect individuals together across national boundaries. This is a shift from controlling individual behavior through mass media messages to the self-organizing of individuals through interpersonal communication. As described by Beniger (1987), the impact of mass media on behavior could be reversed by the interpersonal sharing of messages between people in CMC contexts.

The interpersonal sharing of resources and ideas contributes to the building of social capital. Social capital is a research focus for some CMC researchers (Hampton & Wellman, 2001; Kavanaugh & Patterson, 2001; Wellman et al., 2001). Hampton and Wellman (2001: 477) argue that "community is best seen as a network—not as a local group. We are not members of a society that operates in little boxes, dealing only with fellow members of the few groups to which we belong: at home, in our neighborhood, in our workplaces, in cyberspace." An individual's social network includes kinship, friendship, neighbors, and work ties. People maintain these social ties through multiple mediated options, including telephone, mail, fax, email, discussion groups, and instant messaging.

According to Wellman et al. (2001), social capital includes three aspects: the building of network capital or the relations with family, friends, and co-workers; participatory capital or the involvement in voluntary organizations and politics; and community commitment, a strong attitude toward community and the willingness to mobilize their social capital. Building and mobilizing social capital is both local and global. A number of authors have examined how networks can be used to organize members of local communities into face-to-face interaction (see Horn, 1998; Rheingold, 1993; Schuler, 1996). Or people can globally share their personal thoughts through blogs.

Probably the most well-known social media tool is the weblog. A weblog (also known as a blog) is a personal website that offers frequently updated observations, news headlines, commentary, recommended links and/or diary entries, generally organized chronologically (Werbach, 2001: 21). Blogs change media content by doing two things. First, they enable individuals to have a voice in the media. Blogs can be a form of participatory journalism that is shared on a global level. As a result, mass media news is no longer the only type of authorial voice that is commenting on current events. Second, blogs are connected together through social networks. Social networks foster the formation of new types of electronic communities that share information together.

A goal of blogs is to present a personal point of view in a global village. Bloggers with similar interests will link their sites together into blogging communities. Blogging tools bring people together across time and space. On the opposite side of the spectrum, adding buddy lists and location tools to cell phones enables cell phone users to meet up and physically interact with friends in face-to-face contexts. For example, Ito et al. (2005) explore the social use of cell phones in Japanese life. Thus, social computing directly deals with changing notions of conditions of attendance and how people can communicate and interact across distances and in face-to-face interpersonal relationships.

The sensory bias of computer networks, which extend our nervous system into a global embrace, contributes to our changing notions about real and perceptual space. Because people can now communicate across distances, conditions of attendance in mediated contexts are different from face-to-face situations. Symbolically, people now interact in a perceptual space, often referred to as "cyberspace," instead of a physical one. Thus, the CMC context is abstract and open to interpretation or misinterpretation. This possibility adds a new level of abstraction to the process of understanding messages in mediated contexts, also raising issues about self-presentation and trust. Interpersonal communicators need to envision mental models of their communication contexts to better understand the words being exchanged (see Licklider & Taylor, 1968).

Changing conditions of attendance also alter social behaviors and this is a Faustian Bargain. Separation of people from words leads to the building of social capital as well as socially destructive deviant behavior, such as identity theft and flaming. On a social level, someone can flame another party without having to physically face the wrath of the other person. However, separating people from their actions also contributes to the technology's political bias. National borders no longer bind individuals. Networking technologies reach beyond national borders to enable people to self-organize around local or global political interests and issues. Thus, by examining the directional, spatial, social, and political biases embedded in social media, interpersonal communication scholars can better understand how the shift from face-to-face to mediated communication environments can influence the ways in which people interact. Moreover, this shift raises new technological factors and social issues that need to be considered when conducting interpersonal research.

Summary

The Media Ecological view focuses on the idea that a change in one communication system (such as the Internet) will cause a change in all other communication systems (e.g., human communication). Social Media in the form of Computer Mediated Communication (CMC) is significantly different from face-to-face (FtF) communication, yet it has greatly affected the nature of FtF communication.

Perhaps the most significant change that CMC has had when compared to FtF communication is the time/space bias. No longer do people have to exist in the same space and time to interact, and the use of CMC can manipulate human relationships in four different ways: what individuals choose to disclose in CMC, the ability to easily terminate CMC, the careful edits of information in CMC, and the ability of people to hide their defects in CMC. Social Media, an aspect of CMC, now is a significant aspect of how people meet and make contact with each other. Through an analysis of how the Internet changes the way people communicate interactively across space enables one to understand how the internet changes the way people perceive notions of work and social collaboration.

People can create with Social Media an identity that may be described as a "telepresence," but individuals still have a hard time determining the potential costs and benefits of online relationships. Relationships developed through Social Media can be classified as peer-to-peer networks which enable people to communicate in multiple directions across time and space. The amount of relationships harvested online are now described as social capital, and enables a form of self-expression that not possible with traditional mass media outlets.

The final chapter in this book looks at a form of communication which has been around since days of Aristotle in ancient Greece—public communication. No matter how much Social Media affects humanity, the "good man speaking well" is still an aspect of communication that receives much scrutiny, and will be examined in the final chapter.

Questions For Discussion

1. What is the essence of the Media Ecological view with respect to computer mediated communication?
2. What is the time/space bias? What affect dies this have on communication with social media?
3. What is social capital and how does it apply to social media?
4. What is the significance of peer-to-peer networks in social media?
5. How has social media changed the way you communicate with others?

References

Adar, E., & Huberman, B. A. (2000) "Free riding on gnutella," *First Monday* 5 (10). Available at www.firstmonday.org. (Last viewed September 15, 2005).

Adler, R. B., Proctor, R. F., & Towne, n. (2005) *Looking Out, Looking In.* Belmont, CA: Wadsworth.

Barnes, S. (1999) "Ethical issues for a virtual self." In S. J. Drucker & G. Gumpert (eds.), *Real Law @ Virtual Space.* Cresskill, NJ: Hampton Press.

Barnes, S. B. (2001) *Online connections: Internet Interpersonal Relationships.* Cresskill, NJ: Hampton Press.

Barnes, S. B. (2003) *Computer-Mediated Communication: Human-to-Human Communication Across the Internet.* Boston, MA: Allyn & Bacon.

Barnes, S., & Strate, L. (1996) "The educational implications of the computer: A media ecology critique." *New Jersey Journal of Communication,* 4(2), 180–208.

Baym, N. K. (2000) *Tune in, Log On.* Thousand Oaks, CA: Sage Publications.

Beniger, J. R. (1987) "Personalization of mass media and the growth of pseudo-community." *Communication Research,* 14(3), 52–371.

Biocca, F. (1997) "The cyborg's dilemma: Progressive embodiment in virtual environments." *Journal of Computer-Mediated Communication,* 3(2). Available at www.ascusc.org/jcmc/vol3. (Last viewed May 13, 2003).

Biocca, F., & Levy, M. R. (1995) *Communication in the Age of Virtual Reality.* Hillsdale, NJ: Lawrence Erlbaum Associates.

Burnett, R. (2004) *How Images Think.* Cambridge, MA: The MIT Press.

Carey, J. W. (1989) *Communication as culture.* New York: Routledge.

Carmichael, P. (2003) "The Internet, information architecture and community memory." *Journal of Computer-Mediated Communication,* 8(2). Available at www.jcmc.Indiana.edu. (last viewed September 19, 2005).

Cassell, J., & Bickmore, T. (2000) "External manifestations of trustworthiness in the interface." *Communications of the ACM,* 43(12), 50–56.

Castells, M. (1996/2000) *The Rise of the Networked Society, second edition.* Boston: Blackwell.

Crumlish, C. (2004) *The Power of Many.* San Francisco, Sybex.

Davenport, T. H. (1997) *Information Ecology.* New York: Oxford University Press.

DeVito, J. A. (2004) *The Interpersonal Communication Book,* tenth edition. Boston: Allyn & Bacon.

Doheny-Farina, S. (1996) *The Wired Neighborhood.* New Haven, CT: Yale University Press.

Donath, J. (1999) "Visualizing conversation." *Journal of Computer-Mediated Communication,* 4(4). Available at www.jcmc.Indiana.edu. (Last viewed September 16, 2005).

Dominick, J. R. (2002) *The Dynamics of Mass Communication, seventh edition.* New York: Mcgraw Hill.

Eisenstein, E. I. (1979) *The Printing Press As an Agent of Change.* New York: Cambridge University Press.

Forester, T. (1989) *Computers in the Human Context.* Cambridge, MA: The MIT Press.

Friedman, B., Kahn, Jr., P. H., & Howe, D. C. (2000) "Trust online." *Communications of the ACM,* 43(12), 34–40.

Friedman, T. L. (2005) *The World is Flat.* New York: Farrar, Straus and Giroux.

Garton, L., Haythornthwaite, C., & Wellman, B. (1997) "Studying on-line social networks." *Journal of Computer-Mediated Communication,* 3(1). Available at www.jcmc.Indiana.edu. (Last viewed September 15, 2005).

Gibson, S. B., & Oviedo, O. O. (2000) *The Emerging Cyberculture: Literacy, Paradigm, and Paradox.* Cresskill, NJ: Hampton Press.

Giese, M. (1998) "Self without body: Textual self-representation in an electronic community." *First Monday,* 3(4). Available at www.firstmonday.dk/issues/issue3_4/giese. (last viewed April 14, 2000).

Gleick, J. (1999/2000) *Faster: the Acceleration of Just About Everything.* New York: Vintage Books.

Goffman, E. (1959) *The Presentation of Self in Everyday Life.* Garden City, N.Y.: Doubleday.

Greller, L., & Barnes, S. (1993) "groupware and interpersonal text: The computer as a medium of communication." *Interpersonal Computing and Technology,* 1(2). Available at www.Helsinki.fi/science/optek. (Last viewed April 15, 2001).

Gumpert, G., & Cathcart, R. (1986) *Inter/Media: Interpersonal Communication in a Media World,* third edition. New York: Oxford University Press.

Hampton, K., & Wellman, B. (2001) "Long distance community in the network society." *American Behavioral Scientist,* 45(3), 476–95.

Heeter, C. (1995) "Communication research on consumer VR." In F. Biocca & M. R. Levy (eds.), *Communication in the Age of Virtual Reality,* Hillsdale, NJ: Lawrence Erlbaum Associates, pp. 191–218.

Hewitt, H. (2005) *Blog: Understanding the Information Reformation That's Changing Your World.* Nashville, TN: Thomas Nelson, Inc.

Hickman, L. A. (1990) *Technology As a Human Affair.* New York: Mcgraw-Hill.

Hillis, K. (1999) *Digital sensations.* Minneapolis, MN: University of Minnesota Press.

Hiltz, S. R., & Turoff, M. (1978) *The Network Nation: Human Communication Via Computer.* Reading, MA: Addison-Wesley.

Holohan, A., & Garg, A. (2005) "Collaboration online: The example of distributed computing." *Journal of Computer-Mediated Communication,* 10(4). Available at www.jcmc. Indiana.edu. (Last viewed September 15, 2005).

Horn, S. (1998) *Cyberville.* New York: Warner Books.

Horton, D., & Wohl, R. R. (1956/1986) "Mass communication and para-social interaction: Observation on intimacy at a distance." In G. Gumpert & R. Cathcart (eds.), *Inter/Media: Interpersonal Communication in a Media World,* third edition. New York: Oxford University Press, pp.185–206.

Innis, H. A. (1951) *The Bias of Communication.* Toronto, Canada: University of Toronto Press.

Ito, M., Okabe, D., & Matsuda, M. (2005) *Mobile Phones in Japanese Life.* Cambridge, MA: The MIT Press.

Jones, S. G. (1995) *Cybersociety: Computer-mediated communication and community.* Thousand Oaks, CA: Sage Publications.

Kavanaugh, A. L., & Patterson, S. J. (2001) "The impact of community computer networks on social capital and community involvement." *American Behavioral Scientist,* 45(3), 496–509.

Kline, D., & Burstein, D. (2005) Blog! New York: CDS Books.

Kornblum, J. (2005) "Teens wear their hearts on their blogs." *USA Today* October 30. Available: at www.usatoday.com/tech/news/techinnovations/2005-10-30-teen-blogs_x.htm?POE=click-refer. (Last viewed November 1, 2005).

Laurel, B. (1993) *Computers as Theatre.* Reading, MA: Addison Wesley.

Levinson, P. (1997) *The Soft Edge.* New York: Routledge.

Levinson, P. (1999) *Digital McLuhan.* New York: Routledge.

Licklider, J. C. R., & Taylor, R. (1968) "The computer as a communication device." *International Science and Technology,* April.

Liu, G. Z. (1999) "Virtual community presence in internet relay chat." *Journal of Computer-Mediated Communication,* 5(1). Available at www.ascusc.org/jcmc/vol5/issue1/liu.html. (Last viewed May 13, 2003).

Lombard, M., & Ditton, T. (1997) "At the heart of it all: The concept of presence." *Journal of Computer Mediated Communication,* 3(2). Available at www.ascusc.org/jcmc/vol3/issue2/lombard.html. (last viewed January 18, 2005).

Lombard, M., Reich, R. D., Grabe, M. E., Bracken, C. C., & Ditton, T. B. (2000) "Presence and television: The role of screen size." *Human Communication Research,* 26(1), 75–98.

McLuhan, M. (1962) *The Gutenberg Galaxy.* Toronto: The University of Toronto Press.

McLuhan, M. (1964) *Understanding Media: The Extensions of Man.* New York: Signet.

Majmudar, n. (2005) "College networking puts on a new face." *Democrat and Chronicle,* August 28, pp. 1E, 4E.

Mantovani, F., & Castelnuovo, G. (2003) "Sense of presence in virtual training: Enhancing skills acquisition and transfer of knowledge through learning experience in virtual environments." In G. Riva, F. Davide & W. A. Ijsselsteijn (eds.), *Being There: Concepts, Effects and Measurements of User Presence in Synthetic Environments.* Amsterdam: IOS Press, pp. 167–181.

Marvin, C. (1988) *When Old Technologies Were New.* New York: Oxford University Press.

Meyrowitz, J. (1985) *No Sense of Place.* New York: Oxford University Press.

Murray, D. E. (1991) *Conversation for Action: the Computer Terminal as Medium of Communication.* Amsterdam/Philadelphia: John Benjamins.

Nardi, B., & O'Day, V. (1999) *Information Ecologies: Using Technology with Heart.* Cambridge, MA: MIT Press.

Olson, D. R. (1994) *The World on Paper.* New York: Cambridge University Press.

Ong, W. J. (1982) *Orality and Literacy.* New York: Methuen & Co.

Postman, N. (1979) *Teaching as a conserving activity.* New York: Dell Books.

Postman, N. (1985) *Amusing Ourselves to Death.* New York: Penguin Books.

Postman, N. (1992) *Technopoly: the Surrender of Culture to Technology.* New York: Alfred A. Knopf.

Postman, N. (1995) *The End of Education.* New York: Alfred A. Knopf.

Quan-Haase, A., Cothrel, J., & Wellman, B. (2005) "Instant messaging for collaboration: A case study of a high-tech firm. *Journal of Computer-Mediated Communication,* 10(4). Available at www.jcmc. Indiana.edu. (Last viewed September 15, 2005).

Rafaeli, S., & Sudweeks, F. (1998) "Networked Interactivity." In F. Sudweeks, M. McLaughlin, & S. Rafaeli (eds.), *Network and Netplay: Virtual Groups on the Internet,* Cambridge, MA: The MIT Press, pp. 173–189.

Raymond, E. S. (1999, 2001) *The Cathedral and the Bazaar.* Sebastopol, CA: O'Reilly & Associates.

Reeves, B., & Nass, C. (1996) *The Media Equation.* New York: Cambridge University Press.

Rennie, F., & Mason, R. (2003) "The ecology of connection." *First Monday,* 8(8). Available at www. firstmonday.org. (Last viewed September 10, 2005).

Rheingold, H. (1993) *The Virtual Community.* Reading, MA: Addison-Wesley.

Rheingold, H. (2002) SmartMobs. New York: Basic Books.

Rice, R. E., & Love, G. (1987) "Electronic emotion: Socioemotional content in a computer-mediated communication network." *Communication Research,* 14(1), 85–108.

Sakkas, L. (1993) "Politics on the net." *Interpersonal Computing and Technology,* 2(1). Available: at www.Helsinki.fi/science/optek (last viewed: January 8, 2001).

Schroeder, R. (1996) *Possible worlds.* Boulder, CO: Westview Press.

Schuler, D. (1996) *New Community Networks.* Reading, MA: Addison-Wesley Publishing.

Short, J. Williams, E., & Christie, B. (1976) *The Social Dynamics of Telecommunications.* New York: John Wiley & Sons.

Shneiderman, B. (2000) "Designing trust into online experiences." *Communications of the ACM,* 43(12), 57–59.

Sloan, N. J. A., & Wyner, A. D. (1992) *Claude Elwood Shannon: Collected Papers.* New York: IEEE Press.

Slouka, M. (1995) War of the Worlds. New York: Basic Books. Sproull, L., & Kiesler, S. (1991) *Connections: New Ways of Working in the Networked Organization.* Cambridge, MA: The MIT Press.

Stoll, C. (1995) *Silicon Snake Oil.* New York: Doubleday.

Strate, L. (1999) "The varieties of cyberspace: problems in definition and delimitation." *Western Journal of Communication,* 63(3), 382–412.

Strate, L., Jacobson, R., & Gibson, S. (1996) *Communication and Cyberspace.* Cresskill, NJ: Hampton Press.

Strate, L., Jacobson, R., & Gibson, S. (2003) *Communication and Cyberspace,* second edition. Cresskill, NJ: Hampton Press.

Svensson, J. S., & Bannister, F. (2004) "Pirates, sharks and moral crusaders: Social control in peer-to-peer networks." *First Monday,* 9(6). Available: at www.firstmonday.org. (Last viewed September 15, 2005).

Tepper, M. (2003) "The rise of social software." *Net Worker,* September, 19–23.

Turkle, S. (1995) *Life on the Screen.* New York: Simon & Schuster.

Turner, T. C., Smith, M. A., Fisher, D., & Welser, H. T. (2005) "Picturing usenet: Mapping compu-termediated collective action." *Journal of Computer-Mediated Communication,* 10(4). Available www.jcmc.Indiana.edu. (Last viewed September 15, 2005).

Uslaner, E. M. (2000) "Social capital and the net." *Communications of the ACM,* 43(12), 60–64.

Walther, J. B. (1996) "Computer-mediated communication: Impersonal, interpersonal, and hyper-personal interaction." *Communication Research,* 23(1), 3–43.

Wellman, B., Haase, A. Q., Witte, J., & Hampton, K. (2001) "Does the internet increase, decrease, or supplement social capital?" *American Behavioral Scientist,* 45(3), 436–455.

Werbach, K. (2001, May 29) "Triumph of the weblogs." *Release,* 1, 21–25.

Whillock, R. K. (1997) "Cyber-politics: The online strategies of 96." *American Behavioral Scientist,* 40(8), 1208–1225.

Whittle, D. B. (1997) *Cyberspace: The Human Dimension.* New York: Freeman.

Wiener, N. (1954) *The Human Use of Human Beings: Cybernetics and Society.* Garden City, NY: Double-day Books.

Wiener, N. (1948/1961) *Cybernetics: or Control and Communication in the Animal and the Machine.* Cambridge, MA: The MIT Press.

Wood, A. F., & Smith, M. J. (2001) *Online Communication: Linking Technology, Identity & Culture.* Mahwah, NJ: Lawrence Erlbaum Associates.

Woolley, B. (1992) *Virtual Worlds.* Cambridge, MA: Blackwell Publishers.

Xu, H., Wang, H., & Teo, H. (2005) "Predicting the usage of P2P sharing software: The role of trust and perceived risk." Proceedings of the 38th Hawaii Internation Conference on System Sciences. New York: IEEE Publications [online] number: 0–7695–2268–8/05.

Zuboff, S. (1988). *In the Age of the Smart Machine.* New York: Basic Books.

Chapter 14

Public Communication

Julia T. Wood

The ability to craft and deliver a speech is just as important today as it was over two centuries ago. The ability to gather material, effectively analyze an audience, organize and present a speech is still one of the most important communicative skills an individual can possess. This last chapter introduces the concept of public communication and gives basic guidelines for developing and presenting a speech.

Learning Objectives For This Chapter

- Explain why public speaking is seen as an enlarged conversation
- Identify the main purposes of public speeches
- Understand the difference between a speaking purpose and a thesis statement
- Describe how to organize speeches
- Discuss the types of evidence used in speeches and their uses
- Identify the five delivery styles in public speaking
- Understand how to manage speaking anxiety
- Explain importance of adapting speeches to the appropriate audience

When Wendy Kopp entered Princeton's first-year class in 1985, she didn't realize she was going wind up on the covers of *Time* and *U.S. News & World Report* for launching one of the most effective civic engagement programs for youth in America. Kopp was born into an affluent family that gave her every advantage possible. At Princeton, she noticed that

Julia T. Wood, "Public Communication," *Communication Mosaics: An Introduction to the Field of Communication*, pp. 270–290. Copyright © 2011 by Wadsworth, a part of Cengage Learning, Inc. Reprinted with permission.

her roommate from the South Bronx hadn't had advantages such as excellent preparatory schooling, and that put her roommate at a disadvantage at Princeton.

Kopp decided to do something about the inequities in opportunities. She wrote her senior thesis on her idea for starting a national teaching corps in which college students would spend a year or two after graduating teaching students in low-income communities. Today that organization is well known: Teach for America. It has grown from 489 teachers in its first year to 12,000 today.

To realize her dream, Kopp had to become an effective speaker. She had to persuade people to donate money to start Teach for America, she had to persuade students to give a year or more of their time to teaching students in underresourced schools, and had to inform citizens and media about her vision and, as the results came in, the impressive effectiveness of her program.

Good ideas have to be communicated in order to have impact. That means that each of us will likely have opportunities to speak publicly about issues and causes that matter to us. Public speaking allows you to be an active citizen, an effective professional, and a responsible member of your community and the groups to which you belong. It allows you to affect what others believe, think, and do. Therefore, skill in public speaking is important both for individuals and for society Equally important is skill in listening critically to the public communication of others. People who present their ideas effectively and listen critically to the ideas of others are capable of informed, vigorous participation in all spheres of life. The importance of free speech to democratic life is recognized by the First Amendment (see the FYI box on the right).

This chapter focuses on public speaking. In the first part of the chapter, we will discuss the different purposes of public speaking and its distinctive features. The second section of the chapter provides an overview of planning and presenting public speeches. In the third section, we identify three guidelines for effective public communication: reducing speaking anxiety, adapting to audiences, and listening critically to public discourse. The complex process of public speaking cannot be taught in a single chapter. This chapter's goal is to give you a conceptual understanding of what is involved in public communication. The information we cover will be especially useful in helping you become a more critical listener when you attend to others' public communication.

Public Speaking as Enlarged Conversation

Many years ago, James Winans (1938), a distinguished professor of communication, remarked that effective public speaking is enlarged conversation. What Winans meant was that in many ways public speaking is similar to everyday talk. More than 50 years later, Michael Motley and Jennifer Molloy observed that, "Except for preparation time and turn-taking delay, public speaking has fundamental parallels to everyday conversation" (1994, p. 52). Whether we are talking with a couple of friends or speaking to an audience of 1,000 people, we must adapt to others' perspectives, create a good climate for interaction, use effective verbal and nonverbal communication, organize what we say so others can follow our ideas, support our claims, present our ideas in an engaging and convincing manner, and listen and respond to questions and comments about what we have said.

Thinking of public speaking as enlarged conversation reminds us that most public speaking is neither stiff nor exceedingly formal. In fact, some of the most effective public speakers use an informal, personal style that invites listeners to feel that they are interacting with someone, not being lectured. This means that effective public communication requires and builds on skills and principles that apply to communication in all contexts, as we discussed in Part II.

I learned that effective public speaking is much like conversation when I first taught a large course. Previously, I had taught small classes, and I relied on discussion. In the large class, I lectured in a fairly formal style because I thought that was appropriate for a class of 150 students. One day, a student asked a question, and I responded with another question. He replied, then another student added her ideas, and an open discussion was launched. Both the students and I were more engaged with one another and the course material than we had been when I lectured formally. That's when I realized that even in large classes effective teaching is enlarged conversation.

Distinctive Features of Public Communication

Although public speaking is enlarged conversation, it differs from casual interaction in two primary ways. First, public speeches tend to involve more planning and preparation than informal conversations. Second, public speaking is less obviously interactive than much of our communication. In public speaking situations, communicators are more clearly in speaker and listener roles and the listeners' contributions are less obvious than the speakers'.

Greater Responsibility to Plan and Prepare When a friend asks your opinion on a political candidate, you respond without conducting research, carefully organizing your ideas, or practicing your delivery. Before speaking to a group of 50 people about that candidate, however, you would likely do some research, organize your ideas, and practice delivering your speech. In public speaking situations, you have a responsibility to provide evidence and reasoning to support your beliefs, to structure your ideas clearly, and to practice your presentation so your delivery is engaging.

Listeners' expectations affect the planning and preparation needed for effective public speaking. We expect more evidence, clearer organization, and more polished delivery in public speeches than in casual conversations. Therefore, public speakers who do not prepare well are likely to disappoint listeners and to be judged inadequate. When you are giving a public speech, your responsibility is to analyze listeners, to do research, to organize ideas, and to practice and polish delivery.

Less Obviously Interactive. Public speaking also tends to be less obviously interactive than some forms of communication, such as personal conversations, interviews, and team deliberations. In many contexts, communicators take turns talking, but speakers tend to dominate in public presentations. It would be a mistake, however, to think that listeners don't participate actively in public presentations. They are sending messages even as they listen: head nods, frowns, perplexed expressions, applause, smiles, bored looks. Listeners communicate throughout a speech, primarily in nonverbal ways. As Cheryl Hamilton notes, effective public speakers "realize that successful communication is a two-way street" (1996, p. 29). In other words, good public speakers pay attention to what listeners are "saying" throughout their speeches.

Even though listeners participate actively, public speaking places special responsibility on speakers. To be effective, they must anticipate listeners' attitudes and knowledge and must adapt their presentation to the views of listeners. One of the first steps in planning a good public speech is to ask what audience members are likely to know about a topic and how they are likely to feel about it. Based on what you know or learn about listeners, you can make informed choices about what information to include and how to support and organize your ideas.

While actually giving a speech, you should also adapt to listeners' feedback. If some listeners look confused, you might add an example or elaborate on an idea. If listeners' nonverbal behaviors suggest that they are bored, you might alter your volume, incorporate gestures, change your speaking position, or offer a personal example to enliven your talk. Later in this chapter, we'll return to the topic of adapting to listeners. For now, you should realize that because public speaking gives the speaker primary control, the speaker has a special responsibility to be sensitive to listeners' ideas, values, interests, and experiences. With this background, we're ready to consider the purposes of public speaking.

The Purposes of Public Speeches

Traditionally, three general speaking purposes have been recognized: to entertain, to inform, and to persuade. You probably realize that these purposes often overlap. For example, informative speeches routinely include humor or interesting comments to entertain listeners. Some of your favorite professors probably include stories and interesting examples to enliven informational lectures (see the Sharpen Your Skill exercise on page 272). Speeches to entertain may also teach listeners something entirely new.

Sasha, a student in one of my classes, gave a speech on arranged marriages, which are still common in her native country. Her goal was to inform her classmates about the history of arranged marriages and why they work for many people. Although her primary goal was to inform, her speech had a persuasive aspect because she encouraged listeners not to impose their values on the practices of other cultures. This reinforces our earlier discussion of overlapping purposes in public speaking. Persuasive speeches often contain information about issues as well as content that is entertaining. Speeches intended to entertain may also inform and persuade, perhaps through the use of humor or dramatic narratives. Although purposes of speaking overlap, most speeches have one primary purpose.

Speaking to Entertain. In a speech to entertain, the primary objective is to engage, interest, amuse, or please listeners. You might think that only accomplished comics and performers present speeches to entertain. Actually, many of us will be involved in speaking to entertain during our lives. You might be asked to give an after-dinner speech, to present a toast at a friend's wedding, or to make remarks at a retirement party for a colleague.

Humor, although often part of speeches to entertain, is not the only way we engage others. We also entertain when we engage in narrative speaking by telling stories. We share stories to share experiences, build community, pass on history, or teach a lesson. Parents share with children stories of their courtship; they discuss friends and relatives and keep family memories alive. Stories and the art of storytelling are especially important in cultures that emphasize oral communication (Einhorn, 2000; Fitch, 1999).

Speaking to Inform. A speech to inform has the primary goal of increasing listeners' understanding, awareness, or knowledge of some topic. For example, a speaker might want listeners to understand the rights guaranteed in the Bill of Rights or to make listeners aware of recycling programs. In both cases, the primary purpose is to enrich listeners' knowledge, although each topic has persuasive implications. A speech to inform may also take the form of a demonstration, in which the speaker shows how to do something while giving a verbal explanation. For instance, a demonstration speech might show listeners how to use a new computer program or how to distinguish between poisonous and nonpoisonous species of mushrooms. As Gladys points out, however, speaking to inform may be more successful when speakers also entertain or otherwise capture listeners' interest.

Speaking to Persuade. A speech to persuade aims to change listeners' attitudes, beliefs, or behaviors or to motivate them to take some action. Persuasive goals are to influence attitudes, to change practices, and to alter beliefs. Rather than primarily an entertainer or teacher, the persuasive speaker is an advocate who argues for a cause, issue, policy, attitude, or action. In one of my classes, a student named Chris gave a speech designed to persuade other students to contribute to the Red Cross blood drive. He began by telling us that he was a hemophiliac, whose life depended on blood donations. He then explained the procedures for donating blood (a subordinate informational purpose) so that listeners would not be deterred by fear of the unknown. Next, he described several cases of people who had died or had become critically ill because adequate supplies of blood weren't available. In the two weeks after his speech, more than one-third of the students who had heard his speech donated blood.

Persuasive speeches aim to influence—to change what people believe, think, or do. As communication scholar Cindy Griffin (2006) points out, many of the values and principles of the United States were carved out in key public speeches that changed what people believed and did. Consider a few examples of speeches that contributed to changing America:

- In 1841, Frederick Douglass spoke against slavery.
- In 1848, Elizabeth Cady Stanton advocated women's enfranchisement.
- In 1963, Martin Luther King, Jr. gave his famous "I Have a Dream" speech.

- In 1964, President Lyndon Johnson explained affirmative action.
- In 2001, President George W. Bush announced the War on Terror.

But speeches that change a country's laws and actions are not the only important forms of public speaking. I've seen citizens' votes affected by persuasive speeches that championed or criticized particular candidates. Likewise, I've seen students' attitudes and behaviors changed by classroom speeches that advocated wearing seat belts, giving blood, spaying and neutering pets, and community service. The FYI box on this page provides an example of how one average citizen became a persuasive advocate for stronger laws against drunk driving.

Planning and Presenting Public Speeches

Effective public speaking is a process, not a static event. The process begins with understanding credibility and ways to earn it. The next steps are to define the purpose of speaking, develop a strong thesis statement, and decide how to organize the speech. Next, speakers conduct research to identify evidence that can be used to support their ideas. Finally, speakers select delivery styles and practice the presentation. We will discuss each step. For more detailed guidance, refer to the *Student Companion* to this book.

Earning Credibility

Effective public speaking (and, indeed, communication in all contexts) requires credibility. **Credibility** exists when listeners believe in a speaker and trust what the speaker says. Credibility is based on listeners' perceptions of a speaker's position, authority, knowledge (also called expertise), dynamism, and trustworthiness (also called character). Therefore, to earn credibility, speakers should demonstrate that they are informed about their topics, that they are dynamic communicators, and that they are ethical in using evidence and reasoning.

A speaker's credibility is not necessarily static. Some speakers have high **initial credibility**, which is the expertise, dynamism, and character that listeners attribute to them before they begin to speak. Initial credibility is based on titles, experiences, and achievements that are known to listeners before they hear the speech. For example, Al Gore has high initial credibility on environmental issues.

As Ricardo points out, a speaker without much initial credibility may gain strong credibility in the process of presenting a speech. Speakers may gain **derived credibility**, which listeners grant as a result of how speakers communicate during presentations. Speakers may earn derived credibility by providing clear, well-organized information and convincing evidence, and by an engaging delivery style. Speakers may also increase credibility during a presentation if listeners regard them as likable and as having goodwill toward the listeners (McCroskey & Teven, 1999).

Terminal credibility is a cumulative combination of initial and derived credibility. Terminal credibility may be greater or less than initial credibility, depending on how effectively a speaker has communicated.

Planning Public Speeches

A well-crafted speech begins with careful planning. Speakers should select a limited topic, define a clear purpose, and develop a concise thesis statement.

Select a Topic. Speakers should select topics that they know and care about. When you choose a topic that matters to you, you have a head start in both knowledge and dynamism, two bases of credibility.

Speakers should also choose topics that are appropriate to listeners. It's important to consider listeners' values, backgrounds, attitudes, knowledge, and interests so that you can select topics and adapt how you address them in ways that respect the perspectives and interests of listeners.

Figure 13.1: Organizing Speeches

Topic: Literacy

Speech 1: Temporal Organization

Thesis:	As America changes, so must our way of teaching literacy.
Claim 1:	When America was founded, reading was restricted primarily to the aristocratic class.
Claim 2:	By the late 1800s more members of working class and African Americans were also taught to read.
Claim 3:	Today, America must find ways to provide literacy education to immigrants.

Speech 2: Spatial Organization

Thesis:	Teaching literacy happens in homes, schools, and volunteer-run literacy programs.
Claim 1:	The home is where many children first learn to read.
Claim 2:	Schools teach literacy to many students.
Claim 3:	When home and school don't teach literacy, volunteer-run programs can teach literacy.

Speech 3: Cause-Effects

Thesis:	Literacy programs will increase their productivity, enhance citizens' engagement with society, and reduce incarceration rates.
Claim 1:	People who can read are more economically stable and productive than people who cannot read.
Claim 2:	Citizens who can read more actively engage civic and social issues.
Claim 3:	Literate citizens are less likely to break the law and go to prison.

Speech topics should be appropriate to the situation. If you are asked to speak at a professional meeting, your speech should address issues relevant to that profession. If you are speaking about someone who has won an award or who is retiring, the situation probably calls for a speech that praises the person.

Finally, effective topics are limited in scope. You may be concerned about education, but that topic is too broad for a single speech. You might narrow it to a speech on funding for education or training of teachers or some other specific aspect of your general area of interest.

Define the Speaking Purpose. The second step in planning a speech is to define your general and specific purposes. The general purpose is to entertain, inform, or persuade. **The specific purpose** is exactly what you hope to accomplish. For example, specific purposes could be to get 25% of the audience to sign up to work on a Habitat house, to have listeners give correct answers to a quiz about the spread of HIV, or to get listeners to laugh at your jokes. The specific purpose of a speech states the behavioral response the speaker seeks: "I want listeners to agree to donate blood"; "I want listeners to sign a petition in support of the War on Terror."

Develop the Thesis. The thesis statement is the single most important sentence in a speech. A clear **thesis statement**, which is the main idea of the entire speech, guides an effective speech: "Habitat volunteers build community as they build houses" or "The electoral college should be abolished because it does not represent the popular vote and does not fit the current times." Each of these thesis statements succinctly summarizes the focus of a speech (building a Habitat house; abolishing the electoral college) and the main points of the speech (building community, building a house; unrepresentative, not fitted to current time). Once a speaker has a well-formed thesis statement, he or she is ready to consider how to organize the speech.

Organizing Speeches

Organization increases speaking effectiveness in several ways (Griffin, 2006). First, organization affects comprehension of ideas. Listeners can understand, follow, and remember a speech that is well planned and well ordered. Listeners are less likely to retain the key ideas in a poorly organized speech. Second, experimental evidence shows that listeners are better persuaded by an organized speech than by a disorganized one. Finally, organization enhances speakers' credibility, probably because a carefully structured speech reflects well on a speaker's preparation and respect for listeners. When someone gives a disorganized speech, listeners may regard the person as incompetent or unprepared, which reduces derived and terminal credibility.

Organizing an effective speech is not the same as organizing a paper. Oral communication requires more explicit organization, greater redundancy, and simpler sentence structure. Unlike readers, listeners cannot refer to an earlier passage if they become confused or forget a point already made. Providing signposts to highlight organization and repeating key ideas increase listeners' retention of a message (Woolfolk, 1987).

Consistent with the need for redundancy in oral communication, good speeches tell listeners what the speaker is going to tell them, present the message, and then remind listeners of the main points. This means preparing an introduction, a body, and a conclusion. In addition, speakers should include transitions to move listeners from point to point in the speech.

The Introduction. The introduction is the first thing an audience hears, and a good introduction does a lot of work. It should gain listeners' attention, give them a reason to listen, establish the credibility of the speaker, and state the thesis (the focus and the main points of the speech) (Miller, 1974).

The first objective of an introduction is to gain listeners' attention, which may also provide them with a motivation to listen. You might open with a dramatic piece of evidence, say, a startling statistic: "In the United States, four women per day are battered to death by intimates. Would you know what to do if you or a friend of yours was being abused?" This opening gives a dramatic example and a reason to listen to the speech. Other ways to gain attention are to present a striking visual aid (a photo of a victim of battering) or a dramatic example (the detailed story of a battered woman).

You could pose a question that invites listeners to think actively about the topic: "Have you ever feared for your life and had no way to escape?" Speakers may also gain listeners' attention by referring to personal experience with the topic: "For the past year, I have worked as a volunteer in the local battered women's shelter." Notice that this introductory statement establishes some initial credibility for the speaker.

The introduction should also include a thesis statement, which we discussed earlier. Your thesis should be a clear, short sentence that captures the main idea of your talk and the key points supporting that idea. A good thesis statement presents the principal claim of a speech and the main points by which it will be developed: "In my talk, I will show you that vegetarianism is healthful, and I will demonstrate that a vegetarian diet is also delicious," or "To inform you about your legal rights in an interview, I will discuss laws that prohibit discrimination and protect privacy, tell you what questions are illegal, and inform you what you can do if an interviewer asks an illegal question." Crafting a strong introduction helps speakers earn credibility. In summary, a good introduction:

- Captures listeners' attention
- Motivates listeners to listen
- Informs listeners of the main idea (thesis) of the speech and the key points supporting that idea
- Enhances the speaker's credibility

The Body. The body of a speech develops the thesis by organizing content into points that are distinct yet related. In short speeches of 5 to 10 minutes, two or three points usually are all that a speaker can develop well. Longer speeches may include more points. You can organize speeches in many ways, and each organizational pattern has distinct effects on the overall meaning (see Figure 13.1).

Chronological patterns or *time patterns* organize ideas chronologically. They emphasize progression, sequences, or development. *Spatial patterns* organize ideas according to physical relationships. They are useful in explaining layouts, geographic relationships, or connections between parts of a system.

Topical patterns (also called *classification patterns)* order speech content into categories or areas. This pattern is useful for speeches in which topics break down into two or three areas that aren't related temporally, spatially, or otherwise. The *star structure,* which is a variation on the topical pattern, has several main points (as a star has five or six) that are related and work together to develop the main idea of a speech (Jaffe, 2007).

Wave patterns feature repetitions; each "wave" repeats the main theme with variations or extensions. *Comparative patterns* compare two or more phenomena (people, machines, planets, situations). This pattern demonstrates similarities between phenomena ("In many

Figure 13.2: Types of Evidence and Their Uses

Examples **provide concrete descriptions of situations, individuals, problems, or other phenomena.**

Types:	Short (instance)
	Detailed
	Hypothetical
	Anecdotal

Uses:	To personalize information and ideas
	To add interest to a presentation
	To enhance dramatic effect

Comparisons (analogies) **compare two ideas, processes, people, situations, or other phenomena.**

Types:	Literal analogy (A heart is a pump.)
	Figurative analogy (Life is a journey.)
	Metaphor (The company is a family.)
	Simile (The company is like a family.)

Uses:	To show connections between phenomena
	To relate a new idea to one that is familiar to listeners
	To provide interest

Statistics **summarize quantitative information.**

Types:	Percentages and ratios
	Demographic data
	Frequency counts
	Correlations
	Trends

Uses:	To summarize many instances of some phenomenon
	To show relationships between two or more phenomena (cause or correlation)
	To demonstrate trends or patterns

(continued)

> *Quotations (testimony)* **restate or paraphrase the words of others, giving appropriate credit to the sources of the words.**
>
> Types: Short quotation
> Extended qotation
> Paraphrase
>
> Uses: To add variety and interest
> To support a speaker's claims
> To draw on the credibility of people whom listeners know
> To include particularly arresting phrasings of ideas
>
> *Visual aids* **reinforce verbal communication and provide visual information and appeals.**
>
> Types: Handmade charts and graphs
> Overheads/transparencies
> Computer-created charts and graphs
> PowerPoint slides
> Objects, pictures, handouts, film clips
>
> Uses: To strengthen and underscore verbal messages
> To translate statistics into pictures that are understandable
> To add variety and interest
> To give listeners a vivid appreciation of a topic, issue, or point

ways, public speaking is like everyday conversation") or differences between phenomena ("Public speaking requires more planning than everyday conversation").

Persuasive speeches typically rely on organizational patterns that encourage listeners to change attitudes or behaviors. *Problem-solution patterns* allow speakers to describe a problem and propose a solution. *Cause-effect* and *effect-cause patterns* order speech content into two main points: cause and effect. This structure is useful for persuasive speeches that aim to convince listeners that certain consequences will follow from particular actions.

A final way to organize a persuasive speech is the *motivated sequence pattern* (Gronbeck et al., 1994; Jaffe, 2007; Monroe, 1935). This pattern is effective in diverse communication situations, probably because it follows a natural order of human thought. The motivated sequence pattern includes five sequential steps. The *attention step* focuses listeners' attention on the topic with a strong opening ("Imagine this campus with no trees whatsoever"). The *need step* shows that a real and serious problem exists ("Acid rain is slowly but surely destroying the trees on our planet"). Next is the *satisfaction step,* in which a speaker recommends a solution to the problem described ("Stronger environmental regulations and individual efforts to use environmentally safe products can protect trees and thus the oxygen we need to live"). The *visualization step* intensifies listeners' commitment to the solution by helping them imagine the results that the recommended solution would achieve ("You will have air to breathe, and so will your children and grandchildren. Moreover, we'll have trees to add beauty to our lives"). Finally, in the *action step* the speaker appeals to listeners to take concrete action to realize the recommended solution ("Refuse to buy or use any aerosol products. Sign this petition to our representatives on Capitol Hill").

The Conclusion. A good speech ends on a strong note. The conclusion is a speaker's last chance to emphasize ideas, increase credibility, and gain listeners' support or approval. An effective conclusion accomplishes two goals. First, it summarizes the main ideas of the speech. Second, it leaves listeners with a memorable final idea (a dramatic quote or example, a challenge, an unforgettable computer graphic, and so forth). These two functions of the conclusion parallel the attention and thesis presented in the introduction.

Transitions. The final aspect of organizing a speech is developing *transitions,* which are words, phrases, and sentences that connect ideas in a speech. Transitions signal listeners that you have finished talking about one idea and are ready to move to the next one. Within the development of a single point, speakers usually rely on such transitional words and phrases as *therefore, and so, for this reason,* and *as the evidence suggests.* To make transitions from one point to another, the speaker may use phrases: "My second point is…"; "Now that we have seen how many people immigrate to the United States, let's ask what they bring to our country." Speakers typically use one or more sentences to create transitions between the major parts of a speech (introduction, body, conclusion). A student in one of my classes moved from the body to the conclusion of his speech with this transition: "I have discussed in some detail why we need protection for wetlands. Before I leave you, let me summarize the key ideas."

Researching and Supporting Public Speeches

Evidence is material used to support claims, such as those made in a public speech. In addition, evidence may enhance listeners' interest and emotional response to ideas. Evidence serves a number of important functions in speeches. First, it can be used to make ideas clearer, more compelling, and more dramatic. Second, evidence fortifies a speaker's opinions, which are seldom sufficient to persuade intelligent listeners. Finally, evidence heightens a speaker's credibility. A speaker who supports ideas well comes across as informed and prepared. Therefore, including strong evidence allows speakers to gain derived credibility during a presentation.

The effectiveness of evidence depends directly on whether listeners understand and accept it. This reinforces the importance of adapting to listeners, which we have emphasized throughout this book and which we will discuss again later in this chapter. Even if you quote the world's leading authority, the evidence won't be effective if your listeners don't find the authority credible (Olson & Gal, 1984). No matter how valid evidence is, it is effective only if listeners believe it. Consequently, your choices of evidence for your speech should take listeners' perspectives into account. You want to include support that they find credible, while also making sure your evidence is valid.

Four forms of support are widely respected, and each tends to be effective in specific situations and for particular goals. The kinds of evidence are statistics, examples, comparisons, and quotations. In addition, we will discuss *visual aids,* which are not a form of evidence but rather a means of presenting and enhancing other forms of evidence. For instance, a graph (visual aid) of statistics (evidence) enhances the impact of a speaker's point. Figure 13.2 summarizes the types of evidence and their uses.

Before including any form of evidence, speakers have an ethical responsibility to check the accuracy of material and the credibility of sources. It is advisable to ask questions such as these:

- Are the statistics still valid? Population demographics, social trends, and other matters become quickly outdated, so it's important to have current statistics.
- Does the person quoted have any personal interest in endorsing a certain point of view? For example, tobacco companies' statements about the harmlessness of tobacco may reflect personal and financial interests.
- Is the person an expert on the topic? It is inappropriate to rely on the *halo effect,* in which people who are well known in one area (such as sports stars) are quoted in an area outside their expertise (such as the nutritional value of cereal).
- Is an example representative of the point it is used to support? Is it typical of the general case?
- Are comparisons fair? For instance, it might be appropriate to compare Christianity and Buddhism as spiritual paths, but it would not be appropriate to compare them as religions that believe in a single god.

When presenting evidence to listeners, speakers have an ethical obligation to identify each source, including titles and qualifications, and to tell listeners its date, if the date matters. You can use an oral footnote, which acknowledges a source of evidence and sometimes explains the source's qualifications. For instance, a speaker might say, "Doctor Bingham, who won the 1988 Nobel Prize in physics, published a study in 1996 in which she reported that…" or 'As Senator Bollinger remarked in 1997,…" Oral footnotes give appropriate acknowledgment to the source that initially generated the evidence, and they enable listeners to evaluate the speaker's evidence. Here's another example of an oral footnote that was presented in a persuasive speech advocating stronger gun control laws: "In the June 2006 issue of *Marie Claire,* investigator Jennifer Friedlin reported that it took her only 30 minutes to buy a gun but 4 weeks to obtain a restraining order."

Developing Effective Delivery

As we have seen, dynamism is one dimension of a speaker's credibility Therefore, an engaging delivery is important. **Oral style** generally should be personal (Wilson & Arnold, 1974). Speakers may include personal stories and personal pronouns, referring to themselves as *I* rather than *the speaker.* Also, speakers may use phrases instead of complete sentences, and contractions *(can't)* are appropriate. Speakers should also sustain eye contact with listeners and show that they are approachable. If you reflect on speakers you have found effective, you will probably realize that they seemed engaging, personal, and open to you.

Effective oral style is also tends to be immediate and active (Wilson & Arnold, 1974). This is important because listeners must understand ideas immediately, as they are spoken, whereas readers can take time to comprehend ideas. Speakers foster immediacy by using short sentences instead of complex sentences. Immediacy also involves following general ideas with clear, specific evidence or elaboration. Rhetorical questions ("Would you like to know that a good job is waiting for you when you graduate?"), interjections ("Good grief!" "Look!"), and redundancy also enhance the immediacy of a speech (Thompson & Grundgenett, 1999). The Sharpen Your Skill box on this page invites you to notice oral style in a speech.

Throughout this book, we've seen that we should adapt our communication to its context. This basic communication principle guides a speaker's choice of a presentation style. The style of speaking that is effective at a political rally is different from the style that is appropriate for an attorney's closing speech in a trial; delivering a toast at a wedding requires a different style from that required for testifying before Congress. Each speaking situation suggests guidelines for presentation, so speakers must consider the context when selecting a speaking style.

Extemporaneous speaking allows speakers to be engaged with listeners.

Four styles of delivery are generally recognized, and each is appropriate in certain contexts. **Impromptu delivery** involves little or no preparation. It can be effective for speakers who know their material thoroughly. Many politicians speak in an impromptu fashion ["impromptu" not an adverb] when talking about their experience in public service and policies they advocate. Impromptu speaking generally is not advisable for novice speakers or for anyone who is not thoroughly familiar with a topic.

Probably the most commonly used presentational style is **extemporaneous delivery**. Extemporaneous speaking involves substantial preparation and practice, but it stops short of memorizing the exact words of a speech and relies on notes. Speakers conduct research, organize materials, and practice delivering their speeches, but they do not rehearse so much that the speeches sound canned. Attorneys, teachers, politicians, and others who engage in public speaking most often use an extemporaneous style of presentation because it allows them to prepare thoroughly and yet engage listeners when speaking.

Manuscript delivery, as the name implies, involves presenting a speech from a complete, written manuscript. In addition to the preparation typical of extemporaneous delivery, manuscript style requires the speaker to write out the entire content of a speech and to rely on the written document or a teleprompter projection when making the presentation. Few people can present manuscript speeches in an engaging, dynamic manner. However, manuscript delivery is appropriate, even advisable, in situations that call for precision. For instance, U.S. presidents generally use manuscripts for official presentations. In these circumstances, speakers cannot run the risk of using imprecise language.

An extension of the manuscript style of speaking is **memorized delivery**, in which a speaker commits an entire speech to memory and presents it without relying on a written text or notes. This style shares the primary disadvantage of manuscript speaking: the risk of a canned delivery that lacks dynamism and immediacy. In addition, the memorized style of delivery entails a second serious danger: forgetting. If a speaker is nervous, or if something happens to disrupt a presentation, the speaker may become rattled and forget all or part of the speech. Without the written text, he or she may be unable to get back on track.

When choosing a style of delivery, speakers should consider the advantages and disadvantages of each speaking style and the constraints of particular communication situations. No single style suits all occasions. Instead, the most effective style is one that suits the particular speaker and the situation. Regardless of which delivery style they use, effective speakers devote thought and practice to their verbal and nonverbal communication. It is important to select words that convey your intended meanings and that create strong images for listeners. Equally important are effective gestures, paralanguage, and movement. Because public speaking is *enlarged* conversation, nonverbal behaviors generally should be more vigorous and commanding than in personal communication.

Guidelines for Public Speaking

In this section, we discuss three guidelines for public speaking. The first two pertain to occasions when you might present a speech. The third focuses on effective, critical listening to speeches given by others.

Understand and Manage Speaking Anxiety

One of the most common challenges for public speakers is anxiety. The communication situations that prompt apprehension vary among people, as the commentaries by Tomoko and Trish illustrate.

Both Trish and Tomoko are normal in feeling some anxiety about specific communication situations. Almost all of us sometimes feel apprehensive about talking with others (Behnke & Sawyer, 1999; Bippus & Daly, 1999; Richmond & McCroskey, 1992). What many people don't realize is that a degree of anxiety is natural and may actually improve communication. When we are anxious, we become more alert and energetic, largely because our bodies produce adrenaline and extra blood sugar, which enhance our vigilance. The burst of adrenaline increases vitality, which can make speakers more dynamic and compelling. You can channel the extra energy that accompanies public speaking into gestures and movements that enhance your presentation.

You should also realize that anxiety is common for seasoned speakers. Many politicians feel nervous before and during a speech, even though they may have made hundreds or even thousands of speeches. Likewise, teachers who have taught for years usually feel tension before meeting a class, and such a seasoned journalist as Mike Wallace claims to get butterflies when conducting interviews. The energy fostered by communication anxiety allows speakers to be more dynamic and more interesting.

Although a degree of anxiety about speaking is natural, too much can interfere with effectiveness. When anxiety is great enough to hinder our ability to interact with others, communication apprehension exists. **Communication apprehension** is a detrimental level of anxiety associated with real or anticipated communication encounters (McCroskey, 1977; Richmond & McCroskey, 1992). Communication apprehension exists in degrees and may occur at times other than when we're actually speaking. Many people feel anxious primarily in advance of communication situations; they worry, imagine difficulties, and dread the occasion long before the communication occurs.

Causes of Communication Apprehension. Communication apprehension may be situational or chronic (Motley & Molloy, 1994). Situational anxiety is limited to specific situations that cause apprehension: performance reviews on the job, first dates, or major social occasions. A common cause of situational apprehension is a past failure or failures in specific speaking situations. For example, my doctor called me one day to ask me to coach her for a speech she had to give to a medical society. When I asked why she thought she needed coaching, Eleanor told me that the last speech she had given was eight years earlier, in medical school. She was an intern, and it was her turn to present a case to the other interns and in front of the resident who supervised her. Just before the speech, she lost her first patient to a heart attack and was badly shaken. All her work preparing the case and rehearsing her presentation was eclipsed by the shock of losing the patient. As a result, she was disorganized, flustered, and generally ineffective. That single incident, which followed a history of successful speaking, was so traumatic that Eleanor developed acute situational speaking anxiety.

Chronic anxiety exists when we are anxious about most or all situations in which we are expected to speak. Chronic anxiety appears to be learned. In other words, we can learn to fear communication, just as some of us learn to fear dogs, heights, or lightning. One cause of learned communication apprehension is observation of other people who are anxious about communicating. If we see family members or friends perspiring heavily and feeling stressed about making presentations, we may internalize their anxiety as an appropriate response to speaking situations.

Reducing Communication Apprehension. Because communication apprehension is learned, it can also be unlearned or reduced. Communication scholars have developed several methods of reducing speaking apprehension, four of which we'll discuss.

Systematic desensitization focuses on reducing the tension that surrounds the feared event by relaxing and thereby reducing the physiological features of anxiety, such as shallow breathing and increased heart rate (Beatty & Behnke, 1991). Once people learn to control their breathing and muscle tension, counselors ask them to think about progressively more difficult speaking situations.

A second method of reducing communication apprehension is **cognitive restructuring,** a process of revising how people think about speaking situations. According to this method, speaking is not the problem; rather, the problem is irrational beliefs about speaking. A key part of cognitive restructuring is learning to identify and challenge negative self-statements. Users of this method would criticize the statement "My topic won't interest everyone" for assuming that others will not be interested and that any speaker can hold the attention of everyone. Michael Motley and Jennifer Molloy (1994) report that apprehension decreases when people read a short booklet that encourages them to develop new, rational views of communication.

A third technique for reducing communication apprehension is **positive visualization**, which aims to reduce speaking anxiety by guiding apprehensive speakers through imagined positive speaking experiences. This technique allows people to form mental pictures of themselves as effective speakers and to then enact those mental pictures in actual speaking situations (Hamilton, 1996). Researchers report that positive visualization is especially effective in reducing chronic communication apprehension (Ayres & Hopf, 1990; Bourhis & Allen, 1992).

Skills training assumes that lack of speaking skills causes us to be apprehensive. This method focuses on teaching people such skills as starting conversations, organizing ideas, and responding effectively to others (Phillips, 1991).

After reading about these methods of reducing communication apprehension, you may think that each seems useful. If so, your thinking coincides with research that finds that a combination of methods is more likely to relieve speaking anxiety than any single method (Allen, Hunter, & Donahue, 1989). The major conclusion is that communication apprehension is not necessarily permanent. Ways to reduce it exist. Eliminating all communication anxiety is not desirable, however, because some vigilance can enhance a speaker's dynamism and alertness. If you experience communication apprehension that interferes with your ability to express your ideas, ask your instructor to direct you to professionals who can work with you.

Adapt Speeches to Audiences

A second guideline for effective public speaking is to adapt to audiences, a topic we discussed earlier in this chapter. Listeners are the whole reason for speaking; without them, communication does not occur. Therefore, speakers should be sensitive to listeners and should adapt to listeners' perspectives and expectations. You should take into account the perspectives of listeners if you want them to consider your views. We consider the views of our friends when we talk with them. We think about others' perspectives when we engage in business negotiations. We use dual perspective when communicating with children, dates, and neighbors. Thus, audience analysis is important to effectiveness in all communication encounters.

In one of my classes, a student named Odell gave a persuasive speech designed to convince listeners to support affirmative action. He was personally compelling, his delivery was dynamic, and his ideas were well organized. The only problems were that his audience had little knowledge about affirmative action, and he didn't explain exactly what the policy involves. He assumed listeners understood how affirmative action works, and he focused on its positive effects. His listeners were not persuaded, because Odell failed to give them the information necessary for their support. Odell's speech also illustrates our earlier point that speeches often combine more than one speaking purpose; in this case, giving information was essential to Odell's larger goal of persuading listeners.

The mistake that Odell made was failing to learn about his audience's knowledge of his topic. It is impossible to entertain, inform, or persuade people if we do not consider their perspectives on our topics. Speakers need to understand what listeners already know and believe and what reservations they might have about what we say (McGuire, 1989). To paraphrase the advice of an ancient Greek rhetorician, "The fool persuades me with his or her reasons, the wise person with my own." This advice—that effective speakers understand and work with listeners' reasons, values, knowledge, and concerns—is as wise today as it was more than 2,000 years ago.

Although politicians and corporations can afford to conduct sophisticated polls to find out what people know, want, think, and believe, most of us don't have the resources to do that. So how do ordinary people engage in goal-focused analysis? One answer is to be observant. Usually, a speaker has some experience in interacting with his or her listeners or people like them. Drawing on past interactions, a speaker may be able to discern a great deal about the knowledge, attitudes, and beliefs of listeners.

Gathering information about listeners through conversations or surveys is also appropriate. For example, I once was asked to speak on women leaders at a governor's leadership conference. To prepare my presentation, I asked the conference planners to send me information about the occupations and ages of people attending the conference. In addition, I asked the planners to survey the conferees about their experience as leaders and working with women leaders. The material I received informed me about the level of experience and the attitudes and biases of my listeners. Then I could adapt my speech to what they knew and believed.

By taking listeners into consideration, you build a presentation that is interactive and respectful. As we learned earlier in this chapter, listeners tend to confer credibility on speakers who show that they understand listeners and who adapt presentations to listeners' perspectives, knowledge, and expectations.

Listen Critically

A final guideline is to listen critically to speeches you hear. Because we often find ourselves in the role of listener, we should know how to listen well and critically to ideas that others present. Critical listening involves attending mindfully to communication in order to evaluate its merit. Critical listeners assess whether a speaker is informed and ethical and whether a speech is soundly reasoned and supported.

The first step in critical listening is to take in and understand what a speaker says. You cannot evaluate an argument or idea until you have grasped it and the information that supports it. Thus, effective listening requires you to concentrate on what a speaker says. You can focus your listening by asking questions such as these:

- What does the speaker announce as the purpose of the talk?
- What evidence does the speaker provide to support claims?
- Does the speaker have experience that qualifies him or her to speak on this topic?
- Does the speaker have any vested interest in what she or he advocates?

You probably noticed that these questions parallel those we identified in our earlier discussion of ways to improve your credibility when you are making speeches. The questions help you zero in on what others say so that you can make informed judgments of their credibility and the credibility of their ideas.

To listen critically, you should suspend your preconceptions about topics and speakers. You need not abandon your ideas, but you should set them aside long enough to listen openly to a speech, especially if you are predisposed to disagree with it. By granting a full and fair hearing to ideas that differ from yours, you increase the likelihood that your perspective and ideas will be well informed and carefully reasoned.

Critical listeners recognize fallacies in reasoning and do not succumb to them. To accept a speaker's ideas, critical listeners demand that the ideas be well supported with evidence and sound reasoning. The FYI box on this page summarizes some of the more common fallacies in reasoning in public communication.

Summary

Public speaking has many similarities to social conversations. One would not begin a conversation without some sort of introductory remarks followed by a body of material and some type of concluding comments before the conversation is terminated. The same is true for public speaking. The purposes of public communication also share similarities with one-on-one communication—speaking to inform, entertain, and persuade.

Planning and presenting public speeches is not exactly rocket science, but a speaker must understand how to effectively plan and present a public presentation. The successful selection of a topic is the first step after which the speaker needs to determine a speaking purpose along with a clear thesis statement. Speeches must have a clear introduction that captures the attention of the audience and gives the speech some direction. In the body of a speech the speaker must have the speech organized by a specific pattern which meets the purpose of the speech, such as a temporal, cause-effect, or chronological pattern of organization. Finally, a good speech can be damaged without an effective conclusion that brings the speech to an appropriate end.

Just as essential as the way a speaker organizes a speech is the way a speaker develops evidence for his or her supporting points. Statistics, examples, comparisons, and quotations are supporting materials a speaker can use to give a speech depth and credibility.

Finally, a speaker needs to develop an effective delivery based on the nature of the speech and occasion, e.g., a formal occasion might demand a manuscript speech while an informal occasion might call for an extemporaneous delivery.

Experienced speakers realize that everyone suffers from a speech anxiety, and is able to effectively manage these conditions through methods such as cognitive restructuring or skills training. Even in the age of instantaneous computer mediated communication, the ability to develop, present, and analyze one's speaking effectiveness is a skill which has not changed in the last two centuries.

Questions For Discussion

1. Why is public communication analogous to social conversation?
2. What is a thesis statement in a speech?
3. How can evidence be used to increase the credibility of a message?
4. In what circumstances is it appropriate to give a manuscript speech?
5. How can people manage anxiety associated with public communication?

References

Allen, M., Hunter, J., & Donahue, W. (1989). Metaanalysis of self-report data on the effectiveness of public speaking anxiety treatment techniques. *Communication Education, 38,* 54–76.

Ayres, J., & Hopf, T. S. (1990). The long-term effect of visualization in the classroom: A brief research report. *Communication Education, 39,* 75–78.

Beatty, M. J., & Behnke, R. R. (1991). Effects of public speaking trait anxiety and intensity of speaking task on heart rate during performance. *Human Communication Research, 18,* 147–176.

Behnke, R., & Sawyer, C. (1999). Milestones of anticipatory public speaking anxiety. *Communication Education, 48,* 164–172.

Bippus, A., & Daly, J. (1999). What do people think causes stage fright? NaYve attributions about the reasons for public speaking anxiety. *Communication Education, 48,* 63–72.

Bourhis, J., & Allen, M. (1992). Meta-analysis of the relationship between communication apprehension and cognitive performance. *Communication Education, 41,* 68–76.

Einhorn, L. (2000). *The Native American oral tradition: Voices of the spirit and soul.* Westport, CT: Praeger.

Fitch, N. E. (Ed.). (1999). *How sweet the sound: The spirit of African American history.* New York: Harcourt College.

Griffin, C. (2006). *Invitation to public speaking* (2nd ed.). Belmont, CA: Thomson Wadsworth.

Gronbeck, B. E., McKerro, R., Ehninger, D., & Monroe, A. H. (1994). *Principles and types of speech communication* (12th ed.). Glenview, IL: Scott, Foresman.

Hamilton, C. (1996). *Successful public speaking.* Belmont, CA: Wadsworth.

Jaffe, C. (2007). *Public speaking: Concepts and skills for a diverse society* (5th ed.). Belmont, CA: Thomson Wadsworth.

McCroskey, J., & Teven, J. (1999). Goodwill: A reexamination of the construct and its measurement. *Communication Monographs, 66,* 90–103.

McCroskey, J. C. (1977). Oral communication apprehension: A summary of recent theory and research.'· *Human Communication Research, 4,* 78–96.

Miller, E. (1974). Speech introductions and conclusions. *Quarterly Journal of Speech, 32,* 118–127.

Monroe, A. H. (1935). *Principles and types of speech.* Glenview, IL: Scott, Foresman.

Motley, M., & Molloy, J. (1994). An efficacy test of a new therapy ("communication-orientation motivation") for public speaking anxiety. *Journal of Applied Communication Research,* 22,48–58.

Olson, J. M., & Cal, A. V. (1984). Source credibility, attitudes, and the recall of past behaviors. *European Journal of Social Psychology, 14,* 203–210.

Phillips, G. M. (1991). *Communication incompetencies.* Carbondale: Southern Illinois University Press.

Richmond, V. P., & McCroskey, J. C. (1992). *Communication: Apprehension, avoidance, and effectiveness* (3rd ed.). Scottsdale, AZ: Gorsuch Scarisbrick.

Thompson, F., & Grundgenett, D. (1999). Helping disadvantaged learners build effective learning skills. *Education, 120,* 130–135.

Wilson, J. F., & Arnold, C. C. (1974). *Public speaking as a liberal art* (4th ed.). Boston: Allyn & Bacon.

Winans, J. A. (1938). *Speechmaking.* New York: Appleton-Century-Crofts.

Woolfolk, A. E. (1987). *Educational psychology.* Englewood Cliffs, NJ: Prentice Hall.

CPSIA information can be obtained at www.ICGtesting.com
Printed in the USA
LVOW11s1049300813

350377LV00002B/3/P

9 781621 312987